A RIGHT TO
ROAM

MARION SHOARD

OXFORD
UNIVERSITY PRESS

OXFORD

UNIVERSITY PRESS

Great Clarendon Street, Oxford OX2 6DP

Oxford University Press is a department of the University of Oxford.
It furthers the University's objective of excellence in research, scholarship,
and education by publishing worldwide in

Oxford New York

Athens Auckland Bangkok Bogotá Buenos Aires Calcutta
Cape Town Chennai Dar es Salaam Delhi Florence Hong Kong Istanbul
Karachi Kuala Lumpur Madrid Melbourne Mexico City Mumbai
Nairobi Paris São Paulo Singapore Taipei Tokyo Toronto Warsaw

and associated companies in Berlin Ibadan

Oxford is a registered trade mark of Oxford University Press
in the UK and in certain other countries

Published in the United States
by Oxford University Press Inc., New York

British Library Cataloguing in Publication Data

Data available

Library of Congress Cataloging in Publication Data

Data available

ISBN 0–19–288016–0   100304387

3 5 7 9 10 8 6 4 2

Typeset by Graphicraft Limited, Hong Kong
Printed in Great Britain by
Cox & Wyman Ltd,
Reading, Berks

To
Catherine
and
Dace

ACKNOWLEDGEMENTS

THIS book would not have been possible without the generous help of two institutions: the Nuffield Foundation, which awarded me a grant to look at access arrangements abroad; and the Leverhulme Foundation, which gave me an award to examine the feasibility of introducing a right to roam to Britain. I am extremely grateful to both bodies.

Two people have played a key role in the writing of this book. I met Judith Rossiter at a key stage in the development of my own thinking about access. In 1973, living in a flat in the fairly unprepossessing industrial town of Luton, south Bedfordshire, I looked longingly at the green acres and inviting waters of the lakes, park, and woods of Luton Hoo, a large landed estate on my doorstep whose delights were almost completely out of bounds. I was then preparing a dissertation on the part of the Chiltern Hills in which Luton Hoo lay as a postgraduate student of town and country planning at Kingston-upon-Thames Polytechnic, so I had the opportunity to find out how prevalent such exclusion was. At the time, however, recreation planning orthodoxy was more concerned with protecting the countryside and rural interests from invading townspeople than opening it up to them, so it was enormously helpful to stumble upon somebody who saw the issue from the same perspective as me. From a research directory I was surprised to learn that a Judith Rossiter was preparing a Ph.D. dissertation at Cambridge on the operation of the almost completely ineffective and largely forgotten arrangements devised to enable people to wander freely over stretches of open countryside in the 1949 National Parks and Access to the Countryside Act. Excitedly I telephoned Cambridge and Judith invited me to spend the following day talking to her. That day's conversation in her office marked the dawn of my awareness that access to Britain's countryside involved not only recreation opportunities but profound questions about the character of our society. It was among the most interesting and inspiring days of my life.

Acknowledgements

The second individual who has shaped my thinking is David Cox, with whom I have frequently discussed Britain's rural regime. I am enormously grateful to him for his observations.

I am also grateful to many other individuals. Nils and Lillemor Levan, Michael Jones, Jan Lundegrén, and Jens Christian Hansen provided both generous hospitality and information while I was looking at access overseas. I am grateful to Elizabeth Adams, Margarethe Alexandroni, Anne Caspari, Judith Corbett, and Elke Brown for translating access laws for me, and to Robin Mosses for carrying out document research. My agent Charlotte Howard and my editors at Oxford University Press, Angus Phillips and Helen Cox, have provided valuable support. Carolyn Adams, Fred Beake, John France, Professor Keith Davies, Judith Lewis, Duncan Mackay, Dr Richard Muir, Dr Derek Ratcliffe, Nils Bo Sørensen, Peter Stoll, and Günnar Zettersten looked at parts of the manuscript and I am very grateful for their comments. I am grateful to Samantha Haines for typing parts of the manuscript for me and for instructing me in the use of a new computer when my Amstrad gave up the ghost during the final run at this book. Most of all I am grateful to the hundreds of individuals who have provided me with information, either over the telephone or in person. This book could not have appeared had not countless people been extremely generous to me with their time. Those involved are too numerous to mention one by one, but once more I should like to say thank you very much.

Special gratitude is due to my daughter Catherine. Not only did she help with typing at various stages, but when, during the final stages in the writing of this book, I was laid low (thankfully temporarily) with a prolapsed disc, she shopped, cooked, took me out in my wheelchair, and most important of all, kept my spirits up despite her impending A-level exams.

CONTENTS

INTRODUCTION

AFTER 300 years as one of the world's most urban peoples, the British retain a fierce attachment to their countryside. Indeed the obsession may now be more intense than ever. The country lifestyle long sought after as the prize of achievement is being made accessible by fax and e-mail to people whose work would once have kept them in town. Meanwhile, those not yet able to realize the dream of a country home are presented with an ever wider range of steps towards this goal, ranging from rustic confections and home furnishings to vicarious enjoyment of the gentlefolks' way of life courtesy of the National Trust. Advertisers consider rural associations a reliable way of instilling desire for everything from bread to footwear. Surveys show that four out of five Britons would live in the countryside if they could, and that walking in the countryside is now second in popularity only to gardening among the nation's outdoor pursuits.

For the British, the countryside is a pastoral Eden of peace and spiritual refreshment. Perhaps we should therefore not be surprised that it has become more important to us as the pressures of everyday life have increased in the ever more stress-ridden towns and cities in which most of us still spend most of our time.

British preferences reflect the British idea of the countryside as a repository of tranquillity. The archetypal rural pursuit in Britain is the gentle ramble. Activities associated with the undirected stroll, like bird-watching and picnicking, are also popular. Most of the British seem to want no more from their countryside than to place themselves within it and to roam amongst its treasures.

Ravaged though Britain's countryside has been by building and modern farming, it could still provide very well for this simple need. Seventy-seven per cent of the UK's land is countryside, and this still includes much magnificent scenery. Yet the increasing numbers of people setting off in search of it find their simple quest ends all too often in disappointment and frustration. They can visit the ever more crowded country parks, picnic areas, and other enclaves provided by public and voluntary bodies, but if they try to venture beyond such places and roam freely they soon run up against a harsh reality. Most of Britain's countryside is forbidden to Britain's people. They may look at it through their car windscreens but they may not enter it without somebody else's permission—permission which will be withheld more often than not. The rural heritage they may have loved unthinkingly since childhood turns out to be locked away from them behind fences, walls, and barbed wire. Where they have been expecting relaxation and peace they find instead warnings to keep out and threats of prosecution.

Our law of trespass holds us in its grim thrall throughout our country. Most of us are vaguely aware that those omnipresent 'Trespassers will be Prosecuted' signs are partly bluff. But all of us also know that trespass is indeed illegal, whether or not our wanderings are likely to put us in the dock. When an owner or his representative confronts us, we do not usually choose to argue the toss with him about our right to walk in our countryside. If we did, we should lose the argument. He has the right to use force to remove us. As a result, more than 90 per cent of woodland in Oxfordshire, for example, is effectively out of bounds to the walker.

This dismal state of affairs flies in the face of a key element of our national self-image. The British have been encouraged to think of their distinctive countryside as part of their collective identity. Second World War propaganda, for example, urged troops to think of themselves as fighting for the fields and woods of home. Yet in Britain, the vast majority of the people have so little stake in that countryside that they are not even allowed to enter most of it. Instead, an elect few control it utterly, choosing, for the most part, to use this control to exclude their fellow citizens from entering their holdings even for so harmless a purpose as to wander about looking at the bluebells or listening to the skylarks. For many of these 'owners' of Britain, this right of exclusion is not merely incidental but one of the principal attractions of landownership itself.

Our parents and grandparents took this situation so much for granted that they would have found it difficult to imagine any alternative. Yet the countryside need not be a fiefdom denied to the many by the few. Things were different once and they are still different in countries that are otherwise similar to Britain. Of course no one challenges today the idea of private property. But other societies hesitate to regard the land itself as something that can be owned as absolutely as a piece of jewellery. Our own laws of compulsory purchase and development control implicitly challenge this idea. Deep down we all know it is wrong.

Throughout human history, the notion of which of the planet's resources might reasonably be held as property by individuals has changed as different peoples at different times have developed different ideas of what is right. Prehistoric man's tools, weapons, and ornaments were so much his own property that they were buried with him. Yet the idea that an individual might 'own' the land through which he hunted would have seemed to him absurd, as it still does to surviving primitive peoples. As societies develop, the strong tend to demand the right to use more and more things as individuals—not just land but slaves or womenfolk. In the West, the civilizing process of the past few centuries has included the removal of some of these things from private property status when it has seemed an affront to society as a whole that they should continue to enjoy it. That the landowner's right to exclude his fellows has survived this process requires explanation.

Our Anglo-Saxon forebears did not bar each other from the countryside. Our current landowners' right to exclude stems directly from the particular experience of the Norman Conquest. Effectively, a band of robber barons keen to seize space to pursue their passion for hunting and contemptuous of the claims of the indigenous population grabbed the land from the people. Other particular features of our history served to buttress the grip of their descendants. Because land-ownership came to be seen as one of the fruits of success, owners sought not only to reap economic benefits from their holdings but also to make them the means of proclaiming their status through the pursuit of private pleasures. Other developments ranging from the rise of the wool industry to the introduction of coppicing and pheasant shooting served to entrench a habit of exclusion which might otherwise have evaporated.

Earlier generations of landowners did not escape protest. One of the causes of the Peasants' Revolt of 1381 was the harsh penalties inflicted on those who broke the cruel game laws protecting exclusive hunting forests. Riots against enclosure for sheep farming occurred throughout the seventeenth, eighteenth, and nineteenth centuries. The Diggers of the seventeenth century used direct action against the pre-emption of land for game while people were going hungry. They attacked not just exclusion but its philosophical basis. Their arguments against the absolute ownership of land provided an unwelcome reminder for an élite drunk on property ownership of the distinctions addressed by the ancients between what individuals could own, what the community should own, what no one could own, and what only God could own. As access to the countryside became as important for recreation as it had once been for subsistence, challenges to the landowners continued. The 1930s saw pitched battles between ramblers and gamekeepers over access to Derbyshire's moorlands. Little wonder then, that in our own time public access to the countryside should become an issue of real political importance.

In recent years we have seen the rise of environmentalism create a far more widespread sense than ever before that the land is something in which all have a stake and which owners cannot be trusted to rule as they see fit. At the same time the collapse of deference and the growing clamour for the people to shape their own destiny has made landowners' pleas to act as 'custodians' of the countryside for the rest of us increasingly unpersuasive, particularly as people have become aware of the appalling destruction that has been wrought on Britain's landscape, wildlife, and archaeological heritage by the farming and forestry practices over which these 'custodians' have presided during the last half-century.

Thus it is that we have seen growing resistance to the idea that we should continue to be shut out of what we increasingly see as our own countryside. When the Ramblers' Association began their 'Forbidden Britain' days of protest in 1988, few could have anticipated the extent to which the idea enshrined in their protest would gather force. By the time George Monbiot's 'The Land is Ours' movement was conducting mass occupations of rural sites in the early 1990s it was, however, beginning to be apparent that temperatures were rising. What was to be done in response?

As landowners saw the scale of the potential threat to their own position which was taking shape, they developed an answer of their own. If people were to require access to the countryside, perhaps they had better be given it while it could still be granted on terms which landowners could dictate. Owners who had argued that any extension of public access would make agriculture impossible and devastate wildlife began to change their tune. Instead, they began to suggest that of course access should be improved. However, the most satisfactory way in which this could be done was by voluntary agreement with landowners. Ideally, many of them also thought, they should receive cash payments in return for any access they chose to grant, which might in time prove a significant new form of income for them.

Policy-makers were not inclined to dismiss conciliatory proposals from a group which might be tiny in numbers but which had always been immensely powerful as a lobby, partly because it controlled so much of the land surface. During the 1980s the Conservative government launched schemes which encouraged landowners to open up their holdings voluntarily in return for payments from the public purse. As a solution to the problem, however, this approach could not get very far. Not only were landowners unwilling to open up enough of the land which actually matched public needs; the sums which would be necessary to open up the countryside based on a cash-for-access approach would be far beyond the scope of the cash-strapped public bodies which would be trying to do the deals.

These bodies, mainly local authorities, therefore looked afresh at the machinery already available to them to open up the country-side. Many turned to the public footpath system to see if they could remove the obstructions which were making so much of it useless, or perhaps create some more routes. Desirable though these efforts proved, they too were of limited effect. In a sense they served only to highlight the real problem. Why should elected authorities have to struggle to negotiate access for their citizens along a network of tracks which had grown up at random with no regard to real needs? Why shouldn't people be able to go where they wanted to go?

Thus it was that the idea of general rights of access to the country-side began to swim its way up the public agenda. Alarming though it undoubtedly was to the landowning classes, it was far from a new concept. The people of Sweden, Finland, and Norway have exercised such a right throughout their countryside for hundreds of years. General rights of access to particular kinds of countryside are well established in other European countries including Germany, Denmark, Switzerland, Austria, and Spain. The idea was hardly new to Britain either. As long ago as 1884 the Scottish MP James Bryce introduced into Parliament a bill to provide a right of public access to Scotland's mountains. It was taken extremely seriously, and successor bills might have succeeded had the First World War not swept the issue away along with so much else. By the 1990s the idea had come to fit into the political culture far more naturally than it did in Bryce's day. Talk of a new set of rights and duties for a post-millennial nation seemed to chime well with the idea of a right for the citizenry to walk through their homeland and a duty on landowners to respect this right in return for the many privileges which they enjoy. Not perhaps as awesome as our rights to life and liberty, a right to roam wherever we want through Britain's countryside would nevertheless provide a substantial addition to the attributes of citizenship. No longer would Britons be confined to the margins of their homeland by a feudal law of trespass. Instead they would be liberated from a long-standing indignity, to take their place among grown-up peoples at one with their lands. At the same time, inroads would be made on the practical problem of providing rural recreation opportunities without draining the public purse.

Within Britain's Labour Party, rights of access to the countryside were far from a new idea. Working-class activists had looked to the party for support after the mass trespasses of the 1930s, and the 1945–51 Attlee government had been expected to introduce an access right, but opted instead for other access measures which were to prove ineffective. So it was not surprising that the idea of access to the countryside became a significant theme of the Labour opposition in the 1980s and 1990s. And it was rights of access, rather than other meas-ures, to which the party became committed. In 1994 the party made the creation of a right of access to the countryside party policy at its annual conference. The *Daily Telegraph* called the proposal the most radical of all the party's policies. The idea of a general right of access to mountain, moor, and common land was advanced by successive Labour spokesmen, and the party's manifesto promised that access would be addressed. After the election, in May 1997, the new Labour government confirmed that it would indeed create a right of access to five kinds of countryside, mountain, moorland, heath, down, and common. Michael Meacher, a junior Environment Minister who assumed responsibility for access, promised a consultation paper. Landowning interests threw all they had into a lobbying operation designed to block access rights, staging two highly successful 'countryside' marches on London which bracketed opposition to access rights with other objectives of the rural establishment. Rattled, No. 10 held up the publication of Mr Meacher's paper by more than six months. The landowning organizations argued that legal rights were unnecessary: landowners could provide sufficient access on a voluntary basis.

In February 1998, the government responded by calling the landowners' bluff: the consultation paper appeared, offering landowners the opportunity to demonstrate that they could create access benefits on a voluntary basis equivalent to those which would be provided by a statutory right of access to the five kinds of countryside the government had specified, which would involve between 3 and 4 million acres in all, covering somewhere in the region of 10 per cent of England and Wales. After a three-month consultation period, the government would decide whether to create a statutory right or to allow landowners to create voluntary access opportunities instead. If it chose the latter route, it would review the actual arrangements that emerged, with the clear implication that if these were unsatisfactory it would create a statutory right at some point in the future. If landowners were to escape statutory access rights they would have to show that the voluntary measures they advanced covered as much ground and enjoyed the same permanency as those which a statutory right would create. It is a demand which it is hard to see landowners meeting, since landowners as a group have no means of coercing unwilling individual owners to co-operate, and a mechanism ensuring permanency of access is difficult to envisage.

So a right of access is now a real prospect for at least part of the countryside of Britain. If it is indeed enacted it will mark one of the most fundamental changes ever in our rural regime.

Meanwhile, a separate debate is under way in Scotland. The government has made no commitment on the form new rights of access might take there, having done no more than initiate a debate by asking Scottish Natural Heritage, the government countryside agency, to consult relevant bodies and advise on appropriate changes to the law relating to access in Scotland. SNH has in turn asked not only organizations but also members of the public for their views. The government has not committed itself to any particular approach but has said that it wishes to see access improved in Scotland. Concern about countryside access in Scotland has intensified over the last three decades. Walkers certainly have considerable freedom of movement in the hills but this rests on no more than custom and landowners turning a blind eye to what is in effect trespass, while in the farmed and wooded region of lowland Scotland access is extremely restricted. This situation has produced a debate north of the border concentrating on the idea of a general or universal right to all types of countryside rather than access rights over specific types of countryside of the kind originally proposed by the Labour government for England and Wales. In Northern Ireland there is growing awareness of how greater freedom of movement in the countryside could not only improve recreation opportunities for the Province's own citizens but also enhance the country's important tourism industry. Fundamental questions are being asked about the way in which Northern Ireland's rudimentary access system could be overhauled.

So throughout the kingdom the possibility of new access rights tantalizes walkers and alarms landowners. For both sides in this ancient struggle, this is a matter of enormous moment.

For their part, landowners point out that the creation of a right of access constitutes the expropriation of what up till now has been legally part of their property, namely the right to exclude, without even an offer of compensation. They suggest, however, that they would not be the only losers from the creation of such a right: farmers and foresters would suffer from the damage walkers would cause, and everyone would come to regret the damage done to wildlife by disturbance and to the landscape by litter and vandalism. These arguments need to be faced. Would a right of access enable people to steal crops from farmers' fields? Would walkers on moorland frighten ground-nesting birds off their nests? Would New Age travellers be enabled to set up squatter camps wherever they chose? Would privacy be destroyed? Would landowners cease to care for their holdings if they were opened to everyone else? What good would it do to inherit our countryside at last if we were to destroy it in the process?

Do we really need a right to roam? Are we entitled to one? What are the dangers that would accompany it, and can they be circumvented? What form should such a right take? How could walkers be required to respect any duties which might accompany their new right? How could we accommodate the exceptions and exemptions which legitimate interests might require without emasculating the concept? What can we learn from experience overseas? Is it really ever going to happen? Such are the questions which this book tries to address.

1

TRESPASSERS WILL BE PROSECUTED

FROM a train window, Britain's countryside seems open to all. The fields, woods, rivers, moors, hills, and dales slipping by make up, after all, a vital part of the nation's identity, the homeland for which soldiers die in war. Surely if the train were to stop anywhere amidst this wondrous landscape you could make your way where you chose. Children's picture books, tourist posters, and television commercials all give the impression that the countryside lies at our feet, awaiting entry. But it does not. Whether you try to venture into farmland or woodland, downland or moorland, parkland or waterside, you are likely to find your way barred before very long. The obstacle may be an angry man armed with a shotgun and apparently ferocious dogs. It may be high walls, barbed wire, locked gates, or thick hedges. Often it will be a notice bearing the grim warning with which Britain's soft landscape confronts would-be visitors: 'Trespassers will be Prosecuted'.

This is a potent mantra. 'Trespass', the Lord's Prayer term for transgression against God and man, still evokes its ancient sense of grave wrong, even though its modern meaning is restricted to one of the most questionable infractions in our legal and moral codes. 'Prosecuted' implies the merciless application of the full rigour of the law. 'Will be' (mysteriously bypassing problems of detection and apprehension) announces that such application is inevitable. Whatever meaning now attaches to this message, it is imprinted on the way people think about the countryside and is in itself sufficient to cast a shadow over the souls of those who look to the countryside to escape, not court, confrontation.

In fact, the message carried by those ubiquitous signs is of course a 'wooden falsehood' (in the words of land lawyer C. J. A. Jolowicz[1]). Normally you cannot be prosecuted for stepping onto somebody else's property without permission. You have (normally) committed not a crime or misdemeanour but a civil wrong or tort, for which the wronged party must seek redress against you under civil law. Nonetheless, the power embodied in that civil law is both real and extensive. It is power which is used, regularly and energetically. And the landowner's chances of buttressing the power of this civil law with that of the criminal law on occasion have actually increased significantly in recent years.

The Law of Trespass

The laws of England, Wales, and Northern Ireland give landowners the right to exclude us from all of their land, except for a small fraction consisting of public rights of way, and even here we enjoy an entitlement only of passage. The right of exclusion applies equally to forests and mountains, fields and riverbanks, cliffs, quarries, and heaths, a 1,000-acre parkland or 10-acre meadow. It is enshrined in laws of trespass which provide that if you set foot on British soil you are breaking the law unless the owner of that land has given you permission to be present. These laws entitle a landowner to use 'reasonable force' to eject you if you decline a request to leave. In deterring or ejecting trespassers there are of course limits on what a landowner or somebody acting on his behalf can do. If he uses a considerable amount of force, the trespasser may sue him for assault; threatening behaviour such as waving a shotgun at a trespasser can be classed as assault since you do not need to touch somebody to be guilty of this offence but merely to instil in them the fear that they may be physically hurt.

Whether or not force has been used to get rid of you, the landowner can take action against you in the courts simply for the act of trespass. If you have done no damage, he is usually nonetheless entitled to nominal damages in recognition of the fact that his legal right has been infringed. If he can demonstrate that the trespass has resulted in financial loss to him then a claim for damages will usually be successful. The courts do not welcome actions for damages where no loss can be demonstrated, and a landowner who embarks on such an action may end up having to pay his own costs and yours too. If, on the other hand, a landowner seeks an injunction to prevent

11

a trespasser who does no damage from repeating his trespass, he can expect the full support of the courts for this assertion of his rights under the law. A landowner seeking to prevent you from repeating a trespass on his land simply applies to the county court or to the High Court for an injunction against you. If you breach such an injunction you are in contempt of court, and can be imprisoned. The injunction therefore represents, in the words of Peter Birts QC, an expert on trespass law, 'a truly formidable remedy against trespass'.[2]

Of course there are plenty of landowners who are perfectly happy to tolerate the public on their land. But if a landowner dislikes the presence of the public, he has plenty of ways of getting rid of them. Of course, if he wishes, he can simply remove the feature which attracted trespassers in the first place. If the public are attracted by a stretch of flowery downland he can plough it up, or destroy it with pesticides so long as it is not a site of special scientific interest. A landowner who disliked the presence of climbers on a crag in Derbyshire simply took sticks of dynamite to it and blew it up (though not when the climbers were actually present).[3] People can be deterred from visiting a site through making it difficult to get to it or over it—by planting prickly bushes in the way, placing rubbish at strategic points, stationing fierce dogs or frisky horses along the route, or simply throwing up fences or other man-made obstructions.

Where a landowner prefers to retain whatever attracts outsiders, the law allows him ample scope to exclude them physically. Landowners can erect barriers up to 2 metres high over their land without the need for planning permission, except where a barrier abuts a road or a public path when anything more than 1 metre needs permission. They can top existing or new walls with broken glass, barbed wire, or iron spikes, so long as these are visible in daylight. They can allow savage dogs to roam their holdings, and if such a dog bites you while you are trespassing or making your way legally around the countryside, you will be able to seek redress only if you can demonstrate that the dog has bitten someone before, since every dog, apart from recognized dangerous breeds, 'is allowed its first bite'.

These powers to deter and to deal with trespassers are available to all landowners anywhere in the UK. In other words, the ownership of the land involved has no bearing on the powers available against trespassers. By the same token, no particular form of ownership conveys a legal right for the public to be present. Land may therefore be owned by a public body which nonetheless uses the law of trespass to exclude the public. Thirteen per cent or so of Britain's rural land is owned by the government, local authorities, or other state institutions,[4] yet you will be excluded as effectively from much of this as from the holdings of private individuals. Some landowners, like the National Trust, the Forestry Commission, or the Forest Service of Northern Ireland, do of course choose to allow people a wide measure of access, but we enjoy our visits to the holdings of such owners almost always as a favour not a right. There is no automatic right of public access to 'common land', as is often assumed, or to the Crown Estate. Signs put up to deter entry saying 'Private Property' are in fact redundant: in Britain everything is private property—even public property.

Involuntary entry onto land is not classed as trespass, so if your plane crashes onto a farmer's field, he has to put up with you. To become a trespasser, you have to want to be on someone else's land. You do not however have to know you will be trespassing. So if you misread a map and stray off a public path, you will be just as guilty of trespass as somebody who climbs over a five-barred gate marked 'Private: Keep Out'. 'The wicked and the innocent: the burglar, the arrogant invader of another's land, the walker blithely unaware that he is stepping where he has no right to walk, or the wandering child —all may be dubbed trespassers,' as Lord Morris explained in a court case in 1972.[5]

There is a mysteriously widespread belief that Scotland has no law of trespass or that Scottish trespass law is in some way fundamentally different from English law. It is not. Of course, Scotland's lairds face particular difficulties in enforcing their rights on their often vast and remote estates, yet those rights are essentially the same as those of an English farmer. In one respect, trespass law in Scotland is fiercer than in England and Wales: camping on private land without the permission of the owner is, under the Trespass (Scotland) Act, 1865, a criminal and not merely civil matter. Otherwise trespass in Scotland is a civil wrong as normally in England, with force available to landowners against trespassers who refuse to leave and interdicts from the Sheriff Court playing the part of a county court against repeat offenders. Damages for trespass where no actual loss has been incurred are not however available even in theory in Scotland.[6]

The Trespasser as Criminal

Apart from unlicensed camping in Scotland, trespass is normally a criminal rather than a civil matter only when it involves airfields, railway lines, and embankments, certain ornamental grounds in towns, and military land to which special by-laws forbidding access have been applied. In addition trespassers can be prosecuted if it can be shown they are in the countryside for the particular purpose of poaching. Recently, however, the scope of the criminal law in trespass has been significantly extended.

The Public Order Act of 1986 empowers the police to direct trespassers to leave land if two or more plan to stay on the land 'for any period'. If they fail to leave or, having left, return within three months they are committing a criminal offence and can be imprisoned and/or fined up to £2,500.

In 1994 criminalization took two further steps forward. The Criminal Justice and Public Order Act of that year makes it illegal to hold a 'trespassory assembly'—a gathering on land without the landowner's consent if the chief police officer considers that such an assembly might result in serious disruption to the life of the community or significant damage to land or a building of historical, architectural, archaeological, or scientific importance. Those who defy a prohibition to take part in such an assembly or to organize one may face three months in prison or a £2,500 fine. Also, this same act introduced the new criminal offence of so-called 'aggravated trespass'. This has the effect that any person trespassing on land in the open air who does anything intended to obstruct or disrupt some lawful activity or intimidate any person so as to deter him from engaging in that activity, may, if found guilty, be imprisoned for up to three months and/or be fined a maximum of £2,500. Aimed primarily against New Age travellers and hunt saboteurs, this measure may appear to have nothing to do with ordinary walkers. In fact, however, criminalization of trespass of any kind subtly strengthens the landowner's right to exclude others from his land. The new provision can also catch ordinary walkers directly. In the

Highlands of Scotland, for example, the walker frequently sees notices sporting messages like this one: 'Deer in these hills are shot from mid-August to February for sport, meat and Government control policy. Walkers are therefore warned that rambling on high ground at this time can seriously upset large areas for deer stalking and can be dangerous.'[7] The 'intent' on the part of trespassers to obstruct lawful activity which the act now criminalizes might be deemed to amount to no more than possessing awareness of the probable consequences of the trespasser's acts. If a landowner puts up signs telling people that their presence may disturb deer stalking, pheasant rearing, lambing, forestry operations, or whatever else he likes to specify, he might then be able to claim that a walker who must have seen his notice but still went on to his land 'intended' to disrupt the named activity and was therefore guilty of the new offence. He would then be in a position to call the police. The success of the prosecution of a rambler who merely ignored a sign warning that deer stalking was in progress would doubtless turn on legal argument about the meaning of 'intent'. But the mere possibility that such a prosecution might succeed strengthens the landowner's armoury against the walker.

In 1995 in a policy paper entitled *A Working Countryside* the Labour Party said that it would 'remove the recently imposed threat of aggravated trespass powers against innocent people enjoying the countryside'.[8] By the middle of 1998 this had not been put into effect, and the Crime and Disorder Bill of 1998, which might have been expected to provide the vehicle for repeal, contained no such provision.

The Law of Access

Of course, alongside the laws ensuring you are kept out of most of the countryside are other laws entitling you to be in some parts of it at some times.

Public Footpaths and Other Highways

England and Wales

By far the most important provider of access to the countryside in England and Wales at present is highway law, which entitles anybody to move along predetermined routes across the land, as of right, by day or night. 'Highways' come in five main kinds. On public footpaths you may proceed only on foot; on bridleways you may ride a horse or a bicycle; on roads you may travel in motorized vehicles. On a small number of byways, known as 'byways open to all traffic', you may also take a vehicle, even though the surface will probably be unmetalled; but you are not entitled to take a vehicle or a horse along a small number of 'roads used as public paths'. Together these different types of highway penetrate almost every corner of Britain: everybody knows where roads are and that they have a right to travel them, and even public paths (footpaths, bridleways, roads used as public paths, and byways open to all traffic) are required by law to be signposted where they leave the public road, though this does not always happen. All acknowledged public highways are prominently marked on Ordnance Survey maps.[9]

The walker on a public path is, however, legally entitled only to pass and repass: this means he is entitled to stop and rest, but not to step off the path onto adjoining land and, say, scale a crag rising above the path or to venture down a cave at the end of the path— all these things need the permission of the landowner. At the same time, the landowner has no right to change the course of the path even temporarily without permission: he must allow the public to use it whether he likes to or not. Landowners who wish to eliminate a length of public path or divert it permanently have to submit their proposals to the highway authority, which is the unitary council or, where two tiers occur, the county council. The council will publicize the proposed change in the press and elsewhere. If objections are voiced, a public inquiry will be held and a decision taken by the Secretary of State for the Environment, Transport, and the Regions or the Secretary of State for Wales. Anybody who impedes the passage of the public along any kind of public highway, whether road or path, risks prosecution by the highway authority: a landowner who erects a barbed wire fence, plants crops, or puts up a building across a public footpath is as culpable as somebody who blocks a road. Public highways run with the land—in other words their existence is not dependent on the goodwill of the landowners across whose land they pass. Nor does their presence depend on a particular form of land use: a landowner may wish to turn a field into a forest or a housing estate but he must still work round any of the public roads or paths that exist as slivers of public land inside his own holdings. In some circumstances even the minimum width of public highways is set down in law. If the surface of a highway is interfered with, it must be reinstated, and in such cases public footpaths, for instance, must be at least 1 metre wide, rising to 1.5 metres if they run round the edge of a field.

Our present network of public roads and paths was not of course devised for recreation: by and large, it represents the old communications network of the countryside. The public footpaths and bridleways in particular largely follow the routes established in the days when country people walked or rode on horseback from place to place and the social and economic life of the countryside depended on their ability to do this easily. Today, on top of thousands of miles of road, England and Wales has a total of 101,416 miles of public footpath, 21,450 miles of public bridleway, 4,590 miles of road used as public path, and 2,267 miles of byway open to all traffic—a density of 2.2 miles of public path per square mile of land. In the National Parks and Access to the Countryside Act of 1949 Parliament charged highway authorities with the duty of preparing a 'definitive map' of all routes considered to be public paths in their areas at the time the maps were prepared, mainly in the 1950s and 1960s; these routes were co-ordinated across local council boundaries to form an integrated network. Now highway authorities must keep the maps up to date. When the Ordnance Survey came to use the definitive maps in the preparation of its own maps it chose to use the colour red for public paths, which gives them startling prominence.

Public paths are sometimes eliminated and diverted, but some are also asserted, for example, where walkers can prove that a route has been used by the public without let or hindrance for an uninterrupted period of twenty years and get it added to the definitive map. Highway authorities can also create new paths in cases where they consider there is a need and, if they fail to come to an agreement with a landowner (and secure a public path creation agreement), they can create a path by making a public path creation order. The creation of paths involves rigorous legal procedures with opportunities for path is established by whatever means, it is permanent: 'once a high-way, always a highway' is a deep-rooted principle. Today walkers, riders, and motorists can enjoy views down over Canterbury Cathedral and low-lying marshland beside the River Stour by virtue of a road which runs along a ridge linking the tiny settlement of Stodmarsh to Canterbury. In 1320 this route was but a track, and in that year the authority responsible for maintaining it closed it. Users of the path, mainly monks at a local monastery, were so incensed that they took the case to court. The sheriff ordered that the path be kept open as he judged it to be an 'ancient and allowed highway'. The belief that a public right of way has to be used regularly to prevent its being lost is unfounded, so that temporary circumstances such as obstructions or even lack of use for twenty years or more do not affect the con-tinued existence of a public path.

Nonetheless, a not insignificant amount of the paths network changes, as a result of legal procedures, every year. Setting aside addi-tions to the network, John Trevelyan, the Deputy Director of the Ramblers' Association, estimates that there have been about 20,000 legal events or legal changes to the network since 1983, when the Associ-ation started compiling records. He also told me in 1998 that he thought that the number of changes since 1949 would be of the order of 50,000. Users of Ordnance Survey maps will recognize this small but not insignificant change to the path network. There are enough changes over time—here the diversion of a path round a field edge; there a change of route to make way for a housing estate—to render most OS maps slightly out of date over a period of say ten years.

Of course, not all paths are public paths or even all roads public roads. On an Ordnance Survey map you will see besides the public roads, which are coloured, 'white roads' bounded simply by continu-ous or broken black lines. These roads may be surfaced with fine black tarmacadam and appear to take you where you want to go. But they are not open to the public, even on foot. They are normally private roads whose use is restricted to the owner of the land involved and to anybody he or she chooses to allow along it. Similarly, alongside the public footpaths and bridleways marked in red on Ordnance Survey maps is a much larger network of paths marked only in black along which the public have no right to go. While the public footpaths, bridleways, and other public paths of the United Kingdom total about 130,000 miles, such private paths run to many times this length.

A few of these other private routes can be used by the public as 'permissive paths' or 'concessionary paths'. The status of such paths varies. At one extreme is the owner who turns a blind eye to use of his path by the general public, or perhaps tells people that he happens to meet that they may walk there. In some cases access rests on an informal arrangement with an official from a public agency: the landowner has agreed, shaken hands, and walked away. Such agreements can be useful, but they are not underpinned by any legal security and if the landowner changes his mind the path is normally lost. In other cases, the landowner involved enters into a written agreement with a public body. However, such agreements normally contain a clause providing that either party can pull out at two or three months' notice; agreements also usually stipulate that use of the permissive path shall never be adduced in support of an application for the creation of a public path along the same route. Since use is the main criterion for establishing such rights, a permissive agreement of this kind can therefore be an obstacle to the creation of a public footpath. Permissive paths may also include restrictions which cannot be applied to rights of way, such as a ban on dogs or use outside daylight hours or at certain times of the year. And although such facilities can be important means of enabling people to visit particular stretches of countryside, they are not marked on Ordnance Survey maps, so ignorance of their existence can limit their usefulness.

Nonetheless, the public path network of England and Wales does ensure that you are never too far from a route along which you can penetrate the countryside. In Scotland and Northern Ireland, however, things are very different.

Scotland and Northern Ireland

The familiar 'Public Footpath' (or 'Llwybr Cyhoeddus') signs which spring up along the roadsides fairly frequently in England and Wales are rare in Scotland and almost non-existent in Northern Ireland. The various indicators marking public paths on different kinds of maps are equally scarce in Scotland and Northern Ireland, and often accompanied by a disclaimer indicating that the routes marked are not necessarily rights of way. In these two parts of the UK public paths play no significant role. Some do nonetheless exist, and local councils enjoy powers to create, divert, and extinguish them, while the rights of the general public to pass along them are similar to those in England and Wales. There are, however, important differences in the status of these paths as well as their numbers.

The rule 'once a highway, always a highway' does not apply in Scotland, so paths can be lost if they are not used. If it can be shown that a right of way has been unused for a continuous period of twenty years and that no claim in relation to it has been made, the right can be extinguished. Rights of way in Scotland are considered to run between one 'public place' and another. If a right of way runs through several public places each stretch between one public place and the next is considered a separate right of way. So any one of these stretches is vulnerable to extinguishment through lack of use, at which point the whole route is broken. Loss of a path through lack of use is a serious risk in remote areas where the main potential users are elderly country dwellers. Even if some of them have used a path within the previous twenty years they may die before they can give evidence. In Northern Ireland public paths are permanent, as in England and Wales.

Both Scotland and Northern Ireland lack the definitive map system for public paths which operates in England and Wales. In Northern Ireland district councils have a duty to prepare maps of rights of way in their areas, while in Scotland this is a discretionary power only. In neither case are councils required to carry out surveys to ascertain what rights of way exist in their areas and to prepare the co-ordinated maps, going through a complicated series of drafts which are drawn up before approval. The absence of definitive maps and the preparation process which underpins them is one of the main reasons why public paths in both Scotland and Northern Ireland are so patchily and thinly distributed.

Down District, south of Belfast, for example covers 250 square miles and boasts forty public paths—far more than any other district in the Province. Omagh District, covering 300 square miles of gently rolling glens, forests, farmland, moor, loughs, and rivers in the heart of the

Province contains only seven public paths. Neighbouring Strabane's 336 square miles have fifteen 'accepted routes', along which the current landowners accept a right-of-way status although this has not been vindicated in a court of law and so could be challenged. Fermanagh to the west, which includes farm, forest, open hill land, lakes, and rivers covering an area of 724 square miles, has no public paths whatsoever.

Scotland has a higher density of public paths than Northern Ireland—but nothing approaching the close-knit skein of paths traditionally associated with Britain. The maps of rights of way in Scotland held by the Scottish Rights of Way Society and Scottish Natural Heritage are the only comprehensive collection in the country, and were assembled by the Society through separate visits to local authorities. They show that the vast majority of paths are short routes radiating from towns; they do not link up into any kind of network and many of them are cul-de-sacs. In upland areas, paths are longer, but are usually confined to the lower ground—mountain passes and the bottoms of glens; most follow the old drove roads along which cattle and sheep were driven to market or old military roads used by the English to contain subversion. In the Scottish islands, public paths are virtually absent. In 1998 the Society calculated that Scotland had a total of 10,202 miles of rights of way. Four per cent of these were bridleways; 43 per cent were footpaths; vehicular rights existed on 2 per cent. The status of the remaining 51 per cent has not been broken down.[10] The average density of public paths in Scotland is 0.2 miles of path per square mile of countryside—compared to the average in England and Wales of 2.2.

Even the few public paths that exist in Scotland often enjoy less status than those in England and Wales. Eighty-four per cent of the so-called public paths of Scotland are no more than routes along which a local council believes public rights to exist: these 'claimed' paths have no more legal status than many routes over which claims for public path status languish in in-trays in highway authority offices up and down England and Wales. In respect of a further 15 per cent of Scotland's 'public paths', highway authorities have actually interviewed witnesses; but only 1 per cent are 'vindicated' paths, whose claim to public status has been backed by a court of law. It is only over this fraction of Scotland's supposedly public paths that high-way authorities are empowered to require a landowner to remove an obstruction—something their counterparts in England and Wales can do over all 130,000 miles of their public paths. In the other cases, a council complaining to a landowner that his crops or fences were blocking what they considered a right of way would have to prove the validity of the right before they could enforce the removal of the obstruction. The absence of a co-ordinated network of paths where the public enjoy an unchallenged right to walk means that it is far more difficult to plan circular walks extending to say 20 or 30 miles. In England and Wales many such walks are promoted—like the Dales Way, the Jubilee Way, the Weald Way, the Hangers Way, and so on; but you will not find many similar medium-distance walks in Northern Ireland or Scotland. The National Parks and Access to the Countryside Act of 1949 which provided public path legislation in England and Wales also introduced the concept of the 'long-distance path', now known as the 'national trail'—paths usually at least 70 miles long where the public is able to make extensive journeys on foot, horse-back, or bicycle. Eleven of these have been designated in England and Wales—such as the Thames Trail, the Pennine Way, the South Downs Way, and the Wolds Way. In Scotland, where the powers to designate such paths were introduced in 1967, only four such paths have been designated, and one of these (the Speyside Way) is still in the making. The Ulster Way is the only long-distance path in Northern Ireland. While this provides fine walking through a variety of scenery, it runs for much of its length along metalled roads, state forestry tracks in conifer plantations, and permissive routes, many of them based only on handshake agreements. The informality of these permissive routes leaves the Way vulnerable to closures and unofficial diversions.

Unitary and district councils in Scotland and Northern Ireland have a statutory duty to assert and protect rights of way in their areas. However, in seeking to assert such rights they are denied what their English and Welsh counterparts find one of the most reliable sources of evidence of the existence of such rights—parliamentary enclosure awards. These awards testify to access rights in those 7 million acres of England and Wales which were subject to enclosure by private Act of Parliament, mainly in the eighteenth and nineteenth centuries.

However, enclosure did not proceed through Act of Parliament in Scotland or Northern Ireland. Occasionally ancient parchments indicate a public path, but this rarely amounts to the almost conclusive proof that an enclosure award affords. Almost always highway authorities in Scotland and Northern Ireland must rely on the laborious deployment of actual evidence of long continuous use of the route as of right. To make matters even more difficult, the criteria for establishing that a path is a public right of way are more challenging than they are in England and Wales. Meeting the requirement that a route must connect two 'public places' introduces difficulties of its own. What is a public place? The much frequented summit of a mountain? The beach? In both cases, not necessarily. People have to have enjoyed a legal right to be at the place for it to become a 'public place'.

Even though public footpaths are thin on the ground in Scotland and Northern Ireland, those that exist are not necessarily well known. In England and Wales highway authorities must signpost all public paths where they leave a metalled road unless the parish council agrees this is not necessary. In Scotland and Northern Ireland, signposting is discretionary not mandatory, so councils put up signs only if they wish to do so, and as a result such paths as do exist may go unsung. In England and Wales there is an effective guarantee that a public path will be free of encroaching natural vegetation and that its surface will be traversable without undue hazard because highway authorities have a duty to maintain the surface of rights of way which can of course be enforced in the courts. This guarantee does not exist in Scotland and Northern Ireland. There, local councils are legally required to protect the rights of the public and they can prosecute landowners who obstruct them. But they are certainly not required to keep the surface of paths in a usable state, even though they have a discretionary power to do so. In Scotland highway authorities have a duty to keep public paths in a fit condition for use by the public only if the paths involved result from path creation agreements or orders or diversion orders. The majority of Scotland's paths arise from the twenty-year use rule and in such cases no maintenance responsibility rests either with the public authority or the owner of the land.

Area Access

British law introduces a very sharp distinction between access along routes and over areas. While it allows continuous use along a particular route to become a public right, this is not the case over whole areas. No matter how long the public may have been wandering over a particular place, mere customary use will not become a public right of access.[11] What all this means is that roaming freely is a very different matter from proceeding along public rights of way. There are places where you can roam, but only where special and rather uncommon circumstances have created them.

Legally Accessible Common Land

In England and Wales, the right to roam freely is most frequently encountered on certain stretches of what is called 'common land'. Epping Forest, the Malvern Hills, Wimbledon Common, Ilkley Moor, Berkhamsted Common, and many others—here the public enjoy a legal right of recreation associated with the common land status of the areas involved, enabling them to walk where they will. However, common land is not automatically or even usually open to the public as of right. In total, 1.5 million acres, or 4 per cent of the land surface of England and Wales, is defined as common land. Of this, only one-fifth is open to the public by legal right, though a custom of tolerated trespass—or *de facto* access—exists over much of the remaining four-fifths.

Common land is not, as is often assumed, owned in common by the citizenry. A common is normally a piece of usually private land on which, through ancient arrangement, specified people other than the owner called 'commoners' (often the occupants of nearby cottages or farmland) enjoy a legal right 'in common', i.e. collectively, to profit from the land in specified ways—say, to gather firewood, graze sheep, cattle, geese, or goats, dig peat, or take fish. Less often, land is common land because it is a surviving relic of the waste land of the manors of medieval England and Wales. An Act of Parliament in 1965 required all county councils to prepare registers of common land, and a sight of one of these registers (now held by county, unitary, and metropolitan district councils) reveals an enormous variety in size and type of land involved—a strip of road verge here, a 5,000-acre moor there, a traffic-island of scrubby grassland here, a length of sand dune there.

The public has rights over common land that it does not enjoy elsewhere. In particular, a landowner who wishes to fence a stretch of common land, whether for farming, building, or some other purpose, has to secure the Secretary of State's consent if the work involved would prevent or impede public access to the common. Secondly, a government department or local authority which wishes to compulsorily purchase a stretch of common land for use, say, as a new road or a school, must first seek the approval of Parliament unless it can give to the common suitable land in exchange. Thirdly, the public enjoy a legal right to roam freely over certain categories of common land.

Both Scotland and Northern Ireland contain stretches of land which have some similarity to the common land of England and Wales. In Northern Ireland 'commonages' are usually owned jointly by the people who share common grazing, usually over a stretch of hill country. Around the north and north-west coast of Scotland and in Shetland and the Hebrides lie extensive lands usually privately owned but over which crofters may pasture their animals in common, known as 'commonties'. However, neither category of land is common land as legally defined in England and Wales, and thus the public enjoy no special rights to it.

The types of common land over which the public enjoys a right to wander fall into six main categories. The most important category is undoubtedly commons in urban areas. An extremely significant piece of legislation in the field of access to the countryside—Section 193 of the Law of Property Act of 1925—gave all citizens a new legal right of access 'for air and exercise' over all common land lying wholly or partly within urban districts and metropolitan areas throughout England and Wales. Today, this provision safeguards the public's presence on many small commons as well as over larger well-known public open spaces like Southampton Common, Hampstead Heath, Baildon Common outside Shipley in Yorkshire, Blackheath in south-east London, the Strays of York, Port Meadow in Oxford, the Sands in Durham City, Newcastle Town Moor, and Midsummer Common in Cambridge. Like public footpaths and bridleways, urban commons are open night and day, all year round. Although (unlike public footpaths) their accessibility is not delineated on most Ordnance Survey maps, their long-standing tradition of availability, their closeness to people's homes, and their wild aspect make them extremely valuable.

Around 3,000 villages in England and 140 villages in Wales have areas legally defined as 'village greens', which are usually also common land. Like urban commons, village greens are usually unfenced and legally accessible all the time. Strictly speaking, the legal rights involved extend only to local inhabitants, and then only for active recreation activities, like dancing or playing cricket. In practice, any citizen can walk freely over any village green. In counties with plenty of village greens the access available on village greens can be extremely important. Thus despite its industrial image, Durham has only three small urban commons, but it has 100 village greens.

Apart from these two general categories, there are certain other commons over which a legal right to move freely survives. Dartmoor has been common land for the people of Devon since time immemorial. Today, the main uses of the 90,000 acres of registered common on the Moor are sheep grazing and Army training. Under a unique private Act of Parliament passed in 1985, the Dartmoor Commons Act, the public enjoy a legal right to wander at will (and to ride a horse) over all this land, except that this right is suspended over the military lands when live firing is taking place. Attempts were made during the 1990s to promote a similar bill for the common land on nearby Bodmin Moor in east Cornwall but these were blocked by the landowners and commoners involved.

The freedom of movement the public enjoys over land belonging to the National Trust is usually permissive: it arises because the Trust owns the land and chooses to welcome the public on to it. However, it enjoys no option but to allow the public onto the 163,020 acres of common land to which it holds title. The provision of access to open commons close to towns and cities but also those lying in upland areas like the Lake District was a special aim of the Trust's founders at the turn of the last century. Today, access is required and in practice provided to commons like the Brecon Beacons, Pen-Y-Fan, and the Sugar Loaf mountain near by, Toys Hill and Ide Hill near Edenbridge in Kent, Headley Heath in Surrey, and many others by the National Trust Act of 1907, which laid down that the Trust should keep all commons it owns 'unenclosed and unbuilt on as open spaces for the recreation and enjoyment of the public'.

There is a further category of land over which the public enjoy a legal freedom to wander even though the land involved is not always common land. This consists of stretches of land over which a guarantee of public access is provided by private Acts of Parliament whose prime purpose was to empower public bodies to build reservoirs. The main sites are in the Lake District (31 square miles around Haweswater and Thirlmere) and 70 square miles of land acquired by Birmingham Corporation as reservoirs and water-gathering ground in the Elan and Claerwen valleys of mid-Wales.

In all these categories, there is provision for the behaviour of the public to be controlled through by-laws, which can turn activities which might cause problems, such as lighting fires or playing radios or musical instruments in ways which might annoy others, into offences for which the offender can be prosecuted in a magistrate's court and fined. This is a far easier means for landowners or indeed commoners to control public behaviour than pursuing civil actions using the law of trespass. The authors of the 1925 Law of Property Act clearly considered the power to make by-laws of great importance: they drew up detailed provisions making any rights of access provided under the act subject to any by-laws. They also specified that the right to roam they introduced over urban commons should not include any right to take vehicles or to camp or light fires. Furthermore, they empowered the Minister, now the Secretary of State for the Environment, Transport, and the Regions, or for Wales, to impose conditions and limits on access on the application of the lord of the manor or some other person with a proprietary interest in the common.

Although the 1925 act exempted rural commons from the general right of public access, it allowed for the owners of rural commons to deposit legal deeds of covenant granting this facility with the Minister. Those who did so would benefit from the same provision for by-laws and limitations on access as the owners of urban commons.

Soon after the act was passed a number of such deeds were deposited and around 120,000 acres of common are covered by them, of which 63,000 acres consist of common owned by the Crown Estate, mainly in Wales. Some of the landowners involved seem to have granted deeds for altruistic reasons, but it seems likely that many were attracted by the act's provision for by-laws and the like. During the 1920s many commons especially urban ones but also many rural ones were used by the public for open-air recreation, even though they had no legal right to do so. Landowners found it difficult and expensive to prevent them doing this on the unmanageable open spaces involved, and they found it almost as difficult to regulate and control the behaviour of people they were unable to exclude. At a stroke the act provided landowners with a means of ensuring that public behaviour on their land was regulated at the public expense. For some at least, regularizing public access in this way, even if they would have preferred to prevent it, represented the lesser evil.

Unlike the rights of access provided over urban commons, National Trust commons, the commons of Dartmoor, and land covered by certain private acts, the access granted under deeds of covenant can usually be revoked. When this happens, access may be lost completely or at least significantly reduced. Ranmore Common is on the North Downs in Surrey just over one mile from Dorking. Its deciduous woodland has been used for many years for walks and horse-rides both by people living locally and visitors from London who were able to alight at Boxhill station close by. However, in 1990 a new owner of 130 acres of the common blocked off some of the main tracks with logs; his staff then patrolled the site, ordering people off. Some local residents who happened to be looking into other matters at the public record office at Kew chanced upon a deed of covenant entered into by a previous owner in 1929 which formally granted access to this part of Ranmore Common. They brought this to the attention of the local council, who in turn pointed out its existence to the new owner. He thereupon revoked the deed, thus making people trespassers on land over which they had formerly been roaming legitimately.

British law has no provision for a long-held freedom to wander over land to be transformed into a legal right to move freely, in the way that use of a path can be so transformed. Walkers (and riders) therefore sought to establish public paths over the area by providing evidence of twenty years' use. Three established public paths and one short length of road already crossed the site; local people sought to create seven more rights of way along tracks over the common. These efforts were rebuffed in 1996. An inspector ruled that the paths could not be converted into rights of way because of the existence of the very deed which had legitimized walking over the area in the past. He deemed that the deed gave people permission to use the tracks which they were now claiming as public paths, and you cannot claim a right of way in respect of a route over which you have been passing with permission for some of the relevant twenty-year period. Of course nobody, not even the new owner himself, local people, or the local authorities knew of the existence of the deed: it had simply been deposited with the Ministry of Agriculture which had declined to publicize it. By discovering it, the activists had ironically ruined what would otherwise have been a good means of frustrating, at least in part, the new owner's plans to exclude them.

The local man who had led the fight, Robert Billson, was however not ready to accept defeat and appealed to the High Court. In 1998 a judge upheld the inspector's decision and Mr Billson was left with costs of £50,000. He did not have the resources to take the case to the Court of Appeal though here he might have got a different result. Although the Secretary of State's Inspector ruled against the paths, the Secretary of State himself had earlier disagreed, arguing that the mere existence of the deed was not sufficient to render the access permissive: it would have needed to be conveyed to the public, so that they were aware of it, to have been effective.

The presence of the public on rights of way, certain categories of common land, and on areas covered by private Acts of Parliament involves a number of legal rights. There are also places where people can move around not in pursuit of rights which run with the land for all time but in pursuit of provisions which allow for access only at certain places and in certain times. This can be achieved by compulsion, through cross-compliance (as a quid pro quo for a permission), or through voluntary agreement.

Compulsory Orders

Parliament has provided local authorities with the power to force a landowner to grant access not only to a linear route (as in a public path creation order) but also over the whole of an area of land. The authority for this is to be found in Clement Attlee's 1949 National Parks and Access to the Countryside Act, which devotes one whole section to such access alongside an equivalent section for public paths. But while public paths can pass across any type of terrain, the powers for securing access to whole areas are confined to what was first defined in the 1949 act as 'open country', then restricted to mountain, moor, heath, down, cliff, or foreshore. Today the definitions of 'open country' in the various parts of the UK are similar but differ slightly. In England and Wales it covers mountain, moor, cliff, down, heath, foreshore, woodland, lakeside, riverbank, and canalside (National Parks and Access to the Countryside Act, 1949 as amended by the Countryside Act, 1968). Scotland's 'open country' takes in mountain, moor, heath, hill, woodland, cliff, foreshore, including any waterways in such land (Countryside (Scotland) Act, 1967); and that for Northern Ireland is: mountain, moor, heath, hill, woodland, cliff, foreshore, bog, marsh, and waterway (Access to the Countryside (Northern Ireland) Order, 1983). Access orders may be made only in cases where a local council has tried and failed to secure an 'access agreement' with the landowner involved. It must then secure the Secretary of State for the Environment, Transport, and the Regions (or the Secretary of State for Wales, Scotland, or Northern Ireland's) consent before the order can come into force. In addition to the power to impose access orders, local planning authorities may also buy areas of open country to provide for public access, compulsorily if necessary, although such a compulsory purchase order also requires the Secretary of State's consent. No land, however, has ever been compulsorily purchased for recreation, and only two access orders have ever been made. One covered a stretch of private-owned beach at Seaton in south Cornwall.[12] The other, which is still in force, covers a 514-acre stretch of moor at Wolf Fell in Lancashire. An earlier order under which Lancashire County Council tried to secure access to

Boulsworth Moor in 1956 was turned down by the Minister despite his inspector's recommendation in favour of the proposal. Five years after an order comes into effect, a local council must compensate a landowner in respect of any depreciation in the value of the land caused by the public access. Councils are required to publish maps showing the location of any land covered by an access order.

Cross-compliance

Landowners can be required to grant public access to land as a condition of receiving some benefit from a public body. There are several instances of this.

Tyr Cymen

One case in point applies to farmers in Wales who are receiving grants for agreeing to conserve and enhance the landscape, wildlife, and historical value of their holdings. In 1992 the government agency responsible for conservation in Wales, the Countryside Council for Wales, launched an experimental grant scheme called Tyr Cymen in three districts in Wales (Swansea, Dinefwr, and Merioneth) which together cover about one-fifth of the Principality. Under this scheme, farmers can apply for grants if they agree to undertake conservation work throughout their farm. This usually involves the conservation of existing semi-natural habitats, the protection of archaeological features, and often improving the management and reconstitution of landscape features. If the farm involved includes any open hill land, it is a condition that they have to allow the public the freedom to wander it. By 1997 access was provided in this way over 135 square miles of open hill land, most of it in Merioneth. Farmers who have opted to put their farms in Tyr Cymen also have the option of applying to the Countryside Council for Wales for a payment in return for agreeing to establish new permissive paths. Although the access areas and access paths provided under Tyr Cymen are not shown on Ordnance Survey maps, maps showing the position of these facilities are available at public libraries and local tourist information centres in Wales.

Inheritance Tax Exemption

Another arrangement in which access is required as a condition for the receipt of money for something else operates through the Inheritance Tax Exemption scheme, though here things are less straightforward and transparent than under Tyr Cymen.

In 1976, Harold Wilson's government, faced with protests from landowners at the replacement of death duty with a tax on lifetime transfers called Capital Transfer Tax, introduced exemptions from the tax subject to compliance with certain conditions. This arrangement survived the replacement of Capital Transfer Tax with Inheritance Tax in 1986. Paintings, manuscripts, and 'other museum quality objects' and land of outstanding scenic, historic, or scientific interest can all be exempted from the tax when gifted or bequeathed so long as they are deemed of special quality. In the case of land, the Inland Revenue has to be persuaded by the relevant government agencies responsible for conservation that the land is of outstanding quality. In return for the exemption, owners have to undertake not only that they will conserve the special qualities of the land but also that they will provide 'reasonable public access'. Twenty years after the concession was introduced, a total of 409 square miles of Great Britain involving 189 designations were covered by the arrangements, according to figures provided by the Inland Revenue in response to a parliamentary question in 1996.[13] Although the sums involved in tax forgone frequently run into millions of pounds, the conservation and access benefit to the public is often extremely limited. Conservation gains often amount to little more than commitments requiring a landowner to continue existing land management practices; access benefits are often even more limited. On the prime and extremely valuable Highclere Estate in north Hampshire, which we describe on pages 74 and 82, an inheritance tax exemption does not stop thousands of acres of attractive land from remaining out of reach for most of the year.

In 1998 the government attempted to improve matters. It undertook that in the case of existing schemes there would be 'extended access' and more disclosure of access provisions where access is only by appointment. This restriction to cases where appointment is involved means that any improvements will affect mainly works of art since stretches of countryside are rarely open by prior appointment: any rural land affected at all is likely to be such as may be associated with the few number of houses open by prior appointment.[14] For new schemes, prospects of improvement are better. Here the public will supposedly have 'extended access' to tax-exempt assets; the conditions will be subject to change and there will be more disclosure of conditions of the exemption. If this turns out to be substantial it could be significant, since the arrangements in the past left publicizing any access provided to the landowner concerned. As a result, the existence of access in practice depended not only on whether landowners chose to seek exemption but also how far they bothered to publicize any access theoretically provided.

Whatever changes actually occur are unlikely to contribute much to the overall availability of access to the countryside. The scheme is already attracting fewer applications: in 1998 the Countryside Commission was being consulted on only about a dozen formal applications each year. Any toughening up will make it less appealing still to landowners. The reason for the decline in interest in the conditional scheme is the easier availability of completely unconditional exemption from inheritance tax. In 1992 the Major government granted 100 per cent relief from inheritance tax for all commercial woodlands and for owner-occupied farmland. In 1996 total exemption was extended to tenanted farmland which has been entered into a new business tenancy—in effect most rented farmland.

There is also provision for conditional exemption from inheritance tax if land of outstanding scenic, historic, or scientific interest is given to a public body like the National Trust or a national park authority. This source of accessible land is also likely to dry up with the extension of unconditional exemption.

Planning gain

The town and country planning system assumes that those who make significant financial gains when they are granted consent to develop should share some of the financial benefit they enjoy with the community. This recompense took the form of a financial payment to the state until development land tax was abolished in 1979. Thereafter a new concept developed, known as 'planning gain'. This means the community benefits not through a cash payment but through the provision of other public benefits and facilities. In towns and cities it may mean extra public housing or a meeting hall when a shopping centre is built. In rural Britain, the almost total exemption of the industries which use most of the land—farming and forestry—from the town and country planning machinery means that the opportunities for securing public access through planning gain are very limited. Even developments subject to planning control, like the building of equestrian centres or small-scale housing schemes, are usually considered too small to be subject to planning gain. However, medium and large-scale housing developments, the building of factories and offices, and the construction of large golf courses on rural land do offer scope for this approach. No comprehensive survey has been carried out of the access or indeed other conditions involved in planning gain agreements in rural areas, but my impression is that local councils who decide to seek access as a condition of planning gain seem usually to require that it be permanent or semi-permanent on the grounds that the development itself will be long-lasting. This usually means that the new access must come either through new or diverted rights of way or through the vesting of land in a public body committed to providing access. For example, Newbury District Council in west Berkshire has managed to secure entirely new public footpaths as part of planning gain deals over two eighteen-hole golf course developments which have now been put into effect. The first course has been built on farmland on the Englefield estate at Theale, west of Reading, owned by former MP Richard Benyon (which we refer to again on page 77). The agreement, secured under section 106 of the Town and Country Planning Act 1990, has provided for a new public footpath within the circumference of the course; the agreement also provides for the planting of trees and bushes and for the management of an ancient woodland. The second course, created in a historic park at Donnington Grove on the northern edge of Newbury now owned by a Japanese Buddhist charity, Shi Tennoji International, has led to the creation of three new public footpaths, the repair of Donnington Grove house (a castellated mansion of blue brick described by Pevsner as 'a little Gothic gem'), the management and replanting of wood-land, and the management for wildlife of marsh and reed-bed bor-dering the River Lambourn.

Access by Voluntary Agreement

Access agreements

The same legislation which provides for access orders enables local authorities to arrange public access by agreement. Indeed, as we observed, an authority has to try for an agreement before it can make an order. Authorities can make access agreements with landowners providing for the public to wander freely over stretches of land while existing activities like sheep grazing, forestry, or grouse or pheasant rearing continue. As with orders, only land defined in law as 'open country' can be the subject of an access agreement; we have seen this does however now take in not only moorland, downland, mountain, and heathland, but woodland, foreshore, lakeside, canalside, and riverbank as well in most parts of the UK. Under an access agreement, a landowner agrees not to treat the public as trespassers over an area of his land; for its part the local authority usually agrees to manage recreation by making by-laws and, at popular sites, employing war-dens to enforce them.

An example. In 1996 South Norfolk District Council entered into an access agreement with the owner of a 40-acre stretch of woodland, open heath, and banks of the River Tas 3 miles north of Wymondham known as Smock Mill Common (though it is not a registered com-mon). The area had been open to the public unofficially and indeed certain groups like motorcyclists and New Age travellers were caus-ing erosion. Today the public have the right to be present on the Common, to walk their dogs, to picnic and sit and rest, and a typ-ical Sunday afternoon sees thirty or so people there. By-laws which the council has formulated outlaw the activities which used to cause problems. The agreement provides for no payment to the landowner for the access created; the costs to the council lie in enforcing by-laws through a warden who manages all the countryside sites in which South Norfolk has a proprietary interest.

Access agreements may require the planning authority to suspend access at certain times. Agreements covering stretches of moorland in Yorkshire and Derbyshire (where the majority of access agreements exist which cover substantial areas) allow owners to nominate up to thirty days a year when they can keep the moor to themselves, usually in these cases for grouse shooting; elsewhere access may be suspended on agreed dates to allow for activities which might conflict with public access, such as pheasant shooting or tree felling. Local authorities are usually also free to close access agreement land at times of high fire risk—in contrast to public paths which are always open.

Although the access agreement appears to be a sophisticated and civilized instrument for marrying informal recreation with economically productive rural activities, it actually affects only a small fragment of the countryside. In 1974, when the last comprehensive survey was carried out for England and Wales, land covered by access agreements, access orders, or the purchase of land for access under the 1949 act covered only 126 square miles or 0.2 per cent of England and Wales. In fact it seems that the number of access agreements is greater than it was twenty or even ten years ago and that access agreements may be making something of a comeback. There are still no access agreements whatsoever in Northern Ireland. In Scotland, however, access agreements are not uncommon: Scottish Natural Heritage, which has carried out a survey, estimates that about one-third of all local authorities in Scotland have made one or more access agreements although most of these cover only a small area. This is very different from the situation in the 1980s when only a handful of authorities in Scotland had ever made any access agreements. In England too, use of the access agreement may be becoming more widespread. Sean Prendergast, a student at Manchester Metropolitan University, has received replies on the use of access agreement powers from 80 per cent of local councils in England. Mr Prendergast discovered that in 1994 a total of twenty local councils were party to fifty-nine access agreements, although one authority, the Peak National Park Authority, which administers the Peak District national park, accounted for 44 per cent of the total area of access land, with 76 square miles. Mr Prendergast's figures do not enable us to say for sure how much land is covered by access agreements since he also questioned local councils about other kinds of agreements involving access, such as management agreements including clauses which allowed for public access, as well as agreements providing for access negotiated as 'planning gain'. All told, Mr Prendergast calculated that land covered by all these agreements in England occupied a total of 184 square miles, or 0.4 per cent of England's land. The so-called access agreements that have been made in recent years in Scotland also involve not only agreements under Scotland's equivalent to the 1949 act—the 1967 Countryside (Scotland) Act—but also other types of agreement. In Scotland too a small number of authorities is responsible for most of the access agreement land, notably Highland Council and East Lothian and Stirling District Councils. In both England and Scotland those local councils that make the largest number of access agreements tend to be those which have a history of making access agreements or other arrangements for open-air recreation—a history which sometimes goes back a long time.

Although access agreement land has not been indicated on most Ordnance Survey maps up till now, its existence is usually widely publicized by the local authority or national park authority which is party to the agreement. However, throughout most of the UK there is no guarantee that access provided through access agreements will run for all time: access agreements can lapse if title to the land changes and the new owner does not wish to continue, even if land simply passes from one member of the family to another. They also automatically come up for renewal at regular intervals, usually after twenty or twenty-five years. The exception is Scotland, where access agreements must be recorded in the Register of Sasines (the land register for Scotland) and, once recorded, are enforceable subject to limited exceptions, on subsequent owners.

Access agreements often involve some payment to the landowner particularly in respect of any damage that may be caused to his land, but they do not always do so. There has never been any assumption that landowners would receive payment as a consideration of providing the access itself, although research carried out by Dr Judith Rossiter has shown that where this occurred in agreements made between 1949 and 1968 and still in existence in 1972, the sums involved never amounted to much.[15] Two other key characteristics of the access agreement arrangements are that the selection of sites is based primarily on their potential for affording the public recreation enjoyment; and particularly in the early days this selection was enhanced by provision for the strategic review of access land in every county in England and Wales. The 1949 National Parks and Access to the Countryside Act required all county councils to review their areas to see which land fell within the definition 'open country' and then to see over which of these areas access should be secured in county-wide 'review maps' within two years of the coming into operation of the act. The Scottish legislation in 1967 required the government agency established then to oversee countryside conservation and access provision, the Countryside Commission for Scotland, now Scottish Natural Heritage, to consult with local planning authorities and with owners' and occupiers' representative organizations to ascertain what open country exists and what action should be taken to secure public access to it. In Northern Ireland, district councils have had a duty to consult the Department of the Environment for Northern Ireland as well as the representative organizations of landowners and occupiers in order to ascertain what open country exists in their areas and what action should be taken to secure access to it for open-air recreation. In future the Department of the Environment for Northern Ireland's function in this regard, as in all others mentioned subsequently, will presumably pass to the executive of the Assembly. As we shall see in Chapter 4, provision for a systematic review of open country and access requirements for England and Wales has been allowed to lapse.

Access Payment Schemes

During the late 1980s and 1990s new arrangements for providing access by agreement were launched by the government. However, these differ from the concept of the access agreement in several ways. Most importantly they include the principle that landowners should be compensated for providing access itself, not merely for any loss it may occasion. Under an almost bewildering variety of schemes, flat-rate payments are made to owners or tenants simply for providing access, whether or not people make use of it, let alone whether or not damage results. Nearly all of these schemes involve an extra payment which landowners can opt to receive in respect of land for which they are already receiving public money in compensation for agreeing to avoid environmentally damaging practices. None of the schemes is administered by local councils, and only one involves the strategic assessment of access needs embodied in the review map procedure. None provides for by-laws to control public behaviour on the sites. On-site signs provided by the public agencies which administer the schemes typically ban activities like lighting fires, staying overnight, and allowing dogs off the lead when stock are present, but any enforcement falls on landowners, who must take action themselves or ask the police to intervene if laws are being broken. All the schemes are voluntary and provide no means of imposing access where landowners do not want to permit it.

The vast majority can be conveniently divided into three categories according to the activity for which grant is already being paid when the access payment is added.

Producing Less Food

Since 1992 arable farmers have been entitled to payments from the European Union reflecting the extent of their crop-growing land to compensate them for a reduction in price support from the consumer. To qualify for these 'arable area payments' (which ranged in 1998 from £189 per acre for linseed to £98 for cereals) farmers have to appear to reduce output by refraining from farming, or 'setting aside', a certain percentage of their cropped land. This percentage has been as high as 18 per cent and in 1998 was 5 per cent. Farmers have the option of setting aside a different plot each year or one particular plot year after year. In respect of land in England and Wales which they agree to set aside for five years, they can opt to receive on top of the set-aside payment of £124 per acre an additional annual payment under the Countryside Access Scheme if they agree to allow public access to the land they have set aside. This can take the form of a whole field, part of a field for which the payment is £18 per acre, or strips 10 metres (11 yards) wide usually round the edge of a field, for which the payment is £36 per acre. The payments and the provision of access, including publicity arrangements, are the responsibility of local officials of the Ministry of Agriculture, Fisheries, and Food or the Welsh Office Agriculture Department. The access land provided has to be accessible from a public road or public path. However, its access status is very different from that of a right of way. Even if access takes the form of thin strips, it is not showing on Ordnance Survey maps. What is more, a special clause in the legal agreement between the farmer and the government ensures that continuous use of access land, in particular access strips, can never result in the route being claimed as a right of way.

For his or her part, the farmer must maintain free passage over the access area, establish and maintain green cover suitable for access, and consult the local Agriculture Office official if he or she wishes to put up new fencing on the area or adjacent to it. He must also seek consent if he wishes to close the access area temporarily: this may be allowed for up to ten days each year. Where temporary closure has been permitted, a farmer must post signs giving notice of the intended closure and the reasons for it at each entry point to the access area at least two weeks in advance of the closure. Farmers may also avail themselves of grants to help cover the cost of structures to facilitate access such as stiles, benches, and gates.

Conservation

Another set of enticements to provide public access are on offer in particular stretches of country which have been designated as 'Environmentally Sensitive Areas'. The Lake District, the Somerset Levels, the heaths of Breckland, the north Kent marshes, the Glens of Antrim, the mountains of Mourne, the South Downs, the Shetland Isles, the machair lands of the Uists, Benbecula, Barra, and Vatersay, parts of Scotland's Southern Uplands, the Lleyn peninsula, and the Cambrian mountains are a few of the UK's forty-three separate ESAs. They cover a substantial area, embracing for example 10 per cent of farmland in England. The idea is that these areas retain considerable landscape, wildlife, or archaeological interest, which depends on the maintenance of a particular form of farming that is now less economic than it has been in the past. The Agriculture Act 1986, enacted in response to great concern at the destruction of landscapes and wild-life habitat by agricultural expansion and intensification, provided that in designated ESAs farmers would be entitled to receive flat-rate payments for refraining from destructive landscape change. In 1992 when a reform of the Common Agricultural Policy made provision for member states to introduce 'agri-environment schemes', ESAs started to get 50 per cent funding from Brussels. A considerable number of farmers (landowners or tenants) in the ESAs have opted to receive payments under 'tier one' which essentially involve their carrying on with their existing farming methods and refraining from practices like pesticide use, land drainage, or hedgerow removal which could increase their profits but would harm conservation interests. Two further tiers have been introduced: farmers receive a higher rate of payment if they agree to withdraw land from intensive production and turn it back to the semi-natural habitat characteristic of the area—like chalk downland grass in the South Downs, or lowland heathland in Breckland. A third tier, the access tier, offers owners or tenants an optional additional payment of £102 per mile for allowing people to walk along access strips 10 metres wide along the side or sides of, or across, fields for which they are already receiving payments under tier one or tier two or, in a few of the ESAs £20 per acre for the whole or part of fields up to a maximum of 10 acres. In addition, grants at the level of 80 per cent are available for the provision and restoration of gates, stiles, and footbridges for public access.

So far neither the Countryside Access Scheme nor the ESA access tier has delivered much access on the ground. By June 1996, only 2,453 acres (slightly larger than the area of Richmond Park) had been entered into the Countryside Access Scheme in the whole of England and there had been no uptake whatsoever in Wales and very little in Scotland.[16] ESA access payments agreements are also rare. By November 1997, there was only one in the whole of Scotland (in the Argyll Islands). Thus areas where substantial ESA payments are being made provide for no improvement at all in access. In Hampshire, for example, ESAs have been designated along stretches of the rivers Test and Avon embracing not only the river and its banks but also low-lying often flower-rich grazing pasture and some woodland close by. By the end of 1996, 40 per cent of the eligible area of the Test Valley was covered by ESA agreements and 22 per cent of the Avon Valley. But in neither case was there any access agreement.

However, another of the conservation payment schemes has been far more successful in delivering access. The Countryside Steward-ship Scheme differs from the Countryside Access Scheme and the ESA access tier in that it was introduced and run until April 1996 (when it was transferred to the Ministry of Agriculture, Fisheries, and Food) by an agency whose prime aim is the conservation of natural beauty and the promotion of access to the countryside—the Countryside Commission. Countryside Stewardship applies not to geographical areas but to a range of landscape features wherever they occur throughout England, in particular features whose landscape beauty and wildlife attraction rely on forms of farming which are relatively uneconomic nowadays. For instance limestone grassland, on which plants like the musk, pyramidal, and fragrant orchid flourish, has been reduced to a tiny fragment of its former extent (only 1.6 per cent of the Cotswolds, for instance, where limestone grasslands occurred as vast open downs for centuries[17]). The reason for the loss has been the conversion of grasslands once used for low-intensity grazing to arable fields. Under Countryside Stewardship, farmers and landowners can apply to be paid for refraining from ploughing the land or impairing its wildlife value in some other way. They can also receive £61 per acre if they allow access over an area or £93 per mile for access along permissive paths at least 2 metres (2 yards) wide, with higher rates for paths for riders, cyclists, the disabled, and for educational visits. The other landscape features covered by the scheme are lowland heath, waterside land, coastal land like salt marsh and sand dune, historic landscapes like old orchards, parks and water meadows, upland moorland, arable field margins, fens, and various types of grassland such as upland in-bye pasture, hay meadow, and chalk grassland.

By the time the scheme was transferred to MAFF, 31,476 acres of area access and 294 miles of linear access had been negotiated. During the year after transfer a further 177 access agreements were made. Although all this amounts to far more access than is provided under any of the other payment schemes, the situation on the ground is patchy. In 1996 Dorset, for example, had twenty-five pieces of land covered by stewardship access schemes; the comparable figure for

Hereford and Worcester was only four. Since MAFF took over the scheme, there has been a change of emphasis from funding access over areas of land to access along strips, following the pattern of the ESAs access tier and the Countryside Access Scheme. In 1995 Countryside Stewardship was criticized by the Ramblers' Association on the grounds that in many cases (such as Mam Tor in the Peak District, which is owned by the National Trust) access had already existed to sites now covered by the scheme, so that whatever other benefits the taxpayer may have acquired, additional access was not a significant one.[18] Since then the government has said that applications under all the schemes will succeed only if they offer access to land hitherto inaccessible— although of course the old agreements will still run their course.

General Support for Agriculture

Both Scotland and Northern Ireland have access payment schemes which are available over a very wide geographical area and which essentially involve annual payments to farmers who permit public access usually along defined paths, whether or not they are receiving payments for other purposes. The Scottish Countryside Premium Scheme offers such payments to all farmers outside ESAs (where of course access tier payments are on offer) who agree to allow access across 'in-bye' land on their holdings. In-bye land consists of all farmland which is not rough grazing. Any farmer or crofter who wishes to apply for a Premium Scheme grant must first have a conservation audit carried out on his holding. He then decides which option he would like to apply for. Most of these options are conservation-related, such as the management and enhancement of features like water margins, species-rich grasslands, hedgerows, machair, and moorland. But one of the options aims to provide new or significantly enhanced access opportunities whether through 10-metre-(or 11-yard)wide strips, or areas of land up to a maximum of 4 hectares (10 acres). The scheme was launched in March 1997, and 480 farmers and crofters received payments in the first year. Fourteen of the agreements in question included the access option.

In Northern Ireland a Countryside Access Scheme was introduced in July 1996. Despite its name, it differs fundamentally from the

Countryside Access Scheme in operation in England and Wales, which applies only to set-aside land. The scheme in the Province offers annual payments to landowners who agree to allow access in 10-metre-wide strips (area access is not involved). The type of terrain may be enclosed agricultural land, woodland, open hill (so long as *de facto* access does not already exist), existing permissive paths or 'laneways', which are very common features of the landscape—lanes which service one farm lying behind another farm and over which the farm behind alone has a way-leave. Under the scheme, the Department of Agriculture for Northern Ireland provides annual payments of £61 per acre for the provision, management, and maintenance of the new permissive access routes, while the Environment Department funds capital works which may be needed to make the route functional. The Department of the Environment for Northern Ireland was anxious that any access provided under the Countryside Access Scheme should fit within some sort of strategic assessment rather than, in the words of Ross Millar of the Department, 'farmers just volunteering access that nobody wanted'. The Department therefore requested and secured a precondition that grant will not be paid unless it fits within an access strategy prepared by the local district council. These strategies are not subject to statutory preparation and public inquiry like the review maps provided under the 1949 National Parks Act for local authority access agreements and orders and they vary widely. By July 1998 only one agreement had been secured under the Province's Countryside Access Scheme. However, as more access strategies are submitted by districts, it seems likely that more applications will be submitted. There is no access tier in the Province's ESAs and the Countryside Access Scheme operates within the five areas designated as ESAs in Northern Ireland.

Broadly speaking, all the above schemes follow the general pattern outlined for the English Countryside Access Scheme as far as the temporary recall of access land from the scheme, signposting, and administration are concerned.

The Promotion of Forestry

Foresters as well as farmers have been offered the opportunity to provide access in return for payment from public funds.

Landowners creating new plantations in Great Britain can receive grants (£283 per acre in the case of conifers and £425 per acre for broadleaves). If they are prepared to provide public access, they can receive an additional payment known as the 'community woodland supplement' consisting of a one-off payment of £385 per acre, so long as their plantations lie within 5 miles of the edge of a village, town, or city and there are few other woodlands available in the area for recreation. To encourage the provision of attractive accessible woodland close to major population centres, the government has designated fourteen stretches of land in England and Wales as 'community forests', each of them about 50 square miles in area. The Central Scotland Woodland Initiative provides a similar arrangement at one location. Additionally, a 'National Forest' has been designated over 150 square miles in the Midlands. For all these places, teams of officials draw up plans to encourage landowners (public as well as private) to convert stretches of what is now usually farmland or former industrial land into a woodland-dominated scene which people can enjoy. Those who receive a community woodland supplement payment are required to allow the public into their new plantation for the first ten years of its life. After this time, landowners may choose to bar access, or they may offer it free or they may charge privately for access, or they may take advantage of an annual 'management grant' of £14 per acre in return for agreeing to create, maintain, or enhance public access. As in the case of the schemes related to agriculture and conservation, an additional grant is available for the provision of facilities such as benches and fences or board-walks which could make access easier.

So far, woods covered by one of these access payment schemes are not that common. Thus no more than 0.6 per cent of the woodland of Kent, for example, was so covered in 1996. Kent however contains no designated community forest; within the specially designated areas higher figures are achieved. In November 1997 the Countryside Commission headed a press release, 'Community Forests Open New Gates for Millions of People' and explained that in England they had created 6,671 acres of accessible woodland while nearly 16 miles of paths had been restored, upgraded, and created.[19] Although these figures may sound impressive the area involved amounts only to 0.3 per cent

45

of the total area of woodland in England. It includes land owned by public authorities like local councils and a charity devoted to buying woods and opening them to the public, the Woodland Trust. Much of this woodland was in any case probably already accessible in practice. Unlike the farm and conservation access schemes, the forestry ones do not require that the access for which payments are made must not have existed beforehand. Thus Bob Spence, the regional officer of the Forestry Commission for the Severn, Wye, and Avon Conservancy, whose area includes the Forest of Avon community forest, told me in 1997 that access schemes both inside and outside the community forest often simply formalize *de facto* access.

Grant Schemes: Publicity

None of the access arrangements provided under any of the grant schemes is shown on Ordnance Survey maps. Nor are they assembled and described in any other widely available form. Instead, awareness of the woodland access schemes depends largely on steps taken by the landowners themselves to publicize them. Landowners who enter any of the schemes are given 'Walkers Welcome' signs and discs which they are expected to display on site. Bob Spence told me that in his area he asks recipients of the community woodland supplement to notify their parish council as well as displaying notices on site. 'We insist as a condition that the landowners publicize the scheme and provide signs on site so anyone passing through can see they are welcome,' he said. 'Most of the sites are small and are aimed at people in the parish.' The Forestry Commission does not publish lists of all private woods accessible under these grant schemes though Mr Spence told me he would have no objection to local authorities in his area making the information available: they would be in a position to do this because they know the locations of the sites involved because they would have been consulted when the grant application were made. However, when I telephoned Bristol City Council to ask them about the location of woodlands accessible under the grant schemes, they could provide information only about the three woods the Council owns within the Forest of Avon. They told me that I should ask the Community Forest office for any other information. When I did so, just after 4 p.m. on a weekday in November 1997, an answering machine told me that the office was closed, although I was able to get the information on another occasion.

The Countryside Commission used to be keen that information should be available about sites made accessible by Countryside Stewardship and it pioneered means of achieving this which were adopted by the Ministry of Agriculture when it took over Stewardship in 1996. County-by-county 'Access Registers' provide map references, brief descriptions, and basic maps of sites accessible to the public under Countryside Stewardship. These registers now include access sites created under the ESAs scheme and the Countryside Access Scheme. Thus the Access Register for Berkshire published in 1997 consists of six A4 sheets of paper stapled together describing eight sites in the county. The Ministry sends a copy of the Register to the relevant branch of the Ramblers' Association, local authorities, major libraries in the area involved and information is also placed on the Internet. While such information is clearly better than nothing, the facility is obviously of little use to the visitor from outside who has not planned his or her trip to take in a visit to a major public library or engaged in some preliminary web-surfing. Occasionally information about access provided under inheritance tax exemption agreements is included in the Access Registers but this tends to involve those places whose owners readily publicize the access involved anyway. Both the Scottish Office and the Agriculture Department for Northern Ireland have proposed that local councils should publicize access available under the payment schemes which they administer. In Wales, publicity varies widely. In Snowdonia, the national park authority is responsible for publicizing sites made accessible in Merioneth through Tyr Cymen. It tries to ensure that maps are posted at each end of permissive paths. Maps of open areas available are not however posted on site although these are available at the national park's office and at information centres and public libraries. In response to criticism that it has not publicized these arrangements more widely, the park authority point out that the access provided runs for only ten years and therefore unless it provides new advice each year any advice it does promulgate could be misleading.

Taken together, a great number of different arrangements for providing public access as of right in the British countryside actually deliver very little access indeed. For the most part, therefore, when you go into the countryside you will do so as a trespasser. Your opportunities to do this, and your fate when you do, will then turn entirely on the attitude of the particular landowner on to whose territory you venture. As might be expected, these attitudes vary. At one extreme are those landowners who insist that everyone must stay out, and back up this attitude with formidable barriers. At the other, are the handful who make a point of welcoming in their fellow citizens. In between, there are those who allow on to their land selected individuals—perhaps friends or certain local people such as the local doctor and garage owner, a boy scout troop, the hunt, or people they have invited to fish in a lake or to shoot in a wood. There are those who are fiercely defensive about some parts of their property but more relaxed about others—like the owners of stately homes who allow members of the public to visit the house and parts of their grounds at certain times of the year on payment of a fee but firmly bar them from the rest of their domains. These varying attitudes have different levels of impact on different kinds of countryside in different parts of Britain. To complete our picture of the extent to which you can or cannot walk into your homeland, we must plot what actually happens on the ground.

2

FORBIDDEN KINGDOM

BRITAIN's countryside is famed for its diversity. Field, wood, and down still mingle as in a Constable painting, though industrialized agriculture and forestry have transformed much of the landscape. At the same time there are also the rolling moors of the north and west, featuring peat bog and sub-arctic plateaux. There are heaths and marshes, lakes and rivers, and many different kinds of coastland. Attempting to penetrate these different kinds of countryside in the face of the law of trespass gives rise to difficulties of very different character and degree.

Fields

Of our different kinds of countryside, farmland is the most extensive. Forty-seven per cent of the land of the United Kingdom is enclosed as fields. Just over half of this land is under grass for sheep and cattle and a small amount for horses. Much of the remainder, under crops, is also ultimately committed to stock-rearing as the barley, wheat, and oilseed rape it grows are used for animal feed. Wheat for bread-making covers a small part of our crop land and a small but growing area of arable land is used in the production of industrial products like plastics and diesel oil. About 4 per cent supports vegetables and fruit.

Down on the ground, our fields vary far more widely than these blanket figures on their use suggest. Bounded by hedgerows, stone walls, or barbed wire, Britain's farm fields may be angular expanses of corn and oilseed rape in Essex, rich cattle pasture in Galloway, or tiny meadows snugly enclosed by fuchsia hedgerows in County Antrim. Their agricultural function may be considerable, but, embodying the living expression of one of the most enduring forms of human endeavour, they offer endless fascination to the walker. Because they cover so much of our countryside, they also embrace a wealth of equally enticing associated features—ponds and hedgerows, spinneys and streams, which house much of our wildlife. In the fields stand visible archaeological remains—anything from Bronze Age burial mounds and stone circles to the remains of medieval fish ponds and Second World War pill-boxes. Agricultural imprints too, from prehistoric field boundaries to medieval ridge and furrow, cart-sheds to oast houses and the elaborate machinery of today tell the fascinating tale of the leading part our nation has played in the history of cultivation.

This treasure-house of interest and charm might be expected to attract many curious visitors. Yet the fields of Britain today are striking for their emptiness. At most you glimpse the occasional man with a gun or somebody perched in a tractor; occasionally a solitary line of ramblers snake their way in single file along a fieldpath. The rest of us keep out. Far from treating farmland as an interesting place to be, like the city streets, we treat it as something we expect to view only from the outside. Farmers like to tell us it is their factory floor, the theatre for sensitive operations which urban intruders would disrupt. With the authority of the law of trespass behind them, they back up this message with fences, forbidding notices, and threatening men with guns. Most of us accept our exclusion unquestioningly. Yet it need not be this way.

Elsewhere, particularly in the Third World, farmland is thronged with people, who are not only working it but using it as a place for recreation. In Britain too, farmland was once much more than a sterile production line for agricultural products. I have talked to country people in Lincolnshire, Bedfordshire, West Yorkshire, Suffolk, and Norfolk who have recalled that as recently as the 1940s, people in their country areas often walked freely over meadows once the hay was cut, and picnicked or gathered mushrooms in fields otherwise used for grazing. They walked over arable fields after the last corn had been taken off, crunching the hard stubble underfoot and stopping to admire the tiny wild pansy flowers nestling between the rows. When crops were standing, people simply kept to the field edges and gathered elderberries and blackberries from the hedgerows.

Today, however, farmland has stopped being the natural environment of the community and become merely a tool of businessmen. We are excluded from a field of sheep as thoroughly as from a field of wheat, and the edges of fields, once a universal thoroughfare, have been taken from us with the fields themselves. It makes no difference whether a crop is fully grown or just harvested, whether the land is lying fallow or being 'set aside' in return for public subsidy. Nor whether the farmer has left a wide margin round the field edge for his own use. Farmland is no longer a space in which we all have a stake.

It is not that people are more of a threat to agriculture than they were in the past. It is just that farmers today have a different attitude to the presence of their fellow men and women in their fields. The old pre-war mixed farming regimes, with corn and root crops, sheep, cattle, hens, and geese all reared on the same holding, lent an air of easy-going informality which has been driven out by more industrialized post-war methods. As farming has become far more specialized, farmers have reshaped the environment to cater for its changing demands, ripping out natural features like hedgerows, ponds, spinneys, and streams and in the process denying the rest of us the chance of using the fields to collect wild produce, catch tadpoles, and move around the countryside in an informal, unregimented way. On today's vast, monstrous expanses of prairie and pasture, farmers seem to consider that walkers would be an untidy intrusion.

Such access as now exists to the fields depends almost entirely on the predetermined routes provided by roads and public paths. Roads through farmland are punctuated with signs varying in style from county to county (a green metal sign with 'public footpath' written in white in Buckinghamshire; a small arrow with a walking figure but no indication of the status of the path let alone its destination or the distance in South Gloucestershire, for example) which mark the point at which a public path jumps off through the fields. For walkers these routes are welcome as the only real way into the fields. Sadly even the access they can offer is limited. There are very few public paths across farmland in Scotland or Northern Ireland, and even in England and Wales, many of them are obstructed. Take a walk in the predominantly sheep and cattle-rearing countryside of central Carmarthenshire, say, and you will encounter countless public paths blocked with wire fences or smothered in natural vegetation. There are others marked on the map of which no trace remains on the ground. Dyfed's County Footpaths Officer told me in 1992 that three out of five paths in Dyfed (the Welsh administrative unit which then included Carmarthenshire) were obstructed; what often happens is that 'when a farm changes hands new fences go up. They are just thrown up.' Walkers in arable areas like lowland England face a different difficulty: paths that go invisibly through the middle of a ploughed field or an expanse of crops. If tall crops like maize, peas, or rape have been grown over the path's surface, or if no indication of its position exists amongst deep muddy plough ruts, only the most determined and fit walker will carry on. More than a quarter of a sample of 1,308 paths in Essex surveyed by volunteers for the local Ramblers' Association branch in 1995, for example, were obstructed either with growing crops or ploughed earth. Missing signposts, stiles, and foot-bridges either absent or in poor repair were common problems.[1] The picture varies somewhat depending on the vigilance of local author-ities in enforcing footpath law. Thus surveys in 1993 and 1994 by the government agency responsible for promoting rural conservation and recreation provision in England, the Countryside Commission, found that West Sussex, Cleveland, Derbyshire, and Berkshire con-tained fewer paths which were unusable or in poor condition than Shropshire, Norfolk, Warwickshire, and North Yorkshire.[2]

The distribution of farmland paths is also highly variable. Today's network of public footpaths and bridleways results largely from the communications patterns of past centuries. In former wetlands which were drained relatively recently for agriculture and where movement had hitherto been by boat—like the Somerset Levels, the Wentlooge Levels between Cardiff and Newport, the Fens, and Thorne Moor near Doncaster—there are today very few public paths. In contrast, long settled farmland characterized by a scatter of farmsteads like that of the Gilbert White and Edward Thomas country around Selborne and Steep in north Hampshire, or much of Herefordshire, Essex, and Denbighshire is usually penetrated by a spider's web of paths. Different again in their pattern and density are the paths of the Midlands, where history has left paths fanning out across farm-land from nucleated villages like the spokes of a wheel. In lowland Scotland there are not only few paths, but abundant fencing and the practice of sowing crops right up to field boundaries make trespass-ing more difficult than elsewhere.

Where public paths do exist, their presence, welcome though it is, actually serves to reinforce the idea that away from these routes the fields are off limits. Desperately important though they are in enabling us to penetrate farmland at all, they have nonetheless served to legitimize our exclusion from the farmed landscape as a whole by their implicit message that if we are in the fields we ought to be on a public path.

Just occasionally people can set foot over a whole field, at least on specified days of the year. This is rarely an ordinary field, however: more likely it is a field over which its owner, whether private land-owner or organization like say a county naturalists' trust, has entered into a special agreement such as countryside stewardship in which he, she, or they guarantee that they will farm the land in a certain way. An access option is part of the menu of such agreements and in some cases landowners have taken advantage of it. Travel to the village of Dymock in north-east Gloucestershire in early March, for instance, and you will find certain meadows over which the Gloucestershire Naturalists' Trust has entered into a countryside stewardship agreement in order to allow the wild daffodils which still grow naturally in this area to flourish and where they also permit public access. Similar agreements with access also allowed apply to a few fritillary meadows in Wiltshire and cowslip and orchid meadows in Suffolk, for instance. But all these spots are very few and far between, and they make up only the tiniest proportion of the countryside.

As a result of all this, few of us would think of setting out to roam the fields as our ancestors or even our parents would have done. If we fancy a walk in the lowland countryside which makes up most of Britain we are more likely to head for woodland. A walk in the woods—and woodland still covers 10 per cent of the United Kingdom—still sounds like a reasonable ambition. So what are the prospects of achieving it?

Woods

Woodland offers enormous potential for enjoyment of the open air. For many of us, a walk in the woods is the archetypal rural experience. As we make our way through bluebells and primroses, among the reassuring trunks of ash, oak, and beech, under a leafy canopy alive with the song of blackbird, robin, and thrush, we know we are drinking in the rural heritage of our nation as nowhere else.

It is also a very diverse environment. Walk 100 yards across one of the woods which ecologists regard as 'ancient'—that is, a wood marked on maps which predate 1600 and which may well have existed as an evolving woodland community since the years after woodland clothed land in the wake of the retreating ice sheets 12,000 years ago—and you may well traverse twelve different distinct tree-stand types. Despite its small size and multitude of pressures on its land the county of Berkshire still harbours nearly 500 ancient woods. These woods contain twenty-two distinct tree-stand types, while local variations in geology, geography, biology, and microclimate mean that each wood consists of an intricate patchwork of plant and animal communities. All told, our ancient woods, as well as the deciduous, coniferous, and mixed woods which have emerged later than 1600, play host to 92 of our native bird species, 76 of our flowers, and 105 of our spiders. So Britain's relatively small stock of woodland acts as a treasure-house of our wildlife assets as well as the focus of the rural vision of the nation.

At first glance, quite a lot of Britain's woods appear to be accessible to walkers. A large chunk of land in Great Britain—just over 2 million acres, or 34 per cent of our woodland area—is owned by a public body, the Forestry Commission, and in recent years this organization has opened its holdings to the public as a matter of policy. It not only declines to exclude walkers, it invites them in, offering forest walks, picnic areas, camping sites, interpretation centres, and (usually but not always free) car parking. Travel to Northern Ireland, and though woodland is much scarcer, publicly-provided access appears impressive. The Forest Service of the Department of Agriculture owns 76 per cent of the woodland in the Province—153,000 acres (4.5 per cent of the land surface of Northern Ireland). It allows access on foot over the entire area restricting access only when there is danger to the public, in particular when trees are being felled.

The fact that we are able to walk freely in state woodland is the result of a historical accident. In Great Britain in 1919, in the aftermath of the First World War, the desirability of building up a stock of timber to help the country cope with another war seemed of enormous public concern. As it happened, the way to secure this was seen to be for the state to control production on large areas of land (an approach not applied to comparable activities, agriculture in particular). Private landowners with vast tracts of then unprofitable sheep moor in Northumberland, Scotland, Yorkshire, and Wales were only too pleased to sell to the Forestry Commission, whilst others in areas like east Cornwall and east Suffolk, faced with a requirement to make good forests wrecked by massive and swift felling during the First World War, were also often only too happy to offload. By 1981, the Forestry Commission controlled 5 per cent of the total land of Britain, most of it through freehold ownership. However, by the 1960s it had become clear that the edifice of land and jobs the Commission represented could no longer be justified for the construction of warships and pit props. Recreation was fastened upon as one of a handful of new justifications for the forests and the Commission declared in 1963 that from henceforth it would permit the general public to use all its forests where this could be done without risk of fire and without harm to the legitimate interests of its lessors, tenants, and neighbours. Today, this means that a walk in a forest is readily available, entirely problem free, for many people. Unfortunately, the resource the Forestry Commission appears to provide has been fast disappearing.

One of Mrs Thatcher's first acts as Prime Minister was to issue instructions to the Forestry Commission to dispose of its forests. Eighteen years of Conservative rule saw the Commission selling more than 300,000 acres, in order to raise £200 million. No similar legislation was passed for Northern Ireland however and there the Forest Service has retained virtually all its land over which it continues to allow public access.

The government refused to make public access a condition of sale of Forestry Commission woods for fear of reducing the prices they could command, and many of the new private owners of the woods fenced out the public. As a result, every year people saw their favourite forest walks being closed to them. Strenuous efforts were sometimes made to save them. Brooke Wood, for instance, is one of the few remaining large woods in south Norfolk. Seven miles south of

Norwich, it covers an area of 180 acres (around twice that of St James's Park in London). Travel round it today and you will see a large, mysterious-looking wood, isolated in slightly undulating farmland. No barbed wire keeps people out: instead dense vegetation, only occasionally interrupted by a wide ride, blocks entry. The most visible creature from the road is the pheasant. In fact, entry is also allowed not only to those with an economic or proprietary interest in the wood but to a small number of local people who have been issued with permits enabling them to walk along the main ride and two offshoots. Before 1983 this was a wood to which the Forestry Commission allowed unrestricted access. A retired fire-station officer called George Le Surf, who was area secretary of the Ramblers' Association, made unsuccessful appeals to two government ministers and the Director-General of the Forestry Commission as well as pursuing legal action on two fronts in an unsuccessful attempt to keep Brooke Wood open to all. But they came to nothing.

Strapped for cash, local authorities have found it difficult to purchase woods like this or even enter into access agreements with the new owners—that is, if they managed to find out that a sale was imminent. As a result, of the 135 square miles of woodland which the Commission sold between 1991 and 1995, for instance, access was safeguarded over only 2 square miles.[3] Just occasionally the woods were bought by other organizations which maintained the free access the Forestry Commission had pursued—notably the Woodland Trust. The Trust, set up in 1972 by a businessman called Kenneth Watkins, always permits the public free access over the usually small woods it buys whether from the Commission or private owners.

Loss of access through Forestry Commission sales has been greater than the global figures suggest. Although the woodland sold amounts to only 10 per cent by area, the sales have accounted for almost half— 46 per cent—of the Commission's total number of woods, according to calculations by the Ramblers' Association. This is because the Commission has tended to target small woodlands dotted through the countryside rather than its largest plantations. The Association commented in 1996: 'In some counties, the effect of the sales has been devastating. In South Yorkshire, 73 per cent of all woods have been sold, in Suffolk 60 per cent, West Yorkshire 94 per cent and West

Sussex 52 per cent'.[4] Even when the Commission has held on to free-hold or leasehold rights, it has sometimes tried to meet government financial targets by generating extra revenue from the sale of shooting rights. This has often involved closure to walkers. Just north of Bodmin in east Cornwall stands Pencarrow and Colquite Wood, a mixed wood of oak, pine, and beech, frequented by buzzards and in spring strewn with celandines and primroses. Relatively unknown to tourists, the wood used to be very popular with local people including parents with pushchairs and elderly people attracted by the freedom to roam and also the wide, level paths which the Commission had created. But in the summer of 1992, these people found themselves confronted by locked gates, barbed wire, and notices forbidding access: the Commission had sold the right to manage half the wood, around 300 acres, for pheasant shooting and the new shooting tenant decided to clamp down on access. A protest walk involving thirty local people failed to secure a change of approach; indeed it degenerated into an ill-humoured stand-off. In 1993 however shooting rights were resold. The new shooting syndicate has agreed to allow a permissive path through the woods although it will allow no roaming off this track. In 1997 and 1998 the new Labour government was presiding over continuing sales of Forestry Commission land despite its pre-election criticism of the disposal of public woodlands. And no steps were being taken to open up the woods to which access had been lost during the preceding eighteen years.

The Commission's remaining holdings, extensive in total though they still are, are not as useful a recreation resource as they might appear. One reason is that most of the Commission forests which have not yet been sold are far away from population centres. Its largest plantation, Kielder, sprawls for nearly 185 square miles over one of the remotest areas of England, the Cheviot hills of Northumberland. But the overwhelming reason why access to the Commission's forests—and access to those of the Forest Service in Northern Ireland—is not enough is that, for many people, they are the wrong kind of forests. While a few of the Forestry Commission's woods are deciduous, notably the Lincolnshire lime woods, the New Forest, Wendover Woods, and the Atlantic oakwoods in Argyll, most of their holdings and those of the Forest Service are very different. The Commission's original objectives were far more economic than environmental, and as a result it smothered the landscape with grim ranks of fast-growing but alien conifers. While the tracks and picnic tables they offer may be welcome, the dark and silent shadow of most of these woods is not the setting most people have in mind when they think of a woodland picnic.

Yet if you travel through the small amount of privately owned woodland in Northern Ireland or the 66 per cent of woodland in Great Britain which is not owned by the Commission most of the woods you see are broadleaved or broadleaves mixed with conifers. Suffolk alone harbours 85 square miles of woodland, 16 per cent of it ancient and 70 per cent of it broadleaved; Oxfordshire has about 42 square miles. So what is the position on access to these more typically British woods?

In 1974 Oxfordshire County Council carried out a study of access to its woods. Only 111 acres of the county's 27,000 acres were open to the public all the time—just 0.4 per cent of the total.[5] The percentage is now higher but still not very great. The publication *Woodlands to Visit in England and Wales 1995*[6] lists five woods in the county which are open to the public all the time (one owned by the Woodland Trust, one by the Forestry Commission, and three by the Berkshire, Buckinghamshire, and Oxfordshire Naturalists' Trust). In addition educational tours can take place around the woods on the Blenheim estate by prior appointment. All told the area of the five woods freely open all the time amounts to 1,299 acres—just under 5 per cent of the woodland area of the county.

Nottinghamshire has been the subject of another study. In 1982 Dr Charles Watkins of the county's university carried out a meticulous survey of a 15 per cent sample of Nottinghamshire's woods. Thirty per cent of the sample was found to be freely accessible with signboards and well-marked walks. All this land was owned by the Forestry Commission, apart from small areas owned by the county council and the National Trust. However, in the entire remaining 70 per cent of the sample, all of which was in private ownership, no free wandering whatsoever was allowed.[7]

In 1992 I carried out my own study of access to woodland within a five-mile radius of Perth in Scotland. Three woods were freely accessible: one was owned by the Forestry Commission, another by a local authority, and the third by the Woodland Trust. The presumption over the remaining privately owned woods around Perth, in an area of about 78 square miles, was against access. Few public paths passed anywhere near these woods. In one or two cases landowners seemed to tolerate *de facto* access, but the general rule was fairly energetic exclusion. Local walkers told me of woods from which trespassers returning to their cars might find their tyres slashed.

What actually goes on in these secret woods? The uses to which our woodlands are put are less obvious than those of the fields. The Forestry Commission's woods were originally intended for timber production; recreation provision is a relatively recent bolt-on. In private woods, however, uses are completely different. Alongside timber production, the rearing and shooting of game takes on great importance. Pheasant shooting is as important to the owners of the inaccessible woods around Perth as it is to their counterparts in Hampshire or Cornwall. It is remarkably widespread occurring from west Cornwall to Wester Ross with the highest bags in Cheshire, Lincolnshire, Gloucestershire, Staffordshire, Wiltshire, and the South-East and East Anglia. Twelve million birds are shot every year, 17 per cent the progeny of birds which nested in the wild, the rest that of the 20 million young pheasants artificially introduced into our countryside—mainly into woodland—every year. These birds provide sport for landowners, shooting tenants, and sporting syndicates. Also of great importance is deer shooting: about 800,000 roe deer are shot every year in our woods. Landowners responsible for woods close to towns (372 in England in 1990[8]) have rented out a growing number of them to companies or associations which organize war-gaming: a fast-growing activity favoured by corporate team consciousness builders in which teams of participants fire paintball pellets at each other as they try to capture the flag of their opponents.

Public paths should enable us to cross land whatever its current use and whether or not the owner welcomes walkers. However, if you look for public paths crossing woodland on an Ordnance Survey map, you will soon see that woods are far less well served by public paths than fields. Nowhere is this more true than for the ancient woods. A great deal of these woods are off limits to the general public, for, just as in the fields, the path network through the woods is a legacy of our past. Those ancient woods that have survived often stand at the far edge of a parish: out of the way of the main streams of movement in the past, they are therefore often devoid of public paths today. Where public paths touch upon woods at all, they tend to go round the edge rather than through the middle. These edge paths do not give the experience of being 'in the woods', and are in any case often difficult to follow. The outward growth of branches often leaves the walker squeezed between wood and farmland on a route which the landowner—with countless other private paths at his disposal—will rarely take, and thus has little incentive to keep passable.

For the most part, therefore, the walker is at the mercy of the woodland owner's right to exclude, which is enforced with varying degrees of severity. At one end of this spectrum stand woods where the ordinary citizen is in no doubt that he or she is unwelcome. High fences, barbed wire strung along the top of fences and gates, evidence of exclusive activity in the woods, like the noise of pheasant shooting or paintball firing, often accompanied by exclusion tapes and notices, put out an unmistakable message. Psychological barriers are more widespread, most frequently taking the form of signs festooning woodland edges like 'Private Woods: Keep Out' and 'Keep Out: Trespassers will be Prosecuted'. Or, people may be barred without their realizing any intent on the part of the landowner simply because the means used is natural vegetation—such as a thick, prickly barrier where the wood abuts a road. In the middle of the spectrum is probably the largest category: woods where it is not at all clear what would happen if you stepped inside. Unfenced along the road, or perhaps with the occasional stretch of derelict fencing and peeling 'Trespassers will be Prosecuted' notice, you are aware you have no right to enter but, unless you are familiar with the custom of the area, unsure whether anyone will care if you do. You may move around unnoticed and undisturbed. But you know all the time that the next bend in the path may bring you face to face with a shotgun-wielding landowner or gamekeeper. This may mean an incident which you might find unsettling. All in all, the uncertainty may well be enough to put you off the idea of a walk or a picnic, which usually suits the landowner just fine.

What then of those few broadleaved woods where visitors are welcome? You can consult the new publication called *Woodlands to Visit in England and Wales*, which lists not only woods owned by the Forestry Commission, the Woodland Trust, county naturalists' trusts, and other such agencies, but those owned by private owners who welcome walkers. Perusal of this book brings home the scarcity of public access to woodland and the importance of ownership by organizations like the Woodland Trust. Purchase by the Trust can have a very significant impact locally. In 1985, for instance, it bought a 45-acre oak, maple, and ash wood on the edge of Luton in Bedfordshire called Bramingham Wood. Previously privately owned and fenced off, it now attracts hundreds of visitors every day who are able to feast their eyes on its snowdrops, primroses, and yellow archangel, or, if they are fortunate enough its tawny owls and great spotted woodpeckers. Twenty-five years on, the Woodland Trust now owns important woods dotted all over Great Britain—918 in total by 1998 covering 63 square miles. All told, however, these comprise only 0.6 per cent of our woodland area.

The most recent edition of *Woodlands to Visit in England and Wales*, published in 1995, lists just six woods in Bedfordshire, for instance—three owned or managed by the Forestry Commission, one owned by the Woodland Trust (Bramingham Wood), and two in private ownership—amounting to a total of 1,317 acres. Bedfordshire is one of our more lightly wooded counties but it nonetheless contains a total of 11,700 acres of woodland—an area equivalent to thirty-two Hyde Parks. The area of this which is accessible, according to the book, amounts to 11 per cent. Even then, only the Forestry Commission and Woodland Trust woods listed are open all the time: one of the private woods is open regularly but with some restrictions, the other by appointment only.

Bizarrely, additional access to woodland in Bedfordshire as elsewhere in Britain is coming not through the creation of access to existing, established woods but through the payment of grants to create more woodland elsewhere. These grants often allow landowners to receive an additional grant if they agree to let in the public. Take north Bedfordshire. Here stands the only privately owned wood listed in *Woodlands to Visit in England and Wales* as accessible regularly—covering 277 acres on the 10,800-acre estate of Samuel Whitbread, the head of the brewing family. This particular wood is coniferous;

virtually all of the remaining (mainly deciduous) woodland on this estate (as well as other features including an eighteenth-century parkland) are out of bounds to the general public. An access agreement (or order) or a public path creation agreement (or order) would seem the ideally suited means of enabling the citizens of Ampthill, Bedford, and Biggleswade to explore this resource already on their doorsteps, while allowing existing uses like shooting and forestry to continue. Instead, however, any additional public access to woodland in this region will almost certainly come as a side effect of the creation of new tree cover over the infinitely duller country which abuts the Southill estate to the north. In 1995 the Forestry Commission and Countryside Commission jointly designated 'The Marston Vale Community Forest'—61 square miles of arable farmland now virtually devoid of landscape features together with worked-out brick-clay-pit country, at present resembling a bare lunar landscape. They pledged: 'A third of the area will be planted with trees and the rest will be a mosaic of farmland, villages and areas for recreation . . . the recreational opportunities that the community forest will bring will add a real quality of life.'[9] The Commissions plan to increase tree cover from 4 to 30 per cent by encouraging landowners to take up woodland planting grants on offer. At the same time, since community forests are meant to make accessible woodland available to people in towns and cities, it is hoped that landowners who do receive such grants will opt to receive the additional community woodland supplement to which they are entitled if they agree to allow public access for the first ten years of their plantation's life. A team of Community Forest officers is also trying to persuade landowners to make existing woodland in the area more conservation effective and more accessible by encouraging them to avail themselves of the various management and access grants available.

Unfortunately, the landowners do not seem to be playing ball. By the end of 1997, Marston Vale boasted only one community woodland supplement agreement with a private landowner, covering a mere 12 acres. Although the team has managed to persuade landowners to avail themselves of management grants over a little of the already established woodland, none of this was accompanied by access payments. The four main accessible woods in Marston

Vale are all owned by Bedfordshire County Council or the Woodland Trust. Although the Forestry Commission does have a proprietary interest in one sizeable wood in the area (Wilshamstead Wood), this is not accessible since the Commission leases the wood from a private owner who does not wish to see public access within it; other sizeable inaccessible woods within the Forest's boundary include Sheerhatch Wood, Firtree Wood, Exeter Wood, Wootton Wood, Astey Wood, and Hanger Wood. The four accessible public and semi-public woods could be managed in the public interest whether they were in a so-called community forest or not; while the existence of inaccessible woodland within the Community Forest legitimizes the idea that even there it is all right for landowners to shut people out. Any major increase in accessible land in the Marston Vale Community Forest is likely to come not through the opening up of new or existing private woodland but through the reclamation of a larger area of the brick workings and the creation there of landscape features and a visitor centre, for which the Community Forest has been awarded a grant from the Millennium Commission of £2.4 million. So despite the presence of the Community Forest, it looks as if there will be little increased access to woodland worth visiting in north Bedfordshire in the foreseeable future. Meanwhile the county's glorious woods in private ownership, from the Whitbread woods in the north to the extensive deciduous woods of Luton Hoo in the south, will remain barred to the citizenry.

Mountain and Moorland

If a walk in the woods is not that easy, can walkers at least rely on a hike over the moors? For many, perhaps most, serious walkers, upland country is the terrain of choice. Only moor and mountain provide the space, solitude, and taste of wilderness which these walkers consider essential. Here, you might expect things to be easier. There is no shortage of hill country: nearly a quarter of the land of the UK consists of upland moor and mountain classed in the statistics as 'rough grazing'—rough grassy or heathery vegetation or bare rock. It ranges from Cuilcagh Mountain in County Fermanagh, the Sperrins of Tyrone, and the Mountains of Mourne, much of the Highlands and Islands of Scotland and parts of the Border country, the Lake District, the Pennines through Northumberland, Durham, Yorkshire, and Derbyshire with offshoots like Lancashire's Forest of Bowland, Dartmoor and Exmoor, and large stretches of central Wales, the Brecon Beacons, and Snowdonia. If farmland is thought of as a factory floor, these areas, not only untilled and largely unfenced but apparently largely unused, seem the sort of place where no one could object to people spreading out and enjoying freedom to roam.[10] Even here, however, many owners reach for their right to exclude.

The accessibility of our uplands varies from one part of the country to another. The Lake District has long been associated with the vision we still cherish of the freedom of the hills, and here it survives. It was the custom of tolerated trespass over extensive tracts of grassy fell and mountain that enabled Wordsworth to cover vast distances (around 175,000 miles in his lifetime, according to his biographer Thomas De Quincey) and in the process to teach us to see mountains and moors not as bleak formless places to be avoided but as a natural world in which we should delight. In the nineteenth century visitors were drawn to the Lake District to follow in Wordsworth's footsteps and they trod out paths to the summits of mountains and to viewpoints which became rights of way in the twentieth century, giving walkers a right of passage to peaks like Skiddaw and Bow Fell. Today, walkers in the area enjoy much *de jure* freedom to roam where they like. One reason is that the National Trust owns substantial stretches of common land here. A more particular reason is that since the Lakes happen to have been classed as an urban rather than a rural district, their 25-square-mile common at Windermere, which extends out into the fells in the heart of the region, is accessible by right under the provisions for urban commons enacted in 1925. *De jure* access also arises through the stipulation in local Acts of Parliament establishing reservoirs at Thirlmere and Haweswater that access must be permitted to the adjoining fells; while the authority which has overseen the planning and management of the national park since its designation as Britain's first national park in 1951 has been particularly energetic in acquiring land for recreation.

Similar forces have been at work, though on a more limited scale, in Snowdonia and the Brecon Beacons. In all these areas of mainly rough grass as opposed to heather moorland, private landowners have traditionally tolerated walkers. In Snowdonia there are legal guarantees of access. The area benefits from the historical accident of an urban common (Conwy Mountain); large stretches of the 63,000 acres of Crown Estate common land in Wales to which a deed of access was granted in 1932 (see page 28); and access agreements have been secured since 1949 (notably in the Llanberis Pass and the Nanttle ridge). Public paths are of less use than in the Lake District, since the majority of these follow the passes through the mountains and keep to the lower ground (reflecting the transport patterns of the old farming and mining population rather than the Lake District's tourists), though there is a public right of way up Snowdon itself. Where access does exist over much of Snowdonia it is often permissive and is sometimes withdrawn. Walkers have experienced difficulties in recent years on Moel Siabod, which rises east of Snowdon and affords views of Snowdon on one side and of the Lledr Valley (which some claim as the loveliest valley in Wales) on the other.[11] No right of way climbs to the summit of Moel Siabod and to secure some legal underpinning for the presence of the public there, the national park authority has managed to secure agreements with farmers on some sections under which it pays them nominal sums as compensation for any damage to fences. There remains, however, no long-term agreement. Along the $4\frac{1}{2}$-mile rocky spine of the Arans to the south, which rise between Lake Bala and Cader Idris, farmers barred access (where they had previously permitted it) between 1978 and 1982. Negotiations finally resulted in a concessionary path, or as it was known here a 'courtesy footpath', keeping to the ridge and subject to confirmation or cancellation each year.[12] For the present, however, the public enjoy a wider measure of access on the Arans since several farmers have entered into Tyr Cymen whole-farm agreements which, as we have seen (page 31) require them to permit the public to roam free over their hill land. Indeed, the Arans form part of the 50 per cent of Merioneth which in 1997 was within Tyr Cymen; of that 50 per cent probably two-thirds is open for public access in this way. However, the future is uncertain. The Tyr Cymen agreements last for ten years and have several years still to run. When they do expire farmers in the Arans will have the option of the permissive path agreement (and the payments it involves) with the Snowdonia national park authority. In 1998, a new agri-environment scheme is to be launched for Wales which will be based on Tyr Cymen. At the time of writing (July 1998) the details had not been published but it seemed likely that the new scheme would include the element of cross-compliance access to hill land which is a feature of Tyr Cymen. Snowdonia Park Assistant National Park Officer David Archer told me he thought that many farmers subject to Tyr Cymen agreements would be happy to continue with a similar new scheme despite the access to hill land requirement, because many had come to see that access was not the horror story they had imagined, while the payments, though not generous, provided a reliable income, an important factor at a time of uncertain sheep and beef prices. However, the extent to which free access to hill land continues in Merioneth (now part of Gwynedd) and extends further over Wales through some new agri-environment scheme will depend on how much money is made available and how many farms come in each year. 'I get the impression it will be a little butter spread thin,' Mr Archer told me.

There is yet another reason why public access to the mountains and moors of Snowdonia, though fairly widespread at present, is fragile. Substantial stretches of the Crown Estate commons occur here, part of the 63,000 acres of Welsh common which the Crown owns and which are dotted over Flintshire, Ceredigion, Gwynedd, and Conwy. Some are large; others little pockets of land in the middle of villages or at the ends of people's gardens: they consist of pieces of waste land of the manor which have come to the Crown over hundreds of years. The access deed which the Crown deposited with the Minister of Agriculture, Fisheries, and Food in 1932 declares that all these commons, large and tiny, will be open for the purpose of air and exercise. In practice this means today that walking is permitted over them and that where farmers put up fences, the Crown (often prompted by lobbying from groups like the Open Spaces Society) tries to ensure that stiles are put in to enable movement to continue. However, the deed clearly states that it can be revoked, although it also says that it would require another deed to do this. At present there is no particular reason to suppose that the Crown Estate would contemplate revoking this deed. However, it 'is quite a financial liability' in the words of Sue Jandy of the Agricultural Estates Division of the Crown Estates, and some future attempt to improve Crown Estate profitability could bring about revocation just as the deed granting access to Ranmore Common in Surrey was revoked in 1991 (see page 29).

These predominantly grassy moors in the west of England and in Wales and Northern Ireland tend to provide for more freedom of movement than the moors of the Pennines, Yorkshire, Lancashire, Durham, the eastern Highlands, and the Borders, where heather dominates. Many walkers prefer heather to grass, but though England has millions of acres of heather moor, it is far more difficult to walk on. Essentially, you can expect to encounter difficulties with gamekeepers or other estate staff if you stray off rights of way on such terrain. Visible from miles away across the purple moor, you may well find yourself the target of a landrover patrol which will track you down. The situation is not absolutely uniform. Most of the large estates which control the heather moors of the North York Moors national park do not seem to mind trespass along some of the paths across the moors which are not official rights of way. Try to walk on such paths in Lancashire's Forest of Bowland (an area of mainly open heather moor rather than woodland despite the name) or in the moors of south Durham, however, and you can expect trouble. Throughout these moors, such public footpaths as exist almost always keep to the lower slopes, usually connecting farmsteads; common land with a right of access is rare: Durham, despite its industrial image contains only three urban commons, all small and two of them in or close to Durham City. In certain areas, access agreements permit wandering over a whole area, notably in the Peak District. Overall, such means of legal access are few and far between. The former county of West Riding contained no less than 384,000 acres of moorland over which people had no legal right to walk, according to a study in 1984.[13]

Broadly speaking, variation in the accessibility of our moors corresponds to the relative importance of the land concerned for one particular use—grouse shooting. Four hundred and fifty thousand birds are shot every year in Britain and although the red grouse can live in Wales and Ireland it flourishes best on the drier heather moors of eastern Scotland, the Borders, Lancashire, Yorkshire, Durham, and Derbyshire. In Lancashire's Forest of Bowland, for instance, estates tend to be large (only a handful covering hundreds of square miles of heather moor) and grouse shooting tends to be the priority—unlike, say, Snowdonia, most of which is now largely in the hands of small-scale hill sheep farmers.

Sometimes heather moorland is accessible and grass moorland is not. The Mournes, the steep-sided mountains whose bold, bare granite peaks rise close to the sea 35 miles south of Belfast, are part heather-clad yet are also accessible—so much so that parts are in danger of erosion. Only one public right of way (Traffey Track) penetrates this mountain range and this does not lead to any of the twenty-two peaks. However, the Mournes are too wet for the red grouse to survive, and a tradition of tolerated access has grown up. This is continued by bodies like the National Trust and the Department of the Environment, which have come to own most of the mountains. Yet travel west to the Sperrin hills, an arc of high, dome-shaped hills, smothered in peat and given over mainly to sheep, whose broad curve separates Belfast from Londonderry and which lie mainly in Omagh and Strabane districts, and you will find a completely different picture. Hardly any land in the Sperrins is publicly owned; public footpaths are virtually absent; and while some owners tolerate walkers, others do not. In 1997 the owner of the highest point in the Sperrins, Sawel Mountain, allowed walkers on to his land; his neighbour, who controls access to the second highest peak, Dart mountain, did not: set foot on that and you might be chased off. Further west, public access to Cuilcagh (pronounced Koolka) Mountain south of Enniskillen in County Fermanagh is less promising still. Cuilcagh offers spectacular views over the myriad of lakes of Upper Lough Erne. With a landscape not unlike that of the Yorkshire Dales, its open grassy slopes offer tempting terrain for walkers and countless opportunities for climbers and cavers. However, access over the 27 square miles is permissive, and frequently barred. About half is commonage in which eight or nine people share grazing and have a right to be present—and to throw people off—that entire area. As Richard Watson, the Access Officer for Fermanagh District Council, told me in 1997, 'It only takes one or two of those eight or nine to get grumpy; one man can turn on people and tell them to get the hell out of it.' Over the other half, all in individual private ownership often involving very small

units, farmers also frequently withhold permission or put up warning signs or construct obstructions to walkers. Some have even
gone to the length of placing adverts in the local paper warning that
'Anybody found trespassing on my land will be prosecuted'. Outside
the Mournes, Fermanagh is the most important region of Northern
Ireland for outdoor activities, yet access to ten of the twenty most
popular caving sites, for instance, is threatened at the moment: one
or two of these are closed off completely; for the others, according
to Mr Watson, 'the farmer will sometimes let you and sometimes not—
it depends on his mood'. In 1997 the council received funding to enter
into a lease to provide a permissive route to the summit of Cuilcagh
which will avoid the most problematic areas. However, this route, which
will consist of a long strip covering one square mile, will not enable
free access over the whole mountain nor rights to use particular sites
outside it.[14]

The moors of south-west England also defy the general pattern.
Exmoor, like the Mournes, has been unable to tempt the grouse to a
significant extent, and its dazzling heather and rough grassy moors
are generally accessible either by custom or through ownership by
the Exmoor National Park Authority or through access agreements
it has made. Yet Exmoor has seen the loss of accessible rough moorland to inaccessible farmland as thousands of acres have been squared
off behind fences or hedges to provide intensive grazing lots or even
arable fields.[15] When this happens, the *de facto* access which had been
available simply disappears. Dartmoor is mainly grass rather than
heather, yet here legally underpinned freedom exists to roam at will
over the springy turf, moorland streams, and spectacular granite
tors of the 90,000 acres of common land on Dartmoor provided by
the Dartmoor Commons Act of 1985. On the topographically similar
Bodmin Moor in east Cornwall, by way of contrast, stretches of
grassy common where free wandering is tolerated are interspersed with
inaccessible fenced-off areas and signs bearing messages like this one:
'Notice: No Access to Hawks Tor Summit: Private Land'.

By far the largest area of moor and mountain is the Highlands
and Islands of Scotland and this vast region is too wet or grassy for
grouse to prosper: instead it is given over mainly to sheep rearing
and deer stalking. At present, these uses—over land from the flattish

56 square miles of the heathery knolls, hidden lochans, and peat hags of the Great Moor of Rannoch in the south to the fantastic red sugar-loaf of Suilven in west Sutherland in the far north and occupying 3 million acres in total—coexist with a wide measure of tolerated public access. This current freedom of movement is not, however, underpinned by law. Scotland has no legally recognized common land. Few access agreements have been secured. Public paths are very thin on the ground and those which exist (usually old military or drove roads) rarely climb mountains or run along ridges but keep to the low passes. While some estates are owned by organizations which allow access as a matter of course, like the National Trust for Scotland, the John Muir Trust, or the Royal Society for the Protection of Birds, most is in private ownership. The large size of Scotland's Highland estates and the scarcity of public rights of way mean that one owner's intransigence can have a devastating impact on access over a wide area without the public having any comeback. In any case, informal access is unreliable. In the Highlands you often cannot be sure until you arrive that you will really be able to go where you want. Most Highland estates seek to bar people from the hills during August, September, and October when deer stalking is taking place. During this time, walkers are encouraged to keep to certain areas or on what estates call 'preferred routes' and to telephone estate offices before they set out to find out where these routes run, since their availability and direction will depend on where stalking is taking place at any particular time. Walkers have no way of knowing when they may confront a notice suggesting that they enquire at the lodge before continuing with their walk, with the implication that unspecified unpleasant consequences could follow if they do not. Linda Sharratt from Dumfriesshire wrote in a letter in the magazine *Rambling Today* in 1992: 'Can you imagine anyone walking eight miles, finding such a notice, with no information on how far the lodge is, walking miles to find the lodge, finding someone in authority who knows what's happening on the hills that day, then going back?'[16]

The situation may be improving. In 1992 Paul Van Vlissingen, a Dutch industrialist, and the owner of the 87,000-acre Letterewe estate in Wester Ross consisting of a vast sweep of upland moor and mountain as well as thirty lochs, put up signs banning camping on his land and asking people to keep to footpaths. These signs caused concern among walkers who wished to exercise what they regarded as a tradition of free roaming there. A protracted debate over access ensued. It was finally resolved in December 1993 when Mr Van Vlissingen and representatives of access and conservation groups signed the Letterewe Accord—a sort of access agreement in which Mr Van Vlissingen agreed to allow public use subject to any suspension of access which would be agreed by the signatories. The accord encourages visitors to go in small rather than large groups and to walk rather than drive into the area and to contact the estate for advice on areas to avoid on weekdays from 15 September until 15 November, which is the most important period for stalking.

This agreement has formed the basis for a wider 'Concordat' on access to mountain and moor Scotland. In 1996 walkers and landowners groups including the Mountaineering Council of Scotland and the Scottish Landowners' Federation signed up to an agreement under which landowners accept freedom of access to Scotland's hills and mountains so long as it is exercised with responsibility and subject to reasonable constraints as required for land management and conservation. Walkers agree to respect the needs of livestock and of land management, and landowners pledge that they will make local restrictions on access only if these are essential for land management and that in any case they shall be fully explained and maintained only for the minimum period and over the smallest possible area.

So far the main effect of the Concordat has been to regularize still further the relaying of information to walkers about areas they are encouraged to avoid and 'preferred routes' they are encouraged to use during the stalking season. The Scottish Landowners' Federation and the Mountaineering Council of Scotland have jointly published a book *Heading for the Scottish Hills* which is available at tourist offices and the like, and shows estate boundaries and gives telephone numbers of estate contacts. Since the Concordat was signed, this system has been supplemented by a system of 'hill phones', whereby estates leave a recorded message about where stalking is taking place on any particular day and the areas they would like walkers to avoid. This system does however still have a long way to go: in 1996, when it started, it applied to two estates; by 1998 this had risen to four.

For the walker on the ground in Scotland, the Concordat does not safeguard tolerated freedom to wander over the mountains and moors. While the vast majority of estate owners accept this, a few still do not. John Mackay, the official at the government agency Scottish Natural Heritage responsible for the Concordat, told me in 1997: 'The Concordat is an agreement between organizations but it doesn't, can't control all the individual members of those organizations. . . . The result of the Concordat? It's very difficult to answer that question. There's a better climate of opinion around; we now have the Concordat as a point of peer group pressure—a bit of underpinning.'

Nor does the Concordat do anything to deal with problems which can arise when owners change land use or the intensity of use in ways which can have an impact on free movement. The high fences erected to contain deer or to protect new forestry plantations can cut off routes to the hills; while the spread of new private forestry plantations removes open moorland in the Highlands just as effectively as the spreading intensification of stock rearing on moorland from mid-Wales to Perthshire. Forestry claims 65 square miles of mainly open moor and glen every year in Britain and at least as much is also turned over to intensive sheep grazing systems which involve fencing.

Other Roughlands

Mountain and the moorland which often surrounds it may be the most extensive types of roughland in Britain, but there are several other types which play a different but no less important role in our experience of the outdoors. In spite of our instinctive association of roughland of all types with wilderness, in Britain most of it (including moorland) reflects some kind of human intervention in the past. Ancient forest covered most of the United Kingdom until human beings appeared on the scene. Our forebears in prehistory chopped down most of this forest and then used the rough turf which developed to pasture domesticated animals, thereby preventing woodland from re-establishing itself. Diversity is the hallmark of Britain's rough grazing lands. The clifftops of Cornwall and Pembrokeshire sport carpets of wiry grass studded with pink cushions of sea thrift and bursts of pale blue spring squill. The heaths of Surrey and Hampshire still play host to expanses of purple heather stretching as far as the eye can see. Perhaps most famous of all, because they have been so ably celebrated by writers like W. H. Hudson, Hilaire Belloc, Rosemary Sutcliffe, and Rudyard Kipling, are the turf-clothed chalk downs from the coast of County Antrim to the Wolds of Lincolnshire and east Yorkshire and the Downs of the Home Counties containing as many as forty different plant species per square metre from the rare monkey, musk, and spider orchids to the more familiar blooms of milkwort, rock-rose, and squinancywort. Many of these lowland roughlands, their incidence reflecting the complexity of our geology, nestle cheek by jowl with more or less intensively farmed holdings. This makes their potential for recreation enormous. Ralph Vaughan Cornish, a leading conservationist of the 1930s, recognized what such areas can contribute when he proposed that a belt of roughland 100 yards wide should be set aside right round the coast of Britain.[17] Unlike the moors, which have become synonymous with grouse shooting, the roughlands lying round our coasts and in lowland Britain have never found a particular use which has encouraged owners to keep people off them. Their most frequent use has been low-intensity sheep grazing, and *de facto* public access has often been tolerated alongside this.

Nonetheless, the amount of lowland roughland which survives today is only a tiny proportion of that which Belloc and Kipling would have known. Eighty per cent of Britain's chalk downland turf has gone under the plough during this century.[18] The once vast heaths of Norfolk, Suffolk, and Hampshire have been whittled down to a small number of fragments;[19] while Devon, for instance, saw 69,000 acres of the gorse-strewn roughland which used to clothe countless hillsides (excluding Exmoor and Dartmoor where additional losses have occurred) squared off into farmers' fields between 1900 and 1977.[20] Some of the roughlands which have managed to survive—like much of Cannock Chase in Staffordshire, the Lickey Hills south of Birmingham, and Berry Head in south Devon, are fully accessible through ownership by local authorities which manage them as country parks. A far larger number of the surviving pockets of roughland, which are privately owned, are, however, accessible, if at all, only by accident. Even in cases where roughlands in this latter category are visible from public rights of way, they may not always be stepped upon. Thus in 1998 the 9th Earl of Macclesfield forbade walkers from wandering freely over downland at the Shirburn and Pyrton Hills in south Oxfordshire. In many other cases, pockets of downland are impenetrable because no public right of way comes anywhere near them. The 6,500-acre Highclere estate south of Newbury, for instance, harbours as many as twenty-two separate pieces of chalk downland turf scattered amidst its farms and woods, lakes, estate cottages, and follies. But in 1998 only six of these were accessible to the public all year round. The remainder were viewable only by trespassers. This, even though more than 5,000 acres of the estate is covered by an inheritance tax exemption agreement, providing the 7th Earl of Carnarvon and his immediate successors with tax privileges in return for managing the estate in the public interest. Although the agreement requires the Earl to conserve these pieces of downland, its access clauses cover only the estate's parkland, leaving the bulk of the estate's woods, lakesides, and rough grasslands inaccessible. Here as at the Shirburn and Pyrton Hills and in many other places in southern England, stretches of downland lie within estates in which game rearing is important. Although downland turf alone is not particularly useful for game, it is associated with other types of landscape which provide rough cover for pheasants and partridges and access to it is inhibited because of the customary prescription that game and the public should be kept apart.

The special value of Britain's roughlands for wildlife and landscape conservation as well as recreation has meant that they have been targeted in the various subsidy schemes developed through the 1980s and 1990s to provide for payments to landowners for both conservation and access. Thus the South Downs was one of the first environmentally sensitive areas to be designated, while chalk and limestone turf was one of the first habitats to be included in the countryside stewardship scheme. Behind Folkestone in Kent you will find a concentration of downland conserved through stewardship payments, many of which are accessible to the public because the landowners concerned have opted to enter their stewardship land into the access tier. The largest countryside stewardship site in Kent in 1996 covered 148 acres of chalk grassland on the Folkestone Downs south of Paddlesworth.

In Kent as a whole there were twenty chalk grassland sites covered by stewardship access payment agreements in 1996. However, if you travel west from the North Downs into the South Downs you find a very different picture. In 1996, about one-fifth of the eligible area of the South Downs ESA was covered by ESA conservation agreements, around half of which involved the reversion of arable land to downland turf; the total of 200 agreements covered 42 square miles of land. However, in only three cases had farmers opted to receive the additional payments available under the access tier. The result was an access by 10-metre-wide linear strip over a total of only 3 miles.

Of all our stretches of downland, the South Downs is perhaps the most celebrated. It was proposed for national park designation in 1947 on account of its botanically rich turf, rolling topography, wide views and proximity to centres of population, but was eventually excluded as the parks were concentrated in the uplands of the north and west. A campaign for the designation of the South Downs as a national park nonetheless continues. Today, one of the leading activists is a Brighton man called Dave Bangs. In 1998 Mr Bangs conducted a meticulous survey of public access to a central stretch of the Downs (15.5 miles long by 3 miles wide, running from Shoreham in the west to Newhaven to the east and embracing 47 square miles of land), as the basis for a personal submission to the government's consultation process on improving access. First, Mr Bangs pinpointed surviving areas of semi-natural downland turf: map work backed up by field investigation revealed as many as 180 of these. Many of them however covered only a few acres isolated amidst the arable prairies which have replaced thousands of acres of traditional downland pasture; the largest ran for three miles along the northern scarp slope of the Downs behind Brighton at Devil's Dyke. All told, these fragments occupied about 9 per cent of the chalk outcrop in the study area. Mr Bangs calculated that the public enjoys formal access to no more than 20 per cent of this land, or less than 2 per cent of the chalk outcrop. What this means is that even those who take advantage of the most important recreation resource in the Downs—the South Downs Way, one of Britain's most popular national trails—may fail to experience the area's unique charms. Dave Bangs writes: 'Only one mile of the South Downs Way [out of a total of 22 miles in the study area] crosses flower-rich ancient down pasture. This means that, although the grand scale is wonderful (dramatic long views and open skies), on an intimate scale, thousands of walkers may go away having seen nothing of what makes the South Downs special.'

Mr Bangs's report gives a hint of what the public are missing and of the problems they face. Old Erringham Come is just one of the inaccessible pasture fragments he identifies: 'This delightful, but inaccessible Combe, which is entirely invisible from most viewpoints . . . sports . . . Dark Green Fritillary, Adonis Blue, Chalkhill Blue and Brown Argus butterflies . . . and Autumn Ladies Tresses Orchid.' And on another site, 'Waterpit Hill is a largely north facing slope on the subscarp north east of Sussex University. It is crossed by a bridlepath. Yet any attempt to leave the unfenced path and explore the hillside walk may be met by a challenge from the gamekeeper who polices the St Mary farm shoot. Its long slope is colourful with Devil's Bit and Small Scabious and with Pride of Sussex.'[21]

Parklands

Sought after though roughlands are by those seeking a rustic experience, there is another kind of country whose attractions are even greater. A study of the landscape preferences of the British conducted at University College London in the 1960s by David Lowenthal and Hugh Prince concluded: 'The favoured landscape . . . is a calm and peaceful deer park, with slow-moving streams and wide expanses of meadowland studded with fine trees.'[22] Just why parkland should be the people's choice is not hard to see, since this is the landscape specifically designed to provide society's most privileged with the kind of environment that they would find most attractive. It combines the great shady trees of woodland with the calming grassland of the meadow, the whole set off with paths, lakes, and golden stone buildings. Here we can sit and gaze, read a book, picnic, and watch our children at play. Britain is blessed with lots of parklands. But how often can we get into them?

Engelfield Old Deer Park, first mentioned in records in 1588, just 2 miles from the western edge of Reading, is certainly 'a calm and peaceful deer park'. Today the park provides a scene not that different from that which would have confronted Elizabeth I, who hunted there. Situated on a series of ridges and occupying 39 acres (equivalent to four-fifths the area of Green Park) the park is home to about 300 fallow deer who graze the turf amidst scattered oaks, beeches, sweet chestnuts, hawthorns, and elders. It stands at the heart of an estate owned by Sir Richard Benyon, the Deputy Lieutenant of Berkshire, a former High Sheriff and an MP for constituencies in Buckinghamshire for twenty-two years, and spreads over 12,000 acres of Hampshire and Berkshire—woods, twenty-four farms, housing, polo pitches, a golf course, lengths of the Rivers Kennet and Pang and gravel workings. When one of Sir Richard's forebears decided to add a park to the estate, as was the fashion in eighteenth-century England, he decided against adapting the Old Deer Park and constructed an additional one in front of Englefield House—flatter, larger (at 140 acres two-and-a-half times the size of Green Park) and more formal and picturesque than the wilder Old Park and adorned with a 22-acre lake.

In 1998 both these parks were virtually inaccessible to the general public. The most the would-be visitor could hope for was a partial sighting. You could see part of the eighteenth-century park from a permissive footpath leading to a church and part over or through gaps in a wall alongside a public road. On Mondays all year round, on three other weekdays for four months, and on one Saturday you had another view from a 7-acre garden which was open to the public. You could glimpse the old deer park from a road that rises and dips close by it. But no public rights of way crossed the parks and most of their considerable expanse remained unknowable to outsiders.

In their inaccessibility, the parks at Englefield are not unusual. In total Berkshire has thirty-nine parks. In 1998 only five were open to the public; public footpaths provided limited access to a further nine. The picture is similar in other counties in which country parkland— one of the most admired features of the English landscape—is present. Thus a survey in 1993 found that only four of Hampshire's fifty-nine parklands were open;[23] by 1997, the annual publication *Historic Houses, Castles and Gardens* listed an additional three.[24] In Cheshire the situation is better but far from ideal with a total of eighteen parks open out of forty-eight. Four of these accessible to some degree were privately owned and fourteen in the hands of local council or the National Trust.[25]

Norfolk has particular associations with English country parkland, providing as it does the setting for L. P. Hartley's celebrated novel *The Go-Between* and containing some outstanding National Trust and private parklands, like Blickling, Houghton, and Holkham. But through most of Norfolk, country parklands are not easily accessible. Thus the 350 square miles of rolling country south of Norwich forming the territory of South Norfolk District contains seven country parklands (Kimberley, Broome, Raveningham, Ellingham, Rainthorpe, Hedenham, and Ditchingham). In 1998 not one of these parks was open to the public though some of their gardens were. The District's 180,000 people, who live in its scattered villages and small market towns, must go some way to step inside a country parkland.

Parkland is intrinsically less accessible than woodland. For a start, its topography makes informal trespassing much more difficult. A certain amount of access to woodland involves members of the public walking into unfenced woods without any legal right to do so. Often such trespassers are never spotted simply because the density of the vegetation ensures they are never seen. In parkland, the openness of the landscape means that people are easier to spot. At the same time, they are more likely to be inhibited from attempting to trespass by imposing barriers, often in the form of an encircling parkland wall interrupted by mighty gates perhaps topped by effigies of threatening lions or stags. The walker can be under no illusion that the landowner enshrined behind such defences would welcome him if he stepped in. The wanderer in the woods may have little sense of the existence of the landowner, but his intimidating presence pervades his park.

The vast majority of our country parklands are in private hands and if open to the public at all it is only on payment of a fee and for a limited period. Stratfield Saye park is typical. This park is the centrepiece of the 7,000-acre estate lying in the gently sloping valley of the River Loddon about 7 miles equidistant from Reading (to the north) and Basingstoke (to the south) which was handed to the 1st Duke of Wellington by a grateful nation in 1817. The estate includes woods and farms. On the Ordnance Survey map a stretch of parkland well over a mile long is shown covering 170 acres (slightly smaller than Greenwich Park). On its eastern side the park is bounded by a stretch of the River Loddon and on its western side by a belt of woodland and then to the south by private roads in the vicinity of the mansion, Stratfield Saye house, and two further woods. The access situation in the summer of 1998 was as follows. No public rights of way crossed the park, nor was it visible from any public road or path in the immediate vicinity. However, permissive access existed during June, July, and August and during bank holidays in May and September, when visitors could pay to set foot in the house, gardens, and over a stretch of the park in front of the house including riverside and an arboretum. Visitors could see but not set foot in a larger stretch of parkland as they drove out of the car park close to the house, since the one-way exit route to a lodge-gate on the park's northern side took them along a private road running through a broad sweep of grass dotted with fine trees. Both walking and parking were forbidden along this road: at its start there was a notice saying 'no pedestrians beyond this point'; while signs prohibiting parking had been put up at passing places. To the east the River Loddon was barely visible; a stone bridge across could be seen, but only from a distance.

As on many other country estates, it is not only the core parkland which is out of bounds at Stratfield Saye. That parkland, together with the stretch of river which abuts it, stands in a block of countryside 2 square miles in extent also taking in woods, farmland, and a lake which was penetrated by no rights of way in 1998 apart from one footpath of a quarter of a mile leading to an isolated church. However, 3 miles from the house, the Duke of Wellington welcomes the general public for nine months of the year to a stretch of wood, grass, and flooded former gravel workings called the Wellington Country Park. At this facility, which the estate set up with the help of a Countryside Commission grant, people pay a fee for the opportunity to walk anywhere and enjoy attractions including a children's animal farm, refreshments, and a miniature steam railway. The guidebook to the house explains: 'In 1975, bearing in mind the huge increase of population in this area of the country in the last few years, the present Duke felt it would be appropriate to set aside 550 acres of unspoilt countryside astride the A32 in the north-east corner of the Estate, for public enjoyment as a Country Park. In so doing he felt also he was repaying in some measure the debt of gratitude the family owes to the Nation for the gift of Stratfield Saye.'[26]

Five features of access to the parkland at Stratfield Saye apply commonly at other country parklands: the access is permissive; on payment of a fee; for only part of the year; to only part of the park; a surrounding estate remains largely inaccessible. Nonetheless, such access as exists is clearly much enjoyed by those who take advantage of it. The visitor enjoying rural experiences in Stratfield Saye nonetheless must remain aware of his or her status as a guest invited on carefully defined terms, present usually for a fee in return for which only limited privileges are secured.

It does not seem to make much difference whether the parkland is close to or far from centres of population. Stratfield Saye is in the populous South-East. Floors Castle on the edge of the little town of Kelso north of the Cheviots and inland from Holy Island also boasts wide sweeps of parkland, but here too the visitor was able only to obtain access to a slice of the park during the seven months of the year when it was open in 1998. At Euston Hall outside Thetford in Suffolk, the Duke of Grafton allowed visitors access to a large area of his park, but on Thursday afternoons only for four months in the summer. Haddon Hall outside Bakewell is within the Peak District National Park. Here the visitor pays to go round the twelfth-century Hall and into courtyards and small gardens but in 1998 he or she was not permitted even to step onto any part of the park: instead he looked down from the accessible gardens over an enticing stretch of park through which sweep great bends of the River Wye. This is the Derbyshire domain of the 10th Duke of Rutland, whose base is Belvoir castle 35 miles away to the east near Grantham. Here too the paying visitor to the castle and grounds was also much restricted in the area over which he or she might tread.

At Broadlands outside Romsey in south Hampshire, access was open to the park in 1998 when I visited it last—but apart from occasional events like the Romsey Show only between noon and 5.30 p.m. during the three months of June, July, and August. Even in these few hours, visitors were not allowed to roam the whole park. They could pass along the main drive, park their cars close to the house, and then walk over a few acres of the park near the car park and a few acres of park (in effect riverside lawns) in front of the house. The countless shady spots beneath scattered trees in the rest of the park were out of bounds not only for the nine months of the year when the park was closed but even on the days when it was open as well.[27]

In some parks, the restriction is less on when and where visitors go than on who they are. Thus the owners of some country parklands allow certain local people to obtain permits which give them privileged access. At Rockingham Castle in Northamptonshire, for instance, Commander Michael Saunders-Watson had granted permission to named individuals, such as the local doctor, to walk in the extensive outer park which was closed to visitors to the castle and inner park when I visited the estate in 1982. Sometimes this permissive access is extended to named naturalists, or perhaps to the local scouts for camps at certain times of the year. But its nature is that of widening invited access to an exclusive group. Should the ordinary residents of Romsey write and ask Broadlands' owner, Lord Romsey, for a permit to walk in it, what would he say? 'Definitely not', he told me in 1986. However, Lord Romsey had at that time set aside 3 acres of land on the edge of the park and beside the town where he allowed local voluntary groups like the scouts to hold events rent free.

There are nonetheless some extremely famous and accessible country parklands in Britain. Many of these are in public or semi-public ownership. Petworth in Sussex, Blickling in Norfolk, and Surrey's Polesden Lacey are all owned by the National Trust. Richmond, Greenwich, and Hyde Parks are all royal parks owned by the Crown and managed for the public by the Department for Culture, Media, and Sport. Local councils are the owners of Tatton south of Stockport, Hylands near Chelmsford, and Pitcairncrieff in Dunfermline. As a child living in a tiny cottage close by, Andrew Carnegie had longed to step inside the 70-acre stretch of park, glen, and wooded hills in the very centre of Dunfermline but from which access was then barred. After making his fortune in Canada, Carnegie was able to buy the park and hand it to the townspeople. 'Pitcairncrieff Glen is the most soul-satisfying public gift I ever made, or ever can make,' he wrote in his autobiography.[28]

There is the occasional case in which a private owner has thrown open the gates of a park for 365 days a year for free, for no other reason than generosity of spirit, so that people may wander around under a regime of tolerated trespass. Arundel Park in West Sussex is one such case: here people are allowed to wander over the entire park, around its picturesque lake, and into the surrounding woodland without fear of being thrown off. A similar situation exists over a large stretch of Burghley Park at Stamford in Lincolnshire. Of course such grace-and-favour access can always be withdrawn. The people of Luton, Dunstable, Hertford, and north London had no redress when a new owner of the magnificent 800-acre Southill Park in north Bedfordshire decided in 1964 to discontinue his predecessor's practice of allowing informal access at weekends. Giving bad behaviour by visitors as the reason, Samuel Whitbread introduced a formal permit system under which only residents of the tiny estate village of Southill, bona fide naturalists, and the local scouts and sea scouts would be allowed to stroll in the park or view the calm waters of its beautiful lake.

Perhaps the two best-known privately owned parklands in Britain —Chatsworth and Blenheim—are both covered by the government scheme which perhaps does more than any other to secure more public access to privately-owned parkland—the inheritance tax exemption scheme. As we have seen (pages 32–3), when death brings inheritance tax liabilities to an estate the new owner may be allowed to escape these in return for agreeing to benefit society in some way—say, by opening a house and its treasures to the public or, sometimes, by allowing public access to a park. The financial advantages to the owner can be considerable, especially as he will normally be allowed to charge for the access he deigns to grant. He will also be assured that the entire deal will be kept secret as part of the confidentiality to be expected by a taxpayer from the Inland Revenue, so that visitors to parks have no way of knowing whether or not they are paying for the privilege out of foregone tax.

Highclere Park in Hampshire provides an example of how inheritance tax exemption can work in practice. The park stands at the heart of a 6,500-acre estate owned by the 7th Earl of Carnarvon and his immediate successors in north Hampshire 5 miles south of Newbury. The park with Highclere Castle (a nineteenth-century pinnacled mansion) at its centre was remodelled by Capability Brown and is considered one of his masterpieces. At 430 acres according to the Ordnance Survey map, it is planted with massive cedars of Lebanon and contains hills and dells (it was originally enclosed in 1403), a church and the remains of another church, a ruined temple and several other listed buildings, and two large lakes. Until recently, Highclere was a very private park indeed. In 1978, for instance, it could be seen best from the top of Beacon Hill, a stretch of downland turf which the Earl had dedicated to Hampshire County Council for twenty-one years as a public open space. (In 1998 this was extended for another twenty-one years.) Otherwise it could be glimpsed mainly from a short length of public footpath which ran from a road to a church in an outlying part of the park. The gardens immediately around the house were open three times a year and there was access to the garden shop on two afternoons a week. Apart from this, this park was out of bounds all year round, part of a private kingdom given over to farming, forestry, private fishing, race-horse breeding and pheasant shooting. However, in recent years the park and the house (though not the woods, rough grasslands, lakes, and fields in the remainder of the estate) have been opened to the public. The 6th Earl died in 1987 and an inheritance tax exemption agreement is in place under which the family agree to conserve much of the estate and to allow reasonable public access to it. In 1997, when I last visited it, access to the park was greater than ever before during the last twenty years. The house itself together with parkland immediately beside it and gardens close by were open to the public on payment of a fee (£5.50 per adult) between 11 a.m. and 5 p.m. on five days a week and until 3.30 p.m. on Saturdays, from May until September. Parking was allowed in a car park near the entrance booth. Year round access had become available since the formerly private estate road running east–west across the park had acquired public footpath status as part of the inheritance tax deal. Finally, during the times when the house was open to the public people could also make their way along two permissive circular paths both passing through parts of the park, with one of them affording views of one of the lakes. Not that these arrangements turned Highclere into anything approaching a public park. The presence of the public, when and where it was allowed, was confined to particular spaces. Visitors could see green expanses stretching away beyond them, but for the most part these remained tantalizingly out of reach. Although they might just be able to make out Heaven's Gate, a red-brick, bridge-like folly in the depths of the beech woods of Sidown

Hill which rises 200 feet above the park, they could not venture up there.

By 1998 a measure of public access was afforded to a total of three parklands in Hampshire through the inheritance tax exemption scheme (Highclere, Breamore near Fordingbridge, and Pylewell near Lymington; a fourth, Greywell near Hook, was under negotiation) out of a total of fifty-nine parks in the county. The widening of unconditional exemption which we have already noted (see page 93) is likely to mean that few additions to this list can be expected in Hampshire or anywhere else.

The Seashore

At least it can be said in support of restricting access to parkland that it was usually created for the exclusive use of the privileged. One kind of land which we usually assume should be available to all is the seashore. There is something about the space where sea and land meet, a space usually still untouched by visible human interference, which makes it seem unthinkable that anybody should imagine they could lay claim to the exclusive ownership of it. Surely our children are entitled to build sandcastles with their buckets and spades and watch the incoming tide melt them away? No, actually, they are not. They build their castles as trespassers, tolerated, usually, for the time being, but with no guarantee that they will always be.

The foreshore—strictly speaking that stretch of land between high and low water marks—is owned just like any other stretch of British soil. The apparently free access we seem to enjoy to most of it exists only because of factors which could change overnight. As it happens, the owner of 50 per cent of the foreshore of the United Kingdom happens to be the Queen in her capacity as sovereign and thus inheritor of the Crown Estate. This diverse empire also includes the seabed 12 miles out to the limit of territorial waters, the bed and banks of Britain's rivers where they are tidal, large stretches of farmland and woodland, and residential and commercial property in the West End of London, Edinburgh, Windsor, and elsewhere. It is not public or semi-public land, even though its considerable income does go to the

Exchequer and in return for the sums which the Queen receives for the maintenance of herself and other members of the Royal Family in the shape of the Civil List. The Estate is run on the lines of other private estates by eight commissioners.[29]

As owner of the foreshore, the Crown Estate can generate income by itself engaging or licensing others to engage in a wide range of activities from building ports and marinas, installing fish farms and yachting berths, laying pipelines and cables, and excavating sand and other minerals. And as owner it can stop people walking on the foreshore. In fact, at present, it does not choose to do so, not because it lacks the desire but because it lacks the means. A spokesman told me in 1994: 'People are trespassing, but the Crown Estate tolerates this trespassing because it can't regulate it.' If the commissioners become more concerned to squeeze the maximum return from the asset they administer, we can expect them to look for means of exploiting the exclusivity of the shore. They would be entitled to charge entry fees to Britain's best beaches, and we cannot be sure that some of them will not one day try to do so.

Most of the foreshore not owned by the Crown Estate is in the hands of large estates, though a little is owned by local councils and port authorities. The Prince of Wales as Duke of Cornwall owns most of the foreshore of Cornwall as well as that of the entire Isles of Scilly, while the Duchy of Lancaster owns foreshore in such areas as Morecambe Bay and the northern shores of the Mersey. Other major owners of England's foreshore include the Duke of Beaufort, Lord Montagu, and Lord Rothschild.

All of these owners are legally entitled to stop the public walking on the stretches of foreshore they own, though like the Crown Estate they would face practical problems in trying to enforce this right. Although the general public do not enjoy a right to walk along the seashore, to bathe on it, or to put to sea or land from it, they do enjoy two rights in law which owners must respect. International law entitles anybody to navigate the sea, and when the tide comes in over the foreshore this therefore provides a maritime right of access at least to the waters above it. Secondly, the public enjoy a legal right to fish in tidal waters and this includes a right to fish in waters above the foreshore. Inability to protect fishing rights from seaborne fishermen makes the cost of enforcing exclusion less justifiable. Unless a foreshore owner also owns the land behind the foreshore, he would require extremely expensive fencing to keep people off his property which would bring no economic benefit in return. Allowing access, on the other hand, can generate profit. The owner of a beach may sell concessions for anything from selling ice-cream to renting out deckchairs and surfboards or charging for car parking.

Nonetheless, some foreshore owners do take advantage of their right to exclude, particularly if they also own the land behind the shore. In 1998 if you tried to walk along the New Forest shore just west of Southampton Water, for instance, you would have found your way blocked with fences opposite Cadland House. A little to the west, there were no legal rights of access whatsoever either along or down to the shore along a 5-mile stretch of sand, shingle, mud, and salting, or along the bank of the Beaulieu River for a further 2 miles, or to a hinterland of creeks, lakes, rough grassland, woods, and rivulets as well as a sand and shingle spit.

In Scotland the situation is different. The pattern of ownership is similar, with the Crown Estate owning a great deal of the foreshore and private owners, like the Earl of Morton and the Marquess of Bute, much of the rest. However in Scotland the public do enjoy a legal right to use the foreshore for recreation. Unfortunately the virtual absence of public footpaths north of the border means that it is often very difficult to exercise this right. There is no comparable Scottish equivalent of the long-distance paths which run around substantial stretches of the coast of England and Wales. There are very few public ways down to the foreshore and very often the walker has to pass over private land if he or she wants to reach the shore. Battles over rights of way in Scotland frequently involve tracks down to the seashore along which people try to establish a right of passage. Overall, the inadequacy of rights of access means that the Scottish coast is used far less for recreation than it might be.

Canals

Actual obstruction of access along the seashore in Britain remains of course exceptional. But what happens when we turn inland up our estuaries and try to follow our rivers and streams? A vast network of potential waterside walkways awaits us here, thanks to a dense network of rivers and streams caused by high rainfall and a substantial canal system created during the early part of the Industrial Revolution.

Canalsides are accessible to walkers, by and large, for the same reason as are Forestry Commission woodlands. A state agency, the British Waterways Board, owns the bulk of our canals and decided to permit the public to walk alongside them without charge in 1978 in recognition of its responsibility to the public who own them. Although the privatization of the BWB's canals was discussed during the 1980s, they were saved by their own intrinsic unprofitability in an age when road transport has been made so attractive. The free access of walkers to the paths along canals is paradoxical. Canals were built by private enterprise to generate profit from passage. It just happens that the towpaths created for horses happen to make splendidly flat paths for walkers now the barges have disappeared. In some cases walkers can thank a permissive decree of the BWB for their access (on the Kennet and Avon Canal, for example). Sometimes there is a legal right of passage regardless of the owner since the towpath is also a public footpath (as along most of the length of the St Helen's Canal between Widnes and Warrington). In other cases still, stretches of public path are interspersed with lengths of towing path where the public enjoy *de facto* but no *de jure* right of access (as on the Trent and Mersey Canal). North of Ledbury in Herefordshire are two lengths of dead straight public footpath over dry ground—reminders of the towing path of the Herefordshire and Gloucestershire Canal, which has been filled in.

The access to the countryside provided by towpaths is enormously important. Because the canals were built to connect industrial centres they provide arterial routes from the very heart of some of our biggest urban centres out into the countryside. In Britain towpaths provide 2,000 miles of walkways which are wide, level, and, because they are usually owned and managed quite separately from adjoining countryside, free of the barbed wire obstructions, deep ploughing, and farm animals that can make a walk in the ordinary farmed countryside difficult, unpredictable, and sometimes hazardous. What is more, they offer not only open air and rural sights and sounds but also the additional attractions of aqueducts and bridges, locks and tunnels, pubs, cottages, and the occasional kingfisher. The British Waterways Board estimates that 125 million visits are made every year to our canals. They provide what is often the only stretch of water along which people are allowed to walk and sit for miles around. Where could you take a walk along the water's edge in Buckinghamshire without the Grand Union Canal, in Warwickshire without the Stratford-upon-Avon Canal, in Wiltshire without the Kennet and Avon, in Lincolnshire without the Louth Navigation, or in Shropshire without the Shropshire Union?

Nonetheless, long, safe, and interesting walks along towpaths are not quite the same thing as moving around in the countryside. Because of the canals' history they are concentrated in the old industrial areas like Birmingham and the West Midlands, south of Belfast, the industrial belt of central Scotland and south Yorkshire. The paths are not only level, but dead straight, enclosed with a deliberate boundary, or slightly curved but with dead straight edges. They present a world apart, separate from footpaths and roads beyond their banks and cut off from the workings of the land there too. A walk along a canal can therefore never offer the particular delights to be had from following a babbling brook or mighty river.

Rivers

Rivers, streams, burns, becks, and ditches are everywhere in a country whose varied topography channels away plenty of rainfall. You could put our rivers, let alone their feeder streams, round our coastline many times, yet today, rivers are one of the most secret features of our land. Those rivers along which people may walk—the Thames and the Severn notably—are much visited and relatively well known. But most rivers are not intimately known because they cannot be. Very, very few of the major rivers of either Scotland, Wales, or Northern Ireland can be walked from source to sea. The coastline of Cornwall may be well known, but how many people could name its main rivers? One of these, the Fowey, is accessible on foot (and in a vehicle) for about a quarter of its course, but the Lynher and the Lyd, the Carey,

Cober, Inny, Hayle, Tamar, Helford, De Lank, Allen, Looe, and West Looe, to say nothing of Cornwall's myriad streams, remain virtually impenetrable, glimpsed at the occasional crossing, but their shallows and bends, kingfishers and bridges are almost completely unknown.

Although the water in our natural watercourses is owned by the public, the bed and banks of our non-tidal rivers belong to owners of the land on either side; in the case of substantial stretches of the tidal reaches of our rivers, notably the Thames, Severn, Clyde, Forth, Tees, Tyne, Itchen, Hamble, and Test, the owner is the Crown Estate. On our inland watercourses, there is no equivalent of the public rights of navigation and fishing which help ensure *de facto* access to the fore-shore. Instead, the owners of the bed and banks enjoy the navigation and fishing rights denied to owners of the foreshore around the coast. What this means is that we rarely achieve the tolerated access we know on the coast alongside rivers and streams unless we are pass-ing through unfenced upland moor and mountain. This has come to be accepted, even though we should be shocked to find ourselves sim-ilarly excluded from the coast.

Few of our rivers are bordered on either let alone both sides by public rights of way. Where these do exist for any substantial distance, this is usually the result of the historical accident of a river having been used for navigation in the past—a feature which makes the Thames, now lined on both banks with public footpaths for much of its length, our best-known river partly because it is one of the few we can actually walk along. In the west of England the Severn used to be by far the most important river in the region for commercial nav-igation, and the resulting towpaths alongside it from Shropshire through Stourport, Worcestershire, and into Gloucestershire have become public footpaths, making the river second only to the Thames for accessibility. One person who enjoyed sitting beside the Severn was the composer Sir Edward Elgar, who was brought up in Worcester and wrote later, 'I am still at heart the dreamy child who used to be found in the reeds by Severn side with a sheet of paper trying to fix the sounds.'[30] The public paths along the Severn are not always continuous on both banks (there is a gap for instance at Hallow north of Worcester where walkers have to leave the river and make their way inland past gravel pits and a business centre), but generally speaking access along the Severn is very good—as far as Ironbridge. Above Ironbridge, along the remaining 63 miles to the river's source, there is very little public access. In the case of the Wye the pattern is fairly similar. Although nowadays only the final 37 miles of this river are navigable, a legacy of its navigability in times past is a more or less continuous public footpath between Ross-on-Wye through the celebrated stretches of the river at Symonds Yat and thence across the county border between Gloucestershire and Gwent. Above Ross there are some substantial stretches of public path alongside the river but beyond Hereford there are very few. The Severn and Wye are, however, unusual. The banks of the Teme, which runs into the Severn south of Worcester, were also one of Elgar's favourite haunts. However, the Teme is far harder to get at than the Severn, and the rivers Lugg, Avon, Frome, Dore, Arrow, Leadon, and Onney, with public paths running along a total of no more than a fraction of their banks, are harder still. So although the counties of Hereford-shire and Worcestershire contain hundreds of miles of river, hardly any of this is walkable. There is no tradition of tolerated trespass along-side most of these riverbanks, and people attempting to walk along much of the waterside here are likely to be asked to leave or forcibly thrown off.

In general, access alongside our rivers and streams turns simply on the use and the ownership of the land which abuts them. Visit Selborne in north Hampshire, the village made famous as the home of the eighteenth-century naturalist the Revd Gilbert White, and not only can you wander freely through beech woods and flowery meadows grazed by cows: you can also walk alongside the clear, chalk Oakhanger stream which glides through the land surrounding the village. Here children (and their parents) sail little boats, edge their way across fallen tree bridges, and explore countless bends and twists of the watery environment. This land is owned by the National Trust and as part of its ownership it requires its tenants to allow free pub-lic access. One hundred years ago, Kinnaird Brook north of Pitlochry in Perthshire was similarly accessible. We know because Robert Louis Stevenson brought his new wife and her son here during the summer of 1881, the year in which he wrote *Treasure Island*. From the cottage nearby he wrote in a letter, 'We have a lovely spot here: a little green glen with a burn, a wonderful burn, gold and green and snow-white, singing loud and low in different steps of its career, now pouring over miniature crags, now fretting itself to death in a maze of rocky stairs and pots; never was so sweet a little river. Behind, great purple moorlands reaching to Ben Vrackie.'[31] Stevenson's diary records daily strolls along the brook with his wife sketching and her son sailing boats in the little pools and over the miniature waterfalls. Today the burn can be seen from a road bridge. But you cannot trace the burn as they did: it is closely hemmed in behind a maze of wire fences, as intensive agriculture has taken over from the rough sheep pasture of a century ago.

Such changes have been replayed in countless other places. 'The stream invites us to follow', wrote the nature writer W. H. Hudson in his book *Afoot in England* in 1909 reporting on his attempts to follow the course of the River Exe in south Devon. Hudson went on: 'The impulse is so common that it might be set down as an instinct; and certainly there is no more fascinating pastime than to keep company with a river from its source to the sea. Unfortunately this is not easy in a country where running waters have been enclosed, which should be as free as the rain and sunshine to all, and were once free, when England was England still, before landowners annexed them, even as they annexed or stole the commons and shut up the footpaths and made it an offence for a man to go aside from the road to feel God's grass under his feet.' Hudson was writing before the postwar agricultural revolution which industrialized agriculture and in so doing swept away much of the remaining *de facto* access alongside many rivers and streams. One of the things which has been lost is the ability to paddle and even swim in rivers and streams. Today, you rarely see anyone swimming in the British rivers in which country children learned to swim. A long-time resident of the village of Barnack near Stamford in south Lincolnshire, Albert Corrall, recalled for me in an interview in 1992 that early in this century the local vicar had put up a swimming platform in the River Welland to help children learn to swim. Swimming was not permitted in the lake at nearby Burghley Park although local people enjoyed *de facto* freedom to walk around it. The river, however, seemed somehow to be something no mere owner could deny to the people.

The situation of would-be navigators along rivers is even worse than that of walkers. Navigation rights can be granted by riparian owners and awarded under private Acts of Parliament. However, the latter usually simply empower companies or individuals to carry out work themselves while riparian owners very rarely grant navigation rights. It is possible to establish a public right of navigation by providing evidence of continuous use, but that use has to extend back as far as living testimony can go, in other words sixty or seventy years, compared to the twenty years required for public footpaths—a formidable hurdle in view of the time period involved and the number of riparian owners likely to be affected and whose tacit acceptance that a public right of navigation existed would have to be demonstrated.[32]

For all would-be users of rivers there is one other factor which complicates matters—the value of some inland waterways for fishing. The pursuit of salmon and trout—deemed the aristocrats in the world of fish—ensures that the right of owners to exclude is often more energetically enforced in respect of riversides than it is elsewhere. Glorious rivers like the Tay, Spey, Dee, Forth, Tweed in Scotland, the Test, Avon, and Nadder in Hampshire, the Nidd, Derwent, and Rye in Yorkshire, the Evenlode and Windrush in Oxfordshire, the Foyle, Strule, and Mourne in County Omagh, and the Onney, Teme, and Lugg in Herefordshire belong to fish not walkers. The game fish (salmon, trout, sea trout, and grayling) in the rivers of Yorkshire, Dorset and Hampshire, Devon and Cornwall, Cumbria and Lancashire, and most of Northern Ireland and Scotland are so valuable that they are worth protecting with water bailiffs, who may not distinguish between innocent walkers and poachers. The lesser waters of the East Midlands, East Anglia, and Kent, where only coarse fishing is available for the most part, are often less rigorously policed by landowners and therefore present trespassers with a less forbidding target.

Lakes and Reservoirs

Our countless inland bodies of water—lakes, lochs, loughs, reservoirs, and ponds—are subject to a regime slightly more forbidding even than that governing rivers. In law, the public enjoys no more rights over a large enclosed body of water than over a puddle: as in the case of rivers, the bed and banks are owned by the owners of land adjacent to the body of water; but in this case their ownership also embraces the water. The situation is the same whether the stretch of water is natural or man-made, vast or tiny. The public has no rights to walk along the shores of lakes or reservoirs, and passage over the water itself constitutes trespass unless special laws provide for this. So our ability to glimpse, to sit beside, or to walk along the edge of lakes and the like varies widely. Three factors are especially significant: the existence of special legal circumstances; the ownership of the land; and the use of the lake itself and the land which surrounds it.

Just occasionally the public enjoys the right to navigate over an inland body of water, and where this situation exists, it often incidentally makes possible approach to the lake shore. The most extensive area where this occurs is Lake Windermere: here there is a public right to navigate the whole lake, while a road happens to run the length of one 12-mile lake edge. The public right of navigation on Windermere helped make possible the development of Windermere as a tourist centre and therefore the building of a railway up to the lakeside. Haweswater and Derwentwater also support a public right of navigation and also feature a road along the length of a shore. The other major lakes in the Lake District as well as those in other mountainous areas like Snowdonia and the Scottish Highlands also tend to provide a right of access along one of the long shores simply because they are long-standing communication routes and have been used for centuries for transportation. This does not however mean that the entire lakeside will be accessible. Although a major road runs along the eastern side of Windermere, it does not necessarily provide access to the actual lakeside, and here there are areas characterized by a number of large houses with attractive landscaped gardens reaching down to the lake shore where public access is restricted to the occasional straight line down to the shore and back out again.

Public access to the shores of the lakes of the Lake District is also enhanced by the particular kind of ownership of the surrounding land. Much of the north-western shore of Windermere is owned by the National Trust, and as a result is accessible to the general public. The Lake District has long been a focus of National Trust purchases, while the Lake District National Park Authority owns more land than any other park authority except the Brecon Beacons. Far more than most public authorities, the Lake District authority has targeted its land acquisition in a very precise manner, often with the deliberate aim of facilitating access to the lakes themselves. Thus Bassenthwaite came into the ownership of the board in lieu of inheritance tax. The authority then bought a farm on the shores of Bassenthwaite to provide continuous access to the lake shore.

Nationwide the kind of ownership which delivers most public access to the shores of inland waters is probably that of the British Waterways Board, which owns eighty-nine reservoirs and opens all of them to the public. A large number of reservoirs is however owned by water companies whose policies vary. A path is provided all round south-east England's biggest inland water, Bewl reservoir on the Kent/Sussex border. At Hanningfield Reservoir south of Chelmsford in Essex, on the other hand, public access is restricted to views from a public road and a small permissive picnic site on the 12-mile circumference. The Essex Water Company blocked an attempt by Essex County Council to secure public path status to an existing track which goes down to and along the water's edge.

Outside such lakes and reservoirs where special circumstances apply, any access to inland shores depends on the attitude landowners take to access, which varies according to local custom and land use. Thus at present walkers enjoy *de facto* access to the shores of a great many Highland lochs as well as to the small corrie lakes and tarns in the high mountains of Snowdonia and the Lake District. In Northern Ireland, on the other hand, the largest lakes are tightly hemmed in by farmland, and, in a country with very few public rights of way, public access is often very restricted around the shores of Strangford Lough, Lough Neagh, and Lower Lough Erne. So although Strangford Lough, for instance, has the appearance of a seashore, with its muddy flats and creeks and inlets, the people of Northern Ireland cannot enjoy a walk along its shore as they can along the coast itself.

Farmland has a large number of bodies of water in the form of farm reservoirs, often constructed with the help of a grant from the taxpayer. Some of these are concrete-fringed structures; others are pleasant lakes edged by trees and reed beds, but any public access is purely incidental and where it exists it is for the most part the result of a public right of way which happens to skirt part of the edge. Perhaps our most aesthetically pleasing lakes are those in country parklands. These—like the parklands themselves—are far more numerous than most people imagine—and as access to them depends on access to the parkland itself, the vast majority of such lakes are inaccessible.

Changes in the way in which land is worked can have a huge impact on public access to wetlands. In East Kent, by the villages of Minster and Monkton, for example, people enjoyed *de facto* access until the 1960s to extensive marshlands which were criss-crossed by dykes and streams and used as low-intensity summer grazing for cattle. The post-war drive to increase food production resulted in extensive drainage so that today these areas consist of large fields given over to the intensive production of barley and crops like onions. All the *de facto* access which went with the low-intensity farming use, and with it the chance of a bit of picnicking or tadpoling has gone.[33] However, a few miles away in the valley of the River Stour on the other (western) side of Canterbury, extensive sand and gravel extraction has taken place over the past few decades. Where working ceases, the land is frequently flooded and here the public now enjoys *de facto* freedom to wander round the edges of many of the new lakes that have thereby been created. Whether or not access is permitted to flooded former sand and gravel pits depends, however, entirely on the attitude of the landowner and on any conditions that may have been imposed when planning permission was granted. While the pits in the Stour valley are accessible to walkers, many of the flooded gravel pits in the Kennet, Loddon, and Thames valleys near Reading are not. Janette Skellern, a student at Reading University who conducted a survey in 1993 of recreation provision in Berkshire, writes,

The re-use of water resources on agricultural land and following gravel extraction tends to be for income generating activities such as permit fishing and organised water sports, with very little benefit for unrestricted public access, except in the case of Horseshoe Lake, Sandhurst. This is unfortunate as water resources offer a highly valued environment to informal recreationists. . . . Local planning authorities would have more power to insist on informal recreation benefits if government guidance clearly stated that the question of 'exclusivity' could be a material planning consideration to be taken into account when determining planning applications.[34]

Access to Britain's countryside thus presents a complex picture. Fields are generally out of bounds, woods too unless owned by the state or a semi-public body, though there is a measure of tolerated trespass or *de facto* access to some privately owned woodland. The kind of land supporting most *de facto* access is roughland like moor, down, heath, marsh, and cliff-top, but the situation varies and tolerated access underpinned by no legal right is vulnerable to withdrawal or modification. Country parklands, unless they are publicly owned, offer little tolerated access at least for the general public, with entry usually by payment at restricted times and under highly controlled circumstances. We enjoy a wide measure of access to the seashore but this is at the behest of the owner and can be withdrawn, while the lack of access over land in Scotland often makes it hard to reach. Canalsides are almost always open; riverbanks and streamsides, on the either hand, are very often barred, particularly where there is a strong game fishing interest. The British Waterways Board and some water companies allow access to the edges of reservoirs, but others do not. The sides of lakes, lochs, lochans, and loughs of our hill country are largely open but those of waters hemmed in by intensive farmland and the enticing waters of private parklands are usually forbidden.

Many of us have learned to navigate our way through the nooks and crannies of this maze to find spots where we can taste at least some of the charms of Britain's countryside. Others, lacking special knowledge and the time to carry out intensive research before they go for a walk, have to make do with overcrowded and often unexciting mass venues. None of us can escape the dominant reality that the ordinary citizen is comprehensively excluded from the vast bulk of the countryside, including many of its most attractive places. The peeks and glimpses of our rural paradise available to those who seek them out cannot compensate for the barriers against entry to most of it. Exclusion is however no casual construct. Its roots go deep into our island story.

3

THE ROOTS OF EXCLUSION

THE exclusion of the ordinary people of Britain from so much of their countryside did not happen overnight. It reflects our country's unique history and the distinct attitudes this has engendered over the past thousand years.

Before Exclusion

Back in Saxon times, the notion of trespassing on land belonging to another person seems to have been unknown. Though some land was in the hands of kings and lords, much of England was owned by peasant proprietors or 'ceorls', each with the right to own, bequeath, inherit, and sell land himself and each owning land in order to farm it. Through a broad belt of central and southern England from Yorkshire to Dorset ceorls practised co-operative farming in two, three, or more large, communally worked fields. This system developed into the open-field system established in the eighth or ninth century in which individuals owned the right to farm certain strips in two or three large, shared fields attached to each village. Particular strips were regularly reallocated to different individuals so as to stop the same people monopolizing the most productive ones. Sowing and harvesting of crops on the fields were managed collectively. So was the grazing of domestic animals on common meadows, fallow land, harvest stubble, and over rough grassland and woodland. Where in counties like Devon, Essex, and Cumbria ceorls tilled their land independently outside the open-field system living in isolated farmsteads and hamlets, they still usually relied on communal access to woodland, rough grass, and marsh to graze stock and gather timber, berries, and other natural produce.[1]

In such a world people would have needed to move around freely. Indeed, the open-field system appears to have been designed to ensure that not only people but their animals could make as much use as possible of other people's land as was consistent with the individual holder's needs, although importance was attached to excluding outsiders from the resources of the village community.[2] It has been suggested that the system was arrived at by people who were herdsmen before they became cultivators of the soil and for whom the first necessity was for the cattle to be fed throughout the year.[3] Not only did this mean that the animals should be able to move easily from pasture to pasture; it was necessary for the same crops to be grown in each of the fields and their production synchronized so that they could be harvested at the same time and the land then left free for the cattle to graze it. Whatever the explanation of the development of the open-field system, nobody seems to have thought of trying to impede anyone else's access. The laws of King Ine, who ruled the West Saxons from 688 to 726, have survived. Amongst Ine's seventy-six edicts, many of which were adopted by succeeding Saxon kings like Alfred, there is nothing that remotely resembles our law of trespass. The laws mention fences, both in the common meadows and around homesteads, but their purpose seems to have been restricted to restraining stock: they deal, for example, with what should happen if a cow broke through a fence and ate another ceorl's crops or grass. Were it possible to step back into Ine's kingdom (which roughly covered the area of present-day Surrey, Wiltshire, Somerset, and Hampshire), we should probably see people moving freely over the countryside as we still see them doing in much of the developing world where people go where they can do so without damaging growing crops or otherwise doing harm. Long-distance routes did exist in Saxon England, often along prehistoric tracks like the Ridgeway or lines the Romans had created. These were to make travel physically easier, however, not to mark out the only avenues where passage was permitted. Only one restriction on free movement is recorded in Ine's laws, and that was a crime-fighting measure: 'If a man from a distance or a foreigner goes through the wood off the track, and does not shout nor blow a horn, he is assumed to be a thief, to be either killed or redeemed.'[4] Even here, the fact that blowing a horn was sufficient to secure legitimacy, even for outsiders, actually demonstrates how much more freely accessible even woodland was then than it was later to become.

Space is Seized

By the end of the Saxon period this system of landholding by free peasants had begun to crumble as some of the ceorls had been forced to relinquish rights over their land to territorial lords who agreed to protect them from invading Danes and support them over poor harvests. But it was the Norman Conquest which laid the foundations for the peculiarly British practice of putting the countryside out of bounds which persists to this day. During the bloody years after 1066, the Saxon system based on co-operative and independent farmer-owners gave way to a completely new system of land tenure. Feudalism was not designed to produce the most effective means of sharing the earth's resources among equals: it was a device for sustaining foreign conquest. William the Conqueror made all land the property of the Crown, and then passed on most of it to henchmen who had supported him in battle in return for continuing military backing. About 180 of William's barons received huge chunks of England, much of which they in turn sub-let to knights, who were required in return to contribute troops when required—a system which was extended by later Norman kings to much of southern, northern, and border Wales as well as southern Scotland and the Pale in Ireland. In England, the former Saxon owners usually found themselves able to till land only by leave of a new landlord, who would require in return free labour on land he was keeping to himself plus military service when required. A huge gulf separated these 'serfs' from their new masters, who travelled around on horseback, monopolized the possession of arms and built fortified houses and castles in commanding positions. The countryside became mere property, whose owners did not necessarily work it or even visit it. Instead of living space to be shared with neighbours, rural land became a means of satisfying the needs and desires of a few privileged individuals. This did not immediately mean curbs on public access, but it set in motion a series of developments of which these were to be the outcome.

Game Versus People

England's new Norman lords did not only look to their new holdings to provide food and troops. They were also looking to indulge a particular passion they had brought with them across the Channel —the urge to hunt. One of William's first acts was to claim for himself the ownership of any game he considered worth having—then wild boar and red and roe deer. He decided that huge tracts of his new kingdom would be set aside solely for his own pursuit of deer and boar. These territories, to be called 'royal forest', extended far beyond the lands the king owned personally and included not merely woodland but stretches of marsh, moor and down, pasture and cropland, villages, and stretches of river and lake. By the middle of the twelfth century royal forests covered one-quarter of England's land and a considerable area of Scotland.[5] All were created solely at the behest of the monarch and local people were not consulted, even though they suddenly found themselves deprived of land on which they depended for food and timber. To ensure the primacy of hunting within these 'forests', a string of laws and regulations was promulgated and teams of officials were formed to enforce them. Suddenly large areas of the countryside were subject to restrictions. Forest law outlawed any reduction in the provision of nourishment for deer (which devour not only crops and grass but also woody material) by tightly controlling the ploughing of grass and heath to grow food for human beings, the lopping and felling of trees, the gathering of underwood and the grazing of pigs, horses, sheep, and cattle. Severe fines penalized any infringements, while deer poaching was punished by blinding or castration.

The idea that the privileged few could dictate the terms on which the countryside was used was now up and running. Outside the royal forests, the king granted barons licences to establish their own hunting forests or 'chases'. In the chases, as in the royal forests, special restrictions applied. Cannock Chase in Staffordshire, Dartmoor in Devon, Cranborne Chase in Dorset, and Blackburn and Bowland in Lancashire were a few of the extensive twenty-six private chases of medieval England in which ordinary people had to come to expect that their presence, as in the royal forests, would henceforth involve compliance with strict regulations imposed in the interests of their privileged masters.[6]

Even so, regulation in the royal forests and hunting chases did not go as far as restricting the movement of people directly. The areas involved were so big that this would have been impractical. Fencing them would have been prohibitively expensive and the exclusion of people from such a large area would have threatened social and economic activity on which the landowning élite depended. Nonetheless, the royal forests and chases established the pattern of the countryside as something to be exploited by its 'owners' on any terms they chose. From this it was but a small step to stopping people entering parts of the countryside altogether.

The Normans did not value deer only for the sport they provided. Venison was their most highly prized meat. Those who could produce it were in a position to buy the favours of the king and other powerful figures, in a society in which money was not much used. So alongside the royal forests and hunting chases, another specialized form of countryside came to be designated—the deer park, in which animals were corralled to provide hunting on demand. Once again, William created the first of those facilities with his lords swiftly following suit. Though smaller than the royal forests and hunting chases, the deer parks nonetheless ranged in size from 50 to several thousand acres. More than 1,900 deer parks are known to have existed in England and Wales in medieval times[7]—46 in Dorset,[8] 55 in Leicestershire,[9] 137 in the North and West Ridings of Yorkshire[10] —and they were still being created though at a slower rate in the sixteenth and seventeenth centuries. Unlike the hunting grounds the deer parks were fenced securely, with a bank topped by a hedge or palings. The original purpose of the fencing was to prevent the deer escaping, but those who established the parks felt no obligation to provide gates or stiles to enable people to cross them. Doubtless they also calculated that excluding all access would make it easier to prevent poaching. Since the principle that owners could do what they liked was now well established, the disruption of people's lives caused by the encroachment of free passage did not have to be considered. Thus it was that the first real no-go areas for British people spread across the countryside.

Today there are still places apart from Englefield (see page 77) where we can get a hint of what this development must have meant to our medieval forebears. Travel south out of Stroud, and once through Nailsworth you enter the wide, slightly undulating countryside of the Gloucestershire/Wiltshire borders, now in the new unitary district of South Gloucestershire. At 'Pike Cottage' (presumably the site of an old turnpike station), you turn left past huge dark woods until you come upon a long Cotswold-stone wall which bounds the 2,600 acres of Badminton Park (larger than Richmond Park). For four days each year, in May, Badminton Park is thronged with visitors at what is one of the leading events in the equestrian year. For the remainder, it is normally closed, and devoted to what it was originally conceived for—sport. Thomas le Botiller created this park in 1236. Since then two families have owned it and today it is in the hands of its second long-standing landowning family, the Dukes of Beaufort. Sheep, not deer, graze amidst a slightly undulating mix of green pasture dotted with oaks and chestnuts and copses, and more recent avenues of trees together with ice-houses, lodges, stables, houses—between twenty and thirty listed buildings in all, including a hermit's cell dating from 1750 (wood, with a thatched roof, overhanging eaves, and four large knotty tree trunks at the corners). The deer have given way to sheep partly at least because they are not disturbed by the sport which has taken over from the pursuit of deer with hounds—that of the fox: the present Duke of Beaufort is one of the leading huntsmen in Britain today, and the Beaufort the *crème de la crème* of fox hunts. But although the mounted horsemen and women of the Beaufort hunt can pound over the park wherever the fox leads, the position of other people is ambiguous: the park does not seem any more welcoming for them than it would have done 800 years ago. A single public footpath passes through it, linking the estate villages of Little and Great Badminton which lie on its northern and southern edges. Off this path, the public have had no legal right to tread, although when I visited the Park in 1997 it did not look as if energetic efforts would be made to keep people to the strict line of the path which was unfenced (as is much of the estate, presumably in view of the fox hunting activity there). Not that any signs welcomed people to wander around: the sign greeting the prospective visitor at the main entrance to the park in Great Badminton village simply stated 'Strictly Private'.

Nowadays of course deer parks are no longer a major feature of the English countryside: after the Middle Ages, other forms of land use came into fashion and many deer parks were absorbed into farmland or forest. Yet the era of the deer park left its mark on the attitudes of those who found themselves owning land in Britain. If you wanted to shut people out of your property, that is what you would do, and no one would be in any position to stop you.

From Feudalism to Capitalism

As the Middle Ages progressed, feudalism began to break down. The descendants of William's barons managed to get their military obligations to the sovereign replaced by money payments and then, as these money payments also withered away, landowners became more like those we know today.[11] The ravages of the Black Death in 1349 reduced the numbers of serfs and therefore improved their bargaining power. They were able to persuade their lords to release them from servility and began tilling the land as tenants in return for a money rent. Thus former serfs began to produce for the market. Those who did well were able to enlarge their holdings and even become freeholder yeoman farmers. As this happened, long-established owners lost the symbiotic bond with the landless which the feudal lord's reliance on serfs for military service and land labour had come to embody, and became more straightforwardly committed to maximizing the economic potential of their holdings for their own benefit. Free to pursue their own interests without thinking of the needs of local people whom they might need to rely on in battle, these owners were joined in the mid-sixteenth century by those who took over the one-fifth of England controlled by the monasteries when the latter were dissolved by Henry VIII. The newcomers were lawyers, merchants, or courtiers with little previous connection with the countryside. They were simply the recipients of a new asset from which they hoped to extract advantage for themselves.

Despite the differences in their origins, these various kinds of landowners all came to see their holdings essentially as a theatre for the pursuit of agrarian capitalism, to which the other inhabitants of the countryside would contribute merely as tenants or casual labourers. For these new rural capitalists, the right to exclude which had emerged in the Middle Ages was a potential means of increasing profit. New agricultural opportunities were to provide occasions when this facility could be put to use.

A substantial amount of free movement had survived the encroachments of the Middle Ages. The Normans' seizure of the land had not entailed the destruction of the farming and other practices which provided the country's food, timber, and other natural products. So when the Tudor period began, widespread common rights still provided collective access to nuts, berries, timber, sand, gravel, peat, fish, mushrooms, and some wild animals over untilled wood, rough grass, and marsh. They also made common grazing possible both inside and outside the open fields which had largely survived in central England.[12] Now, however, landowners began to see collective arrangements as an obstacle to the maximization of their own profit. They wanted complete control of what happened on their holdings, and disliked the idea of negotiating common grazing arrangements with serfs or the tenants of other owners which might conflict with their own increasingly far-reaching land management plans. Soon they became intent on sweeping aside the open-field arrangements on which many ordinary people depended, so as to create space in which they were free to try whatever form of husbandry looked most likely to provide the greatest profits. The right of exclusion was to provide a vital weapon in this process.

Enclosure

By the mid-fifteenth century what came to be known as the 'enclosure' movement was well under way. Enclosure meant much more than the closing in of a piece of land with a hedge, fence, or wall. Hedges and fences had existed in medieval Britain, and even individual strips in the open fields were sometimes closed off by movable hurdles. The enclosures which began in the Tudor period, however, entailed the abolition of communal arrangements for administering land like the rotated strip system, the removal of the occupiers of these lands, and the elimination of common rights. In Tudor times the result of the enclosure of farmland was almost always conversion of arable land growing food to pasture for sheep producing wool and cloth often for sale abroad, where prices were rising fast. If any tenants stayed on, their rents were often doubled or trebled.

What had been a piecemeal process came to be formalized in later centuries, with 'enclosure commissioners' acting under Act of Parliament and supposedly providing some protection to those disadvantaged. However, the commissioners' efforts did little to challenge the idea of the landowner's right to absolute control of his holdings. Those who could prove they had owned rights to rotated strips were compensated with fixed patches of ground, turning them too into absolute owners. Though the commissioners were supposed to take account of common rights, they required legal evidence of title to such rights which could rarely be produced. Where evidence of common rights was accepted, it was often converted to cash compensation for loss. So common rights which had existed over open fields and meadows, rough grassland, and woodland disappeared. The commissioners also ordered that the new typically straight-line boundaries they had imposed should be marked out by their new owners, usually with hedges in the Midlands or drystone walls in the Cotswolds and the Yorkshire Dales, creating physical barriers which gave added force to the landowners' power of exclusion. The commissioners also laid down the means by which passage was to occur, specifying the public roads and paths and private routes which were to be used and by implication underlining the absence of access rights elsewhere.

The whole process fed on itself. Larger owners tended to benefit disproportionately from enclosure, and many small owners ended up with such a small block that it was not viable and they were forced to sell out to a larger neighbour. Landowners gaining bigger holdings then became all the keener on maximizing their revenue potential. As people who could prove no legal title to land and others who had depended on common rights were driven out, the population which had kept the countryside accessible by its very presence began to thin out. A thronged and open landscape gave way to an emptier rural world divided up by legal and physical barriers.

Before the enclosures, people would have been visible all over the countryside walking freely along the grassy areas between strips in the open fields, along the streams, in the woods, and over uncultivated land. Their whole way of life seems to have involved constant movement throughout their areas. Agricultural practice seems to have depended on pasturing cattle throughout the year while ensuring the manure provided was used to maximum effect. Sometimes the cattle would graze in woodland or rough grassland beyond the open fields, sometimes on stubble after the corn harvest, sometimes on meadows after the hay had been taken, sometimes on land lying fallow. This meant that all land in any one field had to be under the same regime at any one time, so that cattle would not spoil standing crops when they were supposed to be grazing, say, fallow land. That meant everyone had to see the countryside as a shared resource even though individuals had ownership rights. Typically, a parish in most of Midland England and South Wales had a cluster of houses in the centre with open fields radiating outwards and unreclaimed, often ancient, woodland at the edge of the parish. Because crops would be rotated around the fields, the wheatfield might be to the east of the village in one year and to the west in another. Throughout this area people would be constantly on the move, helping their neighbours harvest, herding their cows, and collecting berries or nuts. No-go areas such as deer parks might have intruded here and there, but until the enclosures this was still by and large a countryside full of people going where they pleased.

The enclosure movement tore this picture apart. Everything from the geography of parishes to communication systems changed. Once sheep in enclosed fields had taken the place of free-ranging cattle, the countryside ceased to be a busy theatre of constantly changing activities conducted by many different people. Instead it became a patchwork of individuals' fiefdoms, each single-mindedly devoted to the most profitable activity which its owner could find for it. The links that mattered now were not paths on which people could wander to the woods but routes along which produce could be efficiently sped to market for sale. New straight roads linking important centres took over from the old network of pathways. This cut down journey distances between towns, but it meant the gradual erosion of freedom of movement within parishes, as owners began to bar access to ancient routes, as well as preventing such people as remained in the countryside from walking round their new field edges and excluding them from uncultivated land. Few records of the reaction of individual country dwellers dispossessed by enclosure survive. One that does is the reported comment of a resident of the village of Tysoe in Warwickshire: 'In the old days' (before enclosure) 'you could walk all through the parish and all round it by the balks and headlands and cut wood on the waste, if there was any. And what can you do now? Make a farmer mad and you be done.'[13]

The parish of Helpston in Cambridgeshire (then in Northamptonshire) was enclosed between 1809 and 1820. It was the home of the poet John Clare. This is Clare describing the experience of walking round Helpston before enclosure:

> How fond the rustics ear at leisure dwells
> On the soft soundings of his village bells
> As on a Sunday morning at his ease
> He takes his rambles just as fancys please
> Down narrow baulks that intersect the fields
> Hid in profusion that its produce yields
> Long twining peas in faintly misted greens
> And wing'd leaf multitudes of crowding beans
> And flighty oatlands of a lighter hue.[14]

And this is Clare again after the enclosure of Helpston:

> There once was lanes in natures freedom dropt
> There once was paths that every valley wound
> Enclosure came, and every path was stopt
> Each tyrant fixt his sign where pads was found
> To hint a trespass now who crossed the ground
> Justice is made to speak as they command
> The high road now must be each stinted bound
> —inclosure thourt a curse upon the land
> And tasteless was the wretch who thy existence pland.[15]

Increasingly movement in the countryside for ordinary people was restricted to predetermined corridor routes, either the new roads or such paths as survived. The spaces in which they had worked and played were closed off one by one. Before enclosure, villagers often used stretches of open meadows or other common grazing fields for open-air games, playing ball, foot races, picnicking, and playing chase. Fairs and festivals took place on these spaces, as whole communities took to them for recreation. There were no dedicated playing fields or showgrounds because people had relied on using the same areas for work and play. Once enclosure converted multi-purpose land into the private property of individuals, people lost much of their opportunity for outdoor recreation. The rector of Hitcham in Suffolk, for example, complained in 1844 of 'how entirely the labourers seem to be without innocent and manly amusements . . . They have no village green, or common, for active sports. Some thirty years ago, I am told, they had a right to a play-ground in a particular field, at certain seasons of the year, and were then celebrated for their football; but somehow or other this right has been lost to them, and the field is now under the plough.'[16] And the Reverend Robert Slaney, who later became MP for Shrewsbury, lamented in 1824: 'Owing to the enclosure of open lands and commons, the poor have no place in which they may amuse themselves in summer evenings when the labour of the day is over, or when a holiday occurs.'[17] The enclosure commissioners did not recognize the loss of recreation space as something requiring compensation, and many landowners welcomed the demise of traditional rural amusements in the belief that it would provide them with a better-disciplined workforce.

Although the main motor of the early enclosure movement was the desire to create profitable, secure sheep pasture, the thinking behind it made its mark in other areas of rural activity. Woodland was enclosed as energetically as the fields, and for the same reason—profit. Indeed, Dr E. J. T. Collins of the Institute of Agricultural History, Reading University, believes that in many areas the enclosure of woodland predated that of farmland.[18] By the sixteenth century, timber had become one of the nation's most important raw materials. It was the main input in building—of anything from market halls to houses great and small, and in manufacturing—of anything from ships to fences, furniture, clogs, toys, crates, brooms, and agricultural and industrial implements. It was the most important fuel. Much woodland which had stood in royal forests had passed into the hands of private landowners as monarchs chose to release areas from forest law to raise cash; while the dissolution of the monasteries' estates had handed forests as well as farmland to new owners from the towns keen to make money. Just as the commercially-minded landowners of the Tudor period were keen to wring as much profit as possible from their farmland, so with their forests. And they quickly decided that the tradition that anyone could walk in the woods to gather nuts and firewood would have to go. They wanted all the produce of their woods for themselves.

Like the fields, woodland became subject to widespread enclosure, not just legally but physically. Banks, ditches, and palisades sprang up around countless woods. By the eighteenth century, the over-whelming majority of English woods had been appropriated by single individuals or families and dedicated to their exclusive exploitation. Woods which had once, Arden-like, been thronged with people, emptied. Country people used to gathering natural woodland produce for free began to face notices like this one in nineteenth-century Hampshire: 'All persons found trespassing in any of the Woods, Plantations, Coppice or Grounds belonging to the Right Honourable Lord Bolton, whether for NUTTING, or any other Purpose, will be prosecuted with the utmost Rigour of the Law.'[19]

If the protection of nuts was one reason why owners decided to enclose their woods, they soon decided there were other good reasons too. Until the nineteenth century, most woodland in lowland Britain was managed as 'coppice with standards'. Under this system, a few isolated trees, such as oaks, were allowed to grow to maturity and then harvested whole and used in the construction of buildings and ships. The vast majority of the trees, typically hazel or ash, were cut down to the base every few years to exploit the ability of the tree to regenerate quickly. The poles that grew up from the stump were cut off every year or two, stacked, and then taken away and sold. The poles were thus vulnerable to theft if woodland was accessible. Also, animals allowed to graze in woods by outsiders might bite off young shoots growing where poles had been cut. In medieval times manorial courts, in which tenants and small freeholders as well as lords were represented, instituted and policed regulations to ensure that grazing, berry-gathering, and so on did not interfere with coppicing, for example by controlling grazing after the poles had been cut. In the Tudor period, the new owners decided it was much simpler to stop anyone from entering their woody domains. Ironically it was in the remnants of some of the former royal forests that movement was least restricted. These woods were heavily used for naval timber, for which coppice poles were not required. Instead they were given over to large mature trees which could not easily be stolen and were therefore not worth fencing in. Both commoners' rights and free wandering often survived here as they do to this day in the New Forest, Epping Forest, and the Forest of Dean.

The Privacy of the Park

The thirst for profit which drove the enclosure process was not to be the only force fuelling exclusion from the countryside. By the eighteenth century, the now all powerful landowning class had come to develop another interest in their holdings besides their potential for profit. The notion of a pastoral sanctuary from the cares of the world, first popularized in the Tudor and Stuart periods, began to appeal to the only people now in a position to put it into effect—the countryside's large-scale owners. They realized that as well as providing economic benefits, their land could give them a particular kind of pleasure, which because it was becoming fashionable could also enhance their status. Unfortunately for the rest of the population, satisfying this new need was to require even more rigorous steps to exclude outsiders. Interest grew in the creation of spacious and peaceful rural enclaves in which landowners could retreat for their own private pleasure. These sanctuaries would be designed not for profit but as 'amenities'—for relaxation, quiet reflection, and creating an impression. Throughout the length and breadth of Britain landowners began hiring men like Humphry Repton and Capability Brown to help them fashion a new kind of landscape in the immediate environs of the mansions they built at the heart of their holdings. In these special areas, utilitarian functions would be specifically excluded in favour of aesthetics. Totally separated from the working agricultural areas of the estates they adorned, Arcadian reserves began to appear, each an idealized vision of the pastoral landscape of the Classical world, dominated by acres of verdant pasture with trees, here singly, there in small groups or copses, and studded with mock Roman temples and columns. These parks were frequently adorned with one or two wide lakes crossed by bridges modelled, as at Blenheim for example, on ancient originals. Central to these parklands was the idea that they were private spaces, to be enjoyed by the privileged in the knowledge that their enjoyment would be exclusive. Very few parks included any provision for a right of passage for anybody other than their owners and those whom they chose to invite in.

Necessarily the boundaries of such a space needed to be clearly demarcated. This was usually achieved by the building of a high wall encircling the entire domain, punctuated by gates often topped by sculptures of lions, stags, or urns. This wall did not simply mark the boundary of the sanctuary. Landowners knew their parks might need to be physically defended from those their exclusiveness mocked. The eighteenth century was known for its riots: there were corn riots in 1757, the Gordon riots in 1780, which had involved attacks on country houses close to London, then the horrors of the French Revolution. The high wall, the guarded gates, the long drive, and the extensive, defended quietude of a park came to symbolize the divide that had emerged between privileged landowners and the dispossessed majority even more dramatically than the enclosed fields and woods.[20]

Appropriately enough, some of the eighteenth-century landscaped parks took in and extended medieval deer parks of the kind which had first stamped the notion of exclusion on Britain's landscape. However, people had been shut out of deer parks as they were shut out of the fields and woods under enclosure to facilitate production. The new decorative parks required outsiders to be excluded for the very purpose of bestowing exclusivity on the space involved. The notion of a rustic retreat in which a privileged individual could remove himself from sight or sound of the uglinesses of the age appealed to people who were not already rural landowners. The park became the status symbol of choice for successful townspeople who wanted to flaunt their achievement. With the cult of the park, the idea of excluding others from attractive landscape became an end in itself.

Enclosure had meant removing people from fields and woods. To create parks, landowners were quite ready to remove people from their homes as well. When Charles Howard, the 3rd Earl of Carlisle, decided to lay out a park round the newly built mansion of Castle

Howard in Yorkshire in the early part of the eighteenth century, he had part of the village of Hinderskelfe levelled to make way for it. The rest of the village was drowned by a new ornamental lake.[21] No records tell of any replacement housing being provided for the people of Hinderskelfe, but in other cases landowners chose to keep a peasant workforce within reach if at arm's length. At Harewood in Yorkshire, Ickworth in Hertfordshire, and Nuneham Courtney in Oxfordshire, to name but a few, replacement dwellings were provided outside the park wall. At Milton Abbas in Dorset, forty white cob and thatch cottages were built to house more than 100 households evicted from a town with its own school, pubs, church, and shops so that Lord Milton could enjoy a park fashioned for him by Capability Brown. Each new semi-detached cottage had to be partitioned to hold four families and up to forty inmates. Over half of the parks and gardens of Hampshire contain village earthworks or an isolated parish church, and the majority of these features were probably the direct result of park creation.[22]

Countless public roads and paths were moved aside to make way for parks. In a book entitled *Polite Landscapes* (since the eighteenth-century park was to be considered 'the landscape of polite exclusion'), historian Tom Williamson writes, 'It is extremely difficult to estimate the number of roads and footpaths affected by emparking but the total must certainly have amounted to several thousand miles, particularly as the long and complex development and staged expansion of the larger landscape parks could (over a period of time) involve the closure of as many as five or ten separate rights of way. Although closed to the public, however, such roads did not always disappear entirely from the landscape. Running as they so often did past the front door of the mansion, they were often retained as one of the principal entrance drives, thus economising on the cost of park-making.'[23] Focusing on one county—Shropshire—landscape historian Trevor Rowley observes: 'The importance of the creation or extension of landscaped parks on the contemporary landscape cannot be overestimated. Many villages were abandoned, moved and radically changed because of emparking, and there are numerous examples of major and minor road diversions throughout the county brought about by park schemes from the sixteenth century onwards.'[24]

The parks thus imposed a new set of obstructions on free movement through the countryside. But not for all. Since a large part of the point of the parks was to enhance their owners' status, they liked other people to visit them—so long as these people were sufficiently important to be worth impressing. Celia Fiennes, a member of the family of Viscount Saye and Sele, chose to tour estates from Penzance and Dover to the Scottish border between 1682 and 1712.[25] She found no difficulty in viewing many fine parks whether or not the landowners were at home: most of them left standing instructions with their lodge-keepers to permit access to the park to people well connected in society. The idea therefore began developing not just that the owner had the right to exclude, but that he had the right to waive this right as and when he chose in respect of those he chose to favour. This was to come to seem more like an enhancement of the owner's power over access than a diminution to those who remained shut out.

Only in the most exceptional cases were ordinary people allowed into a park. Charles I did go too far when he created a new royal park at Richmond in Surrey in 1637 which took in six parishes and included much land subject to common rights. The new park was too near London to escape becoming the subject of discussion in the capital, and Charles finally bowed to public pressure and permitted gates and step-ladders over the walls so that local people could continue to collect firewood. Charles II opened Hyde Park and St James's Park to the public to secure popularity, though Queen Victoria felt confident enough to withdraw this concession in part by excluding from St James's Park lowly members of the public like soldiers.[26]

Because of the sheer size of the parklands surrounding eighteenth-century country houses it is easy to think of their owners as isolated in their spacious domains. The opposite was the case. The Georgian period saw landowners developing consciousness of themselves as a distinct social group, marked by nascent customs and habits. An increasingly formal pattern of social intercourse based on the country seats was accompanied by the annual ritual of the London Season. Everyone knew everyone who mattered, as the numbers involved were small: the core group was the English nobility, who then comprised only 170 individuals knitted together by intermarriage; beyond them the gentry comprised some 890 knights and baronets and 6,000 esquires. As these men and their entourages moved from country house to country house with different but similarly designed country park-lands unfolding at the drawing-room window, the idea of country landowners as a special breed began to take shape. This was not, how-ever, only an age of conspicuous leisure (and conspicuous consump-tion) for the privileged. It was also the Age of Reason, the time when the sons of the élite embarking on the Grand Tour were encouraged to give thought to the way the world was organized. Inevitably the new landowning class therefore turned its attention to considering the legitimacy of its own privilege, which needed of course to be squared with the Christian religion which they remained dedicated to upholding.

A Philosophy of Ownership

Once he delved into the leather-bound volumes in his country house library, the eighteenth-century landowner soon found he was by no means the first to seek philosophical justification for private owner-ship. Intriguingly, Plato and Aristotle, the two leading Greek philo-sophers on this as on so many questions, had both explored the matter and come up with two different models. In his *Republic*, Plato proposed a society in which the ruling class owned nothing whatsoever—no land, dwelling, gold, or silver. Each would receive a daily salary for his services to the state but would be forbidden to possess any private property save personal items like a comb or a toothbrush. These rulers would not even possess homes or special rights over children they had conceived. Instead they would live together in a sort of commune. Anything significant they possessed would be owned in common. They would be specifically excluded from being farmers or merchants or engaging in any other activity which would conflict with their role as rulers. Conflicts of interests were not however the main reason for depriving rulers of property. Plato considered ownership was unsuit-able for those in positions of responsibility because it was inherently corrupting. Were the state's most powerful citizens permitted private ownership they might become indolent and would be more likely to develop into 'enemies and tyrants' of the people.

Plato accepted that it would be difficult to bring this ideal society into being, so in his *Laws* he put forward a second-best model. In this, rulers were not automatically barred from engaging in economic activities, and while half the land would be owned in common the remainder could be owned privately. The form of ownership involved was however to be heavily restricted. No owner could enlarge his holding by buying land, since the buying and selling and the subdivision of land were all forbidden. The owner would have no right to bequeath land other than to his male heir. Since wealth remained a threat to the development of virtue, citizens would be forbidden to use their land for a range of profit-making activities, would be forbidden to own gold or silver, and would be required to distribute the produce of their land in equal shares to citizens, slaves, and artisans.

Plato's approach therefore offered little comfort to the emerging English landowning élite. They were, however, much more encouraged by the approach taken by Aristotle, who was at that time far better known than Plato. Unlike Plato, Aristotle believed private ownership served to make men virtuous. For one thing, it enabled owners to do things for other people. 'There is the greatest pleasure in doing a kindness or service to friends or guests or companions, which can only be rendered when a man has private property. . . . No one, when men have all things in common, will any longer set an example of liberality or do any liberal action; for liberality consists in the use which is made of property'.[27] A second justification for private ownership was that people care more for what is privately owned than for what is communally owned. The private owner develops a more intimate knowledge of his own patch, and is therefore in a better position to know how his ownership can best serve the development of virtue in himself. Aristotle believed human nature required individuals to care most for what they themselves owned, whether it be children, a dwelling house, land, or whatever.

Yet Aristotle did not go on to advocate absolute ownership. Although private citizens owned the title to property, they were obliged to share with others rights to use that property. Aristotle pointed to the example of the Spartans who 'use one another's slaves, horses and dogs in common and when they travel they take what provisions they need from the fields they pass through'. He went on: 'It is clearly better that property should be private, but the use of it common.'[28] Land could not be bought, exchanged, given, or bequeathed: it would remain connected to individual families as a means of producing the family's subsistence. Like Plato, Aristotle firmly believed that excess wealth was a bad thing for human beings so that any unlimited acquisition of property was to be condemned. The ownership of land and other property would enable the citizen to engage in natural exchange to acquire the ordinary things of life he and his family needed. Aristotle's concept of ownership firmly excluded an unfettered right to acquire riches or to build up large quantities of land as an absentee owner or even as a landlord.

Britain's landowners were given further pause when they came on to consider the thinking of the Romans and the early Christians on ownership questions. Here, they came across a distinct and unwelcome emphasis on communality. Although inequalities existed in the Roman world, in particular between free men and slaves, Rome was committed to the idea of equality among citizens. The Roman philosopher Seneca wrote approvingly of an early time when 'Nature was the communal treasure with possession unchallenged' and the earth was used equally by all to satisfy their needs. He quoted a passage from Virgil describing a golden age when

> No fences parted fields, nor marks nor bounds
> Distinguish'd acres of litigious grounds;
> But all was common.[29]

In this world, Seneca noted, 'the miser had not yet barred anyone from the necessities of life by secreting a hoard'.[30] It was avarice that was to impel people to appropriate to themselves property which they did not need.

The Romans acknowledged of course that the world would have to be ordered in a way which took account of the impact of personal avarice but they continued to see substantial scope for public rights in landownership. The Greek Emperor Justinian, who codified the law of the Roman empire in a form which survived for hundreds of years and was used all over Europe, set out a framework of law in this area. He took on board Aristotle's notion that land which was being worked productively could reasonably be owned privately, but he identified other slices of the physical environment which could never be so owned. Justinian excluded four categories of things which could not become personal property. They were: *res communes*—things which were naturally the property of all humanity, like the air and the sea; *res publicae*—things like rivers, parks, and public roads which should be dedicated to public use; *res universitatis*—things like public baths or theatres which were provided by a local municipality for the use of people in general; and *res nullius*—things which had no human owner, such as wild animals or unoccupied land.[31]

The early Christians were even more unhelpfully egalitarian. They began by interpreting the doctrines of the gospel of love and of the equality of all men in the sight of God as pointing towards a socialist theory of property. According to the Acts of the Apostles, those living in Jerusalem 'had all things common. . . . Neither was there any among them that lacked: for as many as were possessors of lands or houses sold them, and brought the prices of the things that were sold and laid them down at the apostles' feet: and the distribution was made unto every man according as he had need.'[32] Later, the principle of the common ownership of property came to be reflected in the organization of monastic life. However, outside the monasteries, the Church came to acknowledge a place for private ownership while, like Seneca, preserving the idea of common ownership as an ideal. For St Augustine, perhaps the most influential Christian philosopher after St Paul, common ownership would have been the condition in Paradise, but private ownership was a feature of the imperfect system operating in a fallen world.

The influential medieval catholic philosopher St Thomas Aquinas, while arguing that a life of voluntary poverty for all was desirable, accepted Aristotle's notion that land was most effectively managed if it was owned by individuals working for themselves. Aquinas nonetheless went further than Aristotle in asserting the requirements of non-owners. Aristotle had argued that a traveller who needed sustenance for his journey should be able to take it from fields which did not belong to him. Aquinas argued that everyone ought to receive whatever he needed from the overall pool of resources. Those in need, he held, had a right to require those of their citizens who had a surplus to provide for them, and those who owned the title to land were obliged to manage what they owned so that they could meet the needs of the poor as well as their own. While the private owner should be free to make up his own mind about how his land should be managed and how the produce from it should be distributed, he should make these decisions 'in the interest of all'.[33]

It was this thinking on which Christian English landowners seized. It appeared to put the landowner in the position of a custodian of natural resources on the part of the rest of society. So long as he could justify what he did—and he was left to be judge in his own cause— he could argue that he was acting for the good of all in doing exactly what he wanted to. The idea of the landowner as a 'custodian' took root and the landowners quickly forgot the less welcome ancient ideas of sharing rights with the landless.

Contemporary thought offered Britain's eighteenth-century land-owners opportunities to build on this fundamental position in a way which was to provide the foundations for a bold new philosophy. John Locke, the leading English philosopher, was anxious to provide some basis for the rights of the landowner-citizen in the face of the poten-tial threat posed by state power after the Glorious Revolution. He held that in the beginning land was not owned communally but owned by nobody, although all enjoyed rights to use that land. Others had argued that even if land had not been communally owned, private ownership would still entail unjustly depriving those who were not to become private owners of their access rights. Locke maintained that this could be justified if the private owner invested his own labour in the land he claimed. He owned his labour, and once this was mixed with something which nobody owned, the unowned thing could rea-sonably become his own. 'Thus labour, in the beginning, gave a right to property.'[34] This idea—that working land entitled people to claim it as their own—undoubtedly reflected an attitude which strikes a chord with many people. But of course it still posed problems for eighteenth-century landowners. They did not work the land themselves, and could not claim that the sweat of their own brows had sanctified the soil to which they laid claim. On the contrary, many had to thank the dubi-ous patronage of William the Conqueror or Henry VIII for the title to their holdings. What is more, Locke maintained that ownership should be restricted to the amount of land that an individual could use himself—a helpful principle for a peasant or crofter but not for a gentleman of leisure in the process of enclosing a vast pleasure ground or even acting as absentee landlord of farms or forests operated by others. Another problem was that appropriation through labour did not obviously entitle those who claimed it to pass on their property to heirs. In Locke's world, a person who cleared unused land and started growing crops on it or building a home there would have title to that land only for as long as he continued to use it. If he stopped for some period of time, the land would revert to its unowned state, ready to be claimed by some other energetic person. Locke also argued, disastrously for country gentlemen, that justification through appropriation was justifiable only so long as there was enough land around for others to appropriate what they themselves could work, for men remained naturally equal in Locke's eyes, and this principle took priority over the right to own.

Though Locke therefore did not intend to justify the behaviour of the landowners of the day, they were able to make use of his writings. Locke did wish to demonstrate that the citizen had certain inalienable rights which predated the invention of government and which government was bound to respect. In linking property with life and liberty, which he also said were natural rights, he enabled himself to be presented as maintaining that the natural right to property was not the equal right of every man to appropriate through labour what he needed for the necessities of life, but the right of every man to keep what he had, however he had acquired it and whether he could use it or not.

It was a jurist who produced the most helpful refinement of current thinking. William Blackstone wrote *Institutes of Natural Law* in 1754. In this book he asserted that it was not working the land which was necessary to justify ownership: all that was required was occupancy. Personal labour might give 'the fairest and most reasonable title', but it was not essential. What is more, Blackstone affirmed that occupancy gave a man 'permanent property in the substance of the earth itself; which excludes every one else but the owner from the use of it'. And all this happened within natural law, before the invention of conventional laws and governments, and so, according to Blackstone, was 'dictated by God himself'. Because private property came before the state and represented the will of God or a natural state of affairs, the state had no *locus standi* in private property. Nothing that might be urged for the common good could then ever justify the violation of private property rights even if the state backed the proposed action since these rights were sacrosanct. The rights Blackstone had in mind were not those acknowledged by Aristotle or Aquinas: they were far more fundamental. In his own words they consisted of 'that sole and despotic dominion which one man claims and exercises over the external things of the world, in total exclusion of the right of any other individual in the universe'.[35] This, at last, was the language the landowners needed.

Yet Blackstone went a stage further. He asserted that the laws of England, which already embodied landowners' claims to absolute ownership, were for the most part not merely a social code but valid declarations of natural law. This thinking was to invest any laws concerned with the protection of private property rights with enormous weight. For anyone who accepted this idea it became unthinkable that the laws of the state should ever threaten private property rights; on the contrary, the prime purpose of those laws was the protection of property: 'The public good is in nothing more essentially interested than in the protection of every individual's private rights, as modelled by the municipal law.'

Blackstone's bold doctrine gave a new edge to the arguments carefully selected from ancient and modern thinkers by the apologists for the landowning class. So too did writings from across the Channel. In France, a group of economists and social philosophers known as the Physiocrats vigorously promoted the notion that the then current arrangements of political and economic power in society were part of the natural order and allowed no interference from the state. For them, land was the ultimate source of all wealth. Trade and industry were of secondary importance, and the protection of landowners' property rights was in the interests of the nation as a whole.

As the eighteenth century progressed, British landowners became convinced that their absolute control of the landscape was not merely a matter of might but of right as well. Henceforth, whether they were enclosing common land, digging mines, or building themselves vast parks, they considered themselves to be exercising their own God-given private property rights. Their dominant position in society meant that the laws and institutions of the country came to reflect this attitude. Gradually, the moral absoluteness of the landowners' attitudes deepened the entrenchment of their grip on their holdings.

The Owners' Sporting Heyday

As in the medieval period, hunting became an important focus of the extension of the landowner's dominion. Justinian might have maintained that wild animals were unownable; even William the Conqueror claimed only the deer and the boar for himself. Yet in the late seventeenth and early eighteenth century Parliament now had no qualms about passing laws which gave a legal right to hunt anything from deer to rabbits to fish only to those with a substantial landowning qualification. The killing of such creatures by non-landowners became a capital offence. Such laws flowed naturally enough from the sense that the state's duty was to further the interests of property-owners. But since such laws were part of God's scheme they would naturally be generally beneficial. The new laws, it was argued, would also protect the poor from their own idleness in that they would 'prevent persons of inferior rank from squandering that time which their station in life requireth to be more profitably employed'.[36]

The notorious Black Act of 1723 created fifty new offences punishable by death, but in fact few people actually went to the gallows for breaking the game laws and poaching, say, a single fish. Instead, the justice of the peace, usually a landowner himself, would often commute the death penalty to imprisonment or transportation.[37] Such judgements not only enhanced the power of the landed establishment over the rest, but encouraged the landless to treat their landed rulers with new deference. Landowners were now poised to take on the moral authority which was to imbue their hegemony in the countryside in the eyes not only of their own kind but of much of the wider community as well. Armed with this new standing they extended their grip even further. Inevitably, landowners who now regarded the creatures of the wild as their absolute property came to make an even more absolute claim to the space which those creatures inhabited.

In the nineteenth century, changing economic circumstances provided new reasons for landowners to exploit more fully the rights they now claimed with such vigour. When the century began, woodland, much of it coppiced, was still producing timber very profitably. Wood remained an important fuel for the burgeoning factories of industrial Britain—as there were as yet no railways enabling coal to be transported long distances. Vast amounts of home-grown timber were used in manufacturing processes—for anything from tanning leather and producing charcoal to making bobbins for textile looms. However, during the second half of the nineteenth century, the market for timber products collapsed. Not only did coal prove a more successful fuel, but the repeal of import duties allowed cheap softwood from overseas to replace coppice as a raw material. At the same time, factory-made products were replacing traditional goods made of locally produced wood. Woodsmen who had rented coppice rights from landowners unable or unwilling to search out new markets for their coppice timber joined the mass migration to industrial towns which was in full swing. As they left the land, the rents landowners could command for woodland fell sharply. Landowners had to rethink the use to which they could put it, and once again their long-standing attachment to bloodsports was to play a key role.

The large and exotic pheasant had been a tempting target for sportsmen ever since the Normans had introduced it. However, it was an elusive quarry, which could usually be killed only in small numbers either with nets or trained falcons because of its irritating habit of hiding in the undergrowth when pursued. A continental invention, the 'battue', got round this by sending a line of men through a wood beating the undergrowth with sticks. They would frighten (or 'flush out') pheasants which would take to the air and which could easily be shot flying away. Then in about 1840 the drive was invented: the guns would remain stationary and the pheasants would be driven by a line of beaters over trees and thus relatively high in the air. During the nineteenth century Britain's landowners seized upon the battue and the drive as a means of turning their problem woodland into a huge new source of pleasure and profit.[38] Once the Prince of Wales had given pheasant shooting social cachet by refashioning Sandringham to provide for it, countless country estates were being replanned to make possible the huge pheasant bags of which Victorian and Edwardian Britain were soon to become famous. Woods with plenty of undergrowth were encouraged (pheasants do not care for draughts) alongside belts of kale and mustard for the birds to feed on, stretches of rough grassland and ponds and, most characteristic of all, long narrow belts of tall trees over which the birds could be driven high in the air for the guns.

Pheasant shooting rapidly overtook timber production in importance. For a time coppicing coexisted with pheasant rearing on many estates, but soon the gamekeepers and game wardens who were becoming a permanent part of estate workforces outranked the wood reeves who were responsible for timber. And if coppicing had involved restrictions on access to woods by outsiders, the effect of pheasant rearing was even worse. Landowners now had a valuable creature to defend against poachers and an exclusive activity which they wished to enjoy in private. The new army of gamekeepers made possible the enforcement of restrictions which it had hitherto been possible to flout.

Landowners quickly realized that the battue and the drive offered them the chance not only of recreation among their own kind: it held out the prospect of real profits as well. The Game Act of 1671 had barred anybody but people with freeholds worth at least £100 per year from hunting. In 1831, as part of the enfranchisement of the middle classes, the landowners' hitherto exclusive right to hunt game was extended to all prepared to pay £3 13s. 6d. per year for a game certificate. However, prosperous townspeople eager to use their new licence came up against the laws of trespass. Landowners seized the opportunity this gave them to charge would-be pheasant shooters dearly for the privilege of pursuing game on their land. Once people were paying for the privilege of shooting, exclusivity of access to the woods became even more important. Devices like the alarm gun and the mantrap appeared to terrorize those tempted to stray into woodland. Not all owners who put up notices announcing 'Beware Mantraps and Swing Guns' had actually installed these devices, if only because they themselves, their gamekeepers, and shooting clients would have run the risk of falling victim to the horrific injuries they could inflict. Nonetheless, the threat was sufficient to make woods no-go areas for more and more country people who had once made use of them. Though alarm guns and mantraps were banned in 1827, nobody knew for sure that some rusty device was not waiting to maim them should they embark on a picnic among the bluebells. Even law-abiding landowners could of course remind would-be visitors that the law was firmly on their side with 'keep out' signs and the like, while notices like this one, nailed to a tree in Broxbourne, Hertfordshire and now kept at the Rural History Centre, University of Reading, littered the countryside: 'Notice: Spring Gun Set. Private Woods. No Footpath: Trespassers will be Prosecuted.'

All this implied a far more vigorous programme of exclusion than was used to defend Britain's first real forbidden territories—the medieval deer parks. The woods now joined the parklands created in the eighteenth century in becoming effectively as private as back gardens. It no longer mattered whether people were being shut out because they might poach birds, because their presence would irritate a shooting party or because a landowner wanted to assert his right to exclude them for its own sake. It was now taken for granted that the woods were out of bounds for ordinary people.

A similar fate to that of the pheasant woods of lowland Britain was soon to befall vast areas of open country in the uplands. By the middle of the nineteenth century, enclosure had transformed vast stretches of upland Britain—Derbyshire, Yorkshire, Lancashire, the Borders, and the eastern and central Highlands of Scotland—into sheep runs, or had intensified existing sheep-rearing there, since wool and mutton were the most lucrative products of an environment whose climate and geography ruled out grain. However, in the 1880s new refrigeration methods enabled lamb from lusher pastures in New Zealand and Australia to undercut home-produced sheepmeat. Landowners had to start thinking of new uses for their hill country, and, as in the case of woodland, sport came to the rescue. The Scottish Highlands in particular had long been known for their game, but now the Romantic movement had made their wild scenery fashionable and the railways were making it accessible.

The key game species in the uplands was the red grouse, and this had been considered a rare delicacy in the days when only landowners were allowed to shoot it. Once the Game Act of 1831 removed the restriction to landowners, the search was on for a means of commercializing the sport. As in the case of pheasants, a means of slaughtering large numbers of birds at a time would be required if Victorian sporting tastes were to be satisfied. In the past grouse had been shot singly or in small numbers by a sportsman using a dog to flush out quarry. As with pheasants, it was the battue and the drive which opened the way to mass slaughter. Soon the moors, like the woods, were dotted with lines of men with guns shooting down birds driven up in front of them by beaters. By 1910, 2.5 million birds were being shot every year.[39]

The red grouse is, however, a sensitive creature. It disdains most food except the flowers and young shoots of heather; shoots older than two years are passed over. Yet it needs high, old heather in which to nest—an important consideration given that the birds' natural lifespan is only two or three years. Attempts to rear grouse outside Britain's northern hills, whether at Sandringham or in Germany, have failed. The bird can live in Wales and Ireland but flourishes best on the dry heather moors of Britain's eastern uplands and Lancashire. To provide what was now a valuable creature with the best possible chance of flourishing, landowners therefore brought large numbers of gamekeepers on to the moors to kill predators like foxes and birds of prey, to prevent poaching and to manage the heather by burning patches or strips in succession to ensure a supply of new growth. As in the woods, the newly omnipresent gamekeepers included turning away 'trespassers' among their duties.

Some of Britain's uplands—particularly the Highlands and Islands —were too wet and grassy for grouse to prosper. Here, though, another game species began to acquire commercial potential. Deer stalking soon had even more cachet than grouse or pheasant shooting among the rich businessmen of England's cities for whom a 'good head' or set of antlers offered a more visible status symbol than a large grouse or pheasant bag. Once Queen Victoria and Prince Albert had bestowed their approval on the sport through annual excursions to the Highlands and then the purchase of Balmoral, the red deer took its place alongside the red grouse as a saviour of the upland economy. As the fortunes of the hill sheep industry declined, more and more land in the west of Scotland was turned over to deer forest. Once again, this meant a more proprietorial attitude to upland holdings and more gamekeepers enforcing the right of exclusion.

Alongside deer and grouse, landowners in the north of England and Scotland discovered yet another profitable sporting resource. The polluted waters of Victorian England were making angling more and more difficult there. The last salmon was caught in the Thames in 1821, and many other English rivers offered less and less to the fishermen. In contrast, the becks, burns, and rivers of the northern uplands offered abundant salmon and trout. The rivers therefore joined deer forest and grouse moor as jealously guarded preserves for the owners and paying sportsmen, policed by ghillies as energetic as gamekeepers in keeping out illicit intruders.

The emphasis on commercial sport coincided with other changes which ensured that the assertive approach of Britain's landowners extended even to the most remote corners of the kingdom. Before Culloden, the Highlands were nominally owned by clan chiefs, but clansmen tilled the land under a co-operative system of agriculture known as 'runrig' which had similarities to the open-field agriculture which had once been practised in England. After the rebellions, the Westminster government moved to co-opt clan chiefs by passing legislation making them outright owners. In their new role, Highland landowners began to adopt the habits and attitudes of their counterparts in the rest of Britain: contact with English landowners gave them a taste for wealth and an aristocratic lifestyle. Many went deeply into debt and the threat or reality of financial disaster forced the majority to sell. This meant that particularly between 1830 and 1850 new owners—landowners, financiers, and merchants from England and lowland Scotland and the occasional American millionaire—took over estates all over the Highlands and Islands.[40] They brought with them the new automatic assumption south of the border that land was the property of its owner, as clansmen found to their cost.

All over upland Britain, social and economic change made the countryside less accessible to people other than paying sportsmen. A population of sheep farming tenants gave way to a smaller number of estate workers largely dedicated to protecting game. Deer stalking provided only 800 full-time and 1,000 part-time jobs at the turn of the century although it claimed a quarter of the entire area of Scotland.

Such free movement of people through the countryside as had been a feature of clan life in Scotland and had survived to some extent alongside sheep pasturing in the hills gave way to corridor access primarily by road. Although sporting activities were confined to certain months of the year, ordinary people were excluded at all times from what were becoming rich men's playgrounds. And so it was that the space which this prized quarry inhabited, however large, was appropriated along with the game itself. As mountaineer E. A. Baker explained in 1924, 'The aim of the owners of deer forests is to create a huge solitude, first by removing such of the human population and their stock as survived the great clearances and then by closing the mountains and glens to the public.'[41] Of Scotland's 543 mountain peaks rising higher than 3,000 feet above sea level, more than 450 were eventually out of bounds to walkers. Notices warning of the dangers of getting shot deterred walkers and tourists, while gates across popular roads were locked. To stop walkers finding somewhere to stay, landowners applied pressure to get inn licences removed and forbade tenants from taking in guests other than paying sportsmen. As vast stretches of Scotland were turned into a huge game preserve, 'the public were gradually man-trapped off everything beyond the high road' according to Lord Cockburn, the then Lord Advocate of Scotland, who lamented that when he was a boy nearly all the countryside around Edinburgh had been freely open to the public, but by the middle of the nineteenth century, not only the open moors but also the riversides and even the seaside had been closed off.[42]

A Century of Farm and Forest

As the twentieth century dawned, much of Britain's countryside was thus largely an exclusive game preserve. This reflected in part a decline in the economic importance of both farming and forestry. The new century was to see this decline reversed, though this, too, would entail further encroachments on freedom of movement. It was the world wars that transformed the economics of the countryside, persuading the nation that food and timber were too vulnerable to enemy action to be left to the vagaries of supply from overseas. Britain, it came to be felt, must have her own strategic resources. This mood was to enhance the standing of landowners engaged in food and timber production and to help secure acquiescence in their own view that they must be left alone to run their holdings as they saw fit.

Foresters were the first to benefit from anxieties generated by war. During the First World War, timber from the countries on which Britain had come to depend like Canada and Norway was threatened by German mines laid at sea. During the war, large stretches of Britain's woods were quickly felled to provide everything from pit props to rifle stocks, and in 1919 Parliament set up a state agency to ensure that the country quickly built up a new stock of standing timber. The Forestry Commission would lease or even buy land itself to establish new plantations. At the same time, private landowners would be offered financial carrots and other incentives to grow more timber. These policies were to mean that much open country would disappear under grim ranks of alien conifers, into which few walkers would wish to venture even if they were allowed to.

Agriculture was to change even more dramatically than forestry. After the repeal of the Corn Laws which had protected Britain's farmers till 1846, Britain had come to rely on produce from Australasia, Argentina, and North America, where crops could be raised much more cheaply than at home, and domestic agriculture became severely depressed. Hitler's U-boat campaign and the shortages it created sparked fears that dependence on food imports might lead to mass starvation. What had been marginal land like the Sussex Downs was hastily ploughed during the Second World War. Afterwards, the post-war government created an enormous apparatus of subsidy which was to transform the prospects for British farming. Later European subsidies through the Common Agricultural Policy combined with UK subsidies to help restore the prosperity of agriculture and reinforce its predominant position in Britain's countryside.

The prospect of high and guaranteed returns encouraged landowners to invest in mass production techniques which would vastly increase food output. The new methods, involving larger fields, more machinery, and more chemical fertilizers and pesticides also had the effect of turning much of the countryside into something more resembling a factory floor than the casual Arcadian tangle of activities which characterized the countryside in the popular imagination and to some extent in reality during the agricultural depression which lasted from the 1840s to the 1940s. Landowners, now convinced of their absolute right to absolute control of the rural environment for generations, proceeded to treat the farmed countryside as factory-owners treated factories. It seemed entirely natural to the post-war farmer that he should exclude casual visitors from his field of operations. The fields were his factory and walkers were inconvenient and untidy. Also, perhaps, their presence posed a subtle affront to the absolute control which the agribusinessman demanded. Anyhow, barbed wire, locked gates, and minatory notices reminiscent of industrial landscapes came to dominate the farmed countryside.

Masters of the Media

The farmers who have controlled access to most of Britain's countryside in the second half of the twentieth century might have been expected to face more resistance than their predecessors. Instead of defeated Saxons or medieval serfs they have been excluding the increasingly assertive citizenry of a mature democracy armed with vigorous communications media and other channels of protest. Yet they have shown great skill in mobilizing features of this new world to support rather than undermine their hegemony. Armed with one of the most potent propaganda machines in British public life, they have succeeded in persuading much of the community that their controlling position in the countryside (and the bars to access it entails) are in the overall interests of everyone.

In advancing the notion that the countryside should be left to them, farmers were able to turn to their advantage the deep divide between town and countryside which marks Britain out from other European countries. As the first country to industrialize, Britain has lost the links between urban dwellers and the villages from which they came which still exist in France. Our agricultural methods also help make the farmed countryside more alien to most people than it is elsewhere. Because ownership of farmland is concentrated in a relatively small number of relatively large units, few twentieth-century British townspeople know a farmer. This has enabled farmers to present a picture of themselves which bears little relation to reality. Though most farmland is in the hands of agribusinessmen committed firmly to the bottom line, farmers' organizations have invited people to think of their members as sturdy yeomen smallholders, fired with a love of their land and its wildlife—characters who must be left alone to grow our food and cherish our landscape and who can be trusted to do both. Invited by the media to field a typical farmer, the National Farmers' Union and the Country Landowners' Association usually put forward not a large-scale, heavily chemical-dependent agribusiness-man but a small tenant farmer of agreeable disposition. As the Country Landowners' Association explained in 1976 in a document entitled *The Future of Landownership*, 'The closer the owner of land, whether owner-occupier farmer or resident landlord, is identified with the small working farmer, the less the likelihood that he will have to bear the brunt of political attack arising from envy.'[43]

These organizations have succeeded in persuading the rest of the community to accept the image they promote because the urban population so long estranged from the countryside remains anxious to sentimentalize it. People want to invest the countryside with the qualities they miss in cities—and they are thus willing to believe that farmers are red-cheeked, decent, and dependable, even if that means we ought to accept their power over the rural environment. One NFU campaign presented farmers as 'The Backbone of Britain'. A typical NFU document was headed 'He Cares'.[44] Typically such offerings show farmers standing beside abnormally small tractors or with sheep dog to heel looking out caringly over a small-scale patchwork of fields, hedgerows, and woods of the kind that has become less and less typical of modern Britain. The farmer is usually working, often at time-honoured tasks like laying a hedgerow, planting a tree, rounding up sheep, or repairing a drystone wall. The press, broadcasting, and advertising have happily swallowed this image, secure in the knowledge that their listeners, viewers, and readers want to believe it is accurate.

Dan Archer has perhaps done as much as any figure, fictional or real, to shape our idea of the farmer. Not everyone knows, however, how much a part farmers themselves played in his creation. The original idea for *The Archers* came from a meeting of farmers invited by the BBC to advise on how farming programmes could be improved. From its inception in 1951 the aim of the broadcast every weekday with a bumper edition on Sundays was largely to support farming, partly by winning townspeople over to the farmers' point of view. Godfrey Baseley, the originator and editor for 21 years, 'had frequent meetings with the Minister of Agriculture and the President of the National Farmers' Union before deciding on Ambridge's farming policy', according to *The Archers* producer and editor for many years William Smethurst.[45] Dan Archer, a working tenant farmer until he died of a heart attack while trying to right a ewe, was presented with a special award by the NFU to mark forty years' faithful and active service to agriculture. You can see why. Certainly if a hard-working, salt-of-the-earth character like Dan told you you had to keep out of the countryside, you would tend to assume he had good reasons for wanting you to.

In rooting their case for the farmer's right to prevail on his direct involvement in manual work on the land, farmers' organizations are continuing to trade on the ideas of John Locke which played such a part in the foundation of the ideology of the landowner. The willingness of the British public to go along with this thinking reflects the deep chord which this ideology undoubtedly strikes. The twentieth century also saw new impetus given to the idea of private landowning from what now looks like a disastrous experiment with the alternative—the short history of communism.

In Britain revulsion against agrarian communism began with the affront it presented to what had come to be seen as the absolute right to own land. But as time passed, the inefficiencies of collective farming seemed to provide practical support for the Aristotelian instinct that only private ownership could secure the efficient harvesting of nature's bounty. The lesson was carefully noted by Britain's landowning community, lending them a new argument should they face any further challenge to their position and renewed confidence that the total control they demanded was not only their entitlement but in the best interests of society as a whole. And the apparent vindication of private landowning provided by communism extended not only to farmers who tilled their land but grander landowners on behalf of whom Aristotle's case could not be made. As collective ownership demonstrated its ineffectiveness, Britain's landowners lost what inhibitions they still felt about their position.

In the absence of any comprehensive land register in Britain like those found in other countries from the United States to France it is difficult to know precisely how much rural land is owned by people who do not farm it themselves, but estimates suggest it is probably about 60 per cent of the total area of Britain. Individuals range up to the 167,000 acres owned by our largest private owner, the Duke of Buccleugh and Queensbury. Many of these people would probably still see their claim to their holdings as Blackstone did, as a natural right. Aware however that this is not universally accepted, they also advance other justifications designed to have wider appeal. Landowners often claim they own land not for personal satisfaction but to serve the needs and desires of society at large, echoing the justification which their eighteenth-century forebears read into the thinking of Thomas Aquinas. They are custodians or, as the then Duke of Northumberland's chief land agent William Hugonin put it to me in 1982, 'They feel they are stewards, that they have been handed down to look after something for a very short number of years which they would hope to leave in a better state than when they took over. They are the arch conservers, and the stewardship involved is management and control.'[46]

Like farmers, country landowners have used the twentieth century's mass media to promote the image they want. But they do not have to rely on outside media. Aiding them in this task is their control of a substantial slice of Britain's heritage industry. Though landowners bar people from many of even the remoter parts of their holdings they have been increasingly ready to invite them into their own homes when it has proved financially expedient. Millions of people every year now visit stately homes, where they are subjected to a very particular view of the role of the landowning class, past and present. Guides are unlikely to explain that the old church standing isolated in the park is all that remains of a village whose inhabitants were driven out by their host's forebears. Enclosure awards, riots against emparkment, and death sentences for poachers pass similarly unmentioned. Instead the visitor is invited to stand in palatial dining rooms and to hear details of the age and style of furnishings while the lords of past ages flattered by the adoring gazes of dogs, horses, wives, and children look down benevolently.

Few rival National Trust-owned hovels exist to present the dark side of Britain's experience of absolute landownership. So people are asked to think of landowners as eminently civilized people living a good life whom the rest of the community should envy perhaps but also respect. Since they have dictated the terms on which people come to them, they can control the way they are represented. They present themselves as important, upright citizens with an ancestry steeped in public service and devotion to duty spiced with a dashing taste for exciting exploits. The emphasis on family helps establish them as caring towards their heritage, their land, and the rest of us. As well as oil paintings of distinguished ancestors, they display lines of current family photographs on occasional tables and grand pianos, just like those on the mantelpieces of more modest semis, flats, and terraced houses.

The subliminal message is that if a good man is in charge of the land, what he does with it will be good too—for us as well as him. Certainly today's landowners are comfortable with the idea that their holdings should be considered as an extension of their personalities. Nicholas Thornhill owns a 1,600-acre farm near Diss in Suffolk, as well as an estate in Derbyshire and a château in France. In Suffolk the clearance of his woods and hedgerows and the drainage of his flowery meadows have given rise to considerable local protest, but Mr Thornhill told me in 1987: 'I see a farm as an extension of one's personality, and you farm as you want to, it is oneself, and that's why I like to see every farmer given freedom. As you go round the countryside you see different farms and you think that's how he farms, and that's how I farm, and it's very much an extension of oneself.'[47] Secure in the knowledge that what they are doing is in everyone's best interests, landowners need not be shy of acknowledging that it is also nice for them. Lord Brocket, who then owned the 5,000-acre Brocket Park estate in Hertfordshire, told me in 1987 why he liked being a landowner: 'I think first because of the privacy it offers. People like to feel that they are nice and private in the middle of their patch whatever size their patch is. Secondly, it offers them a security for the future because landownership has always proved over the last few hundreds of years a good investment for the future and something that people tend to hold on to through its ups and downs in its value: land and bricks and mortar are always the things that people shout about. And I suppose there's a third thing for some people: it's like I think for some people, and I hope not myself, like owning a Rolls-Royce. It makes a statement. It says, "I have arrived".[48]

To encourage people to identify with them, landowners like to present their holdings as simply the home and garden which everyone owns or aspires to own writ large. This has an obvious implication for public access. You wouldn't want strangers wandering around your back garden, would you? So you can see why landowners prefer outsiders to stay off their thousands of rolling acres. Under a reproduction of a painting of *The Montagu Family at Beaulieu* Lord Montagu writes at the beginning of the guide to his country seat: 'My family and I extend a warm welcome to you upon your visit to Beaulieu, which has been a family home since 1538. . . . I believe that the beauty of places like Beaulieu, enjoyed in the past by a few, should now be shared with the people of the whole world. With this spirit you are invited to enjoy this place which has been lovingly cared for by my family throughout the past four centuries.'[49] At Broadlands a few miles to the north, Lord Romsey writes on behalf of himself and his wife and in a guidebook he has signed himself: 'We are both delighted to welcome you to our home and hope you will greatly enjoy your visit and leave with a happy memory of Broadlands.'[50]

The owners of our stately homes have taken the idea that an Englishman's home is his castle and turned it round to suggest that the Englishman's castle is his home. That enables them to go on to maintain that the fields, rivers, and woods around it are their garden, rather than a theatre for generating wealth whether through mining, farming, forestry, leisure sports, or whatever—activities which in the past have not necessarily required that outsiders should be excluded in the way they customarily are from gardens. This identification of the countryside with private gardens has buttressed the philosophical claim of the landowner to exclude and succeeded in winning support for his claim, particularly as home ownership of property has increased rapidly over the past two decades.

Some landowners have tried to use growing fear of crime to reawaken ancient hostility towards strangers who lurk in the woods and bushes. In Britain's countryside strangers have been viewed with

suspicion at least since King Ine required anybody straying off a woodland track to blow a horn. Today a landowner who explains that he
wants his wife and children to be able to sunbathe without fear of
strangers may get an understanding response. And in our anonymous
and urbanized society, there is no obvious way of distinguishing between
potentially dangerous visitors to the countryside and anybody else.
Even ordinary people can be presented as troublesome. Bertram
Sample, the 'resident farmer' of *The Field*, complained in 1990,

What really annoys me about the attitude of the townsman is his seemingly
ineducable ignorance demonstrated by this playground-syndrome attitude
to the countryside. My children, advantaged maybe and fortunate to have
been country-bred and reared, knew instinctively how and when to cross a
stile, pick up a ferret, collect firewood, back away from a bird's nest, feed
chickens, water ponies, control dogs, herd sheep and open or shut gates. In
their early teens they could kill game, drive farm vehicles, mow lawns, mend
fences, shoot straight, work hard and play likewise. They were not paragons
of virtue by any means but they evinced more common sense than the average visitor to the country walking his dog over someone else's land.[51]

In similar vein *Daily Telegraph* columnist Simon Courtauld lamented
in 1993, 'Before the age of the motor car, there was less intercourse
between town and country, and the country was arguably the better
for it. But today our rural areas are burdened with people who have
no understanding of agriculture or country ways.'[52]

The townsman for his part accepts much of this. He senses there
is much he does not know about the countryside and this erodes
his self-confidence as he tries to make his way around it. Education
has not done a great deal to counteract this instinctive hesitation: it
was not until 1985 that the Countryside Commission published a booklet for the public about their rights in the countryside; for decades
up till then they had offered only the Country Code's list of unex-
plained prohibitions.

Though most townspeople are actually rather timid about venturing into it and easily discouraged by obstacles, landowners successfully portray them as a serious threat to the countryside. Almost any
type of recreation from which landowners are not profiting is por-
trayed as a threat to the vulnerable rural environment. Rural pursuits

which clearly do damage ecosystems, like fox-hunting, are nonetheless presented as parts of country life which must be conserved. A nation ready to sentimentalize the countryside easily accepts that what townspeople want to do in the countryside is dangerous while 'rural' activities are automatically a good thing. In the 1960s and 1970s, while agricultural chemicals were wreaking untold damage on wildlife, it was motorists from towns who were presented as the most dangerous threat to the fragile rural environment. Planners considered they had to divert these people to 'honeypots' in which they could crowd with others of their kind and leave the countryside to the men and women whom centuries of wisdom had endowed with a unique ability to care for it.

Today landowners have succeeded in using New Age travellers as evidence that townsfolk are continuing to threaten the countryside. The media moved quickly to vilify this menace, and the government moved in to crack down on the rather limited threat which travellers posed with the Criminal Justice and Public Order Act of 1994, just as the law has moved to support landowners so often in the past.

Exclusion Triumphant

As the millennium approaches, a surprising continuity can be detected between the position and attitudes of landowners today and those of their predecessors over the past thousand years. In Britain, landownership remains essentially absolute, and landowners are as confidently assertive. Ownership remains bound up with bloodsports—just as it was when the Normans first seized the land from the people. The number of pheasants reared on country estates in Britain is actually increasing by 3 per cent a year.[53] Greed, privacy, and the desire for status continue to stalk the countryside, which is still the place to which those who make it big resort to display their triumph. And thus our rural environment remains deeply and intrinsically inimical to freedom to roam in the countryside.

4

RESISTANCE

OVER the last thousand years, the assertion of the landowner's grip on Britain's countryside has not simply been accepted by the rest of the population. The popular fightback we are witnessing today in calls for a general right to walk is the latest of many waves of resistance to which our seemingly placid countryside has played host. Underlying successive skirmishes between owners and landless has been a simmering war of competing ideologies in which the supposed right of ownership of the environment has come up against a growing sense that the earth belongs in some sense to all. The idea of rights which is such a feature of twentieth-century political struggle was identified nearly 800 years ago as the obvious means of eroding landowner power. Paradoxically, it was not the dispossessed and hungry serfs but barons who themselves held large tracts of land and were energetic enforcers of feudal power who were to make the key breakthrough which was to prove the ultimate foundation of today's calls for a right to roam.

Rival Rights

The schoolchild notion that Magna Carta is the root of our rights is not misplaced. It emerged like several subsequent acts of enfranchisement because a powerful group or in this case individual was exploiting his position to such an extent that an implicit understanding about what was acceptable was being broken. In twelfth-century England, King John was seen as a harsh and vicious man. Since both justice and the holding of land issued ultimately from him he could give judgment to spite those whom he disliked, imprison people for years without trial, and extract huge sums when a baron died and his heir succeeded. For pushing all these things to their limit John was renowned. What is more, he had extracted huge sums of money for agreeing to release land his father Henry II had appropriated as royal forest when Henry pushed the bounds of the royal forest to their furthest ever limit. In January 1215 some of John's barons met him in London and demanded reforms. When the king rejected them a second time in the spring they made war on him, marching to London and taking the city by surprise. The result was a meeting of king and barons with clerks and attendants numbering all told hundreds of men on an island of the Thames near Windsor called Runnymede and, after a week's negotiation, the signing of the Great Charter— Magna Carta.

What had fired many of the barons' demands was the notion that they themselves had rights by virtue of their existence independent of the will of King John. This was a revolutionary idea at a time when society was completely hierarchical with the notion of a feudal pyramid and 'no man without a lord' pervading the social structure. Magna Carta ended up enacting that every baron, knight, and freeman (a former serf who had been released) had the right not to be imprisoned except in accordance with law and after having been judged by their peers. This clause, destroying the idea of the higher orders' right to control which was the cornerstone of feudalism, was to form the basis for all those twentieth-century laws granting all men and women rights, and was to help lay the basis for a sense of rights in land directly opposite to the landowners' notion of the right to ownership of land and property. For the charter related its revolutionary thinking directly to land, even though the King remained technically the absolute owner of all of it. Clause 47 declared that all the royal forest which the King had claimed during his reign must be disafforested or released from forest law immediately and that river banks which he had enclosed in similar fashion should be likewise released.[1] Elias of Dereham, the steward of the Archbishop of Canterbury, set off on horseback from Runnymede bearing four handwritten copies of the Great Charter. Within three weeks they had been received in Devon, Westmorland, Shropshire, and Sussex. One hundred and fifty years later, a far larger band of serfs followed where the barons had led.

In the fourteenth century, the idea of Robin Hood, a folk hero who discomfited authority figures by promoting the interests of the poor, became widespread. Whether his feats were performed in the royal forest of Sherwood in Nottinghamshire, or elsewhere in England or even in Scotland, or perhaps only in myth, they captured popular imagination everywhere. Songs celebrating the deeds of Robin Hood were accompanied by other subversive texts. Other ballads like *The Tales of Gamelyn* took as their themes the righting of wrongs inflicted by a harsh system and unjust men, or the downfall of unjust lords.[2] Ordinary people were openly asking why the King or the barons and knights should be able to hunt deer and hare freely in forests, parks, and warrens and take all manner of fish from rivers and lakes while the poor went hungry. Why should a serf be forced to remain with one lord who could require three days' free labour a week, a fine when any of his daughters married, a larger one should they bear a child out of wedlock and his most valuable animal when he died? As these questions gathered currency, circumstances conspired to enhance the apparent value of landless people without rewarding them accordingly. A series of plagues, most famously the Black Death of 1349, wiped out approximately one-third of the population, depriving lords of the labour they needed to till their fields and run their estates. The serfs might have expected the law of supply and demand to require higher wages. Instead the King and his puppet parliament legislated to control wages, at a time when crippling poll taxes were being levied to finance wars in France. These wars meanwhile were themselves playing a democratizing role. The critical role played by archers, all common foot soldiers, at the Battle of Crécy in 1346 helped undermine the previously unchallenged superiority of the mounted knights and barons.

In 1381, a growing band of disgruntled men were yearning to throw off the feudal yoke and move to a system of money rent rather than feudal dues; a temporary move in this direction, hastily withdrawn, fuelled their anger and frustration further. A poll tax riot at Brentwood in Essex stimulated others, and on 11 June 1381 100,000 people marched on London and took over the city for several days. The rebels did not seek to overturn the land regime; all they asked for was the replacement of feudal dues with a money rent. We do not know whether this was because they considered this was all that was practically feasible or because they felt that this was all they were entitled to. They did however also call for a fundamental change in the law on wild animals so that everyone would be entitled to take all fish and game. Although the appropriation of game by land-owners had begun 300 years earlier, this right had therefore clearly not secured the assent of these people.

The sheer numbers of men amassed in the Peasants' Revolt could have overwhelmed the King and his entourage. But these men were not as ruthless or streetwise as their counterparts in Paris in 1793 and when the King told them he would accede to their demands and grant them safe conduct they believed him. The rebels naïvely saw in the youthful King Richard II an ally: they supposed that he was being misled by wicked advisers while his true loyalty lay with the common people. But the rebels' loyalty proved misplaced. They were tricked into submission, their three leaders were killed, and many of their number were later hanged. Yet the incident went into folk memory as a legend demonstrating that resistance to the prevailing order was at least possible. And if it was to be a long time before there was to be any repeat of such action on the ground, the acceptability of the landowning regime had taken a blow from which it would never quite recover.

One of the leaders of the Peasants' Revolt and one of those hanged, drawn, and quartered was an assistant curate from the tiny Essex village of Peldon, named John Ball. Lesser clergymen under-stood and often sympathized with the plight of the serfs since most of them came from peasant families. But unlike their siblings they had to know the Bible. Though attendance at church was compuls-ory, the teachings of Jesus were little known among ordinary people: the scriptures were not even translated into English until the 1390s and then only in the teeth of considerable opposition and danger. Mass dominated time in church and a sermon was a rare event. Once men like Ball discovered what the Christian message actually was, it often had an explosive effect on them. Wandering friars as well as clerics like Ball began to criticize the social order—and the wealth and cor-ruption of the Church—from a specifically Christian perspective. 'When Adam delved and Eve span | Who was then the gentleman?' became their motto. Such thinking was dangerous. Ball was imprisoned and excommunicated before eventually being executed. But his words lived on. In a sermon he preached before a crowd of 50,000 on Blackheath Common on 13 June 1381, Ball declared: 'Ah, ye good people, the matters goeth not well to pass in England, nor shall do till everything be common, and there be no villeins [serfs] or gentlemen, but that we may all be united together, and that the lords be no greater masters than we be. What have we deserved, or why should we be kept thus in servage? We all come from one father and one mother, Adam and Eve.'³ These words were to echo down the coming centuries.

One of the ideas of the time of the Peasants' Revolt which was not to go away was the idea that the landowners' domination certainly should not extend to wild creatures. This feeling survived steady strengthening of the laws against poachers and even the notorious Black Act of 1723 which made it a capital offence to take a deer, fish, or rabbit. Another notion which gained currency was the idea that landowners' rights were less compelling on land which was in some sense unoccupied—land which might correspond to the last of the Emperor Justinian's categories of public goods, *res nullius*, just as wild creatures came within the same group. Thus forest, mountain, rough grassland, and marshland increasingly came to be considered 'common land' by ordinary people.

We shall probably never know for sure precisely how this idea of common land originated. There is reason to suppose that something like common land preceded the development of private landownership. In Saxon times, stretches of land which were too difficult to clear for settled farming but which were rich in natural produce were apparently available to people living in and around the area for the harvesting of all the natural wealth these areas offered, including timber, firewood, stone, berries, mushrooms, and pasture. The Weald of Kent and Sussex was an example. If a Saxon nobleman or thegn sought to appropriate this 'common' land, his ownership could not be absolute, but was subject to the customary rights of others. As population pressure increased over the centuries, not only did these customary rights come to be restricted to people from a smaller and smaller geographical area, but user rights came to be shared out within particular communities. When William claimed the land of England (and his successors parts of Wales and Scotland) he and they allowed the commons system to carry on, both the shared rights over farmland and those over this untilled 'waste'. Presumably the Norman kings calculated that any attempt to obliterate commoners' rights wholesale would stimulate rebellion as well as wrecking the agrarian economy on which their armies depended. But by allowing common land to survive, and with it the implication of communal interests and rights, William allowed a symbol of an alternative approach to Britain's system of relatively absolute individual rights in land to survive and around which those who protested about the land regime could rally.

While a baron needed only the permission of the king to establish a hunting chase and while he was free to make innumerable changes to the management of his farmed land, he was not free to sweep aside all interests over land he owned which was considered by others as common land. We know this because increasing pressure for the enclosure of commons by their usually large-scale owners led the medieval Parliament in 1235 to give lords the right to appropriate such 'waste land of the manor'—but only provided that they left sufficient pasture for their free tenants. The Statute of Merton, as it was called, had obvious limitations. In particular, it provided no safeguards for the mass of the people who were serfs, not freemen. But it did represent some acknowledgement even from the most powerful in the land that there was some sense in which common land was a communal resource, a free good available to all from the richest lord to the poorest labourer or squatter. An uneasy peace over common land and common rights over farmed land seems to have held in the late fourteenth century, with lords holding back from pushing their rights to enclose or otherwise upset commoners too much, at a time when population losses in the aftermath of the Black Death had increased their bargaining power. So a sort of unofficial social contract over the countryside reigned, which alongside commoners' rights also embraced free passage over land outside the deer parks and less rigorous enforcement of the laws in the royal forests.[4]

This relatively progressive feature of rural life was blown apart by massive encroachment upon commons in the early 1500s and the Dissolution of the Monasteries in 1546. This event, bringing into the countryside a new breed of parvenu determined to exploit their commercial rights in land to the maximum, swept aside civilized custom. Common rights were soon being squeezed, and as a widespread assault on the commons and other untilled 'waste' got under way, a new wave of resistance was provoked.

Once enclosure began in earnest in Tudor times this protest gathered pace. Lesser gentry and small freeholders who felt wronged might seek redress at least initially in their local manorial court but frequently they took to direct action or persuaded others to take the action for them, levelling the hedges which had been established to stake out the new property boundaries. In most of these cases, the protests were localized. However, after 1530, as population pressure built up in the arable areas of southern and midland England, the number of riots increased fourfold. It was the lower-ranking members of society who were most often taking part in countless sporadic, local riots, punctuated by larger rebellions. Emparkment was seen as particularly provocative and often provoked not only an anti-enclosure riot but also widespread poaching. Occasionally riots were co-ordinated between villages, most notably in the Midland Revolt of 1607, which led to a month of widespread rioting, often involving several thousand men, women, and children at a time. Protests which started in May of that year in parishes in Northamptonshire which had seen widespread conversion of arable land to sheep pasture and considerable depopulation spread, like the ripples on a lake, to Leicestershire and Warwickshire and then, after a lull involving the defeat of the rebels and exemplary executions, as far afield as Lincolnshire, Derbyshire, and Worcestershire.[5]

Property was the target of the rioters in almost all cases: the risings rarely were directed at people. One particular act characterized these anti-enclosure riots—the levelling of hedgerows. In an age when we celebrate and seek to protect hedgerows as endowing our countryside with its small-scale intimacy and much of its wildlife, it may be difficult to imagine just how much the presence of a hedge infuriated the serfs of medieval and Tudor and Stuart England. For them the hedge symbolized a new exclusion from the land, both economic exclusion and also exclusion of movement. 'By destroying an enclosing hedge, the dispossessed restored, if only momentarily, a sense of community and dramatised their own concept of justice. Thus, their action carried a symbolism of its own,' according to Professor Roger Manning.[6]

After the Midland Revolt, enclosure of commons and wastes like the Fens became the target of many further risings during the first half of the seventeenth century. Such areas aroused strong feeling not only because of their economic value to many people and the communality they embodied, but also because they had actually become home to the growing numbers of men and women who had been driven out of their home villages by the enclosure of the commons. Desperate to protect the waste lands on which they were squatting and frustrated by their inability to cultivate them because of their lack of any legal tenure, these precursors of the New Age travellers of our day found themselves squeezed further by a toughening up of the laws against taking game. These new communities of the alienated and disadvantaged, cut off from the socializing systems of lords and Church, were to form the seedbeds for new thinking about land that was to challenge established orthodoxy. In the middle of the seventeenth century radical thinking on land began to move on from the starting point John Ball had set down.

The revolution that culminated in the execution of Charles I was accompanied by a ferment of ideas about how men and women should live and how society should order itself. Wide circulation of these ideas was made possible by the withdrawal of the strict censorship which had hitherto suppressed unorthodox books. In 1640, newspapers were illegal; by 1641 there were four; by 1645 there were 722. Freedom of assembly enabled people to discuss whatever they wished and with whomever they wished for the first time, and the availability of cheap, portable printing presses unleashed the new communications medium of the pamphlet.

In 1536 William Tyndale suffered imprisonment and execution for taking what had been the dangerous translation work of John Wyclif and his followers in the 1390s a stage further—he was the first Englishman to produce, print, and distribute a Bible in the English language. A hundred years on, the subversive influence of the Bible was beginning to make itself felt. More and more people began to contrast the teaching of the established Church, which had extremely close financial links with the ruling interests, with what they saw as the essential message of the Bible—that men and women were individuals in the sight of God, not mere social cogs, and that God had created all human beings as equals. In a world in which most people still worked the land or laboured in industries based on primary products, it is not surprising that emerging religious groups should have linked what they saw as the Bible's message to the land itself. 'The earth is the Lord's and the fullness thereof. He hath given it to the sons of men in general, and not to a few lofty ones which lord it over their brethren,'[7] declared one of the leaders of the Quakers. Another denounced all 'earthly lordship and tyranny and oppression, . . . by which creatures have been exalted and set up one above another, trampling under foot and despising the poor'.[8] Some of the Anabaptists denied a right to private property while many in the Army making use of enforced leisure after the civil war were asking searching questions about the organization of society. Some called for an upper limit to the amount of land any one individual might own, while others demanded the confiscation of the royalist lords' land.

It was another band of men and women who were to develop the biblical notions of equality into the most sophisticated proposals for land reform, combining direct action with both a philosophical framework and practical recommendations for society at large. Early on 1 April 1649, a Sunday, a group of people congregated on St George's Hill outside Weybridge in Surrey, then common land, and began to dig it up and plant crops. Calling themselves the True Levellers or Diggers, they saw their action as a symbolic call for the men and women of England to be allowed to grow food for themselves co-operatively on the still extensive commons and wastes of England. Their action was also a call for the common people to be allowed to cultivate all forests and wastes. Taking place on the Sabbath it was also a symbolic call for religious freedom, blatantly flouting laws making it a punishable offence to absent oneself from the Sunday service in one's own parish church. Other Digger colonies sprang up soon afterwards at various locations in the Midlands from Gloucestershire to Nottinghamshire, each group digging up common land to plant crops and often publishing pamphlets. It fell to the Diggers' leader, Gerrard Winstanley, to develop the philosophy for the movement which still influences thinking on land questions today.

Winstanley came from an urban middle-class Lancashire background and probably attended a grammar school; as a young man he had never had to work, let alone beg. To set himself up in business, he moved to London, but the uncertainty surrounding the civil war was not conducive to commercial success and, like many around him, Winstanley went to the wall. By the 1640s we find him scraping a living herding another man's cows at Cobham, an area of Surrey where there was still a great deal of country left wild by its owners as habitat for the game which they alone were legally entitled to pursue, yet which also harboured men prepared to challenge their hegemony: at nearby Windsor Great Forest hundreds of men set upon the king's deer in 1641. It was an environment to set a man thinking about land use. Winstanley estimated that between a half and two-thirds of the kingdom could be used far more effectively: 'If the waste land of England was manured by her children, it would become in a few years the richest, the strongest and [most] flourishing land in the world, and the price of corn would fall from 6s or 7s a bushel to 1s a bushel or less.'[9] Collective cultivation of the waste by the poor could allow for capital investment in improvements without any sacrifice of the interests of the commoners, and crops could be grown to feed the nation rather than, like wool, to produce a profit for landowners while the poor went hungry. There was land enough to maintain ten times the existing population and make England 'first of the nations'—if only that land were deployed in the best interests of the people as a whole.[10]

Although the revolutionary thinking of the mid-seventeenth century prompted much rejection of the established Church, it did not lead to mass rejection of religious belief. Far from it. Winstanley himself believed that he had been called by God, insisting that 'a voice within me made me declare it all abroad' and that the origin of his ideas was divine revelation. 'Not a full year since,' he explained in an open letter in 1649 to the Army and the City of London, 'being quiet at my work, my heart was filled with sweet thoughts, and many things were revealed to me which I never read in books, nor heard from the mouth of any flesh'.[11] The key message Winstanley believed that God had vouchsafed to him was that 'the earth shall be made a common treasury of livelihood to whole mankind, without respect of persons'.[12] This being so, his mission was both social and religious for 'True religion and undefiled is . . . to make restitution of the earth, which hath been taken and held from the common people by the power of conquests'.[13] So the will of God would be served only after ownership rights in land had been overturned. 'True freedom lies in the community in spirit and community in the earthly treasury and this is Christ the true man-child spread abroad in the creation, restoring all things unto himself.'[14]

Private appropriation of land was the cause of the present troubles:

The earth (which was made to be a common treasury of relief for all, both beasts and men) was hedged into enclosures by the teachers and rulers, and the others were made servants and slaves: and that earth, that is within this creation made a common storehouse for all, is bought and sold and kept in the hands of a few, whereby the great Creator is mightily dishonoured, as if He were a respecter of persons, delighting in the comfortable livelihood of some, and rejoicing in the miserable poverty and straits of others. From the beginning it was not so,[15]

argued Winstanley and his fellow Diggers at St George's Hill in their declaration, the True Levellers' Standard. It was the Norman Conquest which had thwarted God's plan for the world. Although contemporary landowners had not seized their land by blood and fire, yet they held what was essentially stolen property and thus had no real right to it. Winstanley told lords of the manor: 'The power of enclosing land and owning property was brought into creation by your ancestors by the sword; which first did murder their fellow creatures, men, and after plunder or steal away their land, and left this land successively to you, their children. And therefore, though you did not kill or thieve, yet you hold that cursed thing in your hand by the power of the sword.'[16] Consciously or unconsciously, Winstanley took up the notion of rights in land. He believed that every person, as a child of God, had an equal right to a share of the earth. In his ideal world, it would not be up to beneficent landowners to issue land to citizens whom they deemed worthy or in need; each man, rich or poor, had an inalienable natural right to the land. He wrote, 'The poorest man hath as true a title and just right to the land as the richest man.'[17]

How did the Diggers believe they could achieve land revolution? In fact, they argued that such a revolution was unnecessary since it had already taken place. The abolition of the monarchy and establishment of a commonwealth had removed the linchpin of the property pyramid—the monarch from whom all land was held. Lords of the manor thus had no greater legal claim on land than the common people. Clearly the landowners of seventeenth-century England were not going to give up their lands voluntarily even if they could not gainsay the Diggers' line of reasoning. The Diggers, however, depended on persuasion. They renounced violence: progress must come through change in the hearts and minds of their fellow men and women. Alongside their proposals for land reform they therefore came up with progressive ideas in other areas too: that all men should have the vote, and that education should be universal for both sexes in a form which would alternate academic enlightenment with vocational training. As a more immediate step towards achieving their aims they spoke and wrote widely. Winstanley himself published more than 100,000 words of open letters, pamphlets, essays, manifestos, poems, and songs.

Suddenly, however, it was all over. The restoration of the monarchy in 1660 caused groups like the Diggers to be routed or go underground as a new wave of enclosure swept the countryside and the restoration of censorship ensured that their ideas disappeared too, at least for a time. Protests related to land rights rumbled on—enclosure riots, emparkment riots, and, during the eighteenth and nineteenth centuries food riots developed as landless agricultural labourers on tiny wages found they could not afford to eat the food they produced as it was increasingly shipped abroad. Rioting became an English tradition and the death penalty, introduced for riots involving forty or more people in the wake of rebellions in 1548–9, with the number of people involved being reduced to twelve under Mary Tudor and Elizabeth I, proved unable to stem these disturbances, just as it failed to stamp out poaching after it was extended to the taking of rabbits, fish, and deer in 1723. 'Blacking' attacks, in which gangs of men with their faces blackened to escape detection made night raids into game preserves such as Windsor Forest, Enfield Chase, and Woolmer Forest to get meat for their families continued to reflect an underlying refusal to accept the seizure of the countryside and its contents by the privileged few. Alongside these spasmodic and uncoordinated physical acts of resistance there was however beginning to take place a revolution in the now largely urbanized population's attitude towards the countryside which was to pose what would ultimately prove a far more potent challenge to the landowners' hegemony.

The Recreation Revolution

Before and during medieval times, the countryside had been for most people a theatre for toil and a source of threat. The natural world had been somewhere from which to scratch the means of survival in the face of hostile weather and various dangers: the forbidding mere which serves as the lair for the monsters Beowulf fights could be taken as an apt metaphor for medieval man's idea of the countryside as a whole. The Church taught people to pay little attention to the vale of tears in which they were to live out a brief span before departing for an environment which while unknowable would certainly be very different. Insofar as people took any non-utilitarian interest in their rural surroundings, they tended to prefer carefully contained environments—typically the garden—in which any pleasure to be derived from the contemplation of flowers, butterflies, herbs, and so on could be gained within an enclosure secured from the rigours of the outside world. The Renaissance brought with it, however, the beginnings of the notion that the countryside should be considered as a source of delight and personal fulfilment, not just for country dwellers but for the growing numbers of city dwellers too—indeed particularly for them.

The Italian scholar and poet Francesco Petrarch was one pioneer of what was for his time (the early fourteenth century) a revolutionary attitude to the countryside, albeit one that had its roots in the pastoralism of the ancient Greeks and Romans, ages for which Petrarch yearned: 'I never liked this present age,' he lamented.[18] Rather than regarding mountains and forests with suspicion and distrust, Petrarch chose to live among them: 'Would that you could know', he wrote to a friend, 'with what joy I wander free and alone among the mountains, forests and streams.'[19] Petrarch kept a sort of nature diary recording the habits of wild creatures and he wrote poetry celebrating the joys of the countryside, which he peopled with mythological nymphs and dryads. One day, he suddenly decided to climb a mountain (Mont Ventoux near Avignon) for no other reason than the experience of doing so and of seeing the view from the summit—an action incomprehensible to his contemporaries. Once he realized what he had done, he was overcome with guilt at admiring earthly things,[20] but he had nevertheless started something which was to change completely the role of the countryside in the lives of men. Shakespeare's plays show a delight in wild plants and creatures which would have been fresh in his day, although Tudor merchants were already starting to enjoy weekends in the country: on May Day Elizabethan Londoners 'would walk into the sweet meadows and green woods, there to rejoice their spirits with the beauty and savour of sweet flowers, and with the harmony of birds', according to contemporary reporter John Stow.[21]

During the eighteenth century, delight in the rural scene came to be combined with deepening curiosity about its contents. The scientific instinct which the Enlightenment was fostering found an obvious outlet in exploring the mysteries of the natural world. As Newton and Galileo, Bacon and Boyle provided perfectly logical explanations for activities which had been shrouded in the deepest mystery and magic hitherto, like the movement of the heavenly bodies, the earth and its flora and fauna lost some of the menace they had inspired in more ignorant generations. And as people lost their fear of the natural world, they became confident enough to get to know it better. As they did so they started to find it intriguing and beautiful rather than mysterious and hostile. 'Collecting' suddenly became a mania—shells, fossils, flowers, ferns, skins, stuffed birds, and insects. 'Have got the prettiest fly that ever was seen', enthused Lady Margaret Cavendish Bentinck, an eighteenth-century aristocrat who built up an enormous collection of plants and animals over fifty years, dispatching employees to remote regions of the British Isles to collect specimens while others remained at home to catalogue and paint them.[22]

Scientific developments like the invention by the Swede Linnaeus of a method of classifying plants and animals helped the subject to develop—although many in London's high society, copying those in Paris, preferred the more dramatic descriptions of nature which flowed from the pen of the Comte de Buffon. Dressed in full court costume, the Comte laboured for eight hours a day for forty years at his task—the *Histoire Naturelle*, which was an early publishing success, the initial print-run of forty-four volumes selling out in six weeks.

Dispatched by figures like Lady Bentinck, the eighteenth-century British naturalists soon discovered that the barriers which existed to passage through the countryside presented them with a problem. The muddy, unsurfaced roads were bad enough, but once they left these to poke around in hedges or clamber over rocks hunting plants they faced risks which included finding themselves seized as suspected highwaymen or Jacobite spies. Dr Caleb Threlkeld, for example, was seized upon as a spy while plant-hunting at Tynemouth in 1707, 'because I clambered up the rocks, and kept not the high-road'.[23] Landowners sometimes made special arrangements for genteel botanizers, but by the middle of the nineteenth century it had become clear that interest in rural wildlife would inevitably spread to the lower orders. The Revd Gilbert White's *Natural History of Selborne*, published in 1788, set out a model procedure for the patient observation of individual living creatures which, during the nineteenth century, was seized upon by enthusiasts from many different backgrounds.

Meanwhile, the countryside was increasingly coming to be seen not just as a repository of interesting creatures but as a thing of beauty in its own right. On their Grand Tour through eighteenth-century Italy, young Englishmen came across paintings by seventeenth-century artists like Claude Lorrain and Nicholas Poussin which, through the newly discovered unifying dimension of light, were able to portray an individual stretch of countryside as an aesthetic whole. Those who had discovered these paintings while abroad came back to look around their native land for similar scenes which could be painted or just contemplated out of doors, and developed a new eye for the work of the landscape designers creating parklands at the heart of the domains of the most privileged. Some people began touring the countryside to view its 'scenery' (a word coined in the eighteenth century). Typically they would stand on a viewpoint and look at their surroundings through an instrument called a Claude glass—which produced a miniaturized, subdued version of its subject in which light and shade were exaggerated. The idea was to find stretches of land which fitted an emerging set of rules for what constituted a pleasing landscape such as Poussin might have painted. Particularly favoured was tamed countryside dotted here and there with figures, ruins, or sheep, all placed within a dark frame in the foreground provided by trees or buildings, followed by a second plane of ground more exposed to sunlight, a third again darker, perhaps because overshadowed by trees or a cloud, a fourth, and so on until the plane below the horizon provided a focal point to which the eye would instantly travel since it was suffused with clear yellow evening light. The viewpoint from which such vistas were viewed had always to be high enough to allow the horizon in the distance to be visible; above, the sky got gradually darker, an effect often enhanced by dark foliage at the top of the composition. To appreciate landscapes in this way became an important social accomplishment. But though the formulation of strict rules for landscape quality may today strike us as quaint, the development of landscape appreciation represented a fundamental change in man's relationship with the environment. Here were people looking at the outdoors not as a possession, a source of profit or a theatre for sport but as a spectacle in itself. This new interest inevitably gave people a feel they had a stake in land around them which was bound in time to threaten the absolute control of landholdings cherished by the landowning class.

As the eighteenth century wore on, science inspired a new confidence about the natural world which enabled some people to discover charms not only in the tame pastoral scenes typified by parkland but in wild rough landscapes as well. A new aesthetic category was admitted—the sublime. Alongside the charms of the well-ordered, comfortable, verdant, and fruitful scene, there now emerged the lure of the opposite—lofty mountains, stupendous waterfalls, and rocky promontories. Instead of eliciting terror in the beholder, as they typically had since ancient times, they should, it was urged, inspire exultation and awe, even delight. An English clergyman, the Revd William Gilpin, who journeyed through Britain in the second half of the eighteenth century devising rules for the appreciation of picturesque scenery gradually widened the scope of his aesthetic to take in more and more rough, irregular, wild, and even uninhabited scenery. This development widened the potential claim of the country-lover on the land to virtually all of the countryside. Another new interest soon rendered that claim even more subversive by converting the rural enthusiast from passive external observer into an active participant in the scene he was contemplating.

As the eighteenth century came to its close, the Romantic reaction against the dispassionate scientific objectivity of the Enlightenment and its emphasis on reason began to put its own mark on the emerging habit of rural recreation. The poet William Wordsworth in particular helped move on the cult of the sublime into something quasi-religious. As Renaissance thinkers like Petrarch had gone back to ancient Greece for their ideas, so Wordsworth went back to paganism in search of a link between the earth and the divine. The serfs of medieval Britain may have viewed the countryside as a cruel workplace but for some pagan peoples the stones, the trees, and the earth were gods. Many primitive societies (we may think of the aborigines; Wordsworth looked to the Druids) considered the environment or parts of it sacred, partly because it magically provides the things they need. This sense of the sacredness of the earth is easily awoken even in peoples to whom it is fresh by a determined figure such as a poet. Wordsworth infused the landscape with a pantheistic sense of godhead. This embraced not only the countryside itself but the people within it, who could acquire divinity themselves from their closeness to it so that a rural lass called Lucy, for example, could achieve apotheosis in death by merging with 'rocks and stones and trees'.

Wordsworth's poems were quoted in countless newspaper articles and sermons and made an enormous impact. His followers wanted to wander 'lonely as a cloud' within the landscape; they were not content to view it from outside like the admirers of picturesque scenery. And because imbibing the sacredness of the landscape was effectively a religious experience, it was not something that the earthly property rights of landowners could be allowed to obstruct.

Wordsworth helped establish the idea that the ideal way to experience the countryside was to walk in it, covering long distances, accompanied if at all by one or at most two kindred spirits. The countryside became not merely a workplace but a place of recreation. When Wordsworth bid his sister Dorothy, 'And bring no book: for this one day | We'll give to idleness',[24] he was actually proposing an innovation—namely rural recreation, something which would have seemed bizarre to an eighteenth-century poet like Alexander Pope. For Pope and his contemporaries, the city was the place to be, as the only theatre of civilization and intellectual discourse.

You did not have to swallow whole Wordsworth's rather half-baked pantheistic notions to begin to see something soulful in the countryside which restored the spirits of an increasingly urbanized people. For some the countryside became a place to commune with one's Maker. For the completely godless, however, it began to become a substitute for religion itself, the moods of mountains and lakes amplifying the longings and urges in the hearts of human beings. These human passions were themselves taking on new significance as the individual came to be seen as more and more important. De-medievalization, the Reformation, the Enlightenment, and the Romantic movement itself all placed growing emphasis on the single human being at the expense of the well-drilled mass. The countryside became swept up in this process, as a theatre for self-realization, and this further strengthened the demands of more and more people for a stake of their own in the landscape. The landowners of the enclosure period driving the peasants off their holdings would have been amazed to think that the descendants of those peasants would want to come back to the countryside bringing bicycles and picnics. They shared with their victims a view of the countryside as an unpleasant place from which profit could be extracted. But from the nineteenth century on this attitude was to be entirely eclipsed as the countryside regained the paradisaical image it had enjoyed among the pastoralists of the ancient world. Consequences for the idea of landownership were inevitable. Wordsworth's affirmation that the Lake District is 'a sort of national property' may not have sent a chill down the spines of landowners in late eighteenth-century England, whose confidence was still unshakeable. But their successors would be forced to grapple with its implications.

An Earthquake of Power and Ideas

In the nineteenth century change sweeping the world of ideas was mirrored in the workings of the real world. Britain was being transformed from a rural country into one of large urban populations. In 1815 most Englishmen still worked on the land or in trades connected with agriculture. Yet by 1830 half the population lived in towns and cities, by 1870 two-thirds were urbanized. Once driven out of the countryside by enclosure or attracted to the towns by higher wages most people quickly lost interest in the countryside: conditions in the factories, ports, blast-furnaces, and mines, not to speak of the slums, were of more pressing concern. But their mass movement and the labour they provided helped engineer a decisive shift in the nation's balance of power, away from the landowning class and towards the Whig middle-class industrialists and merchants who were generating the nation's fabulous new wealth. These men deeply resented their near absence of representation in Parliament—Leeds, Manchester, Birmingham, and Sheffield were a few of the burgeoning urban agglomerations which had no MP—while tiny so-called 'rotten boroughs' in rural villages boasted two MPs apiece, ensuring that the Commons remained dominated by the landowning interest. The factory owners were also concerned about the nation's rulers' treatment of the workers on whom their wealth depended. Repression was preferred to concession: rising crime was met with harsher penalties, while not only riots but also mass meetings were broken up harshly, as in the case of the 'Peterloo Massacre' of 1819, when 60,000 people gathered in Manchester to hear a radical orator only to have eleven of their number slaughtered and 400, including more than 100 women, wounded. The urban middle classes, with the still recent French Revolution in mind, feared for the survival of the state. Through political agitation unprecedented in Britain, they forced through the first Reform Bill in 1832. It gave the vote only to a larger number of male property holders and extended parliamentary representation to major towns, abolishing or reducing representation of the rotten boroughs. But the enfranchisement of the Whigs through the 1932 act effectively ended the undisputed landowner hegemony which had obtained in Britain since the Norman Conquest.

The factory owners' revolution was to send ripples through the rest of society. The nineteenth century saw the lower orders starting to flex their muscles as well. A National Union of the Working Class was formed in 1831 and not long afterwards the London Working Men's Association, which drew up a People's Charter urging that all men be given the vote and that the property qualification for MPs should be removed; this charter lent its name to the Chartist riots in the middle of the century. Overseas influences were also undermining the authority of the established orders. America presented an example of a democracy operating successfully after throwing off hereditary monarchy and its associated structures of control as early as 1776. The new French republic, committed to liberty, equality, and fraternity, showed how different things could be only 20 miles away. The French political scientist Alexis de Tocqueville wrote, 'A great democratic revolution is at work among us . . . it is universal, it is durable, it escapes human intervention every day; every event, like every man, furthers its development.'[25] Of course, Britain's ruling class resisted these developments. Thus English-born Tom Paine, who had played a part in the American revolutionary war, was charged with treason for penning his book *The Rights of Man* and had to flee to France to escape trial. But such actions were in vain. By 1859 the philosopher John Stuart Mill was asserting, 'There is confessedly a strong tendency in the modern world towards a democratic constitution of society, accompanied or not by popular political institutions'.[26] Events were bearing this out. Slavery was abolished in the British Empire in 1833, the year after the first Reform Act, then followed the extension of the franchise to working men in towns in 1867, to working men in rural areas in 1884, the Married Women's Property Act in 1882 and finally the extension of the franchise to women in 1928. As the franchise widened, the middle class and the urban working class grew more dominant and socialism, trade unionism, and the co-operative movement sprang into being, the land question could not but find itself drawn back under the microscope.

The philosophers behind the French Revolution had certainly been hostile to large-scale private property. Jean Jacques Rousseau, a philosopher and Romantic, called for a new 'social contract' so that the poor would no longer be oppressed by the rich. 'The first man who, having enclosed a plot of ground, took upon himself to say "This is mine", and found people silly enough to believe him, was the real founder of civil society,' he wrote. 'How many crimes, how many wars, how many murders, how much misery and horror, would have been spared the human race if someone, tearing up the fence and filling in the ditch, had cried out to his fellows: "Give no heed to this imposter; you are lost if you forget that the produce belongs to all, the land to none." '[27] Philosopher Pierre-Joseph Proudhon encapsulated the new mood succinctly in his famous words: 'Property is theft.' In fact, however, Proudhon did not want communal ownership of land but ownership by small-scale peasant farmers, who would themselves possess rights to their property as unassailable as those of the aristocrats they would have to topple.[28] This was to be the actual model for land reform not only in France but in many other countries, including Egypt, Japan, Sweden, Cuba, Tanzania, Germany, Russia, China, Denmark, and Mexico.[29] But what about Britain, a country in which surveys of landownership in the 1870s revealed a huge concentration of landed wealth in the hands of territorial magnates, like the Duke of Buccleuch with nearly half a million acres in fourteen counties from Buckinghamshire to Fife, or the Duke of Beaufort with 51,000 acres from Breconshire to Gloucestershire?[30]

Had the French model been advanced when the enclosure movement was at its height, it might have become the focus of a revolutionary movement here. However, by the time land matters started to be debated seriously in Britain in the nineteenth century, democracy was already developing so fast and on such an urban basis that it did not seem appropriate. Britain's factory workers were not clamouring to return to the land as peasants, even though this thread can be detected even today in some land activists' demands for smallholdings for New Age travellers. Instead, people were concerned about the price of food; the level of rents; the availability of land for homes, factories, and public facilities; and the scope for open-air recreation. Parliamentary reform enabled Sir Robert Peel to achieve a crucial breakthrough on the first of these with the repeal of the Corn Laws in 1846. By opening food markets to free trade, this struck a further devastating blow at the power of rural landowners. It was not long after this step that open-air recreation became a major political issue.

Rus in Urbe

It was in London that the urban population first began to stake a serious claim to the outdoors. By mid-century substantial numbers of both middle- and working-class members of its population of 7 million had taken to spending their free time in woods and on downs, heaths, fields, and riversides around the capital. The open land they sought out was however shrinking rapidly as building developed in the wake of new railway and tram routes which were bringing an ever-widening area within commuting distance. Landowners who could make fortunes from development did not hesitate to sell or lease their hitherto rural holdings and what had been London's great open spaces—Epping Forest, Hampstead Heath, and the commons south of the river—began to look doomed. In 1864 the 5th Earl Spencer, the lord of the manors of Wimbledon and Battersea, decided to sell off around one-third of Wimbledon Common for building. He planned to enclose the remainder, part as a private park, part a public park also to be used for grazing stock and extracting gravel. Had the Earl been making plans a few years earlier, or had the land involved not supported common rights, Wimbledon Common would doubtless have been transformed. However, he fell foul of the post-Reform-Bill Parliament's General Inclosure Act of 1845. This measure was prompted by the rapid enclosure of commons under numerous private acts. It forbade enclosure without the consent of two-thirds of the commoners and, where commons were close to towns, required that the desirability of enclosure must be demonstrated. Earl Spencer believed commoners at Wimbledon to be few in number and expected them to be pleased to exchange their common rights for cash. However, the commoners declined to be bought out. Nor would they exchange their open common for a park. Instead they lobbied influential people who lived close to the Common or frequented it, such as radical Liberal MP and lawyer George Shaw-Lefevre. Together with their distinguished allies, the commoners succeeded in thwarting the Earl's plans through the assertion of commoners' rights in the courts. The Earl was forced to withdraw his bill and place his plans on hold.

It was clear to Shaw-Lefevre and the others involved in the struggle for Wimbledon Common that virtually all the capital's open spaces were at least as vulnerable to development. Only where historical accident conferred common land status on a site could anything be done. In 1865 the Liberal MP for Lambeth, Frederick Doulton, successfully moved the establishment of a House of Commons committee to find ways of conserving for public use such open spaces as remained in the vicinity of London, and the committee urged new legislation. This was enough to prompt urgent action by the owners of a string of open spaces around the capital who feared they might soon be denied the chance of further profit. A new wave of commons enclosures started, threatening Epping Forest, Tooting Graveney Common, Wandsworth Common, Hampstead Heath, Berkhamsted Common, Dartford Heath, and Plumstead Common. Shaw-Lefevre was later to write: 'If these enclosures had been allowed to remain unchallenged, the whole of the London Commons would have been undoubtedly lost to the public.'[31]

Shaw-Lefevre, Octavia Hill (a philanthropist with a special interest in the provision of housing and open spaces for the poor), and lawyer Sir Philip Lawrence set up a new organization to take on these land-owners, the Commons Preservation Society, which launched legal battles to save the threatened commons.[32] Alongside its sober end-eavours, less decorous actions began to occur. At Berkhamsted, a team of navvies tore down the lord of the manor's enclosure railings at dead of night. In 1871 thousands of working men ripped up fences placed round Wanstead Flats during a protracted and bitter battle over Epping Forest which was played out both on the ground and in the courts.

By the late nineteenth century enclosure had reduced the extent of the accessible woodland in the Forest to half of the 9 square miles over which it extends today. Much felling of trees in readiness for build-ing was taking place. Yet the Forest was becoming ever more popu-lar: by the late nineteenth century the coming of railways and trams and the introduction of bank holidays by Act of Parliament in 1871 opened up the Forest to the poorest visitor without any form of per-sonal transport, making it the unofficial back garden of the East End. In 1866 the lord of the manor of Loughton, John Maitland, enclosed without recourse to Parliament 1,300 acres of the Forest, leaving 9 for recreation. A stout fence shut people out of the remainder; within it, Mr Maitland started clear-felling the Forest. Local people had how-ever enjoyed the traditional custom of lopping timber for their own domestic use in the winter months. When 1 November came round, one labouring man called Tom Willingdale and his two sons made their way as usual to the Forest, broke through the fence and started lopping timber. All three were convicted of malicious trespass on prop-erty and sent to prison for two months, with hard labour. One of the sons caught cold in his damp prison cell, developed pneumonia, and died.[33]

This affair caused much indignation throughout East London, and when Tom Willingdale was released from prison the Commons Preservation Society took up his case and sought an injunction in his name restraining Mr Maitland from cutting down the trees and enclosing the Forest on the assumption that a grant must have been made to the local inhabitants in ancient times to lop timber, even though the charter could not be found.

Tom Willingdale did not live to see the outcome of this case. He died before it came to court, after resisting several attempts to buy him off for four years, even though the local establishment made it extremely difficult for him to get work or housing. By holding out like this, Willingdale provided an invaluable opportunity for George Shaw-Lefevre to cast around for another combatant prepared to take on the wealthy and powerful landowners of Epping Forest.

Shaw-Lefevre discovered that the Corporation of the City of London had bought land in Ilford to build a cemetery which attracted common rights over a nearby part of the Forest. He took a deputation to see the Lord Mayor and the City Chamberlain, who agreed to fight the cause of both the commoners and the general public. The ample funds suddenly made available by the Corporation enabled the Commons Society's solicitor, Robert Hunter, to conduct a far more thorough investigation of the records of the Forest. What Hunter discovered was that at Epping a commoner's rights were not confined to the manor in which the commoner lived: the Forest was actually one great common over all of which commoners from every one of the nineteen manors had the right of turning out their cattle, and from which no landowner could therefore bar them. The City of London proceeded to launch a suit against sixteen of the nineteen lords of the manor who had enclosed portions of the Forest in recent years. In 1874 came the final judgment: the Master of the Rolls granted an injunction prohibiting the lords of the manor from enclosing Epping Forest in future and requiring them to take down all the enclosure fences they had erected within twenty years before the start of the suit. As a result, several thousands of acres of land found to have been unlawfully enclosed were thrown open. Once the possibility of development had collapsed, landowners were prepared to sell at a reasonable price, and the City went on to buy Epping Forest and manage it for public recreation, as it still does.

After its Epping Forest victory, the Corporation went on to secure the power to buy and safeguard any land within 25 miles of the City for the recreation and enjoyment of the public under an Open Spaces Act. This enabled it to acquire 1,600 acres of south Buckinghamshire known as Burnham Beeches which was being put up for sale for the erection of 'superior residences'. It drew up by-laws to regulate visitor use and employed an official to enforce them. By 1909, Londoners were flocking out by train to Slough, there to be met in the summer months by a bus service which took them to the Beeches, which were soon fringed by tearooms. A string of purchases of commons in Kent and Surrey followed; the City acquired Ashtead Common as recently as 1991. The City also stepped in to underwrite local initiatives. In the 1890s, lords of the manor sold off two-thirds of West Wickham Common in Kent for building and put up a 'strong unclimbable spiked iron fence' around the remainder. A footpaths and preservation society based in Bromley forced the landowner to offer the land for sale, and when three-quarters of the purchase price was raised locally, the Corporation put up the balance and agreed to maintain the area in perpetuity. In 1892 the Lord Mayor travelled from Bromley station in his state coach and at a specially erected pavilion declared the common 'open to the use of the public for ever'.[34]

Though this extreme energetic promotion of rural recreation was not immediately matched by local authorities elsewhere in Britain, another force for change was emerging—the individual philanthropist. Birmingham was particularly fortunate in this regard. The chocolate-making Cadbury family wanted to provide a congenial environment for their employees both in and out of work time. They acquired a leafy country estate, complete with lake, in which to site their Bournville factory, and started up youth clubs, summer camps, rambling clubs, and summer tours for their employees. They also bought land for open-air recreation for all local people. One site of more than 800 acres which they gave to the City of Birmingham is now a municipal park. South of the City rise the Lickey Hills—more than 500 acres of pine and chestnut woods and sweeps of open heath and bilberry bushes.

Now managed by Bromsgrove District Council as a 'country park' (see page 202), the Lickeys owe much of their existence today to the generosity of the Cadbury family who bought and donated land in the Lickeys to the City in the early 1900s. As a result of their generosity and acquisitions by the City of Birmingham, an area which was once the private hunting preserve of William the Conqueror and in the nineteenth century threatened by building and quarrying is now an important open space and haven for wildlife.

London had individual philanthropists as well as a philanthropic local authority. Octavia Hill, brought up in Finchley, then on the rural edge of London, first concentrated her energies on the improvement of housing for London's poor. With the help of finance from the painter John Ruskin, Hill took over rented property and improved the living conditions of its inhabitants. But she was also appalled by the squalor of their surroundings. 'There are two great wants in the life of the poor of our large towns, which ought to be realised more than they are—the want of space and the want of beauty,' she declared.[35] She set about creating 'an open-air sitting room for the poor' at her first rented property, and a little courtyard was greened and planted, but she came to feel much more was required. She campaigned for the creation of public open spaces in London wherever they could be found. For example, she wanted burial grounds to be released as public open spaces; and she made this plea to the owners of private squares of Belgravia and Kensington:

I hope the day is not far distant when it may dawn upon the dwellers in our West End squares that during August and September not one in fifty of their families is in town, and that it is a rather awful responsibility to lock up the only little bit of earth which is unbuilt over, . . . and that when they leave town they will . . . grant such discretionary power to those who stay in town to admit the power to sit under the trees . . . as they contrast the utmost they *can* give in the somewhat dingy, early dried-up, London plane-tree, with the wealth of magnificent foliage of wood, or park, or mountain, to which they and their rejoicing family, baby and all, grandmother and all, go before the autumn sun dries up poor scorched London.[36]

Octavia Hill, however, wanted the poor to be able to get out of town completely—even beyond the 25-mile radius of St Paul's which the City of London set up as a limit for its acquisitions. Here too the countryside people valued was under threat. Lamenting the loss of footpaths, she wrote: 'As children how we knew them, these little winding, quiet by-ways with all their beauty. . . . through the woods, over the moors, across the fields, by the rivers, and up the hills. . . . Now how they are vanishing. Here, closed by quarter sessions, the poor witnesses hardly daring to speak, the richer dividing the spoil, the public from a larger area hardly knowing of the decision which has for ever closed to them some lovely walk.'[37] In 1894 Hill and other like-minded figures formed the National Trust. Acquisitions in the early years included Hindhead Common, Waggoners Wells, Littleheath Wood, and Selsdon Wood in Surrey, Knighton Woods in Essex, and Little Hampden Common in south Buckinghamshire as well as property in the Lake District. From the start it was all open to the public: the Trust's founders were quite insistent that people should enjoy a general right to roam freely over all uncultivated woodland and other land in the Trust's hands. Hill believed that the countryside should be considered common property. She wrote:

I think men love a country more when its woods, and fields, and streams, and flowers, and lakes, and hills, and the sky that bends over them are visible. I think men are better for the whisper of their quiet voices when the din of the city ceases, and the time of rest begins. I think these little winding ways, that lead us on by hedgerow and over brooks, through scented meadows, and up grassy hill, away from dusty roads, and into the silent green of wood and field, are a common possession we ought to try to hand down undiminished, in number and in beauty for those who are to follow.[38]

Rebellion and Rethinking

Far away from England's conurbations, the absolute power of the landowner was being challenged in a very different way. The tenant farmers working the hostile soils of Ireland had little in common with Octavia Hill.[39] But they did share a sense that the landownership regime was wrong. Most of Ireland had been divided up into large estates owned by English landlords who often lived far away from their estates and held the whip hand over tenants who could be evicted even if they paid their rent, which could be whatever the landlord chose. Many survivors of the potato famine which claimed the lives of about one-eighth of the population in the mid-century had been evicted wholesale from their hovels. By the 1870s, many had had enough. In 1879 tenants banded themselves together into the Irish National Land League, which formally demanded improvements in the terms of rental agreements, but actually embodied the philosophy articulated by Gerrard Winstanley 200 years earlier. League leader Charles Stewart Parnell later recalled: 'We went down to Mayo and we preached the eternal truth that the land of a country, the air of a country, the water of a country, belong to no man. They were made by no man. They belong to the human race.'[40] In taking this view, Ireland's tenant farmers were reflecting an attitude held by serfs in other near-feudal societies, in defiance of their masters. Serfs in Russia, for example, at this time held that the land belonged either to God or themselves, on the Lockean principle that title to land goes 'wherever axe and plough go'. In any event, the Irish tenants pursued their immediate demands with rent strikes and violence which soon threatened to destroy Ireland's landlord class. Gladstone, the Prime Minister, decided to grant security of tenure and judicially determined rents; later he enabled tenants to buy the land with government loans on favourable terms. Within a few years English landlordism in Ireland was overthrown to be replaced by a new ownership pattern of peasant proprietorship similar to that of post-revolutionary France.

Rebellion leapt the Irish Sea. In 1881 fishermen took some of the ideas of the Irish Land League back to the Isle of Skye. They quickly took root. Enclosure in Scotland had taken place more recently than in England and Wales and had been even more vicious. Before the 'Clearances' of the late eighteenth and early nineteenth centuries, the Highlands had been parcelled out between clans. Members of a clan bore the same surname and held the land in common; the clan chief administered justice and a clan 'welfare state', and protected the clan from outside attack by mobilizing clan members. After the defeat of the Scots at Culloden in 1746, the British government, determined that the Highlands should never again prove a breeding ground for rebellion, prohibited the wearing of Highland dress, and abolished the chiefs' judicial powers over their clans. But they also took more subtle steps to undermine the power of the clans, in particular by making chiefs outright owners of a clan's land and making clansmen their tenants.

Clan chiefs thus enriched started to take an 'English' view of their land as a commodity. Some adopted an extravagant lifestyle, sometimes over-reaching themselves, becoming bankrupt and providing opportunities for absentee Englishmen to pick up Highland estates. The English managed to acquire 70 per cent of the Highlands and Islands by the last quarter of the nineteenth century,[41] and their commercial approach to landownership implemented by a new salaried bureaucracy of factors transformed life in the hills.

Scotland's rural underclass found themselves even more hard pressed by these developments than the English poor had been. For one thing there was no common land in Scotland. Large stretches of rough uninhabited land called 'commonties' were not 'commons' as understood south of the border because the rights to use them went with the land adjacent to them, so that they were essentially an undivided part of the private estates which surrounded them. Laws passed soon after the Union, in particular in 1695, hastened their abolition by providing a legal framework for their division between owners. Over tilled land the copyhold tenure based on the notion of customary rights respected at manorial courts which provided limited protection for the poor during England's enclosures did not exist. Land was simply worked on leases granted by proprietors: once the lease came to an end the lessee (and the subtenants and servants who depended on him) could be evicted perfectly legally. No separate parliamentary bills were required to enforce enclosure, as they had been in England and Wales, and there were therefore no enclosure commissioners to supervise the division of land rights and to provide some defence for the weak against the strong. As a result, enclosure was not a legal process as it had been south of the border; estates simply swept away the old system of 'runrig' (akin to England's open-field system and Ireland's 'rundale') and cut down the number of their farming tenants, often at great speed. 'Arguably, nowhere else in western Europe was agrarian economy and society altered so quickly and rapidly in the eighteenth century,' observed Professor Tom Devine of Strathclyde University.[42] A combination of these factors meant that very few of the public rights and concessions that had been granted through enclosure in England and Wales emerged in Scotland. Because there were no commons to divide up, the rural underclass would often be left with no rights whatsoever over land when enclosure took place and they had no option but to quit the land of their forebears; when their descendants from Scotland's burgeoning towns and cities started walking in the Scottish countryside, they found almost no public rights of way on which their passage would be guaranteed, as it would have in England, because it was marked on an enclosure award. A lucky few managed to get themselves allocated small crofts, usually on the edge of the land mass, deliberately made smaller than was needed to support a family so that the crofter would be dependent on seeking work from his landlord.

The crofters on the Isle of Skye who heard of the successes of the Irish Land League proved more responsive to the revolutionary ideas about landownership than even these events might suggest. They had recently been stripped of land known as The Braes on which they used to graze their animals because their landlord, Lord MacDonald, had decided to convert it to deer forest. The crofters drew up a petition asking Lord MacDonald to return them The Braes, but he refused and there was a rebellion which he tried to put down by evicting crofters. A sheriff-officer dispatched to serve the eviction notices was assaulted by a crowd of 150, who burned the notices on the spot. At what became known as the Battle of the Braes, policemen succeeded in arresting the leaders of the uprising. The dispossessed of Skye and many other parts of the Hebrides and Highlands formed a Highland Land League which grew rapidly in both town and countryside. It was not prepared to engage in the violence seen in Ireland, and never achieved the overthrow of Scotland's landowning class, but it did secure crofters a fair rent and security of tenure so long as rents were paid. The political agitation it fostered served to make land a priority issue in Scottish politics. 'The land is our birthright, even as the air, the light of the sun, and the water belong to us as our birthright,' declared the Reverend Donald MacCallum, a leader of the League.[43] Like the Diggers whose words he echoed, MacCallum and his comrades were emboldened by the Bible, which was translated into Scottish Gaelic in 1801. Individualism was not highly developed in Scotland: under the clan system the notion of individuality was suppressed—a man was simply, say, a Mackenzie. The Bible helped the men and women of the Highlands to see themselves as unique individuals in the sight of God. They also saw in the book the story of a chosen people sent into exile whose history they believed paralleled their own in spiritual, social, and political terms.[44]

The Highland Land War left its mark on urban Scotland. Many of those cramped in the tenements of Glasgow, Motherwell, and Dundee had only recently been expelled from the land of their forefathers, and some had seen relatives forced to emigrate to North America or Australia. They lent support to their Highland brethren: in 1882, for instance, 45,000 Glaswegians signed a petition on crofters' grievances. They also took their hostility to landowners into another wider land struggle, this time primarily about urban land which was beginning to gather pace both north and south of the border.

The power of rural landowners was mirrored by their counterparts in the cities to which the victims of the barons of the countryside had fled. The factories, houses, roads, hospitals, and town halls on which urban workers now depended could only be built with the agreement of landowners, who could make their consent subject to whatever conditions they chose. In doing so, they could reap perpetual financial benefit from those who laboured on the land they owned, merely by collecting rent. If the value of land increased because society needed a railway station or houses, those same owners pocketed the benefits of an increase in value which owed nothing to their efforts. In the early explosive phases of urban development, the spectacular transfer of wealth to a privileged few which this process entailed provoked increasing resentment.

An American land radical called Henry George attracted considerable interest with his critique of the whole idea of rent. 'There is in nature no such thing as a fee simple in land. . . . If we are all here by the equal permission of the Creator, we are all here with an equal title to the enjoyment of His bounty. . . . This is a right which is natural and unalienable,' George wrote in *Progress and Poverty*, a work which sold hundreds of thousands of copies in Britain and which George promoted in four British lecture tours.[45] George proposed a tax on all ground rents from land, ideally set at 100 per cent. Landowners would be able to charge a tenant in respect of any improvements they had made themselves, but the state would claim the rent they charged for the land itself—ground rent. In addition, they would be taxed on increases in land values. Not only would all this provide enough money to make income tax unnecessary; it would also force owners to release land lying idle for which they hoped one day to get a higher price. In the 1880s land reform societies reflecting Henry George's attitude to landownership, like the influential English Land Restoration League, sprang up in Britain. Leading Liberals of the early twentieth century like Joseph Chamberlain, Winston Churchill, and David Lloyd George seized on the idea of land taxation, and it became the official policy of the Liberal Party.[46] After dramatic battles over land taxation in Parliament, Lloyd George's proposals for land taxation, including a new Ministry of Lands, were actually being implemented in 1914 before the First World War thrust the matter into the background. Almost identical legislation was approved after a fight by both Houses of Parliament twenty years later, when the Labour government's 1931 Land Valuation Act introduced a tax of 1*d*. in the pound per year on the value of every acre of British land. This time the legislation was a casualty of the formation of the national government in 1931 and Labour's subsequent electoral disaster.[47]

Some wanted to go even further than the disciples of Henry George. The Land Nationalization Society wanted land taxation to be merely a step on the way to the total abolition of private landownership. In its People's Land Charter it called for the state to become supreme owner of all land as well as the minerals it harboured. Once county and county borough councils had been established in 1884, the Land Nationalization Society wanted them charged with the task of administering nationalized land in the interests of the community as a whole. George Bernard Shaw, Sidney Webb, and others in the newly formed Fabian Society advocated something different only in detail. They believed that changes in the conditions under which land was held were an absolutely fundamental and essential first step toward achieving socialism. 'The private appropriation of land [is] the source of those unjust privileges against which Socialism is aimed. . . . Public property in land is the basic economic condition of socialism,' declared Shaw.[48] The Fabians saw the introduction of ground rents as the first step on the way to community control of the land: land would be owned not by the state but by local authorities which would control its use. First, new local or regional bodies would receive the unearned income landowners currently received from rents through a tax on rent. This would generate so much revenue that it would meet the entire cost of local government and of social service provision. As the land tax finally reached 100 per cent it would replace private investment in industry and agriculture. Finally, as well as controlling much-needed investment, the local councils would take over both rural and urban land and manage it in the public interest.

The idea that landowners should be taxed on ground rents or on unearned increments in land value did not go away. In 1975 Harold Wilson's Labour government introduced the taxation of unearned increments on major development through his Community Land Act, which required local authorities to buy land in advance of major development so that the community as a whole could benefit from the resulting rise in land values; this was repealed by the incoming Conservative government in 1980. However, the twentieth century saw landowners successfully reassert the legitimacy of their claim to their holdings in the face of the nationalizer and even the taxers. An assumption took root that landowners were an interest whose rights had to be accepted by the rest of the community in spite of the peculiar character of the asset they controlled. Nonetheless the question mark which had been placed over that legitimacy, however briefly, lurked in the background as the struggle over competing claims on land use continued.

Access by Law

One man who had taken more than a passing interest in the land debates of the 1870s was a lawyer and Oxford academic called James Bryce, who became the Liberal MP for Tower Hamlets. A polymathic geologist, botanist, classicist, lawyer, and historian, Bryce took part in debates on the threatened enclosure of Esher Common and the need to create a public park in Paddington.[49] Then, on a trip back to Scotland, he found that huge areas which had been open to all a few years ago were now shut to walkers. Clearly, land purchase of the kind carried out by the City of London was out of the question: holdings were on a far bigger scale than those, say, around the capital and in any case landowners wished to hang on to them as lucrative deer forest, fishing beat, and grouse moor. Equally, the measures being taken in England to defend public footpaths and common land were of less use in Scotland because common rights did not exist there and public footpaths were almost non-existent: as we have seen, enclosure in Scotland had not been a legal process as it had been south of the border but had simply consisted of the reorganization of individual estates, without any of the concessions for the dispossessed which England's enclosure commissioners had secured.

Bryce concluded that radical action was needed to fill this void. He decided that Scotland needed exactly what is being proposed today—a general right of access, at least to mountain and moorland north of the border. He advanced a private member's bill first in 1884, then in 1888, 1892, and again in 1898 which would have overturned the law of trespass on uncultivated upland in Scotland and replaced it with a new legal right for any person to be present. These Access to Mountains (Scotland) Bills would have prevented landowners from obtaining interdicts against trespassers and would have removed ghillies' powers to get rid of walkers. As a result, the general public would have enjoyed a new legal right to roam at will in the hills. Bryce told the House during a debate on his bill in 1892 that he would like his measure to apply beyond Scotland as well in due course: 'I think, although the case is perhaps hardest on the Scottish people, it is desirable to ask the House to affirm the principle generally for the whole of the United Kingdom.'[50]

The arguments Bryce deployed to win over the House were three-fold. First, he pointed out that access to Scotland's hill country had degenerated markedly over the previous eighty years, in particular as the extent of land given over to deer stalking had increased. Wordsworth and Sir Walter Scott had been able to go wherever they chose in Scotland's hills, but since then the huge expansion of deer forest had led to the closure of vast tracts to walkers. Not only were walkers kept off land by armies of ghillies, but they were unable to find shelter because local people were forbidden by their landlords to take in overnight visitors. Bryce referred to one owner whose territory stretched for nearly forty miles who not only stationed ghillies to defend his domain but had even taken out an interdict against a

crofter to prevent the latter's pet lamb from trespassing into his preserve. Things were getting worse rather than better: indeed over the
previous eight years, since 1884, a further 380,000 acres had been added
to the deer forests. 'The geologist, the botanist, the painter, or the
simple pedestrian, who desires to climb the hills and enjoy mountain
air and scenery, though he is not rich enough to go to Switzerland,
all are treated with equal severity, and even when a man humbles himself to ask permission to do that which he ought to be able to claim
as a right, he usually meets with a refusal.'[51] Secondly, Bryce pointed
out that talking to landowners and sporting tenants, explaining to them
the need for access, and asking them to oblige, simply did not produce results. 'It used to be said—"All that is wanted is to make this
subject known and good feeling will do the rest." But, Sir, we have
waited a good many years for this good feeling on the part of landlords, and we discern no sign of its appearance.'[52] Thirdly, he drew
a comparison with conditions overseas, arguing that, as far as he knew,
the Highlands were the only place in the world where people were
prevented from walking freely over uncultivated ground: 'I have
travelled in almost every country where mountains are found, and
I have made inquiries but I have never heard of a single instance
in which the pedestrian, the artist, or the man of science has been
prevented from freely walking where he wished, not even in those
countries where the pursuit of game is most actively followed.'[53] As
a man who had climbed in Ireland, Israel, Poland, Hungary, the United
States, South America, the South Pacific, Australia, Egypt, India,
New Zealand, Korea, Morocco, Greece, Turkey, China, Japan, and
South Africa by the time he died, Bryce could claim some authority
for this observation. His speech referred in particular to the Alps, where
chamois hunting was not seen as a reason to exclude walkers. These
three considerations led to one conclusion, Bryce told his fellow
MPs: 'The only remedy is to declare that the people have the right
and ought to have the power to go freely over the mountains and glens
of their own country.'[54]

Bryce proposed a number of safeguards to ensure that his measures
did not unduly disadvantage landowners and occupiers. Land close
to dwellings and plantations of young trees were exempted from the
proposed right of access. People were not allowed to take dogs or

firearms or pursue game, to take birds' eggs, to destroy plant roots, to disturb sheep or cattle so as to cause damage to the owner and 'generally it should not apply to anything of a malicious or vexatious intent'.[55]

Perhaps because his approach was so considered, the parliamentary debate, which ran for nearly three hours in 1892, was marked by serious examination of the practicalities rather than impassioned posturing. One concern was that free access might damage deer stalking. Bryce was able to tell the House he had consulted many deer stalkers himself before concluding that free access would not cause any real harm to the sport. However, 'If it can be shown that it will injure sport, still I say the people are entitled to this right all the same.'[56] Bryce said landowners should be entitled to exclude others only around their houses to safeguard their privacy and over cultivated land where walking might cause damage. Elsewhere, land should be shared. 'Property in land is of a very different character from every other kind of property. Land is not property for our unlimited and unqualified use. Land is necessary so that we may live upon it and from it, and that people may enjoy it in a variety of ways; and I deny, therefore, that there exists or is recognised by our law or in natural justice, such a thing as an unlimited power of exclusion.'[57]

Bryce's opposition came mainly from deer stalkers and landowners in Scotland. His main support came from three groups. First, there was the growing band of people who used the countryside to pursue popular interests of the day. Botanical societies, geologists' associations, archaeological societies, and groups of amateur artists were springing up in most sizeable towns and cities. The Glasgow Geological Society, the Glasgow Philosophical Society, the Society of Painters in Water Colours, and the Royal Scottish Academy of Arts were among such organizations which drew up petitions backing Bryce's bill. Then there were the people of Scotland's growing cities who wanted to visit the countryside to escape from the urban environment. Edinburgh, Dunfermline, Paisley, Dundee, and Inverness sent in petitions along with the Convention of the Scottish Royal Burghs, while the people of Aberdeen showed their support by backing an Aberdeenshire MP who seconded Bryce. Finally there was support from some country areas. Sutherland County Council submitted a petition in support.

Bryce explained, 'It is a grievance severely felt that they [poor crofters] should be excluded from what has been recognised as the property of the clan . . . [and they themselves] hemmed in very often by barbed wire fences from going on land which, by right and equity, is the property of the clan, although the title is vested in the landlord.'[58] Bryce ended his speech with a burst of eloquence which retains its relevance:

The scenery of our country has been filched away from us just when we have begun to prize it more than ever before. It coincided with the greatest change that has ever passed over our people—the growth of huge cities and dense populations in many places outside those cities—and this change has made far greater than before the need for the opportunity of enjoying nature and places where health may be regained by bracing air and exercise, and where the jaded mind can rest in silence and solitude. . . . Man does not live by bread alone. The Creator speaks to his creatures through his works, and appointed the grandeur and loveliness of the mountains and glens and the silence of the moorlands lying open under the eye of Heaven to have their fitting influence on the thoughts of men, stirring their nature and touching their imaginations, chasing away cares and the dull monotony of every-day life, and opening up new and inexhaustible sources of enjoyment and delight. It is on behalf of these enjoyments, and those who need them most, and in the hope of preserving for the people one of the most precious parts of their national inheritance, that I ask the House to agree to this Resolution.[59]

In 1892 the House accepted the principle of Bryce's bill, resolving 'That in the opinion of the House, legislation is needed for the purpose of securing the right of the public to enjoy free access to uncultivated mountains and moorlands, especially in Scotland, subject to proper provisions for preventing any abuse of such right.'[60] Bryce pressed the Conservative government to take the matter further, and a few months later a government-sponsored bill similar to Bryce's received its first reading. A month later however Parliament was dissolved and the bill went with it. Bryce's own party, the Liberals, won the election in 1892, and he found himself in the Cabinet. So, however, did several prominent deer-stalking and grouse-shooting Liberals, and the Cabinet would not back him. He managed to present his bill again as a private member, in 1898, but without success. Later, when Bryce had become ambassador in Washington, his brother Annan took up the cudgels with a similar bill which he sought to bring before the House on three occasions (in 1900, 1908, and 1909), always unsuccessfully. Scotland, which had come within a hair's breadth of leading the way on access for the whole of Britain, remained the most cruelly inaccessible part of the kingdom.

The debates about access in Scotland nonetheless fostered interest south of the border. Thomas Ellis, who had been elected as the Liberal Member of Parliament for his native Merioneth in 1886, took up the cause of access to rural Wales, tabling a Mountains, Rivers, and Pathways (Wales) Bill in 1888. Interestingly, he was not a townsman seeking rural recreation but very much a countryman. He was the son of a tenant farmer and members of his family had suffered eviction. An agrarian radical, he believed that all the Celtic nations should unite to overthrow the excesses of landlordism. Many of his constituents were poor tenant farmers and agricultural labourers suffering considerable poverty at a time of agricultural depression and poor harvests, who were subjected to harsh conditions by their landlords. Ellis championed the cause of land reform in Wales and fought for improvements in the conditions of tenants and labourers like those which had recently been won in Ireland. His access bill sought to give the public a legal right 'for the purpose of recreation, or winberry gathering, or scientific research' to move freely over not only all mountains, moors, and wasteland in Wales but also to walk along all Welsh riverbanks, streamside, and lakesides.[61] It would also have provided a right to walk over the bed of any Welsh river, stream, or lake and to ride in a boat over all lakes and rivers. The bill aimed to stem the loss of public footpaths by providing that any paths which had been used for five successive years during the previous forty-nine should again be open to the public. The link Ellis made between the interests of the rural underclass and access together with his emphasis on access to water could have given the access debate a different flavour if his efforts had succeeded. In the event, the second-reading debate was adjourned and never resumed, and no similar bill for Wales was ever promoted again.

England had to wait until 1908 for a countryside access bill of its own. Meanwhile, the struggle there continued to focus on public footpaths and common land. To assert such rights as already existed, direct action was sometimes taken. In 1884, for example, a dispute broke out over the public's right to use paths in the 1,000-acre Knole Park on the eastern edge of Sevenoaks in Kent.[62] The owner, Lord Sackville-West, wanted to close some public footpaths through his park and to downgrade a bridleway to footpath status. He erected stout posts over the bridleway as it entered the park, thereby preventing use by mothers with prams, invalids in bath chairs, butchers' boys with their bicycles, and so on. Both local residents and navvies building a new railway nearby were incensed. One night a crowd of more than 1,000 people assembled and broke down the posts with picks, hammers, and files. A horse was ridden ceremoniously three or four times through the gate to reassert the track as a bridleway. The crowd then marched up to Knole House, a 365-room mansion, hammered on the door, and, when Lord Sackville-West failed to appear, dumped the offending posts there. The following night an even larger crowd gathered, and men dressed up as women wheeled prams up and down the path. Although these men were later prosecuted for trespass, public opinion seems to have favoured the protestors: the *Sevenoaks Chronicle and Kentish Advertiser*, for instance, condemned Lord Sackville-West's action in a leading article in which it linked the dispute over rights of access at Knole with James Bryce's attempts to secure a public right of access to Scotland's hill country.[63]

Footpath societies sprang up to protect rights of access in Kendal, Henley-on-Thames, York, Bromley, Manchester, Edinburgh, and Llandudno among other places. The Birmingham Association for the Preservation of Open Spaces and Public Footpaths, formed in 1883, was typical.[64] As well as saving the Lickey Hills from sale for housing by raising money from the public and the Cadbury family, it used the courts and direct action to defend public rights. Such efforts were particularly necessary in Midland counties like Warwickshire where enclosure had been so thoroughgoing that only a handful of commons had survived. One of the few remaining commons in the county was at Yarningdale, near Henley-in-Arden. Here in 1884 commoners found themselves suddenly prevented from cutting gorse and turf and pasturing their animals over a section of the common which had been summarily staked off with railway sleepers. The Association gave the offender a week to dismantle the illegal enclosure. When he failed to comply, the Association's Secretary supervised the removal of the sleepers by a party of commoners in the presence of the village policeman. The same procedure was followed when stretches of road verge were unlawfully seized. The Association fought many illegal footpath closures in a similar manner, while also trying to get existing footpaths better maintained. Here too their work, and that of other local societies as well as the national Commons, Footpaths, and Open Spaces Preservation Society was echoed by parliamentary activity. In 1888, 1889, 1890, and 1892, James Bryce, George Shaw-Lefevre, and others unsuccessfully sought legislation through private members' bills to protect the public interest in public footpaths and road verges. Thus under their Footpaths and Roadside Wastes Bill of 1888 they tried to get highway authorities in England and Wales empowered to maintain and improve public footpaths, to put up path signposts, and to prepare and distribute maps of public paths in their areas.[65] This bill would also have laid upon highway authorities a legal duty to prevent as far as possible the closure or obstruction of any public or reputed public path within their areas and to take action in the courts in pursuit of this duty which would have been empowered to order that closures and obstructions should be rectified and to award damages. Magistrates would have been obliged to inquire into any obstructions reported to them by three or more ratepayers and to publish a report of their conclusions, and similar provisions would have protected roadside waste.

These proposals were more radical than the measures on public paths which were to come into effect in the 1950s, and Bryce and his colleagues got nowhere in promoting them in the 1880s. Early in the next century, however, it became clear that the public wanted even more extensive provision made for public access to the countryside. A Liberal MP called Charles Trevelyan recognized this and used his success in the private members' ballot of 1908 to promote a version of Bryce's bill which specifically included England and Wales as well as Scotland. As a result, 1908 saw two bills promoted in Parliament—an Access to Mountains (Scotland) Bill promoted by Annan Bryce and an Access to Mountains Bill promoted by Charles Trevelyan relating to England as well as Scotland. Unlike James and Annan Bryce, Charles Trevelyan came from a landowning background (he willed his Northumberland estate to the National Trust). A radical Liberal who later became a member of the Labour Party, Trevelyan became interested in access because of growing demand for a right to roam among his constituents in industrial west Yorkshire. His bill received a second reading, and when the house divided 190 MPs voted in favour of it and 61 against. But its progress in committee was blocked by the delaying tactics of its opponents and it never reached the statute book. So, in the words of one of the leading access campaigners of the twentieth century, Tom Stephenson, 'What had appeared to be a glimpse of the promised land turned out to be a mirage.'[66] The failure of Trevelyan's bill ushered in half a century in which the North of England was to become the focal point of the struggle for rural access.

Battle for the Peak

The moorlands of the Derbyshire Pennines encompass some wild scenery easily within reach of large cities. Public paths are few and far between, yet some of the most remote and rugged areas lie within a few miles of Sheffield, Leeds, Manchester, Barnsley, and Huddersfield. Once the moors were freely accessible, but just as in the Scottish moors and glens, much of them had been closed off within the memory of people still living in the 1930s. Two types of owner were responsible for the closures: the private owners of vast estates who chose to turn their moors over to the increasingly fashionable sport of grouse shooting; and the water boards which gathered water on the moors, whose purity they claimed walkers would imperil, even though they were happy to lease their land for sheep grazing and grouse shooting. In the early 1930s, 15,000 people left Sheffield every Sunday to explore the Peak District, and a similar number flocked out of Manchester, where each Sunday morning queues of ramblers stretched down the approaches to Piccadilly Station. Others used bicycles—young shop and office workers sometimes being followed by their parents on tandems. Local newspapers devoted whole pages of their weekend editions to describing outings and routes to walk in the countryside.[67] The Peak's few paths were so heavily used that the most popular became quagmires in wet weather, while those trudging along them 'looked longingly at the acres of empty peat bogs, moorlands and the tops, which were forbidden territory', in the words of a man who was to play a key part in the drama of access in the Peak, Benny Rothman.[68]

The interests of the thousands of enthusiasts involved were diverse. Botanical societies flourished in the towns and villages of Yorkshire, Lancashire, and Derbyshire, their members including miners, craftsmen, and mill-workers, many of whom lived in grinding poverty yet at weekends rambled for 30 miles or more. 'There are a class of men in Manchester and all the manufacturing districts of Lancashire who know the name and habitat of every plant within a day's walk from their dwellings', wrote Mrs Gaskell in her novel *Mary Barton* in 1848.[69] Geology was another popular passion, but many went to the countryside simply for the release it offered from cramped and smoky towns. One man typical in many respects of the northern countryside activists of the time was Tom Stephenson, who was later to become one of the century's leading access campaigners, serving for twenty-one years as secretary to the Ramblers' Association. On his first Saturday after starting work as a labourer at the age of 13, Tom Stephenson set off out of his home town of Whalley in Lancashire to climb the moorland mass rising above it—Pendle Hill. 'That was on a winter's day in March . . . and it was a wonderful clear frosty day, a bright blue sky. . . . Now from Pendle Hill if I looked southwards I saw a great range of factories, factory chimneys—Colne, Nelson and so on. While the other way . . . I saw right to the Pennines, all covered in snow and bursting in bright sunlight, . . . and it was just wild country, nothing at all. And the great attraction there was that so easily you lost any sense of industrialisation or civilisation for that matter: you felt you were alone in the world,' he told me in an interview in 1977.[70] The lure of the moors was so great that by the age of 20 Stephenson had explored the whole of the Pennines, the Cheviots, and the Forest of Bowland right up to the Roman Wall, 'walking every weekend I could get, taking a bicycle out, dumping it and walking all day.' Men and women like Tom Stephenson were not content to hike only along such roads and public paths as they could find. He told me: 'I like the feel of walking on a completely trackless piece of moorland . . . I would rather walk on the open moor than on a well-made footpath. . . . I like to walk alone and feel I'm alone in the world. And I can get that on the moors more than anywhere else in the country.' Leading activist of the 1930s Phil Barnes explained what he and his kind wanted in a booklet published in 1934 as part of the campaign for an Access to Mountains Bill. In this he makes it clear that his longing to roam free over the moors would require far more than additional footpaths even if these had been on offer. Barnes wrote: 'No true hill lover wants to see more made footpaths in the wild heart of the Peak each nicely labelled with trim signposts and bordered by notices telling one not to stray. What he does want is the simple right to wander where fancy moves him—to seek the highest ridges, to scramble along the rocky sides of cloughs. In a wilderness of this sort a public footpath to which one is expected to stay is a restriction which offends, although the moor may not be fenced off with a physical barrier.'[71]

Matters were exacerbated by the virtual absence of recreation alternatives to the inaccessible moors. Northerners in the 1920s and 1930s seem to have made use of some *de facto* access around field edges just like their counterparts in the south. But in many areas the inhospitable climate and poor soils militated against much cultivation and few fields existed: the built-up area stopped and the moors started. In lowland Britain, in contrast, in a more varied landscape, people could often find somewhere to walk even if they were barred from some large stretches of land, while public paths and roads were far denser on the ground than they were in the heart of the Peak. Most importantly, the north presented no other environment which could offer a sense of wildness, freedom, and 'naturalness'—an experience which southerners were able to gain on the seashore or on the then extensive untilled chalk downlands over both of which *de facto* freedom to roam existed at this time.

Resentment against those who barred workers from the wilderness was heightened by a more generalized grievance against those who were doing the barring. The men who owned the grouse moors or who shot over them were often the owners of the factories, mills, and mines in which the would-be walkers had been exploited at work for decades. People with a strong tradition of nonconformist independence were beginning to discover socialism. Northerners had returned from the trenches of the First World War with the firm conviction that, since they had fought for their country and so many of their comrades had died for it, they ought to be able to walk in its moors and mountains. In the North as elsewhere, the war had served to strip away the last remaining vestiges of Edwardian deference. The Depression of the 1930s hit the industrial areas of Lancashire and Yorkshire particularly hard. According to Benny Rothman, 'Living conditions were desperately bad with bug-ridden and verminous houses. Not many had gardens, there were very few trees, shrubs or flowers in the soul-destroying waste. The only way to enjoy a little fresh air and sunshine was to escape to the countryside.'[72] Growing bitterness was eventually to focus upon a Derbyshire moor which has acquired legendary status in the long struggle for access to the countryside of Britain.

Kinder Scout's peat-topped gritstone plateau rises 3 miles to the north-east of the little village of Hayfield in the far north-west of Derbyshire. The Hayfield, Kinder Scout, and District Ancient Footpaths and Bridle-paths Association was one of the footpath protection societies which had sprung up all over Britain in the 1870s. Public paths crossing the wild gritstone moors of the Peak District were of enormous value for recreation but because settlement in such inhospitable country had been sparse, such routes were few and far between, often embodying old packhorse trails. Thus any attempt by landowners to filch the rights embodied in public paths assumed particular importance. One of the first acts of the infant Hayfield Association was to publish a guide to walking in the area complete with map and footpaths clearly marked 'so as to prevent as far as possible annoyance to landowners from excursionists and others' who might otherwise trespass over the unfenced land on either side of the paths.[73] In spite of this conciliatory approach, the Association soon found itself embroiled in confrontation when in 1877 landowners closed one of the few apparently public paths in the area so as to safeguard grouse shooting. The path involved, which led north-eastwards from Hayfield along a stream called William Clough and under the western edge of Kinder Scout was used for an annual pilgrimage by Methodists in an area in which Methodism was a potent force. A twenty-year struggle during which £1,000 was raised to finance the fight for the path eventually culminated in its ceremonial reinstatement to the accompaniment of a brass band. This victory did not however put an end to concern in the area about access rights. On the contrary, it drew attention to the shortage of access away from the William Clough footpath and gave the people of the area a keen interest in the access issue.

In 1930 members of a group called the Workers' Sports Federation found themselves prevented by threats from gamekeepers from walking over some particularly enticing moors near Kinder Scout. Some of them, including Benny Rothman, decided that an appropriate response might be a mass trespass on this site which had already been the focus of so much struggle. On 24 April 1932, Workers' Federation members and ramblers gathered at Hayfield. The event had been publicized in advance and there was a strong police presence. About 400 set off en masse along the William Clough public footpath. Then, spreading out in a long line, they advanced up the steep, grassy, and forbidden slopes of the Kinder plateau. Here, they encountered a band of gamekeepers armed with sticks. There were skirmishes and one keeper was hurt in a scuffle, though he was able to walk back to Hayfield. At the edge of the plateau top, the ramblers held a victory meeting, then they went back as they had come: 'We were proud of our effort and proudly marched back the way we had come,' recalled Benny Rothman.[74]

At Hayfield, however, Rothman and four of his comrades were arrested by waiting police. The group were tried at Derby Assizes the following July in front of a jury consisting of brigadier-generals, colonels, aldermen, and country gentlemen. They were charged with riotous assembly and assault upon the gamekeeper who was hurt. One of the trespassers, Tony Gillett, a university student who came from a wealthy banking family, was given the chance to have his sentence of two months commuted to a reprimand if he apologized. But when asked by the judge whether he was ashamed of what he had done, Gillett replied, 'No sir, I would do it again.' Gillett and five other trespassers went to prison for terms of up to six months. Even before these sentences were passed, thousands of ramblers assembled at the scene of the trespass to express their solidarity with the accused. Ten thousand people turned up at an annual demonstration in support of an Access to Mountains Bill at Winnats Pass that June. Two further mass trespasses took place in Derbyshire, the second of which was only halted by mounted police with Alsatian dogs. Ramblers in the South showed their support by assembling for a rally at Leith Hill, Surrey, in fifty busloads.

Enacting Access

This upsurge of direct action in the Peak and elsewhere turned pent-up frustration into a significant political force. A perhaps surprising amount of feeling in the country swung behind the mobilizing ramblers and against the landowners. It began to look as though Parliament might at last respond to the calls for public access to the countryside to which it had turned a deaf ear for half a century. In 1938 the Labour Member for Shipley in Yorkshire, Arthur Creech Jones, prepared to introduce an Access to Mountains Bill, which unlike its eight predecessors looked set to reach the statute book. Victory for the ramblers was not, however, at hand. The landowners, now expertly organized, set about trying to savage the bill during its passage through Parliament. Their interests were served, probably unwittingly, by an unexpected willingness on the part of the bill's supposed supporters to make the right kind of concessions. Creech Jones was so anxious to lend his name to the first Access to Mountains Act that he lost sight of the need to ensure that it did its job. The general secretary of the Commons, Footpaths, and Open Spaces Preservation Society, who acted as intermediary between the ramblers and the landowners, was also accommodating. In the end, the Creech Jones bill did become law, as the Access to Mountains Act of 1939, but what it provided was not a general right of access over moor and mountain subject to safeguards to prevent damage, but a procedure for the establishment of legal access over specific areas of land. This fell far short of the aims which campaigners had been pursuing since the time of Bryce, and also fell far short of the provision for general access over all urban commons which had been established in the 1925 Law of Property Act. Under the 1939 act, a landowner, a local authority, or an organization approved by the Minister of Agriculture could submit an application to the Minister for an access order. On land over which an order had been made, members of the public would be entitled to roam freely without being treated as trespassers.

Elaborate machinery provided for the receipt and consideration of objections to an order, if necessary through the holding of a public inquiry. The Minister might then reject the order or impose limitations and conditions on when and how access could take place.

The 1939 act's failure to create a general right of access did not only condemn ramblers to endless battles over individual sites. It also created insurmountable financial problems for them, by requiring applicants for orders to circulate six-inch maps to everyone having a legal interest in the land involved and, at the Ministry's discretion, to deposit money to cover the costs of the public inquiries and any other expenses incurred in making the orders. Once orders were made, the applicants had to erect and maintain notices on the land to which the orders applied; in the Peak District alone this could amount to 500 notices.[75] As only ramblers' groups were likely to apply for orders, it soon became apparent that if they did so on any significant scale they would soon be bankrupted.

Orders had other disadvantages for ramblers besides the cost. People legally present on land covered by an order stood the risk of being treated more harshly in some respects than they would have been if they had been trespassing. Walking on land covered by an order outside the prescribed period became a criminal offence. A range of activities such as dropping litter and taking a plant-cutting on land covered by an order even when access was legal also became offences for which offenders could be prosecuted and fined. In the late 1930s, many ramblers had started to trespass widely over the moors. Access orders could have made their position worse by criminalizing trespass in the lambing, nesting, and shooting seasons and creating legal access only for a few inclement months. In the words of Tom Stephenson, 'That simple little Bill of five clauses was so mauled, mangled and amended by Parliament as to become a monstrous, unrecognisable changeling, not an access to mountains bill, but a landowners' protection bill.'[76]

The access campaigners were left with a dilemma: should they try to make use of an unsatisfactory piece of legislation, or should they lobby for its repeal and replacement with something entirely different? Since it was they who would be most likely to apply for orders under the act, their action would determine the extent to which it was implemented. The outbreak of war resolved the question. They decided to apply for no orders for the time being, making a public statement saying they did not feel it proper to apply for orders at the present time but expressing the hope that landowners would dedicate new paths for public use 'as some contribution to the cause of freedom in which landowners and public are united'.[77] The landowners did not respond.

Action to open up the countryside ceased for the duration. However, the same cannot be said of thinking about the access question. On the contrary, as world war raged, Britain saw more concentrated reflection on the future of the countryside than ever occurred before or since. The War Cabinet were convinced that a working class embittered by the Depression and wary of a repeat of Passchendale and the Somme needed to be persuaded to fight for a country many of them thought of as belonging to the ruling classes rather than to them. Churchill reluctantly accepted that people needed to be promised a fairer post-war future in which all would be rewarded for contributing to victory. A series of committees set to work to shape a new social contract which would provide not only health care, education, welfare, and employment but also a stake in the much-loved countryside of the land for which they were being asked to fight. An architect and town planner called John Dower was asked to devise national parks in England and Wales where none existed at the time, even though they were to be found in imperial territories like Canada and Kenya. Dower came up with the idea of national parks in which land would not be acquired by the state as occurred overseas but would remain in private ownership while being administered by special authorities involving town dwellers as well as local people, which would seek to conserve their natural beauty and to promote outdoor recreation provision within them. However Dower, a keen hill-walker with a long-term association with the open-air movement, considered that parks of this kind would not be enough to meet rural recreation needs after the war. Of the 1939 Access to Mountains Act he complained: 'No access rights whatever are secured directly by the Act',[78] pointing out that it simply provided cumbersome machinery by which access rights had to be fought and won over individual areas. Dower urged that as well as providing national parks, a post-war government should also revert to the Bryce approach to access in the rest of the countryside as well as in the new parks. He proposed a new legal right to roam at will over all uncultivated land throughout England and Wales, whether or not the land involved was included in one of his proposed new national parks. This arrangement would open up vast swathes of chalk downland turf in the south, heathland, moor, mountain and coastline, subject to a small number of regulations to prevent damage and a minimum of excepted areas where free wandering would be incompatible with some other publicly necessary use of the land.[79]

Dower published his report in 1945, and Clement Attlee's new Labour government lost little time in appointing a ten-strong committee to evaluate his proposals. Sir Arthur Hobhouse, who was appointed chairman of the committee, had been a solicitor and a farmer. At the time he was chairman both of Somerset County Council and of the County Councils' Association and a man known for his pleasant personality and conciliatory manner. His committee included a land-owner, a farmer, a county clerk, an officer of the Minister of Agriculture, and ramblers—notably Tom Stephenson and John Dower himself. The Hobhouse Committee endorsed Dower's plans for national parks more or less as they stood, but they set up a separate subcommittee to consider access and footpaths, since it was clear that they would require substantial legislation. Dower's recommendation that the British people should enjoy a legal right to move freely over all uncultivated land in England and Wales secured the committee's unanimous support. It went on to devise detailed proposals for the implementation of such a right.[80]

In one respect the committee went further than Dower. On top of his proposed general right of access to uncultivated rural land they suggested that such a right should also apply to certain stretches of water. In particular they had in mind the Norfolk Broads, man-made lakes over and in which the right to move around had been hotly disputed. They also proposed a public right to navigate freely over lakes nominated by local planning authorities in areas of special landscape importance and those close to freely accessible land. The committee proposed a procedure for exempting land from a right of access—a procedure which would have involved advertisement, objection, and local inquiry—if a piece of land was to be used for a purpose incompatible with freedom to roam, like quarrying or horse-racing. If the land were to be converted to improved farmland or forest (and at that time farming in particular was considered a matter of great national importance) then the committee felt that provision should be made for the retention of footpaths. There would also be provision for the withdrawal of access on a temporary basis, in particular to enable farmers to reseed portions of rough grazing land. In these cases, planning authorities would be enabled to issue a licence withdrawing the land in question from access designation for up to twelve months, with provision for the licence to be renewed for up to a maximum of three years. In addition, authorities would be empowered to limit access to nature reserves and archaeological sites. Access would be extended to all rural commons, as it had already been to urban commons. If an owner or occupier could demonstrate that the rental or capital value of his land had been materially reduced over a period of years by the access designation, then he would be entitled to compensation or to require the authority to purchase his interest. The committee were divided on one detail only: a majority felt that it should be possible to withdraw land from the access designation on the grounds of serious and wanton damage by members of the public. They recommended that the Minister be empowered in exceptional cases and at the request of the planning authority, to withdraw access land temporarily from access designation on the grounds that serious, wanton, and recurrent damage was being caused as the result of its use as access land.

Because the Hobhouse Committee had opted for a right of access which singled out certain types of land which would be covered while leaving the existing law of trespass in place everywhere else, and the land singled out was not always readily identifiable on the ground, they proposed that county councils should as a first step in the introduction of the partial right of access they had advocated prepare maps showing the uncultivated land to which a legal right of access should apply. The draft map, on a 6-inch Ordnance Survey base, was to be submitted to the Minister of Town and Country Planning within one year. Anyone could object either to the inclusion or exclusion of any land on the draft map during a period of six months after this, and all such objections would be available for public inspection. The council would seek to resolve such objections itself, but once six months had elapsed from the closing date for objections, the Minister would appoint an inspector to hold a public inquiry on the draft map and make a report to the Minister, which would also be available to the public. Thereupon the Minister would make an order confirming the draft map subject to such alterations as he saw fit. Finally the planning authority would publish a statutory map at 6 inches to the mile, and deposit and advertise it. If a county council failed to prepare a draft map, the Minister could direct that such a map be prepared on behalf of and at the expense of the authority in default.

At first, it seemed as if Attlee's government would rubber-stamp the scheme sketched by Dower and to which Sir Arthur Hobhouse's committee—not least its farmer, landowner, and Ministry of Agriculture members—had given so much thought. However, as landowners outside the Committee pointed out difficulties, the Cabinet and in particular the man who would be responsible for countryside legislation, Lewis (later Sir Lewis) Silkin, the Minister of Town and Country Planning, began to falter. Under the pressures of government, Ministers lost sight of the wartime vision of rewards for heroes and became bogged down in arbitrating between competing interests. They decided that though there would be national parks, access should be improved incrementally rather than in the big bang of the creation of a new right. And this meant reliance on mechanisms resembling those of the discredited 1939 act rather than Hobhouse's proposals.

A Law at Last

Silkin's National Parks and Access to the Countryside Bill, published in 1949, turned out to be a disappointment for walkers. Silkin clearly did believe it was important that people should be enabled to roam freely over uncultivated countryside: he devoted a whole section of his bill—Part V—to access to what he called 'open country', which his act defined as mountain, moor, heath, down, cliff, and foreshore. But while Hobhouse would have granted a legal right of access to all such land, Silkin chose instead to provide machinery whereby county councils could secure access only over specified stretches of 'open country'. He later advised that they should use this machinery only in cases where they considered this 'necessary'. Thus over land where *de facto* freedom to roam appeared to exist, no action would be necessary and thus no legal right of access would be created.

Nonetheless, Silkin was convinced his measures would bring about fundamental change. Winding up the second-reading debate on the bill in 1949, he declared:

Now at last we shall be able to see that the mountains of Snowdonia, the Lakes and the waters of the Broads, the moors and dales of the Peak, the South Downs and the tors of the West Country belong to the people as a right and not as a concession. This is not just a Bill. It is a charter—a people's charter for the open-air, for the hikers and ramblers, for everyone who loves to get out into the open air and enjoy the countryside. Without it they are fettered, deprived of their powers of access and facilities needed to make holidays enjoyable. With it the countryside is theirs to preserve, to cherish, to enjoy and to make their own.[81]

At first, some walkers were infected by this enthusiasm. At least the 1939 arrangements, which effectively left it to ramblers' groups to take the initiative, were being replaced by elaborate new responsibilities for public authorities. As we have seen (pages 35–8) the basic tool provided by the bill and subsequent act to county councils to enable them to secure access to specific sites was the 'access agreement'—a relatively sophisticated tool which maximizes efficiency by combining recreation with other uses of land, like stock grazing or game rearing, and which also enables the landowner to reclaim total exclusion at pre-agreed times, for instance when he or she wishes to shoot grouse or protect lambing ewes. The act provided elaborate powers to enable the public to take advantage of access where it had been created; and it empowered councils to make access orders where they were unable to secure access agreements. Both councils and the Minister could acquire land compulsorily for access if the Minister considered this absolutely necessary.

To provide strategic logic in the implementation of the Part V powers, the 1949 act required every county council throughout England and Wales to prepare a 'review map' within two years of the passing of the act identifying all the land within its area which came within the definition of 'open country'. Each council also had to prepare a written statement explaining where it proposed to take action to secure access. Any member of the public could make representations about the review map and its accompanying statement, and where an objector and the county council could not resolve their differences, the Minister was required to hold a public inquiry or allow the representations of such people to be considered by an inspector he appointed. Within one year of the completion of its review of open country and access needs, each council had to publish along with a map of open country an explanation of what action it had taken on access. Thereafter it had to prepare, keep up to date, and make available to the public a map of land covered by access agreements, orders, and land purchase, while maps and signs could be posted on the land involved. If the Minister was dissatisfied with the action any county council was taking, he could direct it to make an access order or make such an order himself.

The Wrong Answer

At the time it all seemed quite a business, even though not all were sure it justified Silkin's hyperbole. It seems clear that Silkin himself would certainly have expected that by our own day Britain would be peppered with access sites created under his act. If so, he would have been horribly disappointed. The access provisions of the 1949 act have been one of the most spectacular flops of post-war legislation. Fifty years on, very little land is covered by them. In south-west England, access agreements are virtually non-existent, apart from a smattering in Exmoor. In the Midlands the vast majority of councils have ignored the powers, with the exception of Staffordshire. In the South-East and East Anglia the picture is similar: here Surrey and Hampshire County Councils are a modest exception. A small number of agreements have been made in national parks other than Exmoor, like Snowdonia and the Yorkshire Dales, and in just two of the parks the 1949 provisions have actually made a significant difference. These are the Peak District and the Lake District national parks. The provisions have had no impact on access in Northern Ireland, to which the access provisions were extended in 1983; and although some agreements have been made in Scotland in recent years (using powers granted in 1967), the total amount of land they cover is small. Throughout the United Kingdom, such access agreements as have been made have tended to be haphazard, infrequent, and opportunistic. Access orders have had even less effect: only two have ever been made. All told, land covered by access agreements, orders, and acquisition is certainly no more than half of one per cent of the land of the United Kingdom.

The failure of the 1949 machinery is the more remarkable in view of the success of such agreements as have been made. Landowners and walkers alike are generally happy with arrangements which allow landowners to retain control over their land while councils shoulder the burden of managing public access and walkers enjoy the freedom to roam open spaces, deviating spontaneously from the regular path. So why have the elaborate arrangements of the 1949 act been so little used?

Part of the answer lies in the attitudes of the county councils in England and Wales on which Silkin decided to place so much reliance. In 1949, most of these were Conservative-controlled and not anxious to become the agents of a reforming Labour government. In any case they were suspicious of central government initiatives of any colour, distrusting the metropolitan bureaucrats behind them. They considered Whitehall out of touch with what happened on their own patches and as representing a type which country people of all classes tended to dislike and resent—the invading townsperson. Large-scale landowners played a dominant role on many shire councils (as they still do), and these people were naturally particularly dubious about the idea of public access. Less privileged councillors tended to share their betters' resistance to the idea of the intrusion into their areas of charabanc-loads of walkers. Councillors knew that their local constituents often avoided the access problems encountered by outsiders: landowners who would bar ramblers from the towns might allow local villagers to go where they liked. The shires therefore responded to the new opportunity to open up the countryside with a marked lack of enthusiasm.

Less than two years after the 1949 bill won royal assent, Attlee's team was replaced by the government of Winston Churchill, heralding thirteen years of unbroken Conservative rule. Several members of Churchill's Cabinet were at least as lukewarm as the average Tory county councillor towards the idea of opening up the countryside for the delight of the visiting townsman. Harold Macmillan took over as Minister of Housing and Local Government, presiding over the assessment of many of the review maps and accompanying statements. He had married into the family of the Duke of Devonshire and was often invited to shoot over grouse moors which were barred to walkers, like the 14,000 acres of Barden Moor and Barden Fell, which rise above the little settlement of Bolton Abbey north of Skipton on the Duke of Devonshire's Yorkshire domains. Macmillan considered walkers' demands for access to these moors 'outrageous', according to Dr Judith Rossiter of Cambridge University, who has studied the operation of the access powers of the 1949 act.[82] Certainly the associations and cultural background of Macmillan and his colleagues gave them a different attitude to the proper balance between privacy and public access from that of their Labour predecessors. As the review maps arrived, Macmillan and his successors declined to use their powers to direct that action be taken in almost every case where the issue arose. The first thirty-one councils to acknowledge that open country existed in their areas insisted that no action whatsoever was needed to open it up. Seven councils simply declared that no open country existed in their areas. Even in cases where incontrovertible evidence existed of the public being barred on the ground, as on Devon moorland indicated on the review map as open country but shut off behind barbed wire fences and padlocked gates, the Minister was content to let the matter rest.[83] As so many councils were doing almost nothing, and the government was not protesting, any council thinking of taking action tended to get diverted instead into what seemed more urgent issues.

There were several clauses which enabled Tory councils and governments to subvert Silkin's intentions. The first of these was the restriction of the act's powers to instances where access was perceived to be a problem and where a clear need for access existed. Judith Rossiter explains that advice from the Ministry 'discouraged action by local planning authorities unless there was very strong evidence of interference with *de facto* rights and gave no guidance for situations in which intermediate degrees of inconvenience to members of the public were encountered.'[84] This and subsequent advice from the Ministry enabled local planning authorities to avoid action unless there was very strong evidence of interference with *de facto* rights or unless access was being forcefully barred, and in either case a clear need for access to a particular area also existed. Had the practice developed of making access agreements over stretches of open country from which the public were not being barred and where landowners condoned or even encouraged trespass, things might have been very different. In recent years, many of the access agreements that have been made involve the formalization of *de facto* access. The landowner benefits from by-laws to manage access and the public benefit through the assurance that they have a legal right to be present, together with better information about the site. If the government had encouraged more such agreements to have been made in the early days, councils would have been denied the excuse that there was no need for them to act. They would have built up expertise in securing access agreements which would have stood them in good stead when stepping in where access was denied. Landowners might also have been reassured that they had little to fear from access agreements, and access agreements might have come to be accepted as part of life. As it was, the act's provisions came to be associated only with troublesome situations which councils preferred to avoid.

As it turned out, apparent *de facto* freedom to wander over a stretch of open country was not necessarily to be of much use. The potential for ploughing up such land had been clearly demonstrated during the war, yet the 1949 act offered no protection against the loss of recreational amenity which went with this. The fate of East Sussex shows how blind Silkin was to this danger. In its response to the Ministry in 1951, the council maintained that no action was needed to make access agreements over the rolling grassland of the South Downs because roaming was allowed by custom and many rights of way crossed the area.[85] Over the following thirty years, the Downs were ploughed up even more comprehensively than they had been during the war. By 1980, 95 per cent of the downland turf of the South Downs had been lost mainly to the plough.[86] Access agreements could have checked both ploughing and scrub encroachment, another threat to the turf. The subsidy-driven boom in agriculture encouraged farmers to plough up what had been marginal land. Nearly 70 per cent of the heathland of Dorset, most of it freely open to walkers, was turned over to intensive farmland or conifer plantation in the fifty years up to 1983.[87] Heathland once occurred, though on a much smaller scale, in the South Downs, where assemblies of acid-loving plants grew side by side with lime-tolerant ones on deposits of wind-blown silt or loess which overlay the chalk; almost none of this remains.[88] Today, stretches of open country with *de facto* freedom to wander still exist in corners of Britain from County Antrim to Orkney and from the Scillies to the North and South Downs. But still no machinery exists to defend walkers' interests in these areas when they are threatened by changes of use which would destroy their usefulness for walkers.

If Silkin had legislated for a general right of access over all uncultivated land as Dower and Hobhouse had urged, a new right would have come into being which could not have been removed subsequently without a lot of protest. Such a right would still have had to be enforced, presumably by county councils which would still have been at least as reluctant to perform this role as they were to implement the spirit of the 1949 act. Nonetheless, walkers on uncultivated land would have known they had a legal right to be present even if their local council was not going to help them enforce it, and they would have been more confident because of this. Landowners seeking to exclude them illegally would have faced the considerable problem of creating sufficient obstructions. Walkers would have been able to pressure councils to do their enforcement duty and could have made comparisons with more vigorous authorities—a potent political mobilizer. There would then have been a levelling up process, with ramblers' groups concentrating their resources in areas where councils were laggard. At the same time, Hobhouse's proposals to safeguard the legitimate interests of landowners and occupiers, had they been implemented as well, would have provided sophisticated machinery to enable owners and occupiers to defend their position.

What happened over access under Attlee's government can be contrasted with what happened about planning. Two years before Silkin's 1949 National Parks and Access to the Countryside Act became law, he stripped landowners of a right far more economically valuable than the right to exclude other people—the right to 'develop' land through building or quarrying. The Town and Country Planning

Act of 1947, which nationalized the right to develop and required landowners to seek to get it back through local authorities granting them planning permission, nonetheless came into effect with no great difficulty and no succeeding government has chosen to reverse or even seriously limit it. Why? One reason is that the planning system does not depend heavily on vigorous initiative on the part of local councils: the burden of initiation lies with the landowner, who must make an application for planning permission before anything can happen. The nationalization of development rights therefore proceeded whether councils were enthusiastic, lukewarm, or hostile towards it. The change involved also occurred in one fell swoop, taking in the entire country from top to toe. Thus the nationalization of development rights automatically dispossessed all landowners everywhere, without penalizing a few while leaving others in the clear.

In the 1960s, the idea of improving access to open country underwent something of a revival. Harold Wilson's government extended the power to make access agreements and the like to Scotland in its Countryside (Scotland) Act 1967. This included a definition of open country widened to embrace woodland, hill, and any waterways within or contiguous to such land and to mountain, moor, heath, cliff, and foreshore. The newly created Countryside Commission for Scotland was required to consult from time to time with local planning authorities and with bodies representing owners and occupiers in order to determine what land fell within this definition and to consider what action should be taken for securing public access to it whether by agreement, order, or acquisition. However, local councils were not required to prepare review maps and make proposals which would be subject to government assessment, as those in England and Wales had been in 1949. The Countryside Act of 1968 widened the definition of 'open country' for England and Wales to include all woodland, lakeside, riverbank, and canalside. Then, in 1969, the government announced a new review of potential access land in England and Wales, pointing out that not only had the definition of open country been widened but that demand for access land had greatly increased since the first reviews of the 1950s. However, when Wilson's government gave way to Edward Heath's in 1970, the review was scrapped and no further efforts have been made to breathe life into the access agreement system. Power to enter into access agreements was not extended to Northern Ireland until 1983. The Access to the Country-side (Northern Ireland) Order of that year did not provide for the creation of any Province-wide agency to promote conservation and access on a par with the Countryside Commissions, still less any review map procedure. By 1998 no access agreements whatsoever had been secured in the Province.

Paths Worth Following

Access agreements may have done little to open up the countryside, but the other main device on which Lewis Silkin was relying in 1949 has proved vitally important. This is the public rights of way system, which of course existed before Silkin's legislation but which he nonetheless sought to entrench more formally.

The system to which Silkin turned his attention was already a distinctive and important feature of rural life in Britain. Country people had believed that all were entitled to move freely on certain public routes, whether roads, bridleways, or footpaths for centuries. As long ago as 1285, the Statute of Winchester made maintaining all public highways within each manor the duty of its inhabitants, with-out remuneration or reward. Such maintenance had to include the clearance of any vegetation in which robbers might lurk within 200 yards of either side of public roads. An act of 1555 which was to remain in force for 300 years provided that every parish should appoint a Surveyor of Highways to make sure that its rights of way including footpaths and bridleways were being adequately maintained. When the Surveyor discovered an obstruction, he would stand up in church after the sermon the very next Sunday and denounce the offender, giving notice that if the obstruction were not removed within thirty days he would do it himself and charge his expenses to the parish-ioner responsible.[89] In 1833 a move to ban any ploughing of public paths even during normal farming operations was lost only by the casting vote of the chairman of the committee considering the High-ways Bill.[90]

When the curtain rises on wartime Britain, however, the state of the nation's rights of way is far from satisfactory. Ever more numerous visitors from towns arriving in the countryside lacked the local knowledge needed to tell which paths were private and which public since there was little reliable signposting. The local councils required to maintain public paths by an act of 1894 varied greatly in the diligence with which they discharged this responsibility. Path obstruction was, however, the greatest problem. If a landowner blocked what seemed to be a public right of way or barred certain users, the local highway authority could only require the owner to reopen the route if it could produce clear evidence that the track in question was a public right of way rather than simply a private path along which passage had been permitted. This meant that they first had to establish that the route was a public highway. If this could not be proved say through inclusion of the route as a public right of way on an enclosure award, then the authority had to marshall witnesses who could convincingly testify that use had occurred without hindrance for at least twenty years. Such proceedings could be protracted, bitterly contested, and expensive. Thus John Dower, who expressed concern in his 1945 report on national parks at the 'radically unsatisfactory' state of public footpaths, talked of a case in Cornwall which was finally decided in 1940 after having been in active dispute for seventeen years.[91]

Silkin's solution was to implement the Hobhouse Committee recommendation that the status of rights of way should be established permanently through an ambitious mapping exercise throughout England and Wales. The 1949 National Parks and Access to the Countryside Act gave county councils as highway authorities responsibility for rights of way and laid on them a number of duties. Their immediate task was to survey their entire areas in order to establish the status of every path within them. Those paths which at the time of mapping were understood to be public paths would be entered on to a 'definitive map'. Thereafter, nobody could summarily close them, even if they were hardly used: any closure or even diversion could occur only after the highway authority and the Minister of Town and Country Planning had followed prescribed procedures of advertisement, consideration of objections, and public inquiry if the objections were not withdrawn; in contested cases, the Minister would have the final say. County councils were required to publish the definitive maps, so that all parties—landowners, land occupiers, country dwellers, and visitors from outside—would know where the paths ran. The thoroughness of the procedure, with draft, provisional, and final maps, two opportunities for objection, and scope for public inquiries was seen as offering a good prospect that all parties would accept the definitive maps which emerged as fair.

This hope has been largely fulfilled. Where a public footpath happens to run it does indeed prove a powerful instrument of access for all. The composer Andrew Lloyd Webber was to discover this in 1995 when he tried to get part of a public footpath running through his Sydmonton Court estate in north Hampshire permanently diverted. The length of path in question runs between the buildings which Sir Andrew uses for his business and his house, and he felt that its presence threatened his security. However, after a public inquiry, an inspector rejected Sir Andrew's application because he felt that the balance of disadvantage to the public were the path diverted (in terms of loss of visual amenity, greater length of path, and a soft rather than hard surface) outweighed Sir Andrew's concerns. Of course, many path diversions and extinguishments are successful: around 1,500 formal proposals to alter the network in England and Wales are made every year, and the majority are upheld. Yet the final decision always rests with the Secretary of State for the Environment, Transport, and the Regions and he can only order the closure of a public path if he is convinced that the path in question 'is not needed for public use', since this is the only admissible ground for closure. Some county councils are slow to defend the right to use paths, as indeed some dragged their feet when preparing definitive maps. The North Yorkshire map, for example, was not published until 1965, and then showed the rights of way deemed to have existed in 1956. Nonetheless, after half a century, 130,000 miles of public path remain definitely mapped in England and Wales and in theory at least defended and protected by highway authorities. The same county councils which have so lamentably failed to provide access agreements have done good work on public footpaths and bridleways, not only in keeping them open but in fufilling another responsibility (with some unfortunate exceptions) —to signpost the paths wherever they leave a public road.

The main reason why they seem to have taken their rights of way duties more seriously is that asserting rights of passage which had always existed did not involve anything like such a challenge to the rural *status quo* as creating rights to roam freely would have done. All parties in the countryside accepted that passage through it was necessary for all. Landowners themselves benefited from well-made-up roads to get their goods to market, from long-distance packhorse trails to move their livestock and from footpaths along which country people could get to work. They knew that the economic and social life of their areas depended on everyone being able to move about. They accepted that mere permissive access could not secure this function adequately: they as much as anybody else needed to feel sure that rights of passage on which they depended would be secure in law. Country people also knew that public paths and roads were an indispensable feature of their daily lives, and considered a legal right to use them a necessity. History reassured all sides that this was a right which could coexist with the demands from the countryside of all interested parties. The bodies selected as highway authorities—the shire councils—enjoyed considerable natural authority in the countryside. Parish councils, which would have been far more susceptible to local pressures, had sought to recover control of highways ever since a Highways Act of 1862 transferred control of highways from parishes to highway districts. Nine hundred parishes up and down the country had tried to thwart this process by designating themselves 'urban sanitary districts' in the hope that they could thus retain highway authority status. This loophole was blocked, but even in 1949 Silkin had to resist real pressure to leave the paths to the parishes. Had he given in, it is hard to believe our public footpath network today would have been anything like as impressive as it is.

Silkin did however feel obliged to require county councils to consult parish and district councils over the preparation of definitive maps. This did mean that county councils tended to work from maps originally offered to them by parishes, but at least any complaints about exclusions were then considered at county level. Backsliding county councils could be kept in check through the powers reserved in the system to the Minister.

Although Silkin's measures to prevent local interests from undermining access were impressive, he failed to ensure that every citizen could explore the heart of the countryside by right.

The 130,000-mile network of public paths surviving today is an impressive resource. Yet it has its limitations. Coverage is extremely uneven. Country parklands, woods, lakesides, and riverbanks—key targets for many country walkers—tended to lack traditional rights of way. Parks were of course created with privacy in mind; coppicing and pheasant rearing militated against paths through woods, while conserving fish from poachers militated against allowing waterside routes to be established. The old communications routes of the countryside therefore came to be concentrated on farmland near settlements, and since the public footpath network was based on established use it too became predominantly a feature of the farmed landscape.

The process of drawing up definitive maps introduced new deficiencies. Where landowners were well organized they succeeded in resisting many proposals. Elsewhere the boot was on the other foot. Travel west out of Halifax and above the little town of Mytholmroyd 10 miles away rises a plateau whose sides are criss-crossed by a skein of paths which even the most committed rambler might consider improbably dense. Small-scale farmers here proved unadept at resisting claims that numerous tracks were historic routes. Overall, however, the character of the mapping process tended to mean routes were lost which ought to have been retained.

Both landowners and path users were entitled to make representations on the draft definitive map, but at the next stage, the provisional map, only owners and land occupiers who might be affected were entitled to comment. The position of landowners in the community at the time ensured that they got their way far more often than they might do today. In the 1950s and 1960s landownership still operated as it had for nearly a thousand years through large private estates. Frequently the parish and the estate were one and the same thing, with landowners or their agents chairing the parish council or, in the many parishes which lacked an elected council, the parish meeting. At parish level, landowners wielded enormous power—as the principal employers, the owners of rented and tied housing, the patrons of church livings, and in many other ways. If a parish's leading landowner was not himself the chairman of the parish council, that post was likely to be held by somebody in some way beholden to him. Such figures were inevitably unlikely to go out of their way to propose as public paths routes whose status was in doubt. Without qualified staff, parishes could conduct little systematic research. Some of the maps put forward lacked even a signature to indicate who exactly had prepared them. Local superstition deterring people from using some established paths was enough to ensure they were left off. Mistaken beliefs—such as that the passage of a coffin along a route automatically made it a right of way, or that paths which served no utilitarian function were inadmissible—sometimes held sway. Sometimes tracks were omitted because parish clerks considered that a right of way was not in dispute and that they need only mark rights of way which needed to be asserted.[92] Sometimes it remains unclear how a path on the map got there.

People living outside the countryside in towns and cities had even less opportunity to influence the mapping process than ordinary country dwellers. Until 1974, not just major cities but also large towns were administratively separated from the countryside by the county borough system. It was the county councils which supervised the preparation of the path maps for the countryside of England and Wales. The local authorities responsible for London and the other big towns and cities (and therefore the vast bulk of the population) had discretionary power to prepare definitive maps for their own urban areas but no more influence over the definitive maps of the country-side surrounding their bailiwicks than that of a private citizen. So the interests of a great many townspeople seeking to walk in the countryside—in towns like Exeter, Luton, Oxford, Hull, and many more—effectively went unrepresented in the process of creating the rural public footpath network. Silkin had provided a means by which recreation needs could be accommodated and gaps in the system filled. As well as continuing traditional routes as public paths, shire councils were empowered to create new public paths either by agreement with landowners or by order. But this rarely happened.[93] County councils proved no keener to confront landowners by creating new rights of way than they were to use access agreements and access orders to open expanses of countryside to the public.

The limitations of the 1949 scheme for opening up Britain's coun-tryside became apparent soon enough. Yet as the 1950s got under way, nobody seemed to care. The passions which had provoked the

Kinder Scout mêlée seemed to belong to a bygone age, as people concerned themselves with acquiring new council homes, consumer durables to put inside them, and cars to park in the driveway. Freedom to wander the great outdoors was of little concern to a nation intent on pursuing domestic prosperity. The campaigning organizations became absorbed in trying to get paths recorded on definitive maps, a task which required them to seek out aged countryfolk in a position to testify about long-standing habits of passage at public inquiries.

There Comes a Time

Meanwhile the beginnings of concern for the environment created a mood which militated against the idea of making it easier for people to enter the countryside. The first scare stories in the 1960s quickly created the feeling that the natural environment was being overwhelmed by people, in particular the urban populations whose ever increasing demands seemed to lead to ever more depredation. This notion seemed to appeal perversely to townspeople themselves, who lapped up what became a spate of grim warnings about the threat they posed to the countryside. Planners confidently predicted huge increases in total population in Britain (which never materialized). Michael Dower, the son of John Dower, wrote a ground-breaking book at this time called *Fourth Wave*. In it he warned that we should 'see people like ants, scurrying from coast to coast, on holiday, swarming out of cities in July and August by car, coach, train and aeroplane to a multitude of resorts and hidden places throughout the isles of Britain'. The toughest problem, considered Dower, was the 'invasion of those who pour out of cities by car, coach and train and converge on coast, riverside, common land and forest for a change of scenery. Can we enhance the lives of our people without ruining the island they live upon?' he asked.[94] Such fears produced an official reaction against the drive to improve access to the countryside which had produced the 1949 act. Dower himself warned against the idea of meeting countryside recreation needs by spreading 'a thin layer of gambolling humanity across the whole island'. Instead he proposed that visitors should be decanted into what came to be known as `honeypots', leaving the bulk of the countryside free of the pollution which they constituted.

Rural planners came to see recreation as a threat to the countryside, their task being to corral visitors into 'country parks' and 'picnic sites' where they could do as little damage as possible.[95]

These facilities (sometimes splendid mature woodlands but often constructed out of a disused gravel working or a glorified lay-by) began to spring up close to conurbations in the 1970s. Normally a local authority bought the land involved and dedicated it exclusively to recreation—a very different idea from freeing people to roam over countryside devoted principally to other uses, as access agreements would have allowed. It was also of course extremely expensive, and in the 1980s funds for new country parks began to dry up.[96] By then, however, another shift in prevailing attitudes to the citizen's role in the countryside had begun to get under way.

Environmentalism was growing stronger, not weaker. But as people recovered from the guilt prompted by the initial and often overblown messages of doom, they began to see their surroundings as more than a fragile fabric at the mercy of their own destructive activity. People became far better informed about the countryside and soon realized that their own presence within it was far from being the greatest threat to it. Pressure of visitor numbers might be causing erosion on Box Hill and the Pennine Way. But this was surely trivial compared with the obliteration of wildlife over vast areas of land through the use of herbicides and insecticides and the clearance of woods, heaths, and hedgerows. The farmer, who had been seen as a custodian to whom the countryside could safely be entrusted, emerged as a far greater danger than the urban visitor. Indeed, the farmer, soon seen as ready to commit any act of despoilation which would enhance his profits and subsidies, replaced the townsman as environmental villain. Far from seeing themselves as endangering the countryside, people began to feel that they and their democratic institutions should be working to curb the power of a destructive rural regime.

This thinking chimed with a more general trend for environmental concern to prompt the feeling that the earth is something in which everyone has a stake. As all depend on it for survival, all have responsibilities towards it but all have rights in it as well. People were less ready to leave 'their' countryside to the landowners and farmers who maintained it 'belonged' to them. Subtly the thinking that land is too important to be left to landowners reasserted itself. And people with these attitudes soon recovered the sense of affront that had been instilled in their pre-war forebears by signs warning that parts of the countryside were 'Private Property' and that 'Trespassers will be Prosecuted'. By the 1980s, more and more people were coming into conflict with such messages as the leisure revolution developed a sharper and sharper focus on rural pursuits. Increased prosperity was making people look round for opportunities to enjoy themselves and Britain's countryside proved immensely appealing as the theatre for activities ranging from walking, cycling, and riding to bird-watching, painting, photography, orienteering, and archaeology.

These waves of enthusiasts soon found that the butterflies or prehistoric remains they were seeking would not necessarily be accessible from public footpaths or in country parks. Armed with the new idea that the countryside in some sense belonged to them, they wanted to know why they could not make use of it. And unlike their more deferential forebears, they were not easily going to be fobbed off. The 1980s and 1990s saw a general rise in popular assertiveness on many fronts. People were no longer willing to be told what to do by élites they no longer trusted. A hundred years earlier James Bryce had seen a new legal right of access as the way to reopen Scotland's hills and glens to the people. Now such a right seemed a far more obvious solution to a problem which had become far more widespread than in Bryce's day. The idea of rights had become entrenched in other fields. Why shouldn't people have a right to walk in their own countryside?

Gradually, Bryce's idea of a right of access to the countryside re-emerged as an objective for some countryside campaigners. They included unexpected figures like Norfolk farmer and member of the House of Lords, Peter Melchett, who spoke in favour of the idea as president of the Ramblers' Association between 1981 and 1984. In Scotland, as we shall see later, the Scottish National Party took up the theme with a proposal for a general right of access to all kind of countryside promoted by their parliamentary leader and the daughter of a farmworker, Mrs Margaret Ewing. In the early 1990s the Ramblers' Association formally adopted pursuit of a general right of access to some kinds of countryside as its policy. It began to focus concern on the issue with annual Forbidden Britain Days. In 1991, Forbidden Britain Day saw thirty mass trespasses, protest walks, and rallies up and down the country. The Ramblers concentrated on their traditional stamping ground—mountain and moorland—and when the Labour Party came to make countryside access official policy in 1993, it too committed itself only to opening up mountain, moor, and common land. Nonetheless, the adoption of such a policy by the official opposition made the resurgence in the ancient demand for access to the countryside an inescapable reality. Something, it now seemed, would have to change. But what exactly? If some saw the tide moving inevitably towards a general right of access to all of Britain's countryside, others had rather different ideas.

5

THE LANDOWNERS' SOLUTION

UNDERSTANDABLY enough, pressure for rights of access to the countryside has been something which landowners feel bound to resist. Control of their holdings is not something they will willingly give up. Nonetheless, the growing demand for recreation in the countryside in the early 1990s was not something they could ignore. And at first it looked as if this was something which not only need pose no threat to their power but could even prove a significant new source of profit. In an era in which market solutions had been sought for so many problems, why should a financial mechanism not be the means of generating more access to the countryside? Let people pay for the access they wanted, as individuals or through public bodies, and landowners would provide as much of it as it was worthwhile to provide, where they chose to provide it.

This approach—offering something to walkers while leaving the landowner's power intact and enabling him to turn his right to exclude into cash where he so chooses—won considerable support. Conservative junior environment minister David MacLean maintained in 1993 that landowners should be able to charge a 'stroll toll' for allowing the public to walk on their property.[1] Sir Frederick Holliday, a former chairman of the Nature Conservancy Council and then chairman of the Joint Nature Conservation Committee, called for a system of tradeable permits for public access to the countryside in a speech to the Scottish Landowners' Federation in 1991. He maintained that there was no reason why access to rural areas should not become a marketable commodity: 'Sooner or later, I believe a system of permits has to come', he said.[2] Even popular countryside broadcaster John Craven said: 'Footpaths by credit card? It's not impossible.'[3]

Unfamiliar though the idea of payment for access may seem, the system already operates in embryo all over our countryside, and the scope for expanding seemed obvious. At its most basic it involves a landowner fencing in a beauty spot and putting a turnstile at the entrance—something that has been happening in various parts of Britain for at least a hundred years. Waterfalls seem to have been the favourite early targets for such early schemes, perhaps because they are both spectacular and easily isolated. At High Force waterfall west of Middleton-in-Teesdale, County Durham, you pay 50p as an adult or 25p as a child to pass through a turnstile and walk down to the waterfall. Parking is £1 per car. The money goes to the Lord Barnard's Raby Estate, but visitors benefit from the money the estate spends on keeping the facilities (including toilets) in good repair—between £15,000 and £35,000 each year. The Swallow Falls and Devil's Bridge in Wales, Becky Falls on Dartmoor, and the Ingleton Falls and Upper Aysgarth Falls in the Yorkshire Dales are some of the other waterfalls where charges are made for access. Other turnstile schemes have sprung up on stretches of river valley where access can be restricted easily at both ends; on Exmoor, for instance, at Glen Lyn Gorge behind Lynmouth, and at Badgworthy Water known as 'The Doone Valley' at Malmsmead.

Turnstiles are not only to be found at spectacular beauty spots. Charges are now sometimes made for entry to quite ordinary stretches of countryside, though some particular attraction is usually advertised, for example the opportunity to view unusual animals or wildlife. At Pensthorpe, near Fakenham in Norfolk, you pay £4.50 to walk round 200 acres of wood, meadow, and flooded gravel pit with some water birds. The Fairhaven Garden Trail at South Walsham offers access to a 50-acre wood at a charge of £3. At Mannington 14 miles to the west near Aylsham, though there are no turnstiles, visitors are charged £1 to park their car in an area with little public transport and 50p for a leaflet which shows them a network of permissive paths over pleasant farmland along which they may walk. West Wales has several schemes. In 1994 an elaborate turnstile scheme was set up over 'Cardigan Island Coastal Farm Park'—an area of about 90 acres of farmland east of Cardigan in west Wales which slopes gradually down to cliffs inhabited by choughs and grey seals opposite the small Cardigan Island. No public paths crossed this land although walkers had been in the habit of enjoying *de facto* access along a swathe of rough grassland along the clifftop. Now they must pay to walk over the farm park's network of paths through the mainly arable farmland and along the clifftop which is, however, fenced securely on each side. The entry charge in 1998 was £1.50 per adult and £1 per child. Not far away at Folly Farm near Kilgetty in Pembrokeshire (admission prices in 1997 £3.50 for adults and £2.50 for children) the attractions include go-karting and hands-on contact with farm animals as well as refreshments and trailer rides around the farm; while at Roberts Wall Farm outside Tenby visitors pay not to walk but to drive themselves around on 'quads'—the four-wheel vehicles on which farmers round up their sheep.

The owners of large estates used to charging admission to their country houses sometimes extend the principle to their land as well. Visitors to Broadlands outside Romsey in south Hampshire in 1998 paid not just for access to rooms in the house where Earl Mountbatten of Burma lived but also to walk over an area of parkland fronting the River Test. On the Duke of Wellington's Stratfield Saye estate on the Berkshire/Hampshire borders, adults pay to pass through a turnstile into the Wellington Country Park where they can walk through woodland and rough grass and beside lakes resulting from former gravel working. Private country parks often offer facilities visitors find very useful, such as the adventure playground at the River Dart Country Park at Ashburton in Devon. Landowners who create such parks can get a 75 per cent grant from the Countryside Commission under 1968 legislation, even if they propose to charge for access.

At the Blue Pool, outside Wareham in Dorset, visitors pay to view a strikingly coloured pool, to walk in surrounding woodland, and to use a range of facilities including an educational display and a café. At Old Henley Farm, outside Dorchester, visitors pay to sit in a purpose-built, heated hide in order to see badgers whose sett has been floodlit for the purpose. Not far away at Tregon Farm, a charge is made for access along a network of private roads; for the flying of model aeroplanes at certain times of year; for fifteen days of cross-country riding; for six motorbike scrambling events per year; for access for the air training corps and the scouts; and, mainly during the winter, for deer stalking, for which the charge in 1997 was £1,800 per individual per year.

Where a manned turnstile is not practicable, landowners sometimes invite walkers to buy a permit. This principle is used by the county naturalists' trusts whose members can visit trust reserves which are barred to ordinary people. Sometimes access is provided as an additional benefit associated with another paid-for facility, such as farmhouse bed-and-breakfast or a caravan site with its own woodland walk. Such arrangements have a long pedigree, and grow out of grace-and-favour schemes not originally seen as ways of making money. On the Duke of Rutland's Belvoir estate near Grantham in Lincolnshire, for example, residents from two small villages have long been allowed to move along certain non-public roads. On many estates, naturalists may apply for permits for their own specific purposes. Some landowners grant preferential access by permit to key local people such as their own land agent, the local doctor, and the owner of the local garage.

Increasingly, landowners have been reimbursed for providing access for all citizens by payments from the public purse. As we have seen (pages 42–3) they can receive a flat rate payment of £61 per acre or £93 per mile of 2-yard-wide strip for permitting access on certain types of uncultivated land, such as heathland, waterside, and downland turf, over which they are already receiving an annual conservation payment over a ten-year period under the countryside stewardship scheme. Thus at Tan Hill near Devizes in Wiltshire, a countryside stewardship scheme enables people to wander freely over 165 acres of chalk downland turf affording views northwards over the Vale of Pewsey. The landowner is paid for permitting this access on top of what he receives for retaining the downland habitat. Under the environmentally sensitive areas scheme, landowners can opt to receive £102 per mile for allowing people to walk along access strips 10 metres wide along the sides of or across fields over which they are receiving ESA conservation payments. The arrangements are available only in specified geographical areas (including the Glens of Antrim, Suffolk River Valleys, and the North Peak covering in total 11 per cent of the UK) and the agreements run for ten years. In 1994 the government launched the Countryside Access Scheme, under which farmers can get payment for access along 10-metre-wide strips or over open fields which they are already being paid not to farm under the EU's non-rotational set-aside scheme. These agreements run for five years. Similar arrangements providing taxpayer funds for public access have also been developed for woodland, with landowners who plant new woodland in the National Forest to be created in the East Midlands and in community forests enjoying the option of extra grants if they allow in the public.

Whether a landowner gets a state grant for providing access or charges walkers directly, he is still exploiting his right to exclude for financial gain. Walkers may find they get a better deal, however, when they are footing the bill directly. The owner of a turnstile scheme has a financial incentive to attract as many visitors as possible to his site. He is thus likely to publicize it as widely as he can—flyers for such schemes abound in tourist information offices—and to plough back some of the money he earns in providing facilities. In contrast, a landowner participating in a state-funded scheme like countryside stewardship receives a flat-rate payment for permitting access whether the site attracts one visitor a year or 100,000. He therefore has no incentive to encourage people to make use of the access he is being paid to provide.

The notion of charging others to walk on British soil arises logically from the existence of a right to exclude. Landowners have been trading the right for cash or favours for centuries. In the 1790s William Cowper and fellow hymn-writer John Newton paid the owner of an orchard at Olney in Buckinghamshire a guinea a year for the privilege of crossing an orchard which lay between their homes to avoid taking a longer way around; the area is known as guinea field to this day. Where routes of commercial importance were concerned, revenues could be substantial. In 1770 a pay gate standing across the towpath beside the Thames opposite Eel Pie Island at Ham in Surrey enabled the Earl of Dysart to levy a charge of threepence on each towing horse. The turnpike roads which sprang up in the seventeenth, eighteenth, and nineteenth centuries were based on the notion that landowners could charge for passage, even along a public highway. Private turnpike trusts were empowered to block highways with gates, bars, and turnpikes and demand a toll for vehicular and animal traffic every 3 or 4 miles. In their heyday, over 1,100 trusts charged for passage along 23,000 miles of road. A benefit for travellers was that turnpike trusts were expected to use some of their revenues to maintain the routes concerned. Competition from the railways together with considerable maladministration caused the trusts to be wound up during the 1860s and 1870s, although some charging for passage along routes of commercial importance continued. By then, however, the boom in leisure for the moneyed classes had already pointed the way to charging for access for recreation rather than just passage. Usually charges were levied for access to pursue game, whether deer, grouse, partridge, pheasant, salmon, or trout, rather than merely to walk. But soon in favoured tourist areas like North Wales and the Lake District, landowners were fencing off and charging for access to some of the spectacular works of nature it was becoming fashionable for tourists to visit.

The recent wave of interest in charging for access to rural sites can be traced to the discovery of stately-home owners in the 1970s that entry charges could be their salvation. It was a small step from this to the creation of private country parks. Then came a growing sense that rural landowners would have to find new ways of making money, and that recreation might play a crucial role in this. In the early post-war period, agriculture, propped up by a new array of subsidies and guarantees, seemed set to provide a large and reliable income stream for most landowners. The role of the urban population was to consume the food and timber which an estate produced. Land management involved working out what could best be produced on an estate, bearing in mind its soil structure, pattern of fields, and so on and how best to get that produce to market. Recreation activities tended to involve the upper classes only and were as much a social as an economic function. During the 1960s and 1970s landowners regarded the incursion of the general public into the countryside as a threat to its proper function as their food factory. In the 1980s, however, doubts set in about such complete dependence on agriculture. The huge productivity gains brought about by technological improvements were creating surpluses which taxpayers had to fund. Reform of the Common Agricultural Policy, which guaranteed markets for agricultural produce, came to look more and more probable. The introduction of quotas for milk production in 1984 seemed to herald the end of open-ended largesse for farming from Europe's taxpayers and consumers. And landowners began to cast around for alternative sources of income. New forms of agriculture, such as growing exotic crops or crops for industrial use, seemed to provide one way forward. Increasingly, however, landowners were looking for completely new ways to exploit their holdings. Could an estate provide locations for film-makers or public relations launches? Would a theme park or garden centre be profitable? Could cash be made from the sale of moorings or fishing rights or allowing a sailing school to use the lake? Could a system of toll rides for horse-riders be established; could parts of the woods be let out for war games, or motorbike scrambles? And could money be made simply for charging to walk—either in existing landscapes or in some new specially created environment?

Insofar as there might have been resistance to charges for what had been free, landowners were aided by the spirit of the times. The 1980s saw charging introduced in other areas such as museums and cathedrals as free market thinking ordained that facilities should be paid for by those who used them rather than by the community at large. This was the way to unlock new resources for activities which might otherwise be threatened. Charging could produce the revenue needed to maintain such facilities. Kew Gardens has upped its entrance charge from a nominal one penny to £4.50; the board of trustees which the government set up to run Kew in 1984 said that without charging they would be unable to continue their research programme as the government had slashed its grant to them. In 1993 the Queen introduced a charge of £8 per head to enter the precincts of Windsor Castle, where entry had formerly been free; she also opened state rooms in Buckingham Palace for the first time for two months of the year at a charge of £8 per head. Meanwhile, recreation facilities involving a degree of exclusive access were becoming increasingly popular, whether in the form of golf clubs or holiday villages like Center Parcs. People seemed ready to pay to secure entry to an environment where they could rely upon meeting only a certain class of people or simply feel that their families would be safe in what seemed a more threatening world. All of these phenomena helped entrench the principle that the exclusive use of the earth is something for which people should be expected to pay. At Lyminge Forest behind Folkestone in Kent, two forms of exclusiveness are converging. Here a property subsidiary of the Rank Organization has obtained planning permission to establish an enclosed holiday village in which those who pay for entry can walk, picnic, cycle, eat, and stay overnight in a piece of land outside the public's gaze. The site will cover 436 acres (the size of St James's Park and Hyde Park combined) and will centre on an 'oasis village'—a country club providing facilities for tennis, aerobics, squash, and so on together with a restaurant, golf course, and overnight accommodation. Existing public paths which cross the site will be diverted so that the world at large is kept at arm's length. However as a concession to the local community, Shepway District Council has secured a legal agreement with the developer which provides that over-18-year-olds who live in six local parishes may apply for a 'community pass'; a maximum of 100 such eligible people who have previously booked will be admitted to the site every day except Christmas Day and Boxing Day.

At the end of 1996, the Country Landowners' Association held a major conference at which it put forward proposals to encourage more landowners to open land voluntarily to the public whether under private or state-run schemes. In the document 'Access 2000',[4] the Association suggested that landowners be informed that a 'qualified adviser' was available, presumably through the offices of the CLA, who could carry out an 'access assessment' of his or her land, evaluate existing access opportunities, and prepare an action plan to improve them. The access that landowners might volunteer as a result of such an assessment could take the form of private schemes open to all, or to particular user groups, or they could consist of arrangements for general public access on foot under one of the access-payment state schemes. Landowners would be encouraged, by regional 'access awards' and the naming of 'access champions'—key landowners prepared to commit themselves in public to provide access. It is easy to imagine a future in which the local tourist information offices which now provide space for flyers about private turnstile schemes would sell an array of permits to enter different facilities in return for a cut of the takings. Where landowners receive public subsidy rather than charge visitors directly, steps could be taken to overcome landowners' reluctance to publicize the schemes involved. The public authorities providing subsidies (or tax exemption) could be required to make more information available and such land could be indicated on maps. The Ordnance Survey have said that they are unwilling to incorporate such information since the access arrangements typically run only for a ten-year period, but map-readers could be asked to get used to the marking of temporary access areas whose currency they would be expected to confirm for themselves.

Such a cash-driven route to improving access to the countryside appeared to have substantial advantages. It would encourage landowners not only to seek out and make available to walkers those parts of their holdings which might attract them, but might also encourage them to create new attractive areas (flower-rich downland or water meadows perhaps) so that they might profit from providing access to them. The inflow of funds would also ensure that money was available for the upkeep of the areas themselves and associated facilities for visitors. Nonetheless, as a means of opening up our countryside, this one had obvious shortcomings.

The great strength of private turnstile schemes—that they make money for their operators—has its own downside. Owners are indeed provided with an incentive to attract customers, but this can go too far. Popular sites can become damaged by erosion if an owner seeks to maximize throughput to maximize profit. Such erosion is beyond the control of the planning system. The would-be operator of a turnstile scheme needs planning consent for the construction of new access roads, the erection of visitor centres and lavatories, and the change of use from agriculture to leisure; but erosion, as a natural process, is not something for which planning consent can be demanded. Of course an owner might himself take action to stop his asset being damaged from overuse, but the solution likeliest to appeal to him would be raising charges so he could reduce pressure without reducing his income. This process could create a world in which access to the country's most attractive spots gradually became restricted to the rich. Such a development could change the whole character of the countryside in a way which might make even better-off people feel uncomfortable.

Payment to owners through public subsidy avoids this problem, but is limited by the shortage of public funds. What this means at present is that subsidy tends to be provided where it is administratively convenient to do so rather than where it is most needed. Country-side stewardship and environmentally sensitive areas were designed to conserve landscape features by compensating farmers for managing them in relatively uneconomic ways. The additional payments for access were simply bolted on later. What this means is that the eligible land is often not that most appropriate for increasing access. In the Norfolk Broads and the Somerset Levels—two of the oldest ESAs—the access tier applies only to strips across or along the side of fields over which landowners are already receiving compensation payments for supposedly conservation-friendly farming. In both cases, walkers would have benefited more from being allowed to walk on private, often surfaced, roads and tracks, but the ESA scheme does not allow such an arrangement to be negotiated. The Countryside Access Scheme is a bolt-on to set-aside, a scheme designed to reduce food surpluses. Farmers set aside what they consider their least productive land. This may be unattractive and difficult for walkers to reach (though it must be possible for them to get there), but only set-aside land is eligible for countryside access scheme payments. The inheritance tax exemption scheme similarly provides access not to places where access is particularly needed but to places where somebody is seeking to avoid inheritance tax. This scheme was not designed as a way of improving access but arose from a concession allowing owners of important works of art and outstanding landscapes to receive tax exemption in respect of those items so long as they permitted the public reasonable access to them.

The shortage of resources available to publicly subsidized access arrangements means that even where arrangements exist they are rarely adequately publicized. Tan Hill in Wiltshire is, as we have seen, a site open to the public under a countryside stewardship access scheme. I found out about it in November 1996 by examining the county access register.[5] On the map it seemed as if the site would afford good walking country in a county short of uncultivated land. However, as I travelled along the public road which affords access to the site I could find no sign informing visitors that they were about to come upon an access site, or any suggestion that any parking space was available. Eventually I discovered a map attached to a gate which seemed to match the map in the access register, so I assumed I could pass through the

Most of Britain's countryside is barred to the public. Walkers are not only shut out of springtime woodlands like these in north Hampshire, but are even prevented from following private tracks and roads through the open fields. (*Marion Shoard*)

The seaside is one place we expect to be able to wander freely, as here at Llansteffan in Carmarthenshire. But even the foreshore can be closed off, as it is west of Calshot on the North Solent. (*Marion Shoard*)

Bloodsports are pursued through much of Britain's countryside. Deer-stalking (above) may or may not be used as a reason to exclude walkers; many beautiful riversides like this stretch of the Eden at Great Corby, near Carlisle, are accessible only to game fishermen. (*Glyn Satterley; Tom Finnie*)

Some landowners convert the right of exclusion into income by charging for access, for example at Swallow Falls, near Betws-y-Coed in north Wales. Opposite Cardigan Island in west Wales, people who once walked freely on the cliff-tops now have to pay for the privilege. (*Marion Shoard*)

Most of us depend on public footpaths, like this one outside Banbury in Oxford-shire, to get into the countryside. But they are patchily distributed and often obstructed. (*Dave Ramm*)

Opportunities for roaming freely can be hard to come by. Access agreements between landowners and local authorities, as over this moorland in Lancashire, have opened up a tiny fraction of the countryside. Other opportunities occur where councils have managed to buy pieces of land, as Eastbourne District Council has here in the South Downs, near Beachy Head. (*Marion Shoard*)

Many of our European neighbours enjoy better rights of access to the countryside than we do. In Germany, roads and paths leading to woods, like this one near Bonn, normally have to be open to all. Swedes enjoy a right to roam generally in their countryside, as at this lakeside west of Stockholm. (*Marion Shoard*)

Ramblers have staged many demonstrations against their exclusion from the countryside, like this 'Open Britain Day' walk on Haworth Moor in West Yorkshire in 1995. Yet landowners have mounted a determined counter-offensive. These West Country demonstrators joined the 'Countryside March' on 1 March 1998. (*Ramblers' Association; Eric Roberts*)

gate and wander over the site. However, no notice reassured me that the public were welcome. A survey conducted by Ramblers' Association volunteers in 1995 of 641 of the 811 access sites which had been created in the first three years of the scheme suggests that visiting other countryside stewardship access sites can be just as uphill work as it is at Tan Hill. Thirty per cent of the sites visited had no clearly visible countryside stewardship notice-board at their entrance; and 34 per cent of sites were difficult to find even if you had consulted the Access Register in advance. Nearly half the sites (48 per cent) had access problems or were off-putting to visitors.[6]

Of course, the landowners involved can hardly be expected to encourage visitors as, unlike the operators of turnstile schemes, they have no incentive to do so. If the public authorities involved went in for better publicity they would, however, have that much less left to spend on the subsidies themselves. Even if more public money was made available for access subsidies, there would still be limitations on this way forward. As with turnstile schemes, the approach depends entirely on the willingness of landowners to volunteer to participate. At the CLA's conference on its new proposals in 1996, the then chairman of the Ramblers' Association Kate Ashbrook asked the following questions: 'Can the voluntary approach win a right to roam over the Brontë moors? Can it win freedom to roam over the 90 per cent of the Duke of Westminster's moors to which there is no public access? Can it win freedom to roam over the Sheffield moors?' The three cases to which Miss Ashbrook referred were ones in which her association had been engaged in lengthy negotiations to try to secure additional public access. No answer to her question was forthcoming; and the scheme seems to offer none. Also, access provided whether by public subsidy or turnstile scheme runs for a limited period—unlike rights of way which run for all time. A landowner is perfectly free to introduce or terminate or alter a private turnstile scheme in whichever way he pleases—unless he proposes to do something which would affect planning rules. Once the five-year period expires for an agreement under the countryside access scheme, or ten years for countryside stewardship, Tyr Cymen, ESAs, and community woodland, the landowner is perfectly free to come out of the scheme if he wishes, while if the land's owner or tenant changes the agreement may be terminated. In the long run, schemes would come and go with the varying profitability of private schemes and the availability of funding for public ones.

One additional advantage which landowners' organizations make much of is the idea that access provided under the voluntary approach is 'managed' access. To their members this is presumably supposed to provide the reassurance that they will retain control. But the implication of orderliness is presented as benefiting not only landowners and the environment but walkers too. 'We are keen to see that access is provided but in a managed way, so that the environment does not suffer. . . . The great beauty of managed access agreements in areas where people are allowed to roam and are allowed to use paths is that they are waymarked, they are specific as to where they are, you are safer on those than you are wandering into a farm area,' Julia Page, the Assistant Regional Officer of the South-East Region of the CLA, explained in a television programme in March 1998.[7] In fact, a right of access would of course also be 'managed' insofar as it would be bound to include safeguards for landowners, wildlife, and walkers themselves. But whereas management by owners under voluntary arrangements would be bound to mean management in the landowners' interest, management under a legal right would be aimed at advancing the interests of the whole community.

Payment for access, whether privately or publicly arranged, is likely to undermine opportunities for free access which exist at present. The clifftop now embraced by Cardigan Island Coastal Farm Park used to be accessible to all in practice if not by right. Clearly any such casual unpaid-for walking has had to be prevented to make the payment system effective. Many of the countryside stewardship access schemes involve the public paying for access where once it was freely available by custom: according to the Ramblers' Association's survey, as many as 44 per cent of sites in 1995 had been previously open to the public. Although it is now the policy of the Ministry of Agriculture to pay landowners for access only where this did not exist before, this principle has not been adopted by the Forestry Commission in its provision of access payments. New or not, the introduction of a payment scheme can mean a loss of *de facto* access around the site. My experience of paid-for access schemes is that they tend to spawn

'Private' and 'Keep Out' notices around their boundaries—whether the scheme is private like that by Cardigan Island or a stewardship scheme like that covering grassland alongside the River Rother at Fittleworth, West Sussex. In any case, the idea that payment should be restricted to new access seems unfair on those landowners who turn a blind eye to trespass at the moment or who actively encourage *de facto* access, or whose land supports a high density of public paths.

Payments for access subtly redefine the status of our countryside. Of course, trespass law has always given landowners the right to exclude, which could in theory always have been converted into the right to charge for entry. But while much countryside remained freely accessible in practice, this legal reality lay buried beneath a somewhat different customary practice, so that all could feel they had the opportunity to walk in at least some parts of the countryside. If charging were to become generally accepted, this grey area would disappear to the benefit of the landowner, presented with a new form of wealth, and to the disadvantage of the rest of us, stripped of a benefit we enjoyed in practice if not by right. Inevitably this burden would be borne unevenly, with those too poor to pay turnstile charges and those whose local authorities were least able or willing to pay subsidies suffering more than others. More importantly to some, the idea of payment would change the character of the experience of visiting the countryside in an intangible but disturbing way. It would also redirect into landowners' pockets both public and private funds which might otherwise be used to the greater benefit of the countryside.

Bob Cartwright, Head of Park Management at the Lake District National Park Authority, told me in an interview in 1994 that he feared that the designation of the 926 square miles embracing the national park and more besides as an ESA in 1992 could 'undermine an important tradition of tolerance of access and divert a lot of public money into supporting traditional access probably at the expense of other conservation works'. Christopher Hall, the access and conservation activist and then President of the Ramblers' Association, warned in a speech in 1991 that charging for access could threaten the widespread free *de facto* access walkers enjoy over large areas of the hill country of Scotland and Wales: 'It is one thing for a landowner to charge a fee for a facility, such as a car park or an information centre, that he is providing at his own expense. But it is quite another for an owner to try to extract money from people who simply set foot on his land without intruding upon his privacy or doing any damage to his crops or livestock.'[8] Sir Angus Stirling, the former Director-General of the National Trust, has called the idea of charging individuals to walk in the countryside 'both repugnant and unworkable'.[9]

Nonetheless, hostility to charging has been far from universal. Some local councils, facing strict limits on their own spending, have welcomed private turnstile schemes as a way of relieving pressure on them to provide rural recreation facilities or even to maintain the public paths network. In 1993 I interviewed Bruce Wallace, the Public Rights of Way Officer of Dyfed County Council, an administrative unit replaced in 1997 by four unitary councils. Dyfed covered an area of 2,229 square miles of countryside from Llanelli in the south-east to Aberystwyth on the west coast which took in a western wedge of the Brecon Beacons national park to the east and the Pembrokeshire Coast National Park to the west but also included much other extremely attractive countryside. On the Ordnance Survey map this land appears to be penetrated by a dense skein of public footpaths and bridleways—a total of 5,000 miles of rights of way, a legacy of long settlement, diversified land use, and isolated hamlets. In 1991, however, four-fifths of this network was extremely difficult to follow because of obstruction, encroachment of vegetation, fencing, and lack of signposting. Mr Wallace told me: 'Walkers on the 5,000 miles of rights of way have to have their maps with them. Away from the mountains, they have to have Pathfinder maps, not just Land Rangers. So probably 4,000 miles of that 5,000 are only used by what I would describe as the professional walkers—the ramblers.' Mr Wallace estimated that within the two national parks 50 per cent or more of the paths might be open and used; outside the parks in popular walking areas—on the coast and around the towns—perhaps 30 per cent would be usable and in the rest of the area only about 20 per cent. Mr Wallace saw no realistic prospect of improving this situation very much and welcomed the opportunities increasingly offered to walkers through the many turnstile schemes which are springing up in Dyfed. 'The vast majority of people looking for a walk, locals and tourists, utilize the advertised establishments, finding them either in the leaflets that we produce or in those produced by the private sector. That's the picture really.' When I last visited the tourist office in Cardigan in summer 1996, the only leaflets in the first category related to the Pembrokeshire National Park: there were none whatsoever produced by local councils relating to the remainder of Dyfed. There were, however, many leaflets about private nature trails, open farms, the Cardigan Island Farm Park, and so on.

Because paid-for access often involves strips of land, it undermines the idea of free public paths. Northern Ireland, where virtually no public paths exist at present but where there is considerable *de facto* freedom to wander, is to have what amounts to a paid-for paths system. The government planned that the Countryside Access Scheme which it introduced to the Province in 1996 should cover 621 miles along defined paths by the year 2000 at an annual cost of £250,000. As we have seen (page 44), by the middle of 1998 only one such agreement had been made so the target is at the time of writing academic. However, numbers might well pick up once Northern Ireland's district councils have prepared their access strategies, since until a route has been included in one of these strategies the Department of Agriculture will not agree to payment of grant under the scheme. The government's target spending in the Province if achieved would, however, deliver a density of public paths only one-twentieth of that in England and Wales—0.1 miles of path per square mile of land compared with more than 2 miles of path per square mile of land in England and Wales. Northern Ireland's Countryside Access Scheme may do more to undermine the idea of free rights of way than many of the paid-for public access schemes on the other side of the Irish Sea since the latter may embrace whole areas. Not only is Northern Ireland's Countryside Access Scheme confined to lines of land, but the Department of Agriculture has identified existing permissive paths like 'laneways' as one of the categories of feature which would be appropriate for scheme payments.

Even in England and Wales those access payment schemes which do involve strips of land rather than whole areas also serve to undermine public rights of way where they occur. When in 1991 the Countryside Commission launched countryside stewardship, the emphasis was on area access rather than strips. As the scheme developed, it was felt that the payments for open access were too generous and that in any case it was more appropriate to have the option of a permissive path. In 1996, stewardship was transferred to the Ministry of Agriculture and since then there has been increasing emphasis on offering non-area access in the form of permissive footpaths, permissive bridleways, and permissive paths for the disabled. Now, the majority of the few Countryside Access Scheme and ESA access scheme agreements being made involve linear access. It is true that these access strips are 33 feet wide, while field-edge public footpaths are only 5 feet and public bridleways nearly 7 feet. Nonetheless, on the ground the two types of route look very similar—particularly in cases where both run along field edges. It is hard to find a reason why one farmer should receive £102 per mile for agreeing to allow the public to set foot on a linear route on his land while another farmer has to put up for free with the passage of the public over identical terrain albeit along a narrower route.

The idea that the countryside should be something we pay to enter, like a zoo or a theme park, has attractions for some visitors to the countryside as well as for landowners and public authorities. In an increasingly fearful age, the countryside is seen as potentially dangerous as well as a haven of peace, particularly for lone women and children. Places where entry has been officially licensed, which are securely fenced and perhaps heavily wardened, seem safer than the ordinary countryside—not only from rapists and axemen but from the regular hazards of the working countryside—from bulls in fields to farmyard dogs. Visitors know that if harm befalls them, they will have someone to complain to and to sue for compensation. To some extent this feeling of greater security is well founded, of course. The stout fencing along the clifftop at Cardigan Bay discourages all but the most determined from straying on to the grassy slopes at the top of the cliffs. Private turnstile sites rarely harbour potholes, broken footbridges, or anything else on which visitors might harm themselves, let alone horses, cows, or bulls which might frighten them, and authorities funding public sites obviously start to think about any dangers. Unfortunately, the habit of visiting tamed and secure bits of countryside may make people even more nervous about venturing into the unpackaged version. Would this really be a good thing? The countryside used to be the place where all of us, particularly perhaps children, could get a taste of the hazards from which urban man is protected. If visiting the countryside were to become more like visiting a city park for many people, something very important might be lost.

Certainly the more people visit officially approved sites for rural recreation, the less any of us may be able to visit the rest of the countryside. This is because at present our principal means of penetrating the unofficial countryside is through public paths, and the survival of these paths depends on their being used. Public paths cannot be extinguished simply because of insufficient use, but there is little point in paths being on the map if on the ground they are allowed to become blocked or obstructed. And as the Dyfed case suggests, highway authorities are unlikely to spend money asserting and maintaining paths whose potential users have defected to paid-for farm and countryside parks and stewardship sites. Yet our paths network provides us with what is potentially a far bigger recreation resource than either public or private purses would ever be likely to be in a position to fund through paid-for schemes.

Attractive though payment-for-access must have seemed to many landowners, it came to seem increasingly at odds with the changing political climate of the mid-1990s. As the prospect of a Labour government committed to a right of access to at least some kinds of countryside loomed larger, landowners became more concerned about clinging to control than building a new revenue stream.

They remained determined to resist the creation of any right of access, but calculated that it would hardly make sense to emphasize that people should pay for what new laws might provide for free. So their energies went into arguing that a right of access would create difficulties and was unnecessary—because landowners would provide sufficient access to meet recreation needs on an entirely voluntary basis. Whether or how landowners would be paid for providing such access was a matter shunted into the background—whence of course it might be free to re-emerge should voluntarism win the day.

In its document *Access 2000*, the Country Landowners' Association argued that demands for greater public access should be accommodated but that this could be achieved by encouraging individual landowners to provide more access voluntarily. The deputy president of the CLA, Ian MacNicol, declared at the conference, 'We are seeking a net gain in access but it must be voluntary—with the willing consent of landowners. And it must also be managed—so that access is environmentally, economically and socially sustainable.' Such an approach would clearly preserve the control by which landowners set so much store. But not only would it fail to address the philosophical case for access of right; it was a shaky plank on which to try to build a case that a great deal of access could be made available without the enactment of a right. For landowners are not, on the whole, eager to volunteer access to others.

In the past, few surveys have documented the extent to which landowners would welcome greater public access. One that came up with a perhaps surprising result was conducted by Hampshire County Council in 1997. Of 744 Hampshire farmers asked whether they would consider allowing more access for the general public to their land, 25 per cent said they would.[10] Though this sample is small it shows that not all farmers wish to erect barricades against walkers who might leave gates open, dump rubbish, tamper with farm machinery, and commit all the other misdemeanours commonly ascribed to people venturing on to farmland. However, this result is far more encouraging than those emerging from the only other surveys I have managed to uncover. In 1986, 257 farmers responsible for a representative sample of holdings in parts of the East Midlands, North Wales, Dorset, and the Pennines and Peak District were interviewed at length. The researchers presented figures separately for farmers who already provided facilities for visitors (on top of any rights of way) compared with those who did not. When asked whether there should be more access to the countryside, only 9 per cent of those who already provided facilities said there should, as did 4 per cent of those who did not already provide facilities. Two per cent of the first group and 28 per cent of the second group actually favoured a reduction in public access to the countryside.[11] A recent relatively large-scale survey gives an indication of the attitudes of the owners of woodland. In 1996 three academics questioned a sample of 700 owners of woods scattered through Devon, Gloucestershire, Buckinghamshire, Nottinghamshire, and Cumbria on whether they agreed that the general public should be allowed wider access to uncultivated private land. A mere 2 per cent of these landowners agreed. A few either agreed or were not sure; but 40 per cent of respondents disagreed while a further 34 per cent strongly disagreed. This despite the fact (as we shall see later on page 328) that the majority reported no conflict between their pheasant shooting activity and existing public access to their holdings (mainly by rights of way).[12] No surveys seem to have been conducted on the attitudes of the owners of moor, mountain, down, heath, and common but there is no reason to suppose these differ radically from those uncovered by these three surveys—in other words, by and large, landowners are against, and sometimes strongly against, rather than in favour of greater public access to their holdings.

This conclusion certainly chimes with the attitudes identified at the end of Chapter 3 and my own research for an earlier book, *This Land is Our Land*.[13] There is the occasional landowner who is happy to share his or her land with others, but such people are rare. More typically, landowners cherish their ability to exclude others from their land as one of the benefits of owning it. One Sussex owner wrote to me in 1993: 'I can assure you that owning an estate such as this is about the worst investment imaginable. The return on capital is around one half of one per cent. The only real reason is being able to have some territory which can be kept private, and access allowed only to those who the landowner wishes. It is a very primitive drive.' The success of a voluntary approach to public access would depend on the genuine willingness of landowners to deliver more access, something which landowners' representatives now claim exists. On one of the many television programmes which debated access to the countryside in early summer 1998, Julia Page, the Assistant Regional Officer of the South-East Region of the CLA, said: 'We realise there's a demand for public access and our members generally speaking go with that and actually wish to provide public access.'[14] If so, it is a wish which must have sprung from nowhere fast.

In spite of these difficulties, the CLA remained determined to push the case for voluntary access instead of access rights. When Labour came to power in 1997 committed to rights of access to at least some kinds of countryside, the new government quickly became the target of an energetic lobbying campaign.

The new government had been planning to consult only on the way in which an access right might operate. However, it delayed its programme to allow the landowners to make their case. And in the face of their arguments it made a huge concession. *Access to the Countryside in England and Wales: A Consultation Paper*, published in February 1998, did not only set out proposals for rights of access to specified kinds of countryside. It also invited comments on how an alternative approach to a right of access—'the voluntary solution'—might work. The government said that after the consultation period was over and all submissions had been considered, it would opt for either the voluntary approach if persuaded that this would deliver enough access, or, (if not) statutory rights as originally proposed. Under the voluntary approach, landowners would offer additional access off their own bat to areas of mountain, moor, heath, common, or down instead of being forced to do so. The consultation paper pointed to the experience of bodies like the National Trust and the Ministry of Defence which permit the public to roam free over large stretches of their land even though they are not legally required to do so (except in the case of National Trust commons). It reminded readers that where access has been volunteered by these and other individuals and organizations it appears to cause few problems for land managers; it also argued that there is little evidence that landowners' or occupiers' income has been reduced by the presence of walkers. However, the consultation paper did not simply invite ideas on how a voluntary approach might operate more widely; instead, it sought views on the ways in which a voluntary approach could 'secure access commensurate with that envisaged under the statutory approach'.[15] It went on to set out criteria that would have to be met if the voluntary approach were to be selected. Voluntary initiatives would have to 'deliver substantially greater access in future'. The access would have to be of adequate quality, and permanency, and the arrangements would have to be readily understood and publicized.[16]

These were demanding requirements. It was particularly hard to see how landowners could convince the government that access would be guaranteed permanently to all mountain, moor, heath, down, and common through voluntary arrangements. It would take only a few uncooperative owners to scupper the requirement, and even if all co-operated it was hard to see how permanency could be guaranteed. However, from February 1998, landowners were required to put as much effort as they could into showing that whatever their attitudes had been in the past, they were now determined to open land to the public, at least where this consisted of mountain, moor, common land, heath, or down.

In June 1998, the CLA provided the government with their response to this challenge. It depended largely on the results of a survey which purported to show that voluntary access agreements of one kind or another already cover millions of acres of England and Wales. It argued that growth in voluntary access was taking place at 5 per cent per year and that, if not actually permanent, such access was not usually rescinded. It offered opinion poll evidence that people preferred to follow paths rather than roam freely, and the fruits of other specially commissioned studies aiming to show that a right of access would impose financial costs on landowners and taxpayers and bring few social benefits. It attempted to set out a framework through which it argued that voluntary arrangements could be put on a more formal basis.[17]

Almost all of these elements were individually highly questionable. Together they could not be seen as meeting the tests which the government had set. What they clothed was the resolute insistence that the right to exclude, which landowners had defended for so long, should survive what looked like one of the most serious challenges it had ever faced.

6

IMPROVING ACCESS

If volunteered access is unlikely to prove adequate, what of the machinery which has already been created so laboriously over the years to guarantee us all a foothold in our countryside? It may not have worked yet in the way it was meant to, but could it be made to do so through vigorous refurbishment? In Britain more than many other countries, a variety of devices have been developed to provide some kind of rural access. Almost all of them could be improved.

The Potential of Paths

Britain's public footpath network, for all its shortcomings, is a great national asset. One of its great strengths is that it is universally understood and accepted—even by landowners and even when paths cause those landowners real inconvenience, as where they run a few feet from an isolated dwelling or office, through a cherry orchard or a strawberry field, by pheasant pens or across a golf course. Former gamekeeper Gordon MacDonald of the village of Botesdale in Suffolk told me his boss, Major John Holt-Wilson, had told him that public paths should be respected because 'they are the people's rights and heritage'. In spite of such sentiments, however, much of our current path network is so obstructed that it plays much less of a role than it might in opening up the countryside. There remains nonetheless a consensus that this is wrong. Country Landowners' Association Deputy President Ian MacNicol declared at the Association's conference on access in November 1996: 'We will continue to encourage our members to ensure that all rights of way are open, unobstructed and free for use, day or night, by any member of the public in accordance with the rights which exist.'[1] The public paths system attracts cross-party support and no post-war government has thought of abolishing or even seriously eroding it. For walkers, the paths are overwhelmingly important, providing the ordinary citizen with one of his few opportunities to be in the countryside as of right. According to former Countryside Commission Director Adrian Phillips, the paths are 'the most important recreational facility' in the countryside.[2]

Because of its relatively high density and its evolution to meet the changing social and economic needs of hundreds of years of country life, the network offers all kinds of unexpected delights, providing a means to see at close hand secluded manor houses and lily-covered fish ponds, distant views across many counties and enclosed mossy dells. Public paths link up with other paths in the vicinity and provide complex possibilities for walks. In New Zealand or the United States linear access for walkers exists but is largely confined to special 'walkways' or 'trails' which involve trekking along predetermined routes. Our walkers can 'create' their own walks by choosing their own network of paths to build a particular view of an area. Britain has its own 'national trails' (formerly known as 'long-distance routes')—the Pennine Way, Offa's Dyke Path, the West Highland Way, and so on which enable walkers who are so inclined to proceed briskly. Much more of our path mileage wanders in and out of the inner fabric of our land enabling us to get to know its woof and warp. In the words of the nineteenth-century nature writer Richard Jefferies, 'They only know a country who are acquainted with its footpaths. By the road, indeed, the outside may be seen; but the footpaths go through the heart of the land.'[3] Not only does this mean we can see the working, changing countryside close at hand; we can feel the presence of previous ways of being by retracing the steps of our ancestors along the routes which they have bequeathed to us. But what scope is there for making our paths network do more to meet the growing demands we are making on our countryside?

Improving Existing Paths

In many places the public paths network exists only on paper. On the ground, barbed wire, bulls in fields, waist-high crops of peas or rape prevent anyone wishing to exercise his or her right to walk. The extent of obstruction is wildly variable. In Hertfordshire, a survey in

1993–4 found 76 per cent of paths in satisfactory condition, 19 per cent in poor condition, and 5 per cent unusable; a comparable survey found only 56 per cent satisfactory in North Yorkshire, 23 per cent in poor condition, and more than one-fifth (21 per cent) unusable.[4] A sample survey of paths in the former counties of Gwent and the three Glamorgans for the Countryside Council for Wales in 1992–3 found 30 per cent in poor condition and 20 per cent unusable.[5] Sometimes paths are simply absorbed into cropland. When local Ramblers' Association volunteers surveyed the condition of cross-field paths in Gloucestershire in 1995, they found 52 per cent of them submerged under growing crops or ploughed earth.[6] These variations in the walkability of paths in different parts of the country result partly from the differing attitudes of highway authorities. The Isle of Wight is said to have the densest network of rights of way in England—3.4 miles of path for every square mile of land. The island's council sees the paths as a key to attracting tourists and in both 1997 and 1998 was spending £80,000 to try to ensure that all its paths are maintained and signposted by the year 2000. Other councils spend far less; and even within counties variations occur. Thus the paths of east Herefordshire are in much better condition than those in the far west although they are all the responsibility of Herefordshire Council. Such local variations often reflect the relative pressure mounted by walkers' groups and the amount of use the paths receive (east Herefordshire abuts the Malvern Hills and is within easier reach of people living in the West Midlands than the west of the county). Public paths in popular walking areas close to conurbations like the Chiltern Hills or the Peak District National Park tend to be in good order.

No amount of deliberate action by highway authorities can, however, match the effectiveness of the instrument which kept the paths open in past centuries—the daily passage of large numbers of actual human feet. Now that fewer people live in the countryside, and most of those who do travel by road, the paths network has become primarily a recreation resource. In past centuries, if landowners or farmers obstructed paths, local people well aware of their rights would simply remove the obstructions. Today's visitors to the countryside may walk long distances along footpaths but they frequently do this in many different areas and even if they concentrate their walks in one area they are unlikely to be as aware of where they have a right to go as the old rural population would have been.[7]

Landowners used to see a need to keep paths open so their workers could get to work. Now this imperative has gone, and landowners do not rely on the public paths crossing their property for their own passage. They tend to move around their property by vehicle, driving along the tracks over it which are not public rights of way or even straight across fields. Increasingly, they now see public paths as an obstacle to their own operations. To have to reinstate paths after ploughing and to put up with the presence of strangers on their land seems a nuisance to many. Far from wanting to keep public paths open, they have an incentive to let them become obstructed. The surface of the vast majority of public paths is owned by the highway authority,[8] so any encroachment on the paths either by mounting obstructions or growing crops over them is in effect the illegal seizure of a public asset. But not all farmers see things this way: some consider public paths an unfair burden. Thus farmers and landowners may feel no shame about obstructing public paths. They may sympathize with those of their peers who transgress in this way.

A serious effort to remove obstructions to public footpaths might involve the following elements. More money could be spent on path maintenance if necessary at the expense of other recreation investment. In 1990–1 less than £27 million was spent on public rights of way in the whole of England and Wales.[9] The councils that spend most on rights of way tend to be relatively wealthy councils with substantial urban areas (like Cheshire or Hertfordshire), or national park authorities, which receive a block grant from central government. Councils in remote areas much visited by the public but without any designated national parks have a legitimate claim on more money for path maintenance from central government. Much could also be done to improve the marking of public paths. At present, highway authorities are required to put up signs indicating where public paths leave a metalled road. These signs vary greatly from county to county. Some suggest a public right through green-painted metal signs with the words 'public footpath' or 'public bridleway' in white lettering. Others, however, simply state 'footpath' on wooden signs which are easily missed and which the passing public may well not realize they are entitled to use. Some simply display a tiny and mysterious symbol which would mean nothing to the uninitiated even if they managed to spot it. Few signs anywhere indicate the destination of the paths or the distances involved. The obligation to signpost paths where they leave roads has never been extended to Scotland or Northern Ireland: it could and should be. Furthermore, highway authorities could also be required to mark paths at points along their route where walkers could easily take a wrong turning or where paths meet. Some do this with simple yellow arrows and clarifying signs at junctions; but many do not. Here too we could learn from the reliable and uniform systems used in continental countries like France.

More Paths

Even if all existing public paths were maintained in tip-top condition and were clearly signposted and waymarked, many areas would still suffer from their absence. Footpaths may be one of the great glories of England and Wales, but Scotland and Northern Ireland have very few public paths indeed, simply because the legislation requiring highway authorities to draw up definitive maps of rights of way was never extended to those countries. Even in England and Wales, many substantial stretches of riverside, areas of farmland, whole woods, parks, and moors lack any public paths at all. For the walker the situation is bafflingly arbitrary. The woods, deer park, and farmland which make up the parish of Boconnoc near Lostwithiel in Cornwall contain no public paths whatsoever; neighbouring Lanreath parish has eighteen. In 1997 the new county of Lincolnshire inherited a public footpath density of 1.1 miles of path per square mile of countryside compared with a density of 2 miles per square mile in Northamptonshire, for example. The density of public paths in Norfolk is only one-third of that in Suffolk.[10]

The architects of the 1949 National Parks and Access to the Countryside Act were well aware that the network of public paths which existed then, reflecting as it did the pattern of routes country people had been using to get to work, would fall far short of what would be required to meet the burgeoning demands for recreation. Sir Arthur Hobhouse's Committee on Footpaths and Access to the Countryside envisaged a new world in which 'new footpaths can be created with reasonable facility wherever there is a public need'.[11] In the influential magazine *Out of Doors* countryside writer Thomas Sharp explained in 1948:

Our present field paths are a brief though lovely suggestion of what is required. But they are unrelated, ill-defined, insecure. They should be co-ordinated and extended into a complete system—a network of footpaths running through field and copse and wood, along streamside and riverside, along the margin of the coast, through parkland, past farmyard ponds, low in the valleys, high on the hilltops, wandering across the plains—a systematised network of paths, tracks and bridleways, that will enable a man to walk ten or twenty miles a day if he wishes without ever having to pass along a busy road.[12]

To secure such a radical widening of the network, the 1949 act empowered county councils to create entirely new paths either by entering into agreements with landowners or, failing agreement, by making orders which would be subject to confirmation by the Minister, now the Secretary of State for the Environment, Transport, and the Regions.

Unfortunately, the pervasive network of new paths of which the 1949 legislators dreamed has failed to materialize. The most obvious reason is the inhibiting scale of the task confronting a local authority seeking to create a new path in the teeth of landowners' objections. It can be done in theory, but the process is always laborious and can require the payment of compensation which is often prohibitive. This is because a landowner is entitled to be compensated not only for any depreciation in the value of his interest in the land in question but also in respect of any damage he has suffered by being disturbed in his enjoyment of it. So if a new path will pass close to a farm building, compensation might include the cost of providing more secure doors. If a new path is to pass across the heart of inaccessible land valued for its privacy and to which sporting rights have been let, far greater compensation claims are likely. Usually, a plot of land crossed by a public footpath is significantly less valuable than one without. Woods crossed by public paths may have only two-thirds the value of woods without, so local councils have to be very wary of opening up many woodland paths. In 1986, Oxfordshire County Council successfully imposed a public path creation order along an outer part of Wychwood Forest,—a 1,550-acre ancient woodland outside Charlbury virtually devoid of any public access. The 2nd Baron Rotherwick, its then owner, said he wanted £1 million from the council to compensate him for the disruption of his commercial deer and pheasant shooting; the compensation claim was still unresolved at the end of 1997.

Even where compensation claims are less daunting, any local authority knows that embarking on footpath creation will soak up much office time as the resistance of landowners has to be countered. Although landowners are less dominant in rural areas than in the 1950s, they are still an extremely significant force, and most councils hesitate to confront the people who are often their most influential citizens.

Local authorities do nonetheless sometimes create entirely new public paths, but straightforward cases tend to involve public owners. For example, when Berkshire County Council discovered that the Environment Agency intended to build a new flood relief channel between Maidenhead and Datchet to reduce flood risk in Maidenhead, it stepped in to ensure that public paths were established along the entire length. The path creation process went smoothly until Eton College objected to a half-mile stretch on the edge of their grounds because it would erode their privacy. The College proposed that along that stretch the path should be switched from the southern to the northern side of the channel. Berkshire County Council opposed this idea as it would have placed the path between the new flood channel and the M4—a far less appealing situation than the one they had originally proposed, which provided views of the relief channel on one side and trees, playing fields, and college grounds on the other. The county council's view was supported by the inspector at a public inquiry and subsequently by the Secretary of State for the Environment in 1994; the way was clear for the path to be open.

The Long Haul

In recent years, attempts have been made to create long-distance footpaths along charismatic routes such as the course of the River Thames. There are however no special procedures for achieving this and local authorities have to use the same methods as for any other form of path creation. Central Scotland has seen one of the most dogged attempts to set about this. It was in 1970 that local councils proposed a 'Clyde Walkway' should be established along a 40-mile stretch of the River Clyde from the spectacular Falls of Clyde through woodland past New Lanark village (a nominated UNESCO world heritage site) and then through farmland including fruit-growing fields and industrial and post-industrial derelict land to Glasgow. Twenty-six years later, when South Lanarkshire Council took over responsibility for most of the river after local government reorganization, the project was still incomplete. Paths already existed along most of the river's edge: some were for fishermen and some for farmers, but *de facto* access for all existed along many of them. Some rights of access have been secured by path creation agreements, but the council has had to resort to path creation orders (and the difficulties this process brings) in two cases where agreements have not been possible. The first order affects only 0.6 miles of path but it runs along an extremely important stretch of the river—immediately downstream from New Lanark village in a stretch of river valley which the old Clydesdale District Council designated an 'outstanding conservation area'. The second section involved only 624 yards near Crossford, but without that link a 6-mile stretch of the route would have been incomplete. In the first case the council had to pay compensation; by April 1998 (the time of writing) no claims had been lodged by the owner of the land affected by the second case. So, nearly 30 years on, just over half of the 40-mile route is established walkway along which the public have a legal right to pass and over which the council is empowered to take action should problems of maintenance or obstruction arise.

Like the Clyde Walkway, other widely publicized national trails and medium-distance routes established in recent years have usually been cobbled together with difficulty through agreements or orders providing links between existing rights of way. Oxfordshire County Council, for example, made an order at Moulsford, south of Wallingford, in 1996 to fill in a missing link along the Thames Trail where walkers had hitherto had to take to the road. The route of the South-West Coast Peninsula Path has more to do with the habits of smugglers and coastguards in days of yore than the ambitions of the Countryside Commission.

The Thrall of Paths Past

Virtually all the paths on the definitive maps are there not because new rights of way have been asserted to meet contemporary needs but because access rights have been established in the past. This happens because a path cannot get on to the definitive map unless it can be demonstrated that a landowner has dedicated it for public use either expressly or by implication. Under express dedication, a landowner announces that he will allow certain routes to become accessible to the public as of right and gives his blessing to public path creation agreements or path modification orders which alter the definitive map to include the new paths. The most celebrated (and probably by far the most extensive) instance in recent years involved the Labour peer who is now executive director of Greenpeace, Peter Melchett. Lord Melchett expressly dedicated 7 miles of new public footpath over his 800-acre farm in north Norfolk during the 1980s in order to increase public enjoyment of the area. Implied dedication is altogether less deliberate. A landowner does not have to be heard to say he is granting the public a right. If it can be shown that members of the public have freely used the route in question without let or hindrance for twenty years continuously, then it is assumed that such access rights have been ceded. What this means is that in almost all cases putting paths on to the definitive map does not of itself involve the creation of new rights of access but simply enshrines rights which already exist and which the public are already entitled to exercise.

Clearly, a public path network thus based on a combination of historical habits of passage and the ceding of rights by landowners will be unlikely to match walkers' needs today if only because there will be many areas where for reasons of geography and topography, patterns of passage were never established—to mountain summits, for instance, or land liable to flooding or where local feeling discouraged passage, for instance close to burial areas and battlefields. Because rights of way grew up to meet transport needs, rural paths are more common close to houses and settlements than away from them. In places where landowners were particularly keen to exclude the public, paths are scarce indeed.

Not surprisingly, thousands of claims for additions to the definitive maps have been made since the original maps were drawn up. Sometimes claims involve anomalies in the system or the status of paths, but many are based on claims that routes still denoted as private on the map are in fact public rights of way which were omitted first time round either wrongly and deliberately or through an oversight. Many of the people now making claims for rights of way are the inhabitants of London and the county boroughs omitted from the definitive-map-process in the 1950s and 1960s who resent both their disenfranchisement from the path allocation process at that time and the excessive influence wielded then by parish councils and the landowners who dominated those councils at that time. Such complainants cannot often get new public paths created. Instead they must cast around for evidence that the routes in question were used as public paths in the past but that for some reason or other (which they do not need to discover) the routes were omitted during the drawing up of the definitive maps. These claims frequently come down to seeking an attempt to demonstrate past use.

The Anarchy of New Claims

The distribution of claims for new paths is, however, only a little less random than that of the established network. In 1991, a new owner blocked access along a path beside the River Dee near Llangollen close to a packhorse stone bridge predating the cross-river structure for which this spot is most famous—Telford's aqueduct of 1805. Recorded history of use of the path went back to the time of the poet Percy Bysshe Shelley, whose companion Hogg reported that he and the poet came upon a crowd of Welsh Anabaptists there in 1851. Early twentieth-century postcards show hundreds of people gathered along the path for mass baptisms, while others picture bathers in swimming costumes using the path as a place to get on to their unofficial local beach. The name of a rock outcrop in the river—'Roman Ford'—suggests that the path may be of much greater antiquity. However, the path involved, which runs for only 70 yards, was not included in the definitive map of rights of way which the old Denbighshire County Council prepared during the 1950s and 1960s for the situation which existed in 1952. The local community council (the Welsh equivalent of the English parish council) at Llangollen was dismayed by the loss of the path but believed it could do nothing to save it once it had been left off the definitive map. A Chester man called Gordon Emery heard about the case, however, and decided to pursue it. He collected a total of 129 signed statements from local people testifying they had used the path as if it was a public right of way. Mr Emery applied to the old Clwyd County Council and when that got him nowhere to the Secretary of State for Wales, then John Redwood, for a public path modification order adding the path to the definitive map. This would have enabled the walkers' claims to be tested against the owner's contention that the path had always been private at a public inquiry. Mr Redwood rejected the application, but Mr Emery, now supported by the Ramblers' Association national office, took the case to the High Court, which overturned Mr Redwood's decision. Not to be defeated, the Secretary of State for Wales, now William Hague, appealed to the Court of Appeal. Mr Emery was, however, upheld here and awarded costs, which of course the taxpayer has had to pay. Users of this Deeside path were lucky that Mr Emery was so persistent.

The vast majority of applications for paths to be added to the map never get as far: they sit in pending trays in council offices up and down the country. When a route through Pencarrow and Colquite Wood near Bodmin was barred in 1992 after the Forestry Commission sold shooting and with them access rights to a new tenant (see page 57 above), local people submitted a claim to Cornwall County Council, as their highway authority, that the route in question should be added to the definitive map through a modification order. However, Cornwall Council has a backlog of hundreds of similar claims to consider and little chance of clearing them in the foreseeable future. The longer a claim has to wait to be considered, the less likely it is that the claim will be successful, since people who might have used the route will have died. Before doing so, they may have deposited signed forms testifying to their use of the path, but such evidence carries more weight where witnesses can turn up at path inquiries and testify in person and be questioned about their use. One of the reasons why councils still face large backlogs of unresolved claims is the cost of processing them. But it is not only relatively poor councils like Cornwall which harbour large numbers of unresolved claims and thus tie up a potentially large amount of extra access to their areas. At the beginning of 1998 both Hampshire and Suffolk County Councils, for example, had about 300 outstanding claims. The backlogs reflect not only lack of resources but also the difficulties of making progress: labour is involved, and it often leads to conflict. It is far easier for councils to concentrate on promoting their existing paths, for instance through inventing new circular routes, than to create new ones.

Extra cash from central government earmarked for the purpose of sorting out unresolved path claims would of course help the path creation process. The government could also require all councils to undertake entirely new reviews of their definitive maps with a view to adding lots more paths—some of which would arise from unresolved claims but some of which could come from other sources. Until 1981, highway authorities had to carry out formal reviews of their definitive maps every five years. However, many of them lagged behind, while the large number of cases which had to be considered at one time threatened to overwhelm the government's rights of way inspectorate. They are now therefore required to conduct continuous reviews. However, this does not necessarily mean that all highway authorities are systematically examining their definitive maps to see whether particular additions, diversions, or deletions need to be made. Instead some are interpreting continuous review as simply involving the consolidation on to the definitive map of changes which have been made for one reason or another over the years, for instance to accommodate new building or to facilitate farming. Far, far more could be done. To achieve it, central government could make more resources available for footpath work and it could announce new formal reviews.

A formal review which systematically examined the case for new public paths from one end of a county (or unitary authority area) to another could usefully look to several key sources. First, there are the claims made by members of the public and user groups which in some places amount to several hundred and would take several years to clear without extra effort. Secondly, highway authorities could carry out a systematic comparison of their definitive maps with other maps, like old Ordnance Survey maps, so that they could be sure they had not omitted paths which are in fact rights of way. At present, such discoveries happen largely by chance, usually when access is barred or when somebody happens to be examining a map for some other purpose. Thus in 1997 I was examining the 1905 Ordnance Survey map of the land now covered by the Cardigan Island Coastal Farm Park while trying to work out how that area had been changed. I noticed to my great surprise that a path was marked on the map along the very route along the clifftops which people now have to pay to access. If that path can be shown to be a right of way, then the toll along the clifftop will have to be modified so as to allow free passage along the line of the right of way. A turnstile preventing such free passage would constitute an illegal obstruction. It would be possible to charge for entry to the farm park while allowing free passage along the right of way (the National Trust charges for entry to Winkworth Arboretum outside Godalming, Surrey, though it has to allow free passage along a public footpath which bisects the land involved). Yet the profitability of a turnstile scheme whose principal attraction is a clifftop stroll would obviously suffer. The existence of a clifftop path opposite Cardigan Island has been spotted by another member of the public who put the matter to Ceredigion Council, which in 1998 passed it to the Welsh Office for a decision.

A Future from the Past

Another field of study which could unearth extra paths is examination of maps even older than the 1905 Ordnance Survey maps. These can often throw up all manner of questions about the existence of rights of way and the status of existing public paths. One source is the tithe maps which were prepared in the 1840s by tithe commissioners who surveyed the countryside of England and Wales to identify land over which tithes should be paid to the Church. These men were not concerned primarily with identifying the status of roads and paths, but the tithe maps they drew up usually show routes fairly accurately; what is more, public highways such as public roads and bridleways are picked out on the maps through the use of colour, since they were exempt from the imposition of tithes. Being shown in colour on such maps is not conclusive proof that a path was a public highway at the time of the map, but it can provide extremely useful supporting evidence for claims, as well as an indication of where a claim might usefully be examined.

Perusal of the tithe map covering the core of the Duke of Wellington's Stratfield Saye estate on the Berkshire/Hampshire borders, for instance, throws up a host of interesting questions. When I visited the estate in 1998, a 2-square-mile core of it including parkland, a lake, a 1.5-mile stretch of river, woods, and farmland appeared completely inaccessible save for a short stretch of public path to a church and permissive access mainly to the park but only for three months of the year (see page 79 above). Yet the tithe map, dated 1839, shows a network of roads and bridleways, both clearly coloured and thus possibly public and if so open to all. For example, the private road along which visitors at present drive as they leave the estate—a road on which they may not stop, or walk, and which was in any case out of bounds for the nine months of the year when the house and grounds were not open to paying visitors in 1998, looks like a public bridleway on the 1839 map. So too does a completely inaccessible private road which leaves the exit route and swings over to the east across a bridge over the River Loddon. This apparent bridleway continues over farmland to woodland through which it provides a kidney-shaped circuit. Also apparently a public bridlepath is a continuation of the present public footpath which terminates at the isolated church. This extension carries on past the church over another, southern crossing of the Loddon. These are not the only stretches of apparently public highway on the tithe map; the biggest surprise is a public road which swings roughly north–south, bounding the park along its northern half. Of this there is now no trace whatsoever, even as a private track, on the Ordnance Survey map.

What happened to all these apparently public highways? How have they come to be lost? Nobody seems to know. The map which Stratfield Saye parish council submitted to Hampshire County Council in the 1950s and which formed the basis of the definitive map which exists today provides few clues. These maps which parish councils submitted to county councils were extremely important in dictating the subsequent definitive map and Stratfield Saye is no exception. In the case of Stratfield Saye, the public paths marked on the map lodged at Hampshire County Council which it received from the parish are identical to those on the present-day definitive map for the area. However, that parish council map bears no signature, no name, no date, and no explanation, so it is impossible to tell why routes clearly marked on the tithe map were left out ninety years later. The minutes of Stratfield Saye Parish Council of 11 December 1953 report that the draft footpath map had been received and that 'it was resolved to raise no objection to same'. But we do not know who drew up that draft map.

A claim to modify the definitive map now in order to include all these paths could be made and it might succeed. The estate would doubtless maintain that the routes identified were not really public highways in 1839 or, if they were, that they have been closed at some time during the intervening period. This would have been the case if a magistrate had made a stopping-up order over the routes or part of them. Very few such orders have been made, but there is no co-ordinated record of them, and checking requires going back through years of records. I asked local history researcher Robin Mosses to investigate the matter for me and he could find no record of these paths —if they ever existed as public paths—having been stopped up. A highway authority which felt confident about routes such as these would apply for a modification to the definitive map and then see if the landowner or landowners could produce any convincing evidence that a magistrate had stopped up the public route.

If a tithe map is not usually taken as conclusive evidence of a right of way having been given in the past, there is one other archive source which more often is: an enclosure award. When landownership was reallotted through Act of Parliament, as occurred in many places in the eighteenth and nineteenth centuries, enclosure commissioners indicated on maps how existing land rights were to be reallocated. This included marking on maps and setting down on paper the routes of new and existing roads and public paths. Today these awards exist as parchment in county record offices—accessible to the general public but not that easy for the lay person to interpret. Few of the county councils which drew up the definitive maps or the parish meeting or the parish councils on which they depended for much of their source material consulted enclosure awards. If routes marked on enclosure awards as rights of way were missed off the definitive map, this archive evidence ought to provide clear proof that they should now be included. Since no new creation would be involved, no compensation would be payable to landowners.

A park was created at Stratfield Saye as long ago as 1261, and although enclosure awards exist in the Stratfield Saye area, they do not affect the park itself or the core area of extremely attractive landscape around it, so they can throw no light on the routes identified in the tithe award. However, when Robin Mosses and I examined one of these, the enclosure award for the parish of Heckfield which abuts Stratfield Saye parish to the east, we found no fewer than 7 routes clearly described as public which fail to appear on the definitive map; neither Mr Mosses nor I could find any record of their having been closed.

Not far away, there are two other parks to which access to the general public was in 1998 in the first case virtually non-existent and in the second permissive only and then for only three months of the year (see pages 77 and 80). The first is Englefield Park just west of Reading. An enclosure award dated 1829 for Englefield marks more than one mile of public road skirting a corner of the park and then following what is now a private road past the village church, Englefield House, and on through some woodland. In this case, a closure order was obtained from quarter sessions in 1854 and a former public route through a parkland has been converted into a private drive (a process identified on page 112). At Broadlands, outside Romsey, the situation is less clear cut. The enclosure award of 1807 divides routes into 'public roads', 'footways' and 'private roads'. The status of the footways, whether public or private, is unclear, and while the description of some of them includes the word 'public', in others it does not. One intriguing path listed as a footway in the award but without including the word 'public' in its description runs north–south for a distance of 2.4 miles over what is normally inaccessible land.

None of this proves there were ever more rights of way in any of these areas than exist now. If there were, they might well have been legitimately removed. Yet further inquiry in such cases throughout the country might well lead to the recovery of lost public highways. If it turned out upon closer examination that any lost routes were made public highways by an enclosure award, and had not been closed legitimately thereafter, it would now be possible for the highway authority to reassert them. Enclosure awards remain legal documents with at least as much force as the definitive maps.

Paths out of Paths Chaos

Were councils to make systematic searches of enclosure and tithe awards it seems likely that many public paths might be rediscovered and large stretches of path added to the network. Such a search could be undertaken at present: highway authorities are perfectly within their rights to initiate search of archive sources with a view to amending the definitive map. However, were the government to announce a new review by all highway authorities, with appropriate finance to help with the research and default powers to require any authorities which dragged their feet to take action, then more might be achieved. Action could take other forms. At the very least, government could make extra resources available to highway authorities to clear their backlogs of unresolved claims. It could also make resources available to councils to investigate enclosure awards and check to see that all the routes designated within them as public highways are on the definitive maps. Rather than councils adding such routes when they choose to invest-igate them, the government could institute a fresh review of the path network along the lines of the original definitive map surveys so that additions and any necessary deletions could be made in a systematic way. This would be a step entirely in keeping with what highway author-ities have seen as within their purview. New surveys of paths could follow closely the procedure introduced in 1949 for the original definit-ive maps, although it would be important to introduce extra safeguards to ensure that the process was not influenced too heavily by local interests represented by parish councils on the ground. New surveys would be a far less daunting task than in 1949, since a huge amount of expertise has built up amongst highway authorities and land-owners' and ramblers' groups on the public paths system. In any case, the highway authorities even in the 1950s were able and often willing to draw up the original maps while being reluctant to take on other areas like access agreements.

Whether or not new reviews of the definitive maps are instituted in England and Wales, new surveys of paths with a view to preparing co-ordinated definitive maps are essential in Scotland and Northern Ireland. New legislation should bring the powers and duties of highway authorities in line with those in England and Wales, particularly in the areas of the signposting and maintenance of public paths and the preparation of definitive maps. Councils in these areas could be given a new legal duty to survey, map, and classify all public rights of way in their areas. Procedures could be similar to those used in England and Wales, with steps to prevent the community councils which are the equivalent in Scotland of parish councils and community councils in England and Wales from playing too large a part in shaping the network. (There is no equivalent of parish or community councils in Northern Ireland.)

Throughout the United Kingdom there are certain kinds of route over which right-of-way status could usefully be provided without any need to demonstrate 20 years continuous use or to produce documentary evidence. The most obvious is canal towpaths. At present, the vast majority of towpaths are treated as if they were public rights of way because the British Waterways Board which owns the canals allows the public to walk, and in some cases also to ride or cycle, along most of the wide, flat towing paths which run alongside. These towpaths provide enormously important waterside access in counties in central England like Buckinghamshire and Wiltshire where few accessible bodies of water exist. Yet since the towpaths are not in law rights of way their contribution could disappear if the British Waterways Board were to change its mind about access to them or if it were to be privatized or suffer the kind of privatization by stealth which has been so destructive of access of former Forestry Commission woodland. Reclassification of towpaths as public paths would not only guarantee a right of passage twenty-four hours a day: it would also guarantee a right of free passage. If the paths were all deemed to be public footpaths, walking along them would be free but it would still be possible for the British Waterways Board to charge cyclists to use them, as that would be deemed to be a private use of the path. The BWB has started restricting cycling along its towpaths to people in possession of a licence, although in 1997 a charge was made for such licences only along the Kennet and Avon Canal, where they cost £12.50 per year. However, were the towpaths all deemed to be bridleways, cycling and riding along them would have to take place by right. There is no existing right to bridleway status for towpaths, since the original main use of the paths by horses towing barges required payment, confirming that any bridleway passage is a permissive use; in fact the BWB prohibits riding on its towpaths.

Another category of route which could usefully be classified as public right of way automatically is disused railway lines. The Beeching cuts may have occurred many years ago, but stretches of disused line still exist, many the result of those closures and some the result of more recent closures, for instance lines to quarries which have closed. When such lines do close, no right of way is deemed to exist and once the tracks have been taken up, the land is often absorbed into neighbouring private holdings—unless special steps are taken. These steps can involve considerable expense and may not in any case be successful. Thus the inhabitants of the village of Coalburn in hill country north-west of Douglas in South Lanarkshire had been in the habit of walking along a length of disused line exercising a right which they presumed but did not in fact enjoy. Coalburn is an old mining village, as its name suggests, and many settlements thereabouts are characterized by sudden eruptions of council housing in open moorland built for miners and their families. The environs of Coalburn are now bleaker still: after the closure of deep mines open-cast mining has arrived and the village now boasts the largest hole in western Europe. In such a grim environment, every little bit of access provision and environmental improvement helps. In the late 1980s the former Clydesdale District Council sought to upgrade the path from an overgrown track, retaining its clinker, to a path which would be attractive and comfortable to walk along. It took the council more than three years of correspondence and negotiation to create a half-mile public path, and it eventually had to resort to a creation order. The long delay was the result of difficulties in seeking out the owner and then dealing with him. He lived abroad and objected to the establishment of right-of-way status along the track on the grounds that he wanted to build a house over it. Eventually the Scottish Office confirmed the order and the path was upgraded.

It could be argued that the public has a special claim to routes along former rail lines since payment was made to the original landowners as compensation for building the line. Morally, then, when the railway line closes, the route should remain with the public. At a time when we are not seeing a spate of railway line closures this question might not seem too urgent. Yet things could change. The continued viability of some of our most remote routes (like the West Highland line or the West Coast of Wales line), which also often go through extremely attractive scenery, is frequently questioned. Rising sea levels could swing the balance still further against the many routes which pass for a short or long distance close to the seashore—not only the west Wales coastline but also that between Swansea to Carmarthen along the shore of Carmarthen Bay, in the Dedham Vale area just south of Colchester, the line running west from Exeter along the Exe estuary, and the east Kent line near Herne Bay.

Plenty of benefits could thus flow from a determined attempt to improve and extend the public footpath system. Even so, any new review of the public paths network would still leave inaccessible the countless private tracks penetrating valuable countryside. The creation of new rights of way will continue to depend on wearying case-by-case struggles. Landowners who continue to enjoy the use of a host of private routes are unlikely to bother overmuch to ensure that any public paths over their land remain walkable. In any case, whatever happens to the paths, they can provide linear access only, and for many it is not satisfactory to be confined to corridors through the countryside, however many there are. However, in 1949, another apparatus was devised to complement public paths by opening up whole stretches of countryside for free wandering—the access agreement.

Roaming by Agreement

Part V of the 1949 National Parks and Access to the Countryside Act provided powers for local authorities in England and Wales to make access agreements, or failing agreement, to make access orders or purchase land compulsorily for access. In the 1960s these powers were extended to Scotland and in the 1980s to Northern Ireland. In fact, there has been virtually no use of the compulsory powers to acquire land or to make access orders: instead, those councils which have chosen to use the powers have either made access agreements or they have acquired land for access without the use of compulsion, and so far only a tiny amount of land has been either subjected to agreements or acquired. Here, it might well be thought, there must be scope for improvement, both in the use of the existing powers and in the approach on which they are based.

Clearly acquisition of more land for access will depend on the availability of public funds. Large-scale acquisition is clearly out of the question, so the only part of the Part V powers that leaves is the access agreement and order.

Public paths and access agreements share one key characteristic: they allow for existing land uses to continue but superimpose a legal right for the public to be present as well. In the case of the public path, the presence involves only the right to pass and repass; in the case of the access agreement, it involves a right to move in any direction over the land concerned—or indeed to sit or stand still on it. The men and women who created the concept in 1949 did so in the belief that recreation in Britain could not be based on areas wholly dedicated to this purpose—such as sites bought by local authorities. They believed that in our crowded island the countryside would have to be shared. But while this idea has worked well where public paths are concerned, it has never really caught on for whole tracts of land. Could it be made to?

In the few instances where access agreements have been made, all parties usually seem to be happy with them—walkers, landowners, land occupiers, and local authorities. A large proportion of the very few access agreements made since 1949 survive to this day—even in cases where the agreement was originally achieved only in the face of considerable reluctance and even where the land involved is very extensive. One of the most controversial agreements—and one covering a considerable area of land—was that secured in four stages over 14,000 acres of grouse moor known as Barden Moor and Barden Fell. These formed part of the 11th Duke of Devonshire's Bolton estate north of Skipton in the Yorkshire Dales. The trustees of the private family trust in which the Duke of Devonshire's land was vested, the Trustees of the Chatsworth Settlement, already had experience of an access agreement: they were the first private landowner in the country to sign an access agreement—in this case over 5,600 acres of moorland near Edale in the Peak District National Park which had long been available for *de facto* access. In 1957, the trustees were prepared to extend this area by 9,400 acres, also over Peak moors tenanted for grouse shooting. At Barden Moor and Barden Fell, however, where the shooting was managed directly by the estate, only those walkers prepared to run the gauntlet of the Duke's gamekeepers could savour the wild beauty of these moors away from the few public paths which crossed them. Both moors were guarded all year round so that, for four weeks of the year, the Duke and his friends could enjoy the shooting themselves. Yorkshire ramblers campaigned for a decade to open up this area. In 1958, for instance, between 1,000 and 2,000 people attended a rally on Ilkley Moor urging access to Barden Moor and Barden Fell. It was only after the inspector at a public inquiry into access needs in the old West Riding of Yorkshire had come out in favour of access agreements over five areas including Barden Moor and Barden Fell, together with a change in the political complexion of the council and the appointment of a new county planning officer, that the trustees finally agreed to sign agreements opening up the total of 14,000 acres in four stages by 1974.[13]

Yet today the agreement at Barden Moor and Barden Fell seems to work well. Around 30,000 people visit Barden Moor and Barden Fell every year, while sheep grazing and grouse rearing are under way. When shooting takes place, the agreement provides for the closure of the moor for up to thirty days a year, yet this does not seem to cause much resentment amongst ramblers, perhaps partly because most of the shooting takes place in the middle of the week. Shooting is not allowed on Sundays, and is avoided on Saturdays for fear of shoot saboteurs. Closure of the moors midweek is effected solely by the posting of notices at each of the twenty-one access routes onto the access agreement area, as well as at car parks in the neighbourhood. When shooting is taking place and the access agreements are suspended, the public rights of way across the moor remain open, but the estate and its keepers ensure that any walkers are not harmed: if keepers are beating across the right of way they will ask walkers to stand still for a few minutes. Twenty-one by-laws drawn up by the national park authority provide a framework for reducing any further conflict. The majority of these ban or control obviously disruptive or dangerous activities, such as damaging shooting cabins, stone-rolling, or the light-ing of fires; one of them requires walkers to seek permission from the estate before flying a kite on the access land, for fear this may frighten grouse. Dogs are not allowed. Although the access agreement provides for the local council to reimburse the trustees for damage to the area occasioned by public access, the trustees have never made a claim in respect of damage by fire since the first agreement was made in 1960. The only path erosion for which the national park author-ity has had to pay involves a stretch of less than half a mile leading to the main viewpoint on the site, Simon's Seat.

As we have seen earlier (see page 190), there was considerable anti-pathy in the early decades to the use of access powers granted by a government with a strongly socialist image on the part of county councils which were in the main Conservative. It may therefore come as a surprise to learn that in 1995 the select committee on the environ-ment of the House of Commons (which included eleven Conservat-ives among its twenty-two members) came out strongly in favour of wider use of access agreements: 'We feel that access agreements can contribute to resolving the conflicting interests of walkers, farmers and landowners. We urge the National Park Authorities, local author-ities and the Ministry of Agriculture, Fisheries and Food to pursue access agreements with vigour. We believe that access should be significantly increased by the year 2000.'[14] A side effect of access agree-ments has been to conserve wildlife habitat. Councils have been able to insert clauses into agreements forbidding the conversion of the land covered to 'excepted land', like intensive farmland, and this facility has protected areas covered by agreements which might otherwise have been vulnerable to ploughing, such as the chalk downland turf of southern Britain. Nonetheless, as things stand, the chances are that fewer rather than more access agreements will be made.

An Instrument in Decline

Where landowners are prepared to tolerate public access at all they are increasingly finding it more financially attractive to make arrange-ments other than access agreements. Thus at Aysgarth Falls in the Yorkshire Dales National Park, a landowner came out of an access agreement with the park authority and is now charging the public to view the site under a private turnstile scheme. Some landowners still prepared to enter into agreements with public authorities prefer the various access payment schemes available under the Countryside Stewardship and the Environmentally Sensitive Areas, since these schemes require commitment for shorter periods (ten rather than twenty or twenty-five years) and provide generous guaranteed payments per acre simply for the access provided. While the 1949 legislation provides for landowners entering access agreements to be paid in respect of the access itself, a great many of those that have been made include either no such payment or one that is merely nominal, since the local authorities involved have extremely limited funds. There is usually only provision for the reimbursement of landowners for any damage caused. Another benefit that landowners often derive from an access agreement is the provision of by-laws to regulate public activities, which of course local authorities and statutory bodies like the National Trust can create but individual landowners cannot. These by-laws together with arrangements for car parking, litter collection, and wardens to manage sites, have provided advantages which some landowners have valued. Understandably, however, the advent of the new access payment schemes have made them expect more so that new access agreements are only now being made in rather special circumstances.

Gone are the days when access agreements were used—as at Barden Moor and Barden Fell—to open up land which the public wanted to use but where access was denied. Instead, agreements made today almost always involve land on which a considerable amount of illegal trespassing already occurs, which the landowner hopes to contain through the by-laws, litter removal, and wardening which come with an access agreement. Agreements made in this way may still open up valuable areas of countryside, like, as we have seen (page 35), Smock Mill Common in Norfolk, which was signed in 1996. But where landowners feel no need for regulatory machinery, they have little interest in access agreements, even though these agreements still offer great advantages to the rest of the community. Payment schemes like Countryside Stewardship end up providing access on a more or less random basis in areas which have been designated as special for some other purpose and where owners volunteer to participate. Sites affected must always be small since the payments involved would otherwise be insupportable. Access agreements are, on the other hand, designed to cover tracts of country which the local authority considers valuable for recreation. Councils select the areas on which resources are to be targeted —a selection initially shaped by the procedure introduced in 1949 requiring all councils to prepare 'review maps' of open country in their areas and draw up proposals for securing access where they consider this necessary. The local authority also controls the publicity for access agreements and other access arrangements that result. The 1949 legislation also provided machinery for central government to amend councils' access plans where it considered that they were not up to scratch.

Access agreements and the like may have been relatively little used over the UK as a whole, but extremely valuable experience of making and publicizing agreements has been built up, and not only in national parks. Since those access agreements which have been made tend to be in places subject to the most extreme recreation pressure, experience of managing access agreements in the most challenging circumstances is well established. This experience has been built up not only in national parks but in areas as different as Surrey and East Lothian. The councils responsible for these two areas were committed to opening up the countryside to visitors from towns long before the 1949 act. They sought and secured powers through private Acts of Parliament in 1931 and 1936 respectively to enable them to acquire land for outdoor recreation provision; when the access agreement powers came along these were welcomed as a useful addition to each council's repertoire. Today, Surrey County Council has four access agreement areas, embracing a total of 2,241 acres of woodland, heath, river, and lakeside, much of it in the North Downs and northern Weald between Guildford and Dorking. Since the mid-1990s, landowners responsible for two of these have been prepared to extend the areas involved by an additional 200 acres or so in each case. The council has long publicized the access agreement areas in a leaflet about Surrey's open spaces which also includes information about National Trust land as well as land the council owns. East Lothian District Council has twelve access agreements. Through these access agreements and through land it owns under purchases made often many years ago, the council now controls 80 per cent of the coast stretching east from Edinburgh past towns like North Berwick and Dunbar. The control the council enjoys over such a large proportion of this land enables it to promote selectively (through publicity and car parking provision) different areas both in order to provide a variety of recreation opportunities and to protect lengths of fragile sand dune and maritime grassland.

The expertise of these two councils and other bodies like the Peak District national park authority could be passed on to other councils were the access agreement concept to be relaunched. Such a relaunch could take various forms. One of the most obvious would be a statutory review along the lines of the reviews of open country and access requirements introduced for England and Wales by the 1949 act. Councils could be required to prepare maps of all 'open country' in their areas and to draw up proposals for securing access agreements and the like where they considered this to be desirable. These would go to central government, allowing for extra-local input.

Review maps prepared today would stand a better chance of producing useful results than they did in the 1950s. For one thing, councils are better equipped to prepare maps of 'open country' nowadays. Many councils have already prepared habitat maps of their areas; while every national park authority has had a legal duty since 1985 to prepare and revise regularly a map of all mountain, moor, heath, down, cliff, foreshore, and woodland within its area to monitor changes of land use, in particular the ebb and flow of intensive agriculture. Thus, the authorities involved are well placed to spot the best prospects for access agreements. As we have seen, though access agreements are few, councils with experience of operating them successfully do exist, from Stirling and East Lothian to Lancashire and South Norfolk. What is more, the concept of 'planning gain' which has pointed the way to the possibility of securing access in return not for money but for other public favours has given a larger number of local councils experience of securing legal agreements with landowners over the related areas of landscape conservation and reconstitution. Any new move to draw up review maps and proposals systematically for the extension of access would probably be extremely successful now that town and country planning has become more proactive than it was in the early post-war period. Furthermore, the development of structure planning in the 1970s and 1980s has given councils much experience of involving the public in drawing up plans.

New review maps could proceed along the lines of those provided for by the 1949 act. Or, perhaps particularly in Scotland and Northern Ireland, they could be combined with or take place in close association with reviews of public rights of way with a view to drawing up new definitive maps. Or, they could form part of reviews of recreation needs which embraced not only walking but other activities too. One way in which this system could also be improved is through a widening of the definition of 'open country' to embrace parkland. South Norfolk, for instance, contains seven private parklands, all of them inaccessible. In an area with so little public space it would seem entirely natural to examine the desirability of securing public access to these areas along with the woods, riversides, heaths, and so on which would automatically be covered.

Perhaps the most sensible way of giving new life to the access agreement idea would be to take an altogether more radical approach. At present, local authorities are not required to devise an overall plan for recreation in their areas in the way they are required to show how they propose to discharge other responsibilities. Although highway authorities are required by law to keep public paths open, they are not required to say whether what they have in the way of provision is adequate or not. So if an authority's network contains just one path and it keeps that path open it would be meeting the statutory requirement at present. There is a clear need to review the whole path network and determine whether it is adequate. The same goes for the whole field of recreation provision. At present a council may choose to spend money on the provision (and usually costly maintenance) of an elaborate leisure centre, whose use will come mainly from fit, young, affluent people, even though the community as a whole might prefer resources to be spent instead on subsidized transport and tickets to enable poorer people to use existing facilities or visit the countryside. Each local authority could be required to produce a plan showing how it would meet all recreation needs and how it proposed to prioritize the conflicting demands on available resources. South

Norfolk District Council is one authority which is beginning to do this: it has set up a community leisure services team bringing together countryside access, the arts, children's play, sports development, and museums. It is also carrying out a parish-by-parish survey, asking people what facilities they would most value. If all councils were required to produce recreation plans, rural recreation would find its place within them, access would be dealt with as part of this, and the council would then see how and where it needed to create new access agreements to meet goals which would be clearly stated, reported to central government, and subject to local consultation.

For councils which already do much on the access front, like South Norfolk, even a simple review along the lines of the 1949 act could provide a useful additional bargaining counter in securing further access; while for councils where few or no access agreements have been secured to date, like those in Northern Ireland, they could provide a useful means of injecting strategic thinking about access and a spur to the use of powers councils already enjoy. In Northern Ireland in particular, much access to date has been *de facto* and is threatened by everything from agricultural expansion and intensification to more energetic use of the trespass laws. More than two-thirds of the Province's district councils have appointed access officers since the mid-1990s, partly in recognition of the important part which access plays in attracting tourists. The Province's own special Countryside Access Scheme requires these councils to prepare access strategies before farmers and landowners can receive payments under the scheme. The ground is therefore prepared, and a co-ordinated survey, district by district, of open country and access needs with a view to the co-ordinated securing of access agreements could be highly productive.

However, even if all this took place, there would still be limits to what could be achieved through access agreements. The most that could be hoped for would be a lot of case-by-case agreements, rather than the opening up of the countryside as a whole. Landowners would still be reluctant to enter into agreements now they are looking for more money than councils can afford to pay. The power of the access order would remain but in reserve is where it would tend to stay, since a council that makes an order must pay compensation to the landowner and taking compulsory action against individual landowners is seen as victimizing particular people.

Even authorities keen to use the existing powers have found themselves unable to do so to a substantial extent. Oxfordshire County Council would like to secure a legal right for citizens to roam free on several hundred acres of chalk downland turf on the Shirburn and Pyrton Hills. However, the landowner refused to enter into an access agreement, and the council was reluctant to proceed to an access order because of the liability to compensation this would bring at a time when its social services are seeing substantial cutbacks because of lack of money. Even in the Peak District—the area in which access agreements are generally considered to have been most successful—only a third of land falling within the definition of 'open country' is accessible to the public. Much woodland and riverbank in the Peak remains barred to the general public. The 76 square miles of moorland covered by access arrangements in the Peak together with another 19 square miles accessible through ownership represents only half of the total area of moorland in the national park. Negotiations which the Peak park authority started in 1982 to seek to extend access agreements over additional areas have not resulted in any new agreements being concluded simply because landowners have been unwilling to enter into them, apart from one deal with Sheffield City Council and one with a private owner involving an inheritance tax exemption.

When the Peak District national park authority's existing access agreements expired in 1993, negotiations to get them renewed took more than four years. The struggle revolved around two points. First, money. The Peak authority had already agreed to pay landowners and occupiers with agreements on their land sums in respect of each mile of internal drystone wall, of external drystone wall, per ewe grazed on the land, and per acre of access land. When the renegotiations took place, landowners sought to get the standard rates increased sevenfold. The final figure was less than this but higher than the original, so that compensation now costs the authority £70,000 each year. The second sticking point involved advance publicity for the dates on which tenants wished to shoot and therefore close the moors. Shooting tenants cited fear of disruption by shoot saboteurs as the reason for declining to publicize shooting in advance, with the result that people would turn up at a moor only to find it was closed for the day. The Park authority has been unable to get shooting tenants to reinstate the former arrangements for advance publicity: a compromise scheme provides that telephone numbers will be issued so that walkers can telephone on the morning of their walk to find out whether the moor they wish to visit is closed that day. The authority hopes to reduce the area closed at any time by drawing up shooting management plans, which may for instance close different sections of a moor at different times of the day, rather than the whole moor for the whole day as has tended to happen up till now.

The length of time needed to renew the Peak access agreements and the fact that they have resulted in new relatively high rates of compensation payment does not bode well for the future of access agreements in Britain, particularly in view of the fact that the Peak Park is usually held up as the place where the access agreement has been most successful. Already the new scale of payment has had knock-on effects elsewhere. Thus Alan Oakley, who managed Surrey County Council's access agreements and other county estates until 1997, told me that the new payments in the Peak have forced Surrey Council to make higher payments to landowners than hitherto for access agreements, so much so that the council seriously considered pulling out of one of its agreements (covering 1,300 acres of land) in 1996. Altogether, the access agreement road, promising though it must have seemed in 1949, offers an uphill path towards limited benefits.

7

A RIGHT TO ROAM

Volunteering more access to the countryside and reforming existing arrangements to extend it both involve working within what have become conventional assumptions about where rural power should lie. Yet these assumptions spring from a notion of landowner rights which would amaze many of the peoples of other parts of the world, not to speak of our own Saxon forebears. We do not really accept that the 'owners' of land should have absolute rights over their property, even though they have managed to equip themselves with a law of trespass. At some level we know we ought to be able to walk in our countryside without either paying those who 'own' it or seeking their permission. The exclusion rights which landowners are trying to defend or sell are remnants of a feudal Britain whose day is gone. The obvious way to enable us all to use our countryside for recreation is to reclaim the birthright which was stolen from us with the Norman Conquest—the right to walk where we will. Access to the countryside is something which ought to be ours by right, like the vote or trial by jury.

After a thousand years when such a right has been energetically denied in practice and in law, this may seem a fresh and somewhat startling idea. But formulating a new right of access, subject to limitations to protect landowners' specific needs, could crack the problem of access to the countryside far more decisively than any other approach. The benefits for the people of Britain would be dramatic. They could expect to find their way not only to new corners of the landscape but also to new kinds of understanding of aspects of their homeland which have been closed to them up till now along with the land itself. In north Hampshire archaeologists would be able at any time they chose to approach if not stand next to the 48 of the area's 50 prehistoric sites which are at present out of bounds, according to local archaeologist Nicholas Riall. People would be able to seek out and follow the courses of countless rivers and streams—thus redis-covering the intimacy with our inland waterways which our fore-fathers knew hundreds of years ago. They would be able to trace old ways through the woods free from the fear that the next twist might bring them and their children face to face with a gun-toting land-owner or gamekeeper who was perfectly within his rights to throw them off that land. On moor or down they would be able to exult in a freedom to roam where the mood took them rather than find themselves shut out or confined to a strip peppered on either side with 'private' signs. They would regain the opportunity to picnic under the spreading branches of trees or beside still or running water. They would be able to make their way along countless currently private roads from which they are now barred by locked gates or forbidding signs. Above all perhaps they would feel for the first time at home in a coun-tryside they had a right to inhabit instead of existing within it on sufferance. So a right to roam would not only provide a means of meeting growing demand for rural recreation but would change the meaning of citizenhood. It would not only enable people to find their way to places from which they are at present barred, but would allow them to feel secure in other places where their presence is currently hedged around with uncertainty. It would foster a new sense of one-ness between people and their environment which none of the half-measures employed up till now could begin to achieve.

The Philosophical Case

These benefits for all would of course come at the price of disadvantage to a few. A right of access for all would mean the end of the right of exclusion for Britain's landowners and their tenants. For them, this would mean not only the infiltration of specific intrusions into what had been their private space but a more general erosion of their feel-ing of control over their holdings. Theirs would be a real loss which needs to be justified. How? The answer is that the right to exclude others from walking on land is not something that ought to have belonged to its 'owner' in the first place—that land should not be con-sidered a chattel to be owned absolutely. Instead, as part of the envir-onment, it has to be seen as something in which individuals should only be accorded limited rights. Land, like the sea, the air, and outer space, was not created by man but by God or Nature, according to one's belief. True, the kaleidoscope of light and shade, form and colour which makes up a landscape is the result of a dialogue spanning millennia between Nature and the activities of man. But humanity cannot create a single blade of grass, let alone a spider or a woodland ecosystem. The land was not made by man, and it is central to the lives of all living things on the planet, human and non-human, living and as yet unborn. Land is the source of most of the food we eat, the minerals from which we build shelters and tools and fuel machines, the timber from which we manufacture buildings, tools, newspapers, and the plants and animals from which we derive medicines and clothing. It is the source of the space we occupy, and part of the collective identity of tribes, peoples, and nations. Such a resource cannot simply be treated as private property.

These characteristics of land put it in a different category from other things that people believe they own, like buildings or consumer durables. This is reflected in the special meaning which many societies have accorded to land at different times. Individual landowners may have their own objectives for their holdings: they may see them not only as a source of profit but also as a means of expressing their personality, a source of privacy, source of power, or as a place to entertain people of their choosing. But society too cannot but make its own demands on these same holdings to meet the inevitable needs of the rest of the citizenry including generations as yet unborn. This reality has often been articulated in the past. More than 150 years ago, the philosopher John Stuart Mill declared in *Principles of Political Economy*, 'No man made the land: it is the original inheritance of the whole species. . . . The land of every country belongs to the people of that country.' The Diggers' leader Gerrard Winstanley declared that 'The earth shall be made a common treasury of livelihood to whole mankind'. Charles Stewart Parnell, the leader of the Irish Land League, held that, 'The land of a country, the air of a country, the water of a country, belong to no man. They were made by no man. They belong to the human race.' Against such fundamental perceptions we have to set the circumstances in which individuals achieve title. In the land rushes of the Wild West, men on horseback lined up to be unleashed on virgin territory by a shot from a starting pistol. Those who reached plots first kept them and handed them on to their descendants who now often behave as if they consider their ownership God-given. The present-day feudal landlords of large estates in South America can trace their claim back to the Spanish and Portuguese *conquistadores*, who seized the land from Inca people engaged in an early form of collective farming. In Britain, somebody paying good money for a piece of land today is usually buying a title ultimately handed down from the barons who seized it at the time of the Norman Conquest. Insofar as the land belongs to all the people, those who buy it for themselves inevitably are buying what is in some sense stolen property. That part of the property which constitutes the right to exploit it economically can be reasonably accorded to those who acquire it. But not the right to abuse it or to exclude harmless walkers from it.

If you buy a table or a television nobody disputes your right to do whatever you choose with it, even if you want to take a hammer and smash it to pieces. You do not enjoy such rights over your children, however, or even your pet goldfish. Over these things your custodial rights are limited. If society considers you are neglecting your child or your pet it can enter your house, if necessary by force, and take it away from you. Land is equally something whose ownership is normally subjected to limits of one kind or another. In Saudi Arabia, if an owner leaves land idle for three years the government can take it off him and give it to somebody else. In France all sales of farmland are monitored by statutory agencies which can force an owner to sell to them if he proposes to sell instead to someone unlikely to work the holding in the best interests of French farming. There are also limits on the amount of land which new purchasers may farm. In Norway and Denmark, nobody may buy farmland without first obtaining a permit from the government indicating that he or she has the necessary technical qualifications to farm land.

Some peoples find it difficult even to understand the idea that particular individuals should own virtually all rights over a block of the earth's surface. The North American Indian chief Seattle asked the Washington government in 1852, 'How can you buy or sell the sky, the warmth of the land? The idea is strange to us. If we do not own the freshness of the air and the sparkle of the water, how can you buy them?'[1] Where the law does acknowledge the private ownership of the earth, citizens often question its validity. Serf folklore in nineteenth-century Russia held that land did not really belong to their feudal masters but to God; earthly title should follow not pieces of paper but 'wherever axe and plough go'. In Britain our own ambiguity over the nature of landownership permeates the same laws which appear at first sight to entrench landowners' rights. We outlaw trespass, but treat it as a civil wrong rather than the criminal offence it ought to be if it really constituted theft. Even squatting is not criminal, and occupiers can acquire rights in land without actually buying them. Landowners are therefore wary of using the powers they have on paper and the police are often reluctant to assist them in taking action against squatters or those committing criminal trespass. Why do we feel it is an affront for an owner to keep a house empty while we do not mind somebody owning a television but never turning it on? The answer is that we share at some level the ancient notion that land should not be held by those who fail to use it productively. The idea that a man can own a mountain strikes us as oddly as it did the Emperor Justinian, who believed unoccupied land ('res nullius') could not be privately owned. In some sense we also concur in Justinian's view that public parks, rivers, the air, wild animals, and the sea cannot be personal property either. Our public footpaths and access orders (rare though the latter have been) themselves imply disbelief in the absolute rights of landowners. We do not allow 'owners' to pump pollutants onto land just because it is 'theirs'. If the community wants a new road or other facility it will overrule the landowners involved if necessary with the power of compulsory purchase. Planning laws have removed the individual's right to build or quarry on 'his' land without the consent of his local authority, even if that building involves no more than a house extension.

If we now decide to widen our constraints on landowners' powers by curbing the right to exclude, we shall not be entering uncharted waters. A right of access to the countryside may sound novel in Britain, but it is extremely familiar to some of our European neighbours. Cross the North Sea and in Scandinavia you find that our landowners' right to exclude is as puzzlingly unfamiliar as a right to roam seems to many in Britain. In Sweden, Norway, and Finland the notion that every person has the right to move freely around the countryside is as much a feature of national life as, say, democracy is in Britain. All three countries experienced the imposition of feudalism as we did. However, the pattern of large estates which survives in Britain was largely replaced by a new ownership structure in which relatively small-scale farms dominate. This and other cultural and historical factors shaped attitudes to the countryside different from our own. In particular perhaps, the long Nordic winter made travel difficult for all, wealthy and poor, feudal lord and landless serf. In a country in which made-up roads were thin on the ground and often buried under snow, it was in everybody's interest to allow passage in any direction. This tradition, perhaps coloured by even older folk memories of shared ownership in the Viking era, helped ensure that a right to roam over the countryside would prevail over private landownership rights in Scandinavia to this day.

It is in Sweden where the right to roam, known as 'Allemansrätt' or Everyman's Right, is most comprehensive. In 1988 I went there to find out what this fabled entitlement means on the ground. I travelled in the countryside with native Swedes, going where they would go; I stayed with a family in a country cottage close to Stockholm and shared their use of the environment; and I talked to landowners and farmers as well as their representative organizations, walkers and conservationists, the Swedish Natural Environment Protection Agency which oversees Allemansrätt, as well as officers in local councils responsible for administering it on the ground.

The essence of Allemansrätt is that it gives the citizen the right to go wherever he or she wants except where this would conflict with rather obvious claims, such as a citizen's right to privacy in his home or a farmer's right to preserve his crops from being trampled.[2] Such concerns are respected without any need to rely on a blanket right of exclusion. People are not allowed to walk across fields of crops, but they are allowed to walk along field edges or along the gaps left by farmers where one crop gives way to another. They may walk where they like over fallow land or set-aside. Fields of pasture are accessible all year round, but it is up to the walker to assess whether it is prudent to advance. Thus in practice you can climb over a fence and cross an enclosure in which animals are grazing but it is up to you to take precautions or keep out if you think they might be dangerous. The right of access includes a right to picnic: it is not confined to passage as on a British right of way. So you can simply settle down wherever you like—in the forest, by a lake, or perhaps on a rock outcrop in a field giving views over a lake. Once settled, you can picnic or paint, read a book, or simply soak in the fresh air. Parkland is not out of bounds. Nor are lakesides and riversides. Indeed Allemansrätt goes beyond the right to walk and engage in associated informal activities: you have the right to swim, sail, canoe, or row in lakes and rivers and even tie up your boat and go ashore if you wish. You can even pitch your tent and camp if the mood takes you.

What can't you do? If you wish to camp for several nights, you must ask permission of the landowner. Swedish farmhouses are seldom patrolled by fierce dogs and you can usually ask on the spot. If in doubt as to who the owner is, you can inspect a public register of landownership at the local council offices. Although you can moor your boat on an inviting looking stretch of riverbank, you have to ask permission to use somebody's jetty. If you propose to take a party of people with you (as in an organized walk or school party for instance) or if you wish to engage in an organized group activity, like orienteering, you are also expected to secure the landowner's consent. And if you have a dog you must make sure it does not disturb wild-life by keeping it under close control during the spring and summer. Anybody who drives a four-wheel drive or other motorized vehicle off the roads or on roads closed to traffic can be prosecuted; those who damage land or leave litter can be fined under the Penal Code. None of this dents the exhilaration a trip to Sweden can induce in those who are used to being confined to public paths lined by 'Keep Out' notices.

The Allemansrätt arrangements seem to work as well in the busy countryside around Stockholm as in the unpeopled arctic forests. In Sweden's far south, arable farmlands are interrupted by lush pastoral oases surrounding seats of the aristocracy, as, say, in Hampshire, yet here both farmland and parkland are effectively shared by all. The difference goes beyond the right of access itself to underlying attitudes to landownership. One estate I visited was Övedskloster, which covers more than 11,000 acres near Sjöbo in Malmöhus county, and I put it to Count Rammel, the estate's owner, whose family's ownership dates back to the seventeenth century, that some British landowners would not feel it was worth owning land if they could not keep people out when they wished. Count Rammel replied: 'I don't need that power. I can grow what I want to; I don't need the feeling that I am more important than other people—have them bowing everywhere.' The unostentatious interiors of houses like Övedskloster lack the large canvases of past owners lording their power over people and land from the back of a favoured steed which so often adorn British landowners' houses and reflect a difference in outlook between Sweden's largest landowners and those of their British counterparts who pride themselves on maintaining stately homes as proud monuments to the feudal past. In Sweden, the assumption that the attractions of the countryside are for all to share is not just the official line of landowners' and farmers' representative organizations but fully felt by ordinary farmers. Ragnar Sandberg, for instance, owns 250 acres of woodland and 75 acres of arable land on the edge of a village close to Jönköping in central Sweden's industrial area. Around 50 people walk through Mr Sandberg's land every day and he told me, 'People walking do no damage', though he does have trouble with motorcyclists whose activities are not endorsed by Allemansrätt. When I asked him what he would think if Allemansrätt were abolished, he said that would be terrible: 'It's nice to meet people in the forest and nature is something we should all share wherever we live.'

The twenty-one county authorities which administer Allemansrätt undoubtedly find their task made easier by the general support which the system enjoys. Nonetheless, sanctions are available where enforcement proves necessary. If a landowner puts up a new fence, he has to make sure there is a way through it for walkers. If he fails to provide one, the local council can require him to, and if he neglects to, it can do the work itself and send him the bill—a system similar to Britain's machinery for removing illegal obstructions from rights of way. If a landowner were to put up a notice forbidding access then the local authority could require him to take it down. If he failed to do so, it could take it down itself and send him the bill.

Allemansrätt is not officially enshrined in law but simply respected as custom. Swedes have been reluctant to turn it into a law because they feel that definition of the right could mean the narrowing down

of the freedom of movement they enjoy at present. There are indica-
tions that they may be right. The citizens of Norway enshrined their
own right of access to the countryside in the Outdoor Recreation Act
of 1957, which was amended most recently in 1996.[3] Broadly speaking,
this gives Norwegians similar rights of access as Swedes but guaranteed in law not just custom. In both countries people are expected to
respect the privacy of houses and gardens. But whereas Allemansrätt
simply forbids anybody from pitching their tent close to a dwelling-
house, the Norwegian legislation forbids camping within 150 metres
of a dwelling. In Sweden, most people probably would not camp closer
than 130 or 150 metres to an ordinary occupied home but they might
not consider it necessary to give a summer house in a forest clearing
such a wide berth, particularly if there clearly is no one at home. Neither
Swedes nor Norwegians are as territorial about their homes as the
British. People often do not fence in their gardens and I have come
across imposing, isolated manor houses in southern Sweden where
landowners encourage people to inspect their home at close quarters
by posting up notices drawing their attention to particular features
of architecture rather than keeping them at arm's length as is so often
the British way.

A Right in Britain

The idea of a right of access like that enjoyed by Scandinavians was
perhaps bound to find adherents in a country with such a long tradition of struggle over land rights as Britain. From Magna Carta on, the
British had seen entrenching rights rather than relying on grace-and-
favour concessions as a natural means of redressing grievances and
asserting the needs of the weak against the demands of the strong.
The idea of rights was one of the lasting legacies of the Enlightenment in Britain, with Tom Paine helping America's revolutionaries
define their own rights culture. As the nineteenth century saw new
rights being created for groups like women, it was perhaps inevitable
that the idea of a right to access to the countryside should eventually
take shape, as it finally did in James Bryce's bill in 1884.

Ever since then, the idea of a right of access to the countryside
has been somewhere on the agenda, dormant much of the time but

exploding in occasional eruptions, like the mass trespasses of the 1930s. Sixty years ago, H. G. Wells spelt out the case forcefully: 'Every man, without distinction of race or colour, is entitled to nourishment, housing, covering, medical care and attention, employment and . . . the right to roam over any kind of country, moorland, mountain, farm, great garden or what not, where his presence will not be destructive of its special use, nor dangerous to himself nor seriously inconvenient to his fellow citizens.'⁴ Our own era has strengthened the people's claim to the countryside. Two world wars which saw so many people lay down their lives for their country have made it seem stranger that their country should be a place in which they have no right to roam. This idea certainly helped fuel the mass trespasses of the 1930s and it retains its force today. Jack Ibbott, a 76-year-old Ramblers' Association stalwart, fought his way up most of Italy and landed in Normandy. He comments, 'I didn't serve my country for five years so as to be kept off four fifths of it for the rest of my life.'⁵ Some people thus feel that citizenship ought to entitle them to a right of access to their homeland as much as a right to vote or to receive equal treatment under the law. Access achieved through landowners' grace and favour would not be enough for them. At the same time, the contemporary idea that the natural environment is the responsibility of everyone (and thus something in which we all must have some kind of ownership rights) also conflicts with the notion that land can be treated simply as private property. So it is not surprising that the citizens of the 1990s are less and less prepared to accept the idea that they are to be treated as trespassers in the rural environment because individuals think they own it. As people interpret democracy ever more assertively, the private power of landowners thus seems likely to grow further out of step with contemporary attitudes.

However, the argument in Britain has not revolved simply around a universal right of access to the whole countryside, albeit subject to exceptions, of the kind that exists in Scandinavia. While people like Wells have instinctively seen the issue in universalist terms, many of Britain's most influential activists have come to favour a different approach. They have argued that instead of providing access throughout the countryside, it need be provided only to certain particular types of terrain. Such a partialist approach had of course already been evident in Bryce's nineteenth-century bills, which referred only to uncultivated upland in Scotland, and it was Bryce's bill which gave later activists their model. Bryce and his associates were particularly exercised by the impact on the walker over Scotland's hills of the creation of huge deer preserves during the previous eighty years. The virtual absence of public footpaths and common land in the High-lands suggested some other means of opening the hills was needed, but since the problem was then seen as overwhelmingly an upland one, a universal right of access did not suggest itself. This historical accident was not, however, the only reason why the idea of a partial rather than a universal right of access subsequently came to the fore. Bryce himself concentrated on uplands not only because this was where the urgent problem was occurring but also because of his own special affection for mountain and moorland terrain. From boyhood, he was passionate about Scotland's hills, and as an adult, he was a keen mountaineer, climbing in some of the remotest regions of the world. This personal preference for mountain, moor, and hill turned out to be shared by many of the countryside activists who came after, for some of whom the countryside meant the uplands. Lowland woods, vales, riversides, and farmland were not the places where they wanted to walk, so the problem of access to these kinds of countryside did not overly concern them.

Professor George Trevelyan, the historian, was a one-time president of the Youth Hostels' Association and chair of the estates committee of the National Trust. He was also the brother of Sir Charles Trevelyan who in 1908 tabled the first right to roam bill for mountain and moorland in England (see page 176). In a lecture in 1931, Professor Trevelyan tried to explain the preference of his ilk: 'Nature, no doubt, acts as a comforter and giver of strength even in the southern wood-lands and on smooth hillsides. But to many of us the moorland and the mountain seem to have more rugged strength and faithfulness with which in solitude we can converse and draw thence strength and comfort.'[6] The identification of rural recreation with upland country among activists was not confined to an educated class still in thrall to Wordsworth's vision of the magic mountain. As hiking became a pastime of growing importance for the northern working class, their leaders also focused firmly on the hills. It was no accident that the mass trespasses of the 1930s, involving many workers from industrial towns, were directed at the moors of the Peak District rather than lowland countryside. Tom Stephenson, who as we have seen on page 178 was the Ramblers' Association's general secretary for twenty-one years, came from a thoroughly working-class background in Lancashire. He told me in an interview in 1977, 'I've learned to endure lowland scenery. I realize that you can't help but admire a mountain, but to appreciate the more subtle lines of a lowland landscape is more difficult—I think it's got to be acquired.'[7] Stephenson devoted much attention to the moors of the Pennines, but his favourite landscape in Britain was even more rugged: 'Above everything I would put the Cuillins of Skye because they are gaunt, almost black at times—gabbro and basalt. They are shattered and pinnacled and you can see almost from one side of the mountain to the other through cracks in the rocks.' When Stephenson invented the concept of the long-distance path he helped ensure that the first such path was the Pennine Way. The influence of him and his kind also helped ensure that when the National Parks Commission established in 1949 came to create Britain's first national parks, they were pointed in the direction of upland countryside. The Commission was enjoined by statute to bear in mind proximity to centres of population, yet spurned areas like the South Downs and the Chilterns, which might have served Londoners, to concentrate virtually all of Britain's parks in the uplands of the north and west.[8]

Just why Britain's rural activists have been so fixated on the hills is debatable. Perhaps the trauma of our rapid industrial revolution, concentrating people suddenly in polluted and congested cities, created an intense yearning for lofty, open spaces among our more vigorous spirits. Such people felt hemmed in, not transported, when they were let loose in bluebell woods, and confined, not delighted, by flower-strewn meadows. In 1977 I interviewed at length five leading figures in the English outdoor movement about the special attraction all of them felt for moorland scenery. Lady Sylvia Sayer, who founded what was to become one of Britain's most influential pressure groups, the Dartmoor Preservation Association, recalled experiencing Dartmoor for the first time; 'Plymouth in those days was rather a smoky town. One never noticed that until one stepped out of the rather tiny train at Princetown station. As a child the very air was magic because it was so different, so clean and absolutely heady . . . But of course it was primarily the wildness, the feeling of freedom. . . . Instead of being in a terraced house in Plymouth there was all this lovely wild freedom.'[9] The other people I interviewed were Tom Stephenson; Kate Ashbrook, then 24 years old and working for the Dartmoor Preservation Association, by the mid-1990s general secretary to the Open Spaces Society and chair of the Ramblers' Association; Gerald McGuire, who worked for eighteen years at the head office of the Youth Hostels' Association and had served on the Countryside Commission and the North York Moors National Park Committee; and Malcolm MacEwen, who led a campaign to halt the ploughing of moorland on Exmoor and went on to write two books about national parks. All regarded the moors as a unique refuge whose remoteness cuts them off from the man-made environment. Only moorland and mountain could provide an environment in which the individual could break free of man's works and enjoy a 'wilderness' experience. Moorland, my five interviewees explained, offered a combination of openness, asymmetry, homogeneity, height, the absence of obviously human handiwork, and freedom to wander at will which answered a deep need within them.[10]

In view of this, it becomes easy to imagine the anger which must have gripped Britain's would-be hikers during the 1920s and 1930s when they contemplated vast tracts of moorland on the doorstep of our northern cities. Unlike an inaccessible wood, which few may see into from the outside, hikers who tramped to the edge of the built-up area of northern cities like Sheffield could see wide open hillsides from which they were barred staring down at them. And even activists far from the moors considered they were being barred from the kind of terrain on which their spiritual well-being depended. Thus it was that access to moorland rather than the countryside generally became the subject of the fierce struggles of the 1930s. The idea took root in this period in the minds of those who cared most about the subject that access to the countryside meant access to moorlands and that a right of access to uplands rather than to the countryside as a whole was all that was required. Insofar as they were interested in access rights in the lowlands at all they tended to concern themselves with wilder landscape types, usually downland turf and heathland.

Partialism in Practice

As it happens, the idea of a partial right of access—to limited types of country only—has already been tried out not too far from Britain just as a universal right of access already exists in Scandinavia. Germany is a particularly clear case of a country which has proceeded on the partialist model. For the Germans, however, it has not been upland country which has been the priority target. Their own historical and cultural circumstances preoccupied their activists with a different concern—forests. Forests have long had a mystical significance in Germany, at least as strong as the spell exercised over Britain's hikers by the hills. As hiking gathered popularity in twentieth-century Germany, the forests seemed the obvious destination, yet although access was tolerated in some woods, in many others it was barred. Inaccessible forests were mainly owned either by large-scale proprietors or smaller-scale owners who had banded together to form hunting co-operatives, both of which groups leased out hunting rights at high prices to wealthy Germans. By the 1960s, at both federal and provincial level there were politicians who wanted to provide for general access to forests. They had in mind a civil law giving landowners a duty to tolerate access to their land, but the burden this would impose on civil courts deterred governments from action. However, in 1969 the government of one of the country's most popular *Länder*, North-Rhine Westphalia, whose 17 million inhabitants include the citizens of Bonn, Cologne, Aachen, and Düsseldorf, grasped this nettle and passed its own Forest Law, which granted the public a right to enter all wooded areas for the purpose of outdoor recreation. Six years on this served as the model for a forest law applying to the whole of the former West Germany: at a stroke the Federal Forest Act of 1975, passed after difficult negotiations, granted a legal right of access throughout all forests, large or small, state or privately owned.[11]

Huntsmen and forest owners opposed the 1975 legislation, arguing vehemently that public access would cause damage, disturbance of game and wildlife, and more forest fires. By the mid-1980s these fears were proving more or less groundless, and the Bundestag widened the scope of the law. Now, in what used to be East Germany as well as the West, a right of access to particular types of countryside has opened up not just woods but rough grasslands, heaths, marshes, meadows not in agricultural use, fallow land, land in set-aside, and all roads and paths, including privately owned paths unless they pass close to a dwelling or through a farmyard. This last element not only provides a legal means for people to reach many stretches of legally accessible open land or woodland from which they would otherwise be cut off, but it also opens up other landscape features like watersides, so long as they are not immediately bordered by farmland: access to the coast, lakesides, and riverbanks arises either because of the presence of paths or by virtue of the right of access to uncultivated open land alongside. The countryside access laws do not affect rights of passage along public footpaths and roads, which are guaranteed under separate legislation.

Though only certain types of landscape are accessible in Germany, exemptions are available within these types as they are in countries where a blanket right of access operates. As in Sweden, exemptions are mainly to meet the needs of agriculture, forestry, nature conservation, and privacy around people's homes. In spite of their early objections, Germany's landowners and huntsmen now seem to have learned to live with public access to the woods. Visit woodland around Bonn today and you find a near absence of litter and few signs of landscape erosion. Doubtless what is now a sophisticated access management system helps secure this happy state of affairs. The many paths and minor country roads which pass through woodland and which are accessible to riders, cyclists, and wheelchair users as well as walkers are not open to vehicles except those owned by people who have obtained a special permit, usually because they live or work in the vicinity. Such roads may be gated or may exhibit a special sign. Other laws forbid the dumping of rubbish except at special dumps. These arrangements not only protect the countryside from damage but enable visitors to enjoy high-quality countryside on the edge of the towns where they live. If they drive to the popular areas of countryside they have to leave their cars at car parks; many prefer to use impressive public transport facilities. In 1993, the House of Commons Environment Committee investigated the impact of public access on woodland in Germany. After a four-day visit, the Committee, chaired by Conservative MP Robert Jones, concluded in a report entitled *Forestry and the Environment*: 'In Germany, where there is a general right of public access to all forests—in private as well as public ownership—there appear to be no real problems, either with the public's use of woodlands or with the perceptions of landowners.'[12]

Denmark is another country in which access has been provided partially—to specific types of countryside rather than universally. In this very maritime nation, it was not woods but seashore which was singled out for priority attention. In 1917, a legal right to walk along the seashore was introduced, and in 1937 the government required landowners to obtain permission for most changes made within 100 metres (109 yards) of the shore, such as building and tree planting, partly to prevent the construction of houses along the seashore which might impede public access. In 1995 this zone was extended to 300 metres. The Nature Protection Act of 1992 now provides a right of access for walking, bathing, standing, sitting, or lying on beaches, the foreshore, and other coastal areas. A farmer who wishes to fence down to the seashore needs permission from a local conservation board, though if consent is withheld, he can appeal to Denmark's state conservation agency. For their part, the public must keep their dogs on a lead from 1 April until 30 September. They need consent to camp but have a right to bathe or stop for a short period and walk on the shore even if they are within 50 metres (55 yards) of a dwelling.[13]

Heathland is also culturally important in Denmark and this became the second category of land to which the public were granted access. Now the 1992 act provides for public access to uncultivated, unfenced areas, opening up not only heaths but also uncultivated areas alongside streams and behind the coast. If the land involved is privately owned, walkers must keep off between sunset and 7 a.m., and while they may pass they must not stop within 150 metres (164 yards) of a house or a building devoted to farming or forestry. Dogs must be kept on a lead and the local council is empowered to suspend access if it deems this necessary to safeguard wildlife while the police may do the same to reduce the risk of fire.

Danes do not enjoy quite as much freedom of access to woodland as do Germans. Thirty-one per cent of the country's woodland is owned by the state and the public enjoy a right of general access all over these woods, whatever their size, at any time of the day or night, on or off roads and tracks. (In Britain although public access to Forestry Commission woodland is extensive, it is at the Commission's discretion and may be lost when the Commission sells freehold, leasehold, or shooting rights; see page 56.) In Denmark a general right of access also extends over woods owned by local councils, the country's official church, and public institutions. One-third of Denmark's privately owned woods are deciduous (beech is the national tree) and they are used for pheasant shooting and deer stalking as well as timber production. Over the years the Danish ramblers' organization and the Danish Outdoor Council, an umbrella group of ninety nongovernmental groups including ornithologists, scouts, and walkers, have pressed for greater access in privately owned woods and this has been achieved in stages. In 1969 Parliament provided a right of access along all roads and paths in large privately owned woods; in 1984 the Nature Conservation Law provided that people should enjoy a right to walk along the roads and paths in all privately owned woods over 5 hectares (12 acres) in extent so long as there is some legal means of reaching them. The 1992 law extended the provision to woods under 5 hectares unless an owner under certain conditions puts up notices to the contrary. Again as with access to heaths, access is not allowed between sunset and 7 a.m., dogs must be on a lead, and walkers may pass but not stop within 150 metres (164 yards) of a dwelling or farm or forestry building.

Zealand, the island on which Copenhagen stands, is Denmark's most populous area. The Ledreborg estate, owned by Count Knud Holstein Ledreborg, stands on the edge of the small town of Roskilde (population 50,000), 8 miles from the capital. At nearly 4,500 acres, it is broadly comparable to Highclere, the Hampshire estate near the medium-sized town of Newbury. In both cases an imposing house is surrounded by a park with farmland and woodland further out. An estimated 10,000 people visit Ledreborg's woods every year, yet not only does timber production proceed unhindered but 4,000 pheasants are reared every year to be shot by the family and a syndicate. Around 250 roe deer living in the woods are also successfully hunted.

While parts of Highclere Park are open for only part of the year in addition to the single public footpath which now crosses it and the short one which leads to a church (see page 83), the Ledreborg park is open all year round during daylight hours including Christmas Day. The law requires the Count to allow people unfettered access along the many paths and roads through his woods. For five days each year, during November and December, he closes his woods to enable pheasant shooting to take place, as he is legally entitled to do. I asked him in 1988 whether the public access caused problems for the management of game on the estate. He replied:

'You have to learn to live with it. You know you can't put your table in the road: it would be driven down. . . . Pheasants get very used to people: they don't really mind. The problems only occur with people who bring dogs. [But] more than 95 per cent of people keep them on a leash. Those that are let loose are often fat little things that don't do any harm. A big dog can create some havoc. You must learn to put the pheasants where the public don't go. We put them down in small areas in fields, say along some hedges, and in the woods where by experience we know people don't pass by. A few people will go near the pheasants anyhow, but that doesn't matter. Roe deer thrive very well with the public. If there are too many people, roe deer can move quickly from one part of the woods to another.'

Poaching is not a problem either. 'The public is so numerous about here. We haven't caught any poachers for years. Of course one thinks that a person driving a car through may shoot a roe deer, but it is not important: we haven't had any of that for years.' Trouble with the public is possible but avoidable. 'You can make a conflict if you sit there and think you can shoot roe deer on a Saturday afternoon: you do that and you can provoke a conflict. We have to learn to adapt ourselves.' The Count believes problems could arise with orienteering exercises, but these require his permission and he ensures that they take place on days when they will not adversely affect his own land and game management regime. On access generally: 'The closer you get to a big town, the more social your attitude has to be. If you live far from a town and see only two tourists a year you can allow yourself to be infuriated. You adapt—it's human nature.' Count Ledreborg has posted a sign 'Velkommen tu Ledreborg' at the entrance to his property. This did not seem to be some kind of public relations exercise. He did it, he said, because it seemed natural to him to do so.

Switzerland is another densely populated country where partialism has provided access to certain types of countryside.[14] Whereas in

Germany and Denmark rights of access have been gradually introduced and extended often in the face of landowner opposition, in
Switzerland a freedom to walk in the mountains, upland pastures, and
woods is an ancient custom given legal standing in 1907 in the Civil
Code, which declares: 'Everyone has free access to other people's forests
and grazing lands and may take berries, mushrooms and other small
fruits, in accordance with local custom, except where the competent
authority has imposed special bans, limited to particular areas, in order
to protect land under cultivation.' In addition the Swiss enjoy a right
of access on most paths and tracks across cultivated land. The British
climber E. A. Baker visited Switzerland in the 1920s and was struck
by the contrast between the treatment of tourists in Switzerland and
Scotland, where vast areas were still barred to walkers in the interests of deer stalking, grouse shooting, and game fishing. 'Imagine what
Switzerland would have been had the Swiss allowed the mountainous portion to become a great closed area where private individuals
stalked deer', Baker wrote. 'Europe would have been deprived of that
area within its bounds where nature is most lavish of splendour and
majesty.'[15]

Rather than extending the categories of land over which a right
of access exists, the Swiss have refined their procedures for defending
that access and for resolving potential conflicts with other activities.
Forest assessment exercises now enable citizens to argue that an area
on which native woodland trees have been planted has become forest, to which public access should therefore be available. Since 1991,
cantons, which are responsible for administering the system, have been
empowered to restrict access to forests in order to protect the arboreal environment. As a result, public events such as marathons and
festivals in woods require the consent of the cantonal authorities. In
the interests of nature conservation, walkers are sometimes confined
to paths, as in the Grisons National Park, where rangers, who are part
of the police force, can impose on-the-spot fines for dropping litter.
Huntsmen pursue their quarry of foxes and deer singly or in small
groups and have to pass tough examinations before they can hunt.
Walkers take special care during the hunting season, but hunting is
not considered a sufficient reason for excluding walkers. Access can
be withdrawn when felling is taking place or new plantations are being

established. An owner who wishes to close off a piece of woodland as tree felling is to take place does so himself when the work is about to begin.

Recently attempts have been made to create a right of access to lakesides in Switzerland. A federal law passed in 1979 required the relevant public authorities to keep free of buildings the sides of lakes and watercourses and facilitate passage along their banks. This sought to enshrine an ancient custom of access along lakeshores which had been lost as people enclosed lakeside gardens to their houses and mansions, but those who own such properties are often wealthy and powerful citizens. Nonetheless several cantons have taken steps to establish greater public access along lakesides. Thus in 1982 Berne passed a law which requires local commune councils to establish walkers' paths along riverbanks and lakesides throughout the canton.

Northern Europe therefore offers examples of how both partial and universal rights of access to the countryside can work successfully on the ground. The choice between partial and universal has reflected the history and culture of the individual countries. In the UK, however, where we are starting almost from scratch, we can make our own choice between the two approaches on the basis of which would work best here. The fundamental difference is that any partial system maintains the principle of the landowner's right to exclude but removes it in specified cases. A total right of access, in contrast, would turn the law of trespass on its head and give people a general right to move freely, though it might in practice exclude as much or even more of particular types of land through exemptions than a partial right of access. In neither case would such a 'right to roam' mainly affect rambling at will across trackless expanses, since people tend naturally to take to paths. More important in practice would be the opening up of existing linear routes such as private paths and roads along which most movement would naturally tend to take place.

Partialism Triumphs

In Britain, our own heritage provides pointers to both partial and the universal approach. A partial system might satisfy the activist moorland enthusiasts who have been the noisiest advocates of enhanced access, but it would fail to meet the demands of those like H. G. Wells who have felt that Britain's freedoms are incomplete without a total right of access which would give people a right to move freely as a matter of principle. It was, however, the idea of a partial right of access confined more or less to uplands only which came to the fore during the access debate of the 1980s and 1990s. This was largely the result of the stance taken by the country's leading lobby group for walkers, the Ramblers' Association.

The Ramblers' Association was founded in 1935 in the wake of the mass trespasses and rallies in the Peak District. Hill walkers from northern England preoccupied with freedom to wander over moorland have always been an extremely significant if not the dominant element within the organization and the Association's pronouncements have frequently assumed that the uplands should be walkers' priority concern. *We Demand the Freedom of the Hills*, a campaign document issued in 1945, typically urged 'as a fundamental right of citizenship access to all uncultivated mountains and moorlands'. In fact the association did not push hard for a right of access of any kind during the 1960s, 1970s, and 1980s. When the issue resurfaced in the late 1980s and early 1990s it was not absolutely certain which way the Association would jump. The idea of a right of access to green belt land was floated by some, an idea which although apparently partialist was clearly at odds with the upland partialism of the 1945 document. Since green belts contain different kinds of landscape linked only by their proximity to population centres, such thinking might have taken the Association ultimately in a universalist direction. In 1988 the Association formally called for at least half of all set-aside land to be automatically accessible;[16] once again this was an apparently limited notion which could have opened the way to a far broader approach. However, the RA was still dominated by people particularly fond of the hills. Although Kate Ashbrook, who held the positions of vice-chairman and then chairman between 1995 and 1998 (she continued to chair the important Access Committee of the Association), lives in Buckinghamshire and clearly enjoys walking lowland footpaths and over the open downland of the Chilterns, her devotion to the countryside cause sprang from a deep affection for Dartmoor; her choice of university (Exeter) was shaped by her desire to live close to the moor. Janet Street-Porter, the RA's president from 1994 to 1997, had loved hill walking since her child-hood experience of Snowdonia; she has had a second home in the Yorkshire Dales for many years. At an RA rally on the moorland mass of the Forest of Bowland in Lancashire in 1994, she enthused: 'I walk for hours near my home in Yorkshire now over moors, on and off tracks. It clears my head as well as my lungs. . . . The human spirit needs to experience the emptiness and solitude of places like Bowland now more than ever.'[17]

As calls for a general right of access to the countryside began to be made outside the organization in the late 1980s, the Association found itself required to define its position on a general right of access. Calls for a legal right to roam were beginning to be heard and the organ-ization was in some danger of being left behind. It set up a working party in which Kate Ashbrook played a leading part to determine its own position on the issue. A campaign document entitled *Head for the Hills* published in 1990 made it clear which way the Association had decided to go. In this document, the RA pledged that it would seek 'to persuade Parliament to make a new law to recognise and protect existing access to mountain and moorland and to create a right of access where none currently exists to open country'. Three years later, on the anniversary of the birth of Tom Stephenson at an event on the Pennine Way, the Association unveiled another paper called *Harmony in the Hills*, which set out the scope of a possible right to roam and invited comments from walkers. By this point, the emphasis on upland partialism had become entrenched, although some of the types of lowland landscape most akin to hill country, like downland and heathland, got a mention. The aim of a new right was seen by the association less as providing the citizen with a means to move freely around his or her native land than as a device enabling walkers to stray off the existing public paths crossing open, uncultivated moun-tain, moor, down, or heath and enjoy the experience of roaming freely: 'Walkers navigating over wild, uncultivated land need freedom to explore summits, valleys, waterfalls and crags, whether or not such places are accessible by rights of way', *Harmony in the Hills* explained. The document assumed that mountain, moor, heath, and down would be covered by the right of access which the organization would demand, though it did ask whether foreshore and woodland, which also fall within the definition of 'open country' used in current access law, should be included. The membership's answer to this question was a resounding yes: of the 2,300 members of the Association who returned a questionnaire, 82.5 per cent asked for riverside and canalside to be included.[18]

When the RA came to draft an Access to the Countryside Bill in 1995, it included not only moor and mountain but the other types of land which fall within the legal definition of 'open country' for England and Wales (heath, cliff, foreshore, downland, woodland, riverside, and canalside) as well. Still partialist in principle, such a bill if enacted would nonetheless have embraced a substantial slice of Britain's countryside. Though committed to its bill in theory, the RA's campaigners continued however to emphasize moor and mountain in practice. All three of the sites at which the Association launched its bill were north country moors. In 1996 the Association published a document called *Freedom with Responsibility* to explain and promote the bill. The front cover showed hikers on the moors. Inside, lengthy articles concerned themselves with access problems over certain Pennine moors and Welsh mountains; woodland hardly got a mention except in the context of the loss of access to land once controlled by the Forestry Commission. One of the RA's officers explained to me that woodland might not be appropriate for a right to roam because the existence of trees in the way of the walkers prevented the free wandering which was viewed as the whole of a new right by so many RA activists.

In January 1996, Paddy Tipping, the Labour MP for Sherwood in Nottinghamshire, introduced a private member's bill entitled *Access to the Countryside*. Based on a draft prepared by the Ramblers' Association, this bill spelt out what a partialist access regime might actually comprise. It sought to give a right of public access to virtually all land which falls within the definition 'open country'. There would be several categories of land which while 'open' would be exempted from the right of access, such as land covered by buildings or the curtilage of buildings, railways, racecourses, quarries, and gardens. The bill provided for any person having a legal interest to make an application to his or her local authority for a declaration that a particular stretch of land was not 'open country'. Such people and also English Nature and the Countryside Council for Wales (the government agencies with statutory responsibility for nature conservation) could apply for a 'temporary prohibition order' to suspend the right of access to a stretch of land for up to three years in order to preserve or restore land for rough grazing; protect recently planted trees; protect or restore plants or animals on the land; or prevent accidents at ponds, quarries and the like. English Nature, English Heritage or the Countryside Council for Wales could also apply for temporary suspension of the right of access in order to protect geological, physiographical or archaeological features or areas or to protect or restore the natural beauty of the land or its suitability for open-air recreation. If any person complained to his local authority that the means of reaching a stretch of 'open country' was inadequate, the authority, if satisfied that this was so, would be under a duty to provide a remedy. People obstructing access to 'open country' or displaying notices containing any false or misleading statement likely to deter the public from entering such land would be guilty of an offence and could be fined. The new law would apply to all 'open country', including that in the hands of the Crown Estate and government departments. The bill was debated briefly: a number of objections were raised by the Conservative member for South Suffolk, Tim Yeo. It was then put to the vote, and while 60 MPs voted against it, 144 voted in favour, including Tony Blair. In July 1997 Mr Tipping tabled his bill once more and it was debated briefly but not put to a vote.[19]

Although Paddy Tipping's bill had embraced a wide range of landscape types, after the vote on the Tipping bill, discussion of a right of access to the countryside came to revolve almost wholly around the upland partialist approach. Not only the Ramblers' Association, but other outdoor bodies took it for granted that a right of access would mean a right of access to the hills. A formal commitment to partialism rather than universalism on the part of the leading walkers' body, coupled with a practical commitment to upland partialism, had a great deal of impact on the overall discussion. Other groups and bodies followed the RA's lead, sometimes seeming to take it for granted that a right of access to the countryside should mean a right of access to the hills. The Council for National Parks, for example, said that it wanted a right of rural access, but only over 'open country', as defined in the 1949 National Parks Act. Rural activists inside and outside the

RA were not led only by their preferences in opting for the hills. They also felt that it was less defensible for people to be excluded from open moors than from say fields, woods, and riversides because up there walking seemed less likely to interfere with economic activities than it might in the busier lowlands. Another factor inevitably in play was the fateful British belief in compromise. If a universal right of access, albeit subject to exceptions, provoked resistance from landowners, concentration instead on what seemed the most important kind of countryside seemed a sensible halfway house. Surely, if campaigners laid off the lowlands with their elaborate farming operations and jealous owners of prestigious parklands designed by Capability Brown, would they not have more chance of depriving the owners of empty moorland acres of their right to exclude? Perhaps the landowning enemy could be divided between lowland owners who would be let off the hook and their upland counterparts, who appeared to have less to lose anyway by allowing access.

Then came what looked like a clear sign that access might indeed be significantly extended so long as this was done in an upland, partialist way. In 1996 the Scottish Landowners' Federation signed a 'Concordat' with the Ramblers' Association Scotland and the Mountaineering Council of Scotland in which the Federation formally acknowledged a freedom to roam over Scotland's hills.[20] Such a freedom had existed in practice for much of the twentieth century, but now ramblers gained formal recognition of their right to walk the hills. As we have seen (page 71) under the Concordat, landowners agree to respect *de facto* access to Scotland's open hill country so long as ramblers avoid active stalking areas during the shooting season, though it involves no sanctions on either side. Brokered by the government agency Scottish Natural Heritage, the Concordat entrenched the idea that as long as access to Britain's countryside meant access to only a part of that countryside then it might be realizable.

Certainly when politicians felt obliged to confront the increasingly urgent question of access to the countryside, they seemed instinctively to prefer the partial to the universal approach to access rights. On the face of it, the Conservative governments of 1979 to 1997, with their links to landowning interests and firm commitment to property rights, were fiercely opposed to any kind of a right of access. In 1986 they actually toughened up the law of trespass in their Criminal Justice and Public Order Act, even though this measure, aimed principally at New Age travellers, posed a clear threat to ordinary walkers. In 1997 John Major condemned the idea of a right to roam as 'a charter for rural crime',[21] while Michael Heseltine, then Deputy Prime Minister, pledged that his government would continue to resist calls for access rights. He told the CLA's conference on access in 1996: 'Those who manage the land are best able to decide what additional access—over and above that offered by the rights of way network—should be made available, and how that access should be managed. . . . Voluntary agreements are the best way to secure additional benefit for the public without damaging local interests.'[22]

All the same, even the Conservatives showed that they were prepared to countenance some extension of access rights of a very partial kind, albeit only briefly. In this case the type of countryside involved was not moorland, but common land. In 1986 a twelve-person group including a representative of the RA, the Country Landowners' Association, and a range of conservation and land tenure groups called the Common Land Forum recommended that the public should enjoy a legal right to roam over the 1.5 million acres of common land in England and Wales along with new measures to conserve the commons.[23] The Conservative government accepted the recommendations of the forum and promised to act on them in the run-up to the 1987 election. As it happened, the Conservative government reneged on this commitment in 1991 fearing a defeat in the House of Lords, but the fact that they were even prepared to consider such a change was a clear sign that access rights had found a place on the political agenda at least in their partialist form.

As the Tories' prospects of remaining in power diminished, access seemed certain to rise higher up the agenda, particularly in view of the opposition parties' apparent emphasis on strengthening community. Perhaps surprisingly, one party determined that even partial rights of access should continue to be resisted was the Liberal Democrats, which turned out to be even more hostile to a right of access of any kind than the Conservatives. The party Spokesman on Rural Affairs, Paul Tyler, MP (North Cornwall) condemned the idea of a right to roam on philosophical as well as practical grounds at the CLA conference.

'The claim of a "right to roam" is fatally flawed', Tyler argued. 'Nobody has the "right" to intrude into another's property, be it in towns or in the countryside . . . An unrestricted "right to roam" will cause untold damage to the more fragile ecosystems and possibly ruin the finer qualities of our rural environment. The object has to be agreement on access.'[24] Whether this line reflected the Liberal Democrat's links with the rural establishment or a particular reading of the philosophy of Liberalism, it was however soon apparent that their stance would make little difference. Even before the outcome of the 1997 election it was apparent that the Labour Party was likely to dominate the political environment of the *fin de siècle*, and this party had a very different attitude to rights of access from both the Liberal Democrats and the Conservatives.

Labour's roots in proletariatism and egalitarianism inevitably pre-disposed it towards the idea that the many should enjoy more of a stake in a countryside held firmly in the hands of the few. Some of the party's early figures, like George Bernard Shaw, had favoured full-scale land nationalization, and the link between walkers' activism and the political left was long-standing. Benny Rothman, one of the leaders of the Kinder Scout trespass, had been an official of the radical British Workers' Sports Federation, while, as we have seen (page 179), many of the rambling clubs which spearheaded the struggle for access to moors and mountains were formed in the industrial North and included many men and women active in the early trade union, co-operative, and Labour movements.[25] The party involved itself in the struggle over access in the 1930s and went on to pass the 1949 National Parks and Access to the Countryside Act which gave local authorities their well-intended if ineffective powers to make access agreements and access orders.

When some Labour people started again to think about access to the countryside in the early 1980s, it was the universalist approach which initially seemed to capture their imagination. An influential figure was the hereditary Labour peer Peter Melchett. Melchett was a child of the 1970s wave of environmentalism, a socialist with radical views, an old Etonian, a keen walker and naturalist, and the owner of an 800-acre farm in Norfolk which he had inherited from his father. On this farm, the energetic and young Melchett set about working out ways in which he could put his socialist ideas into practice on his own land: he gave his farm manager ownership rights on a par with his own and created a 7-mile network of entirely new public footpaths for the enjoyment of visitors. But Melchett was even more anxious to shape Labour Party policy and to this end he set up the Socialist Countryside Group which produced policy papers. As a farmer Melchett was in a position to see what the effects of greater access would really be for the average British farmer on the ground. He concluded that the supposed difficulties had been massively exaggerated. The Group's paper published in 1983 on *Access to the Countryside* stated unequivocally in a section which I drafted, 'There should be a general right of access to the countryside, subject to safeguards that prevent damage to crops, harm to wildlife and intrusion into people's privacy. This is the basis of the law in Sweden and other countries and it works well there. Ideally, Parliament would legislate to provide a right of access on foot to all woodland, parkland and rough grassland, lakeside, riverbank, field edge, farm track and forest path. The new right would apply whether land was owned by private individuals or public authorities, including the Crown. . . . the deliberate prevention of access to land covered by these provisions, other than for some reasonable purpose such as restraining stock, would be an offence.'[26]

It was not only Melchett who, as a peer wielded little real power in the party and who in any case shifted his focus from Westminster to become executive director of Greenpeace in 1989, who was prepared to support universalism in the Labour Party. Even members of the front bench were prepared to put their name to something not far short of it. In 1990 Bryan Gould, the Shadow Environment Secretary, launched a policy paper entitled *Out in the Country* and declared 'The next Labour Government will provide a new legal right of access to uncultivated land. Countless private tracks, woods, lakesides, riverbanks, mountains, moors and heaths will be opened up to those who wish to walk or ride on them, subject only to an obligation to respect the rights of landowners and the flora and fauna.'[27]

Soon, however, these early signs of universalism among Labour's thinkers on access began to give way to the upland partialism predominant among the lobby groups with whom Labour politicians came into contact. There was no formal conversion. The party did not immediately rule out a right to roam over countryside other than upland and roughland; it simply started failing to refer to other kinds of landscape in its statements. The shift seems to have been not simply the desire to conform to what lobbyists seemed to want, but also a reflection of the caution with which the party was approaching the prospect of power. New Labour did not relish the prospect of noisy battles with landowners, and it looked to party policy-makers as if a right of access confined to moor and mountain could be achieved with less fuss than a universal right. In any case party figures involved shared much of the bias towards moorland which infected the leaders of bodies like the Ramblers' Association—for similar reasons. The kind of people who became Labour spokesmen shared much of the outlook of activists in bodies in the Ramblers' Association. So they too often identified the countryside with the hills. John Smith, who succeeded Neil Kinnock as leader in 1992, was an enthusiastic hill-climber in his native Scotland. He was often joined on the mountains by his shadow frontbench colleague and namesake, Chris Smith, who became spokesman on countryside matters, including access. When John Smith died suddenly in 1994 it seemed natural to many in the party that a right to roam should be pursued as a memorial to the party's lost leader, but given that leader's tastes it also seemed natural that such a right should concentrate on upland Britain. When Chris Smith came to promise a 'John Smith Memorial Act', speaking as spokesman in 1994, he said it would 'enshrine a "right to roam" on open country, mountain and moorland for the ordinary people of Britain'.[28] At the party's conference that year he declared:

'Finally, let me say this: there is another environmental right. It is the right to walk freely in our countryside. Over the mountains and moorlands. People have fought for hundreds of years for the right to roam where there is still fresh air and beauty to be enjoyed. We will enshrine that right in law— so that this land can be *our* land—and not just the Duke of Westminster's. I'll tell you one man who would have dearly wanted us to do it. John Smith. On Easter Monday only this year I stood with John at the top of a mountain in the far north of Scotland. The snow was hard underfoot. The cloud was blowing across. We could see for miles, and John looked and felt on top of the world. He would have wanted—as I want—*everyone* to know the exhilaration of such moments.'[29]

From that moment the Labour Party's policy on access reflected the RA's. At the CLA conference at the end of 1996, the party spokesman on rural affairs, Elliot Morley, made it clear that the right to roam to which his party was committed would apply only to 'open areas, of mountain, moorland and existing common land'.[30] Common land managed to creep in alongside moor and mountain because there was a long-standing party commitment to enact the recommendations of the Common Land Forum, and policy-makers thought it would arouse little opposition. (After all, even a Conservative government had been prepared to contemplate access to commons as of right.) In any case, most of the common land in Britain is in fact moor or mountain land and thus already covered. Mr Morley went on to say that land covered by the new right would be identified on maps and wherever possible by signposting. Helpful though these steps might be to walkers, they would of course serve to emphasize that the law of trespass would remain in place except where land had specifically been taken out of its orbit.

Weeks after the 1997 election, Michael Meacher MP, a junior Environment Minister, announced that the new government would launch a consultation exercise on the implementation of a right to roam over mountain, moor, and common land. Six months later, though the consultation paper had failed to appear, Mr Meacher suggested that the new right might also apply to down and heath. The party had wavered on this point in the past: although Elliot Morley insisted in 1996 that the new right would be confined to moor, mountain, and common land, Labour Environment Spokesman Frank Dobson had talked at a rally the year before of a right to roam over mountain, moor, and open country, without defining what 'open country' might mean. Mr Meacher also made it plain that any new right would be confined to England and Wales, with any new proposals for Scotland and Northern Ireland arrived at separately. In practice this seems bound to mean that access in Scotland will become a matter for the Scottish Parliament, with access in Northern Ireland a matter for the Northern Ireland Assembly. When the government suggested in its consultation document that it might rely on voluntary arrangements for England and Wales rather than a statutory right, it made it clear it was still concerned only with the categories of land it had specified.[31] So England and Wales seem destined for a partialist approach, even though this is far from being the sensible compromise it may seem, and may in fact create even more problems than a universalist solution.

A Wrong Turning?

A right of access to moor, mountain, heath, down, and common land in England and Wales would affect between 3 and 4 million acres.[32] This is only between 8 and 12 per cent of the land of those territories, but landowners would not view this as getting off lightly, and would be able to make telling objections to it. At the same time, walkers would find it failed to address some of their most important needs.

A partial right of access to the countryside would not only fail to meet but would specifically deny the philosophical case for access on which its intellectual respectability depends. 'The Earth is the Lord's and the fullness thereof' has been the driving idea behind 1,000 years of reaction against the Normans' expropriation of Saxon people's land rights. People like John Ball, Gerrard Winstanley, and Henry George all took it for granted that the bounty of the earth should be shared. They would not have understood why only certain parts of the earth were being exposed to the workings of what they would have seen as the natural moral order. If, as the seventeenth-century Diggers put it, the earth is 'a common treasury', in which the rights of the many have been usurped by the few, then a reforming government should not be entrenching the usurpation of all but a part of that common treasury. If 'The land of every country belongs', as John Stuart Mill contended, to 'the people of that country', then a universal right, however much it might be subjected to exemptions and exceptions for whatever reasons, would make more sense than any right applying to only selected kinds of countryside.

If we are to live in a society which offers citizens sensible rights in return for sensible duties, then the kind of right of access to the countryside which makes sense is a general right constrained where this is required for reasons which society can accept, not by crude differentiation between categories of landscape. We live in an age which has been civilizing itself partly by promulgating rights which have won assent. If these are to be convincing they need to be universal in their application, at least in principle. We did not provide women with a partial right to vote. We do exclude peers and the mentally ill from this right, but these are specifically justified exceptions to a rule which is fundamentally general. Of course, a right of access to the countryside cannot be absolute: it must be balanced against other rights like our right to expect our wildlife to be protected and the right of a landowner to gain a living from his land without undue interference. But arbitrarily applying access rights to some classes of land but not others is clearly no way to secure a proper balance.

A right of access ought to be a right to the land restricted only for good reason—a right to the earth which is the common environment of all. We need a world in which people care for the environment because they think of it as their own living space. We are widely supposed to be putting aside the 1980s mindset that only individuals and their families matter to rediscover a sense of community in which all recognize their obligations to promote the common good in return for sharing in it. If this is so, a universal right to walk in the countryside ought to make that much more sense. A partial right, reinforcing the owner's right to exclude outside its remit, would reflect the values of the past.

It is not only the philosophical tenor of the age that a partial right of access to uplands and common would fail to match. It would also fall a long way short of solving the real practical problems that exclusion is currently creating for people who want to visit their countryside. The minority of heavy-duty walkers who only walk on moorland might feel they had achieved their objective. But the far greater numbers of ordinary people who would like to enjoy the countryside in a less organized way might notice little difference.

Vast stretches of our countryside would be unaffected by a right to roam even if down and heath were opened up as well as moor, mountain, and common. Both Scotland and Northern Ireland are omitted from Labour's so far published plans. Within England and Wales, counties like Hertfordshire, Essex, Warwickshire, Lincolnshire, and Somerset have only the tiniest amount of land falling into any of the categories which the government has so far contemplated rendering accessible. Those parts of the country to be significantly affected will be overwhelmingly those dominated by upland moorland, like the Lake District, the North York Moors, the Cheviots, or the Brecon Beacons. In lowland counties like Gloucestershire, Hertfordshire, Hampshire, Suffolk, Warwickshire, or Cheshire such common land as exists is often the one kind of country which is already legally accessible. The addition of chalk downland and lowland heath will not make much difference on the ground. Only 4 per cent of the land covered by a mountain-moor-common-heath-down right of access of such land would be heath and down: it has been suggested that the total area covered by such a right would be around 3 million acres; but chalk downland and lowland heath cover only 128,440 acres.[33] Clearly there will be areas of common land in lowland England and Wales which will also be covered, but as common land in total covers only 4 per cent of these two countries and as the vast amount of it is in the uplands, the availability of common land is not going to alter the situation that much either.

Since most towns and cities are in the lowlands, the parts of the countryside which would be least affected by the kind of access right currently proposed are the areas where most people live. What is more, they are the areas which most people want to visit. Some of the most influential rambling activists and Labour politicians may be wedded to the moors. But the evidence suggests that most other people prefer lowland countryside. It is our patchwork of field and hedge, down and stream which forms the backcloth to television advertisements idealizing our countryside—not Dartmoor or the Cheviots. When in 1971 the *Geographical Magazine* asked its readers: 'If you had a choice, which other areas would you designate as National Parks?', the Cotswolds came out top of the readers' preferences; eight of the top ten proposals were in lowland Britain and included the Dorset Coast, the Weald, the New Forest, Norfolk Broads, and the North Downs of Kent and Surrey.[34] We have already seen (page 76) that the survey of landscape tastes conducted by David Lowenthal and Hugh Prince concluded that 'the countryside beloved by the great majority is tamed and inhabited, warm, comfortable, humanised. . . . What is considered "essentially English" is a calm and peaceful deer park, with slow moving streams and wide expanses of meadowland studded with fine trees. The scene should include free-ranging domestic animals. . . .

When it is arable land, hedgerows and small fields are usually obligatory.'

Moorland enthusiasts are captivated by the notion that they should be able to roam at will—off paths—and that this is only practicable in upland and roughland. Most people are, however, content to walk on linear routes when they are out of doors—whether it be along tracks and footpaths or along towpaths and the edges of fields, as the Countryside Commission study mentioned on page 317 has shown. Simply by opening up currently private tracks, paths, and roads, a universal right of access would do far more for most walkers than the right to roam free on moors will do for the few. In any case, this latter right is of limited practical value. Much moor and mountain land is too boggy, rocky, or otherwise difficult to be of much appeal to walkers. And surprising though it may seem, the legitimate case for excluding walkers from upland areas is often stronger than in lowland areas—so much so that whether a right of access is partial or universal it is likely to require exemptions for much upland country for a significant amount of the time. Grouse shooting, on which the survival of heather moorland depends, could require temporary exemptions from a right of access over a wide area when the birds are nesting, since grouse rear their young in the wild, unlike pheasants which are mostly artificially reared. Closures could then be expected for another thirty days or so per year from 12 August when shooting is actually taking place. Farmers would want restrictions for at least a further six weeks during the lambing season. Not just farmers and landowners but conservationists would want walkers barred from both heather and grass moorland during spring and early summer, since this is the season for the many often scarce species of wild birds which happen to nest on moors, since they all nest on the ground, unlike woodland birds which mostly nest in bushes and trees. These ground-nesting birds, like snipe and curlew, hen harrier and golden plover, are undoubtedly vulnerable to disturbance. On top of all this, midsummer closures for fire risk are likely to become increasingly necessary if drought, as expected, becomes more common. Already, the 7,000-acre Barden Fell and Barden Moor in the Yorkshire Dales has had to close for weeks at a time to avert the risk of a blaze. All in all it could well be argued that if a right of access were to be limited to one kind of countryside only, then moor and mountain would be among the least suitable of types of countryside to choose. Certainly when all the necessary periods of exemption are taken into account it becomes clear that a right of access to the hills alone will not create all that many months of extra walking time.

All this is not to say that there should not be a right to roam over moorland in principle, only that singling out this kind of country seems more and more peculiar the more you consider the implications. But singling out any kind of countryside creates problems that do not arise with a universal right. A peculiarly difficult problem is defining whatever kind of countryside the partial right of access is to apply to. It is not as easy as it may seem to say what exactly moorland, for example, actually is. You can try relying on a vegetation indicator—such as the existence of a certain percentage of heather. You will soon discover, however, that the amount of heather present varies not only according to natural factors like geology and geomorphology but also according to the management of the land. Large numbers of sheep on land lead to the replacement of heather by grass; periodic burning, as is done for the benefit of grouse, encourages heather to dominate. This will mean that what is 'moorland' and what is not will keep varying, so you cannot mark it on a map and walkers will be unsure where they can go and where they cannot. And of course landowners who do not want walkers can take steps to ensure that heather gives way to grass. Suppose instead you define moorland as any land used as rough grazing in upland Britain. In the middle of Kinder Scout or Rannoch Moor most people would be in no doubt as to what was involved. But travel through a valley in mid-Wales and you will probably see a continuous greenish mish-mash of rough grazing interspersed with pasture of a slightly greener hue where artificial fertilizer has been applied to improve the nutritional quality of the grass. Once this has happened, the grazing is presumably no longer rough. Yet to the untrained eye, the two types of vegetation are not easily distinguishable and the whole scene appears uniform because sheep graze everywhere with no fences to separate improved from unimproved grass. Amidst a tumble of hills and ridges and occasional plateaux, the brighter green pasture can turn up in the most unexpected places—sometimes high on the ridge tops, sometimes as an isolated sprawl over a rough hillside. And this is without farmers taking deliberate action to make nonsense of a law many of them would hate.

Necessarily, whatever definition were settled upon would have to be arbitrary, and would thus be a recipe not only for confusion but for conflict. Inevitably people allowed to walk on some spaces will want to walk on other similar spaces even when they know they are not supposed to. What about stretches of land enclosed by stone walls or wire fences whose vegetation is actually more interesting than neighbouring unfenced moorland—say an enclosed area now strewn with foxgloves which many people might find more attractive and more 'natural' than an area above, which may be rocky and strewn with gorse and where sheep may actually be more numerous? What about a meadow grazed by a solitary Shetland pony or an enclosure confining no grazing animals at least for the time being, not necessarily in mid-Wales but say on the outskirts of Bath? What happens when a stretch of rough grass and bracken is being slowly invaded by scrub and birch trees? When is this land 'woodland' and thus exempt from the right to roam and at what stage is it moorland and legally accessible?

Such efforts as have already been made to map moorland highlight these difficulties. Since 1985 national park authorities have been required to prepare maps of uncultivated moor, heath, woodland, and foreshore within their areas and to publish them. The Snowdonia National Park Authority has done so for the country north of Machynlleth—and a very complicated picture it presents.[35] It is possible to refine and bring these maps up to date to follow the ebb and flow of agricultural 'improvement' as farmers 'improve' some areas through the application of fertilizers while leaving some other land once improved to revert to natural vegetation. Yet the process requires sophisticated computer mapping techniques using satellite imaging. Ordinary families going out for a Sunday walk could not be expected to arm themselves with the latest edition of a complex plan before deciding where they would go.

If moorland presents one set of problems, mountain presents another. Where does the foot of a mountain lie? The government's consultation paper said it would include all land above 600 metres (1,969 feet) as 'mountain'.[36] But how are people to know when they have reached 600 metres? What happens if the 600-metre line is covered in a plantation? If defining moor and mountain poses problems, the two further categories of lowland landscape which the government proposed to embrace create even greater difficulties of definition. The inclusion of heath and down appears to meet a possible objection from the owners of moors and mountain land that the original proposal would have singled them out unfairly. However, defining, let alone mapping, heathland and downland would be a daunting task indeed. The edges of moors and mountains may be hard to pin down but at least we all think we know what moors and mountains are.[37] Yet how exactly does downland differ from the many kinds of pasture land from which it must be distinguished, and what exactly is a heath?

As we have seen, chalk downland and lowland heath, whatever exactly they are, cover a tiny area of land compared with mountain and moor. But although the area is tiny, it rarely forms conveniently continuous expanses like moorland and mountain. The chalk downland turf which runs across southern England up to the Yorkshire Wolds has been in the forefront of the post-war expansion and intensification of agriculture. This process has not only cut down its area massively: it has also sliced it up. Salisbury Plain, with 27,000 acres of downland turf in three large blocks, accounts for over one-third of Britain's total downland (though much of this would presumably be exempted on account of the Army training which takes place there). The remaining stretches of downland turf are in the main small and fragmented. A survey of twenty-nine sites in Berkshire in 1985 revealed that 79 per cent were less than 25 acres; while 97 per cent of sites in Lincolnshire were less than 13 acres in 1990.[38] Lowland heathland is if anything more fragmented: a survey of forty-seven sites in 1996 revealed that 66 per cent of them occupied less than 25 acres.[39]

The question of unfairly singling out one kind of land rather than another is not solved but pushed further down the line. Some people will ask why down and heath are to be included while other types of rough grassland are not being included as well. If semi-natural grassland surviving on chalk is to be covered surely semi-natural grassland on limestone must also be included. And why not semi-natural grassland on neutral soils? For the system to work, of course, walkers will have to be able to tell the difference. Yet for the vast majority of people down and heath are indistinguishable not only from the rough, grassy vegetation that grows up on alluvial, clay, loam, gravel or sandstone soil but also from grasslands which are not semi-natural but whose vegetation has been modified sometimes slightly, sometimes radically, by human intervention. For many people it will seem completely illogical that one stretch of down supporting a flock of sheep should automatically become accessible whereas another rough meadow, low-lying beside a river perhaps and grazed by a few shaggy horses, should be exempt. Take a train ride through almost any part of lowland Britain and see if you know what is down and heath and what is not. In fact, you will probably see very little vintage down and heath. You may well see some rough pasture on ridge-and-furrow in say Buckinghamshire, and you will also see plenty of rough grassy areas—rough fields, unused land here and there perhaps partially invaded by scrub. Most of this would not be included in a bureaucrat's likely definition of heath or down. A little would be. How is the walker to know which areas are being opened up on his or her behalf and how are the landowner and farmer to be reassured that their rough meadows will not be invaded by walkers mistakenly assuming them to be down or heath?

As if this were not all challenging enough, the government muddied the waters still further in the definition of 'down' put forward in its consultation paper. 'Down', it asserted, 'is characterised by semi-natural grassland on shallow, lime-rich soils associated with limestone escarpments'.[40] The map with which it accompanied its comment seemed to show most stretches of rough semi-natural grassland on chalk and limestone outcrops in England and Wales. But how thin does the soil have to be to meet the definition's requirement of 'shallow'? How calcareous does it have to be to be 'lime-rich'? Traces of lime can be found in many kinds of soil, particularly as farmers commonly add it to soils in which it is naturally lacking. The map does not show only escarpments, but if the land involved has only to be undulating, is all land to be included which is not actually flat?

Because down and heath are so hard to distinguish from other types of pasture, the land actually covered would have to be shown on maps. Not only would this be an enormous undertaking, it would require a delay between the enactment of the new right and its coming into effect. During such a period severe environmental damage might occur if landowners decided to protect holdings from being overrun by walkers by changing their character. Landowners can plough up or afforest or apply herbicides and fertilizers to down and heath without the need for any consent (unless the land happens to be a site of special scientific interest). Downland and heathland are extremely vulnerable to such action already. The impending threat of public access, which could be avoided by a reclassification of the land involved, might persuade many more owners to make the switch. Downland and heathland might be ploughed up or turned into ryegrass through the application of fertilizer and herbicide. Trees might be planted, or a few trees sown amongst any shrubs and saplings which were invading the site anyway. All these things could spell environmental disaster for the heath or down in question—an unfortunate consequence since down and lowland heath are now scarce in spite of their outstanding and unique botanical and herpetological interest.

On top of all this, the scattered character of down and heath in particular would mean that the access provided would be of little use in many cases because the sites involved would be cut off from walkers by land which is inaccessible. As we saw on page 74, there were sixteen fragments of downland turf in Highclere which could not be reached from rights of way in 1998. To overcome this problem an array of new subsidized access agreements or path creation arrangements would be required—a development neither easy nor likely.

Common land is a rather different matter. Definition does not depend on the character of vegetation or height above sea-level, but on legal actuality already documented as a finite number of pieces of land listed on registers. Furthermore, a system providing a right of access to certain commons has been up and running for seventy years. The 1925 Law of Property Act granted a legal right of access to all urban commons, and similar arrangements have been extended to some rural commons, most significantly through the Dartmoor Commons Act of 1985. Though the Moorland Owners' Association opposed the idea of a right of access to common land in the early 1990s so effectively that a Conservative government withdrew a pledge to provide such a right, this was at a time when more radical proposals for extending access to the countryside were not on the horizon. Today, moorland owners—and country landowners as a whole—might be readier to sacrifice common land as a concession helping them fend off the prospect of access to other kinds of countryside. Comprehensive registers of common land exist in local authority offices and maps could in theory be drawn up showing boundaries which would not change as often as those of moors, though owners of common land do try to get it deregistered and would probably do so even more if it was always to be open to the public. On the ground, however, there would be no way a walker who had not studied these maps could identify common land as it does not consist of only one landscape type. The ninety-six registered commons of Somerset, for example, take in saltmarsh, sand dune, moor and heath, woodland, dense scrub, limestone grassland, marsh and bog, and a 3-mile stretch of shingle and shore around Bridgwater Bay, as well as stretches of road verge.[41] In Derbyshire there are eighty-six separate registered commons, which embrace marsh, old quarries, limestone grassland of high botanical value, heath, and many stretches of road verge less than 1 hectare (2.47 acres) in extent.[42] Even if the boundaries of these odd patches of land could be successfully communicated to walkers they might reasonably wonder why they were being directed to them rather than more apparently suitable land nearby. Both Somerset and Derbyshire desperately need more land accessible to walkers, yet common land occupies 1.5 per cent and 0.1 per cent of their land areas respectively.

All of this further suggests that a partialist approach involving different types of landscape might be more successful than one concentrating on moor, mountain, and commons. The Spanish manage to define the coast: their Coastal Act 1988 guarantees access to a 6-metre-wide stretch above high-tide line, or 12 metres if passage is difficult. Woods, paths and currently private roads are also clearly definable. In 1996 Elliot Morley, then party spokesman on rural affairs, muddied the waters by suggesting somewhat ambiguously that the new right of access might apply not exactly to moor, mountain, and common but merely to 'open land' within these categories. This might not make that much difference on moors and mountains but could prove another rich source of difficulty on common land, where owners would be able to argue that even where their own holding is indisputably 'common land' it is not 'open', thus excluding wooded commons, for example. The Tipping bill attempted to deal with confusion in this area through the creation of a legal category called 'non-conforming land'. This would enable landowners or tenants to apply to the authority in charge of the right to roam for a declaration that their land was not 'open country' and thus not subject to the access right. The bill suggested that 'In an application for a declaration of non-conformity the applicant may claim that the land is agricultural land but agricultural shall not be deemed to include land which is agricultural land by reason only that it affords rough grazing for livestock.' Unfortunately the introduction of the concept of specifically identified 'non-conforming land' only gives rise to further difficulties. Landowners understandably objected that once 'non-conforming land' had been identified, the public would start imagining it had a right to walk over any other 'open country' which had not been specifically exempted as 'non-conforming'. The further complication for the public trying to understand another separate category on top of mountain, moor, common, down, and heath, not to speak of the prospect of endless judicial review of local authority decisions on nonconformity, demonstrates the can of worms which is opened by opting for a partial rather than a universal right of access. Yet there is more still to worry about.

To deprive one group of owners of a right but to leave others untouched may strike not only those disadvantaged but other people too as unfair. It may be justifiable to remove the right to exclude from all landowners if you believe that a right to roam ought to take precedence over it. But if you are only removing the right to exclude from some owners you obviously cannot claim one right is simply giving way to another. Owners of moorland are likely to be considerably more incensed if they are singled out than they would be if they saw all landowners getting the same treatment. And they may find support for their complaint in the judicial system. Arbitrary impositions on one group while other parallel groups go untouched fly in the face of the presumption that citizens should enjoy equal treatment before the law. Aggrieved moorland landowners might well be able to take their case with some hope of success to the European

Court of Human Rights. There is every indication that they would take this course. The CLA say in their document *Access 2000*: 'A legal challenge (to the right to roam) would be inevitable—e.g. on the grounds of unfair discrimination between landowners'.[43] A successful challenge of this kind could entitle moorland owners to considerable compensation. If this became a serious prospect it might inhibit a government from embarking on the whole idea of extending access to the countryside.

Certainly there is every reason to suppose that moorland owners would use every weapon available to them to protect their rights. The assumption of some ramblers that such owners would not really care about intrusions on their empty acres is not borne out by the evidence. It was the Moorland Owners' Association who persuaded the Conservative government to renege on its promise to legislate to grant a right of access to common land—even though the recommendation had the official support of other landowning organizations. Moorland owners seem to feel as possessive about their holdings as any other landowners. Many moors have remained within the same family for generations—like those of Sir Anthony Milbank, the chairman of the Moorland Owners' Association, whose 4,000-acre Barningham Moor on the borders of Durham and North Yorkshire has been in his family for 300 years; or those of Britain's largest private landowner, the Duke of Buccleuch and Queensbury, whose vast moors in the Scottish borders have been part of his family's estate since the seventeenth century. Lord Downe chooses to keep 10,000 acres of unprofitable heather moorland as part of his estate west of Scarborough in the North York Moors. Although the shooting rights only just enable the moor to break even, Lord Downe told me in an interview in 1983 that he would not consider selling it: 'I keep the moor because it's been in the family for years and because I want to look after it for everybody who cares about it.' Such aristocratic figures would be able to call on the support of a very different and perhaps more media-friendly group. Hill farmers, a byword for struggle against the odds in a hostile environment, might attract more sympathy than grouse-moor owners if they demanded to know why they were being singled out for apparently arbitrary and unfair treatment. Were any proposal to be extended to down and heath, those owners too might be expected to put up a fight, like the 9th Earl of Macclesfield, who has strongly resisted attempts to secure access over his downland in south Oxfordshire (see page 74).

The Universal Alternative

If a partial right of access to mountain, moor, common, down, and heath only might cause more trouble than a universal right, as well as failing to satisfy the needs it is designed for, there is clearly a case for reviewing the rush into partialism which has overtaken the access debate in England and Wales. A universal right of access to the countryside, subject to exceptions, would bypass the philosophical, legal, and practical difficulties in which access to the countryside in Britain is in danger of getting ensnared. By creating a readily understandable new right, it would hit landowners firmly but fairly and provide real benefits to the many would-be countryside visitors of our lowland towns and cities and not just hill-walking enthusiasts. In fact, the force of the case for universalism has been evident to some, even as the moorland partialists have appeared to carry the day.

H. G. Wells wrote his letter to *The Times* demanding a right for everyone to walk on farmland and parkland as well as moors and mountains in the immediate aftermath of the mass trespasses and pitched battles which had seen the access movement focus on moorland. Thereafter the logic of universalism continually made itself felt. Sir Arthur Hobhouse's wartime Committee on Access to the Countryside were particularly anxious to deliver access benefits to the whole of the population, not just those close to the moors of the north. To ensure that their recommendations did not benefit only those interested in solitary walking on upland moors, they focused on the sea-shore as an area which 'affords sheltered spots much appreciated by picnickers, sunbathers and other holiday-makers'.[44] They were also particularly anxious to ensure rights of access over the Norfolk Broads. When the government came to act on Hobhouse's report in 1949, it baulked at much of his prescription, but not at the idea that access needed to be extended throughout the countryside and not just to the hills. Its 1949 act was called the National Park and Access to the Countryside Act, sending out a very different signal from the Access

A Right to Roam

to Mountains Act sought by Charles Trevelyan, James and Annan Bryce, and the 1939 legislators, and, effectively, by the dominant activists and politicians of our own day. Though the 1949 act's access agreements and access orders may have been ineffective, they were clearly aimed at all kinds of countryside.

Within the ramblers' movement itself there have been prominent figures committed to a universalist stance on access to the country-side. Christopher Hall was chairman of the Ramblers' Association while it was highlighting access problems in its Forbidden Britain campaign but before it settled on the kind of right of access it should promote. Hall articulated an unambiguously universalist position in an inter-view with me in 1987 for the television programme *Power in the Land*. He said:

I think the answer to access problems is to reverse the whole notion of land-ownership and trespass and what those kind of concepts mean in this country. At the moment you're not allowed to go anywhere in the countryside unless there's a specific sign or indication that that's where you can go because it's a public footpath or access land or a common or something of that kind. It seems to me that the sensible civilized thing to do would be to put that the other way round and say you can go where you like provided that you don't get in the way of people's privacy, provided that you don't do damage, and obviously provided you know that you don't harm the animals and this kind of thing. Now that sort of system exists in a greater or lesser degree in a num-ber of continental countries, it exists in perhaps its most advanced form in Sweden, where there is a general right there of that kind, it exists to some extent in all countries subject to the Napoleonic code as far as mountains and uncultivated landscape are concerned, and I think that it would cut through at one stroke a great deal of the hassle and nonsense that there is about what private landownership means, and where people can go in this country.

The changing attitudes that accompanied the rise in environ-mental awareness in the 1980s implied a universalist rather than par-tialist approach to the question of access to the countryside. As a child myself of the surge in environmental awareness of the early 1970s and a victim particularly of constraints on access in lowland Britain, I did not think of suggesting a right of access limited to certain types of terrain, and certainly not only to upland. If humanity was charged with a duty to care for the earth and that in some sense gave us all a right to it, then I would not have been able to explain why access rights should apply to only bits of it. Thus in a speech at a rally organized by the veteran Kinder trespasser Benny Rothman in the Peak District in 1982 to mark the 50th anniversary of the Kinder trespasses, it did not occur to me to suggest a right should be other than universal.[45] In 1987 in a book called *This Land is Our Land* I gave an account of the role a universal right of access might play in a more democratic rural regime, which evoked considerable approval. One reviewer said: 'In Sweden there is a customary right of *Allemansrätten* authorising anybody to walk over anybody else's land providing no damage or disturbance is caused. One of the many admirable objectives of this book is to have such a principle instituted in our own laws'.[46] Channel 4 saw fit to accompany the book with a documentary which unequivocally advocated a universal right of access.

Today, the increasing involvement of those with an urban background in rural affairs and the spread of environmentalism have helped foster renewed commitment to the universalist route among some of those who have grown interested in access rights. The Green Party made a universal right to roam part of its manifesto for the 1997 election: its Press Officer told me that the party saw access to the countryside as inextricably linked with its demand for a more just system of land tenure reflecting the view that land is an asset belonging to the community as a whole. Individuals who promote the universalist position nowadays often bring to bear a historical perspective. David Grosz, the RA chairman since 1998, who once proposed an equivalent of Allemansrätt, is a former history teacher. A retired history lecturer, John Alexander, pushes for a universalist right of access within the RA from his base in Hampshire, an RA area where there is particular concern at the failure of the Association's partialist bill to open up kinds of land locally considered important, like field edges.

The convergence of environmentalism and land rights was thoroughly embodied in *The Land is Ours* movement. Its leader, George Monbiot, outraged by a landownership regime which seemed to exclude the poor, modelled his movement on the Diggers of the seventeenth century. Echoing Winstanley's vision of the earth as 'a common treasury for all mankind', Monbiot and a band of 300 young men and women arrived on 23 April 1995 at a disused airfield and some unused woodland alongside a set-aside field at Wisley in Surrey and, living in tents, started to cultivate a small area of ground and to harvest the herbs on the set-aside land for food and medicine. They chose the site and the date to coincide with the Diggers' first land occupation—at St George's Hill, Weybridge in Surrey on 23 April 1649. This was the first of several mass occupations of land by *The Land is Ours*, all designed to promote a claim to universal entitlement to the earth. A universal right of access is one of the reforms urged by *The Land is Ours*, and to make their point they have conducted direct action occupations at three inaccessible sites, all in lowland England—Wychwood Forest, the Shirburn and Pyrton Hills (both in Oxfordshire) and Luton Hoo, Bedfordshire. In 1998 Luton Hoo was up for sale and at their occupation in the grounds the activists met estate workers who were facing the prospect of being barred from the delights of an estate whose amenities they had both enjoyed and worked hard to create if they should lose their jobs and the tied housing going with them under a new ownership regime. On the eve of an attempted trespass at Stonehenge Monbiot declared,

It is, in truth, not we who are the trespassers but the landlords. They are trespassing against our right to enjoy the gifts that nature bequeathed to all of us. We must challenge this intrusion by demanding a statutory right to roam, which would require the owner to produce a good reason for excluding us, rather than requiring us to produce a good reason for being there. In the meantime we should, like the people who will try to enter Stonehenge this week, heed John Major's call for a classless society by trespassing in the countryside as often and as comprehensively as possible.[47]

It might be expected that wildlife conservationists would be wary of measures increasing public access in view of landowners' claims that walkers disturb wildlife. In fact, however, the state's nature conservation bodies[48] welcome the public to most of the sites they own, whatever kind of habitats involved. Temporary exemptions from general access and visitor management techniques encouraging people at some sites to keep to paths usually protect any specially vulnerable wildlife. This reflects a growing feeling on the part of conservationists that wildlife benefits more from the public enthusiasm that comes with access than it might lose from disturbance. Effectively English

Nature and the like operate a universalist right of access insofar as their sites embrace a range of landscape types.

Some naturalists have advocated a universal right of access more explicitly. Naturalist Richard Mabey, who owns a 16-acre wood outside the Hertfordshire town of Berkhamsted, makes a point not only of opening it to the public but of welcoming them to share in the delights of its bluebells and badgers. In an interview in 1987 I asked him what he thought of the idea of a universalist right of access for the UK. He told me: 'It would seem to greatly enhance the appreciation and enjoyment of natural history by the people of this country, and to put into practice what I believe should be natural law. I think that in their hearts most of the people in this country support that as well, they think that the surface of their own country is a place they have a right to walk on. And I think that by allowing that with the kind of reservations that you described would actually be restoring the situation to what it really ought to be.'[49]

There are even farmers who support the universalist approach to access rights. Oliver Walston grows cereals on 2,000 acres in Cambridgeshire but is embarrassed at the large state payments he receives and believes taxpayers are entitled to receive more in return for their largesse. In an article in *Farmers' Weekly* in 1993 Mr Walston urged that farmers should 'give to the public one of the things that makes farming so splendid. We should give them—as a right and not a privilege—total access to the countryside. Every single member of the public should have the right to walk anywhere on any farm.' The only condition should be good behaviour. Any farmer who resisted the idea was, in Mr Walston's view, 'neanderthal'. Former editor of *The Times* Simon Jenkins agreed that rights of access should not be restricted to the uplands. 'Mr Walston has to be right', he wrote in an article later in 1993. 'This year, more than £3 billion is being spent subsidising farms. This is more than is spent on Britain's entire employment and training programme. If such money is to be given to one small group of businessmen they must surely offer in return more than generalisms about food security and the vagaries of past farm policy. . . . If taxpayers are to give an annual grant to a farm to uphold a traditional way of life or preferred landscape, then these benefits must be made accessible.'[50]

A Right to Roam

The greatest impetus for a universalist right to roam is now coming from Scotland—ironically perhaps, given that it was James Bryce's nineteenth-century Scottish bill which set the access movement on the road to upland partialism. Since James and his brother Annan tabled their succession of Access to Mountains Bills, Scottish people have noticed that they now face greater problems of access in the lowlands than on the hills. Because Scotland was excluded from the definitive mapping process which gave England and Wales a web of public paths and because Scotland also lacks urban commons, the Scots have few legal means of penetrating intensively managed farmland which separates most of them from the hills or to enjoy their leisure on this land closer to their homes. This has caused the access debate in Scotland to 'come down the hill' and concern to develop in the lowlands as well as the highlands, though people are still irritated by new obstructions constantly being created by conifer afforestation and fencing for sheep grazing.

An awareness of the ownership of rural land and of folk history and culture far greater than in England give Scottish people a new cause of grievance about the land crimes of the past and make them readier to contemplate action more radical than the English. In his explanation of the approach to rights of access of the Ramblers' Association in Scotland, the RA's Scotland Officer, Dave Morris, told a conference in 1998: 'There is no connection between the proposals of the RA Scotland and those of the RA south of the border'.[51] Morris worked for the Nature Conservancy Council in England on the wild-life value of field edges before returning to his native land and he believes that Scottish people should enjoy a right to walk along field edges and, when these are overgrown, tramlines through the crops. Pressure from activists like Morris and a climate in which a general right of access is debated to a far greater extent than it is in England helped persuade the Ramblers' Association to make an exception for Scotland in framing their stance. Since 1997 the Association has advocated a universal right of access north of the border while claiming only a strictly partialist one for England and Wales. Not that the RA is the only organization urging a universal right for Scotland: it has been outflanked by the Mountaineering Council of Scotland which has called not only for a right of access in Scotland but also for a right to fish for species other than salmon and sea trout (the old common law position which was removed by legislation in 1973), a right to picnic, to ski, to swim, and on hard tracks though not driveways a right to cycle and roller-skate.

Campaigners for a general right of access in Scotland are not only pressure groups. They also include individual activists, some local authorities, and others whose interest lies in a concern for land reform for economic reasons. One of these is Dr James Hunter, a former Secretary to the Scottish Crofters' Union and the author of a major study of the Clearances. Hunter has long campaigned for land reform in the Highlands and Islands for economic reasons, but he has recently added a right of access to his demands. He told me in 1998:

I think the whole notion of a right to roam is very deeply embedded in the way Scottish people feel about the countryside and the way they define themselves. The notion that people have a right to be on the hills is deep seated in the Gaelic tradition. You find evidence in the old Irish law codes, and of course the Gaelic tradition came from Ireland. What's very evident in that material is a major distinction between material and assets which are the production of people—like a ploughed field—and hill grazings, woodland and water, which pertain to everybody and everybody had rights over them. To this day in the Highlands and Islands the Gaelic saying that everyone has a right to a tree from the wood, a fish from the river and a deer from the hill is generally accepted. This thinking is of very ancient origin but it is still something that people here feel.[52] Thus we do not regard poaching as a crime. If you poach a salmon you may go to prison but although it's a legal crime it's not regarded as a moral offence in the way that robbing a bank would be. Another aspect I feel quite strongly about is that official bodies like Scottish Natural Heritage have tended to approach landowners to seek agreements for access with them and then proclaim these as great achievements. To people like me that notion is anathema. For the moment you enter into an agreement you concede the landlord has the right to keep you out. I believe we have an absolute right to be in the hills.

Unlike the parties to the south, the Scottish National Party has come to take a thoroughly universalist stance on rights of access to the countryside. The SNP opposed every aspect of the Criminal Justice and Public Order Bill in 1994, and while campaigning during the 1997 election proposed that a right to roam on the Swedish model should be enshrined in a written constitution. In 1993 the party had the chance to flesh out this objective when Mrs Margaret Ewing, the SNP MP for Moray and leader of the SNP's parliamentary group, moved a bill under the 90-minute rule to give a right of access to all the country-side of the United Kingdom 'for the purpose of open-air recreation'. This proposal, three years ahead of the Paddy Tipping bill, was called the Freedom to Roam (Access to the Countryside) Bill. It was the first parliamentary measure ever to have been moved in the UK embody-ing a universal right of access.[53] The bill did not list types of land to which the measure would apply: instead while providing a general right of access it listed categories of land which would be exempt. These included: agricultural land but not pasture, whether rough grazing or more intensive pasture; nature reserves; land covered by buildings or the curtilage of such land (this would include farmyards); and town parks, pleasure grounds, and gardens. Other exemptions were quarries, railways, golf courses, sports grounds, playing fields, racecourses and airfields, land covered by works used for the purposes of a statutory undertaking or the curtilage of such land, and land on which development was being carried out. In addition, Mrs Ewing's bill empowered the Secretary of State to make an order by statutory instrument to exclude any land if it appeared necessary for him to do so, or to impose any limitations he considered fit for one of the following reasons: the protection of wildlife, the preservation of objects or buildings of historical interest, the protection of the public, or because public access would seriously prejudice the use of land for farming or forestry.

The bill embraced a right for people to bathe in non-tidal water unless a notice had been displayed near the water prohibiting bathing and which had the approval of the local planning authority. It also embraced a right to cycle and ride in that these activities were not covered by prohibitions. Such prohibitions covered the following activ-ities: driving a vehicle; lighting a fire; taking a dog not under proper control; wilfully disturbing or harming plants or animals; hunting, shooting, or snaring animals; wilfully damaging the land; obstructing the flow of any drain or watercourse; breaking through any hedge, fence, or wall; neglecting to fasten any gate. As a private member's bill which had no support from John Major's government, Mrs Ewing's bill did not of course receive a second reading.

One effect of the creation of the Scottish Parliament could be progress on access north of the border on a far more fundamentalist basis than the Labour government at Westminster currently seems ready to envisage. In 1998 three major reviews of rural policy were afoot which could all bring with them a strengthening of access rights. These reviews have been prompted partly by the prospect of elections expected in 1999 to the Scottish Parliament and the drawing up of party manifestos beforehand; they cover national parks (Scotland has none to date although the concept was invented by a Scot called John Muir); land reform; and access to the countryside.[54] The Blair government has shown itself to be responsive to the complaints of vested interests, so much so that by April 1998 there were fears that it might abandon the idea of a right to roam completely in the face of landowner objections. A Scottish executive might be bolder. It looks likely that Labour would not have a majority in a Scottish Parliament, and whereas all English parties are more hostile to access than Labour, the second largest party in Scotland, the SNP, which has already taken an interesting position on access rights, may prove more assertive in this area. Whether or not the SNP actually participated in a coalition government, its views could help shape opinion. The Labour Party in Scotland is very urban and has even fewer links with the countryside than its English counterpart. The Liberal Democrats have a strong link with the old Liberal Party in Scotland whose antecedents were supporters of Gladstonian liberalism and land reform. Should the executive of a Scottish Parliament opt for significant proposals, these would not have to run the gauntlet of a second chamber stuffed with landowners like the House of Lords. If a right of access were to be created by the Scottish Parliament, it would be that much harder for the Westminster government to drag its feet in according a similar right to England and Wales, particularly as many Labour Party supporters in Scotland would be likely to support moves to improve access in Scotland.

Those who favour a universal right of access for the UK as a whole must in the meantime decide how to respond to the upland partialist approach with which the Westminster government seems set to proceed. It could be argued that they should oppose any partialist moves on the grounds that they will become accepted as the last word and perhaps give the whole idea of a right of access to the countryside a bad name because of the problems of definition and unfairness they would throw up. In fact, however, universalists are likely to judge, probably rightly, that a partial right is likely to turn out to be a step on the way to a universal one. The very illogicality of a partial right may create pressure for its extension once people wake up to the realities involved. Certainly the experience of countries like Germany, Switzerland, and Denmark suggests that partial rights tend to get extended. In all these countries initial rights of access relating only to certain categories of land were succeeded by further measures embracing more categories. Would Switzerland today be taking on the millionaire owners of mansions around Lake Geneva to secure a right for the people to walk along the lakeside if it had not nailed its colours to the mast of a right of access to woodland and mountain pasture in its Civil Code nearly a century ago? Would Denmark's ramblers' organization, Dansk Vandrelaug, be notching up a legal right of access to the tracks in small privately owned woods if it had not already successfully secured a right of access to the seashore, heathlands, then large private woods, then medium-sized ones? Would Germany's citizens enjoy a right along paths and tracks if the 1975 Federal Forest Act, granting a legal right to roam over all woodland, had never been enacted? The fact of the matter is that at present in England and Wales partialism is a politically achievable step while universalism may not be. The likeliest route towards a universal right of access is through building on a partial right, as lowland landowners currently opposing the proposed upland access right are all too well aware. Both sides in this profound struggle have reason to see the Labour government's apparently modest plans as the way to a fundamental transformation of the rural regime in Britain which will only really come with a universal right of access.

8

MAKING IT WORK

IF a universal right of access to Britain's countryside makes sense in theory, would it work in practice? What form might it take? What would it mean on the ground? Would it apply to groups as well as individuals? At night as well as by day? Could people exercising the new right take a wheelchair with them? A pram? A dog? A horse? A canoe? A four-wheel-drive vehicle? What exemptions would be needed? Would these have to be temporary or permanent? How would grouse shooting and strawberry growing, paintball gaming, and deer stalking be affected? What conflicts might arise between such activities and unlimited public access and how could these be resolved? Where would the new right leave the existing law of trespass? What about owners' liability to claims for negligence from walkers? What would become of the rights of way network and existing payment-for-access schemes?

Who and What

A new right for all to go where they like subject to exceptions would turn the existing law of trespass on its head. At present you have the right to go nowhere except where you are specifically allowed; a general right of access would mean you had the right to go anywhere except where you were specifically forbidden. Where you were excluded, from buildings and gardens, say, the law of trespass would effectively continue to apply. It would however have to become illegal for landowners to obstruct walkers from entering their property deliberately, just as it is illegal now for them to block public footpaths. A locked gate into a field to protect stock from rustlers would be unaffected by a right of access. Walkers would, however, be entitled to climb over it. Barbed wire placed on top of it to discourage this would become an illegal obstruction. A farmer concerned about damage to gates

308

being climbed over by walkers could consider creating stiles. Clearly there would be plenty of room for argument in all this (what about impenetrable shrubs planted deliberately to obstruct?) but the principle would be clear: walkers must be allowed on to 'private' land.

Even where deliberate obstruction was not taking place, a new general right of access would not of course in itself make it physically practicable for walkers to move wherever they wanted. People would still depend on public paths, pavements, surfaced paths alongside main roads, and roads themselves to make journeys on foot, and there would continue to be a need to extend the public paths network. Yet a right to be present would henceforth exist in principle everywhere else not specifically excluded. This new right could be upheld in law and action taken against encroachments upon it. This right, to make sense as a fundamental entitlement, would need to apply irrespective of the number of people taking advantage of it and their motives for doing so. If they chose to do so as a group, even a large group, that would be up to them so long as they were not causing damage. Clearly a large group might cause damage through erosion of the surface or disturbance of wildlife or livestock which a small group might not. Although much of the use would probably be for some sort of recreation, the right should not itself depend on a particular purpose—such as a right to enjoy open-air recreation. Not only might people wish to be present for other purposes, like scientific study for instance, if the right is to be fundamental it should be available without reference to motive just like the right to walk on rights of way.

In practice, of course, exclusions to any such general right of access would have to be considerable. In other countries where a universal right of access exists, permanent exclusion from that general right for certain classes of land is always built in. Land on which crops are growing and buildings and their immediate surroundings are usually exempted, and obviously would be exempted in Britain too. Almost equally inevitable is temporary suspension: in certain places where activities which are incompatible with the presence of the public take place intermittently—such as shooting game, felling trees, or deliberate firing of a heather moor for grouse management. Some forms of permanent exemption could be specified in legislation, but a more flexible mechanism for adding to (and removing) such exemptions might also be useful. There is a much stronger case for day-to-day machinery for adjudicating on temporary exemptions: as well as a law, there should therefore be an agency providing ongoing administration of access rights. This could be an existing or new agency of central government, local authorities, or a combination of both.

Landowners express understandable concern about the implications of any duty of care which they might owe walkers—a liability which might increase insurance premiums. However, a right to venture into the countryside need not embrace a right to protection from harm that might befall you there. Legislation providing access can also provide that it is at the walker's risk. Insofar as man-traps, bulls in fields, or dangerous chemicals could be shown to be deployed with the deliberate intention of endangering walkers, criminal sanctions rather than a civil obligation ought to be the remedy. Equally, criminal sanctions should be the means of containing vandalism and littering by walkers. The difficulty of detecting such activity could be offset by the severity of the penalties imposed where detection occurred.

A right need not include the right to cause damage or annoy the owners and occupiers of land. It should embrace activities like sitting down whether to rest, paint a picture, read a book or picnic, but not to leave anything behind or take things away. This means blackberrying would not be embraced by a right of access. Its status—and that of taking all the other fruits of the earth which have been the subject of so much concern to commoners over the ages—would be unaffected. A right of access, like highway rights, should apply by night as well as day, but should not include the right to camp, which has implications which go beyond mere presence. Sleeping in the open air could be permitted, but erecting a tent would be a different matter. A right of access is not a right to create encampments. In practice most picnicking and sunbathing would be likely to take place on areas of land like woods, heaths, and set-aside land rather than on paths or field edges.

A right for a human being to go somewhere immediately raises the issue of what he can bring with him. A dog, a horse, a bicycle, a canoe, a motorbike, a jet-ski, a four-wheel-drive vehicle, a caravan? Clearly there is the potential for a harmless right to be transformed into something which would not only create real problems for landowners but could reduce the attractions of the countryside for others. Of course, those involved in noisy or disruptive outdoor pursuits have legitimate demands, but their needs are separate from the need for a right to roam on foot. Such a right, if it is to work as a theoretically universal entitlement, must be restricted to being just that. Apart from walking, wheelchair and pushchair use ought to be included since the vehicles involved provide the equivalent of walking for human beings who have no alternative. Other demands should, however, be separately dealt with. Riders may find this irksome, but horses' hooves often change the landscape whereas human feet do so only occasionally. For the huge numbers of dog-owners who want to unleash their pets in the countryside, this may seem unfair. Yet dogs create problems—fouling places where children play, disturbing wildlife (particularly ground-nesting birds), and disrupting livestock—which mean that they should not have the whole countryside opened up to them. Their needs should be met in specially designated areas, and not through a right to roam on foot. This may mean the public acquisition of land specifically for dog use (perhaps funded by a reintroduction of the dog licence) or perhaps paid-for use of private land. Stiff penalties should be imposed on anyone abusing the right to walk by trying to turn it into something more disruptive, although dogs can already be taken along public footpaths if on a lead or 'under close control'.

Even walkers may be disappointed at first by the limitations which remain even under a right to walk. There will be a great deal of land which is physically impossible to reach—marshes and mires, rugged cliffs and gorges, and so on. The existence of a mere right will not create boardwalks over reed-beds or new paths down slippery slopes. It would make sense for society to take steps to improve opportunities to exploit the right, and I shall later suggest ways of doing this, but this is a separate matter from the enactment of the right itself. Nonetheless, the new recreation opportunities which the right will create at a stroke—even for wheelchair users and pushchair pushers—should not be underestimated. In particular, the opening up of all currently private roads and paths would in itself provide enormous opportunities for enjoyment. All of us should find a new world at our feet—of rarely glimpsed lakesides and riverbanks, of secret grassy rides through the woods, of private beaches and mountain peaks. Most important for most of us would probably be the ability to move around the familiar yet rarely mundane countryside close to towns, cities, and villages—the lanes at present gated, the field edges, the secluded parklands, and the countless little patches of roughland near our homes but currently barred to us.

Existing Uses

A general right of access should obviously disrupt existing activities on rural land as little as possible. Exemptions from the right of access, both temporary and permanent, would need to be a key element. Legislation could recognize a class of activities to be exempted automatically, while providing machinery to exempt other activities temporarily.

The obvious qualification for permanent exemption would be the existence of a use that would be made impracticable by public access or which would significantly endanger walkers. Take golf courses. Walkers come close to golfers on courses crossed by public footpaths and on other land where a public open space surrounds or abuts the course.[1] But if walkers were allowed to roam freely over fairways, let alone greens, they would ruin the game and also endanger themselves. Exemption for land as long as it was being used as a golf course would obviously therefore be sensible. The same applies to military land while firing is taking place or where security needs to be maintained. At present the armed forces make voluntary concessions on public access in some cases but not in others. There is a warning here for legislators that exemption could be abused if they did not specify carefully that the supposed cause for permanent exemption must apply all the time over all of the land over which it was claimed. Permanent exemption could nonetheless obviously be claimed for racecourses, airfields, railways, and motorways and their associated facilities, land which is in the process of being built upon or excavated for minerals or in the process of some other type of 'development' as defined in planning law (building, engineering, or mining operations on, over, or under land or the change of use of buildings or other land), and land covered by works used for the purposes of a statutory undertaking or the curtilage of such land (sewage works, electricity and gas installations, waterworks). Fortunately, most of these types of land use are easily recognizable, people expect to be excluded from them and their recreation value is limited (though birdwatchers might disagree about sewage works). In the case of such permanently exempted uses, the law of trespass and other laws (which for instance make unauthorized entry onto airfields a criminal offence under the Civil Aviation Act 1982) could continue to apply.

It is important to recognize that exemption should be tied to the use and not the land itself or its ownership, so that change from an exempted to another use would involve loss of the exemption.[2] Over time, a case for changing categories of permanent exemption might also arise. Thus in the 1920s it was generally accepted that the public had to be excluded from quite large stretches of land around reservoirs lest water was infected with typhoid. Advances in water treatment technology have since removed this danger and many reservoirs have themselves become recreation centres, as well as the water-gathering grounds around them. It is possible to imagine similar progress making it easier to open the sewage works currently eyed up by birdwatchers.

Perhaps we can learn a lesson here from the way in which planning law was drafted. In 1947, Parliament decided that all farming and forestry operations (apart from those involving building) were so completely unthreatening to the conservation of natural beauty and so completely compatible with all other desirable activities in the countryside that they should be completely omitted from planning law. As a result, these activities were given exemption from the definition of 'development' for which planning permission would be needed, putting them quite outside planning law. In fact, it was not long before it became clear that while many farming and forestry operations posed no special conflict with other interests, some (like the removal of hedges, the drainage of wet meadows, and the afforestation of hillsides) posed a very serious threat. The blanket exclusion for farming and forestry has meant it has been very difficult to secure any adjustment to the town and country planning system to take in certain farming and forestry operations. Yet, the 1947 legislators did create another class of activities under what was called the general development order—activities for which planning permission was in theory required but for which planning permission was deemed to have been granted—like certain temporary uses of buildings and land or the building of walls up to a certain height. Provision was made for local councils to retrieve this deemed permission in special circumstances after securing the approval of central government. These general development orders have allowed for much greater flexibility, and had farming and forestry operations been simply placed in one of these orders, change would not have been so hard to achieve. Thus while the erection of farm buildings to a certain size, for instance, was granted as deemed planning consent, local councils have over the years revoked that permission in certain sensitive areas with government approval, while central government has adjusted the general development order itself to restrict the activities for which planning permission is deemed to have been granted, to reflect changing circumstances.

Permanently exempted uses could thus be provided for under something comparable to the general development order. In the case of golf courses, we might note that some of them have been established over large stretches of sand dune—an attractive and often scarce feature of the landscape and one which may provide the only extensive example of roughland for miles around. If one of these courses was not much used a case might be made for allowing the public some access to the roughs on the dunes. Here deemed exemption could be retrievable by local authorities (or the supervising access agency if that was not local councils), subject to central government approval.

The expiry of 'permanent' exemption once the exempted use disappears would have very real application, particularly in the case of mineral workings. Disused quarries and excavated areas, whether they be flooded gravel pits or overgrown limestone, sandstone, clay, granite and chalk quarries, can offer many opportunities for open-air enjoyment particularly for those interested in geology or botany, as can even disused rubbish dumps. The worked out gravel pits of Ham River Lands near Teddington in south-west London accommodated builders' spoil and rubbish from the London blitz up to and including a double-decker bus. Today its rough grass, scrub, and woodland boast a vast array of plants—168 species in all—while 32 bird and

19 butterfly species are known to breed there, including green and great spotted woodpeckers, stonechats and linnets, and peacock, holly blue and purple hairstreak butterflies. The area is used enthusiastically for walking, birdwatching, picnicking, and so on by large numbers of people. Sewage works, too, are clearly exemptable when active but would be of interest to birdwatchers once redundant.

What machinery would most effectively ensure that any land yielded up from mineral working or electricity generation or sewage treatment or whatever would automatically become accessible under the general right of access? It would be helpful if future planning consents for such uses specified at what point accessibility should resume. At present, planning permissions for mineral excavation for example make detailed provision for the aftercare and restoration of the land, and it would seem sensible to deal with access there. Where land already granted planning consent ceases to be used for the special intensive use, then there would be an automatic presumption of its becoming accessible. Provision could however be made for the access agency, say local councils, to require access and for members of the public to make applications to their local councils that such orders should be made. As we have seen (page 274), Swiss legislation provides for citizens to argue through forest assessment exercises that an area of plantation has become of a size and age as to render it 'woodland' and thus available for public access. In Norway citizens are told that once trees have grown to knee height, then the plantation is accessible.

Since land used for quarrying and so on would automatically become exempt from the right of access once quarrying commenced, it would be natural for local planning authorities to take this into account when they assess planning applications. This would also apply to land to be used for other activities for which temporary exemptions would have to be granted, like, say, the use of woodland for war-gaming. At present 'exclusivity' is not a recognized planning consideration except occasionally. As we have seen (page 212) Shepway District Council in Kent did make provision for some local permissive access to continue once a large stretch of Lyminge Forest had been turned over to a holiday village. This is probably an exception because the area to be enclosed is so large. Usually, however, local councils granting planning permission for new uses in the country-side bear in mind wildlife and landscape conservation matters and local disturbance that the activity may cause through, for instance, noise and traffic congestion. They have not considered the extent to which the new use will render land more exclusive—understandably since most sites for which planning permission is sought have little public access in the first place. Once a right of access to the countryside was in place, conversion of land to a use which only one group in society would enjoy would involve a net loss of access, often to a substantial extent, just as the enclosure of the commons deprived the community of a resource. Janette Skellern, the Reading University planning student who made a special study of the recreational use of land in much of Berkshire (see page 95), suggested a new 'exclusivity' consideration when councils assess planning applications for formal recreation uses; her special concern was the exclusive use of flooded gravel pit lakes for activities like jet-skiing and fishing by private fishing clubs in an area where there is much demand for access to the water-side for the whole population. The introduction of a general right of access might make landowners even more concerned to legitimize formally exclusive uses of land so as to render it exempt from the general right of access. So the case for an exclusivity consideration where planning applications are assessed would be even greater than it is at present.

Farming

Airfields, golf courses, racecourses, scientific installations, sewage works, and so on are limited in area, self-contained, and readily identifiable. Farmland, covering 76 per cent of the countryside, is the countryside of most of Britain. It does of course vary enormously, some of it being cropped, some pasture, some intensively cultivated, some open moorland grazed by sheep. Farmed land is intimately bound up with ponds and streams, archaeological remains, and belts of flowery unused land in hollows and on hillocks. There are rocky outcrops in the fields and leafy corners. Fields of land lying fallow and stretches of set-aside interlock with expanses of wheat and rape. Farmland plays host to a loose skein of linear features—roads and paths (some public, many private, some surfaced, others no more than the wide prints made by tractors). In addition, there are the field edges, often with a belt of roughland beside a hedge, or a belt of bare earth which has been specially sprayed by the farmer to prevent the spread of weeds into his crop.

Obviously this kingdom is so large that it cannot all be permanently exempted from any meaningful general right of access to the countryside. Equally there must be provision to ensure that public access does not mean people trampling crops or disrupting sensitive operations. Countries which already operate a general right of access have had to confront this reality. In Germany, for example, the Nature Conservation Law of 1987 provides a general entitlement for the public to be present at their own risk on roads and tracks in farmland and in fields which are not in use. Individual German states (or Länder) have to interpret this law more precisely. Article 49 of North-Rhine Westphalia's Landscape Law, 1991 lays down that access is permitted to private roads and paths, the edges of fields, non-railway embankments, fallow land, and other areas not currently used for agriculture. Private paths include the paths made by tractors and other machines. Effectively this Article is enough to provide North-Rhine Westphalia's citizens with most of the access they actually need without enabling them to interfere with any agricultural operations. It would also provide a useful indication of the sort of land that would become available under a new right of access in the UK.

A general right of access in Britain would automatically provide a similar right to walk on the enormous network of private roads and paths over farmland. Although the principle of a right to roam freely is philosophically and psychologically important, in practice most people would continue to walk along linear routes. A study of the walking habits of residents of Alton in Hampshire, Burnley and Clitheroe in Lancashire, and Whitby in Yorkshire by consultants acting for the Countryside Commission in 1996 found that between 85 and 90 per cent of walking in the countryside at present makes use of obvious paths: these are not just public rights of way but also canal towpaths, and field edges.[3] Another Countryside Commission study has revealed that while one-third of walking in the countryside takes place on public paths, a further third makes use of country lanes, roads, pavements, and roads through villages.[4] And as roads and paths are already devoted to human movement (as opposed to, say, rough-lands whose prime purpose may be game rearing or stock grazing), they ought obviously to be the first target of any real attempt to improve access to the countryside even if that were not being pursued through the mechanism of a general right to roam. In some parts of the countryside, private paths and roads are frequently surfaced, which could make them of special value to people in wheelchairs or with pushchairs. Access to tracks like these by walkers should pose no real risk to farm operations. The next most obvious opportunity for walkers in farmland is presented by the edges of arable fields. Few farmers grow crops right up to the field boundary, and many delib-erately leave a strip of bare earth between the hedge or fence and crops or between breaks in the crops, partly to stop the spread of weeds. Access just to these field edges, combined with private roads, tracks, and paths, would not only enable walkers to get into farmland but would also enable them to get to other features, like woods, which would be theoretically accessible under a general right of access but often inaccessible in practice. This alone is reason enough why farmland would have to be penetrable in any effective access regime. Set-aside land too could prove very beneficial. Farmers now have to set aside only 5 per cent of their arable acreage but that nonetheless comprises 758,000 acres of land. Sometimes this land is on the edge of settlements, sometimes it is in the depths of the fields. It repre-sents a considerable potential recreation resource.

Since access to private routes and field edges could achieve so much, walkers would have no problem if land under crops received a blanket permanent exemption from a general right of access. In Scandinavia, such an exemption does not apply after crops have grown. After the harvest, people can walk over stubble, and when land is covered by snow and ice they can pass freely over it not only on foot but also on skis. In Britain it is probably not worthwhile complicating matters by creating such an exception to the exemption, even though people once swarmed over stubble to pick up bits of corn as well as to play games. Today, British farmers rarely leave much time between tak-ing in the harvest and sowing the next crop. However, it would make sense to keep such a general exemption under review, just like other exemptions. If global warming reroutes the Gulf Stream and gives us a Scandinavian climate, we too might take a fancy to cross-country skiing.

Grazing land is of course very different from cropland. It includes the moorland which has been the prime target of the serious hiker for generations, and there is clearly often no conflict between walkers and livestock. We in Britain already have quite a lot of public access through fields containing grazing animals, since many public paths pass through such land, and grazing animals are frequently present, even certain bulls.[5] As we have seen (page 274), Swiss law entitles people to be present in grazing lands: in practice you can walk into any field containing cows so long as you close the gate behind you. A similar freedom exists in Sweden: I have toured the countryside with native Swedes well versed in Allemansrätt who cheerfully climb over the fencing of a paddock in which horses are grazing, en route to some other feature rather than for the joy of walking in horse paddocks. In many cases no problems should arise, but where conflicts do occur it should be possible for farmers to apply for exemption from the right of access to reduce any conflict with the rearing of livestock, whether farm animals or horses. Exemptions might for instance be regularly granted when ewes are lambing or when suckler cows are present with young calves. It would be hard to distinguish between different types of pasture such as down and meadow since the difference is not readily apparent even if satisfactory definitions could be arrived at. Any system expecting walkers to rely on much use of maps and signs differentiating apparently similar kinds of land would clearly be doomed, particularly as the boundaries of pastureland are constantly being changed. Instead, the general right of access could apply except where permanent or temporary exemption was in force.

It could be up to farmers to go to the trouble of applying for exemptions where they thought the disruption caused by walkers justified the effort. Some would bother; some would not. Fine. Obviously where disease was a problem, exemption would be easily secured, so long as the threat was real and not just an excuse. Some people have suggested that fox-hunting can spread the sugar beet disease rhizomania. However, Jon Austen of Heacham Bottom Farm near King's Lynn in Norfolk commented in a letter in *Farmers' Weekly* on 16 October 1992: 'I manage 470 acres of sugar beet on this estate and we welcome the hunt here every year. I do not believe the hunt transports any more soil than 4,000 pink-footed geese, partridges, hares, deer or tractor and lorry tyres.'

Intrusion by the public into farmland under a right of access is unlikely to cause significantly greater difficulty than occurs under existing arrangements, but that is more limited than might be thought. In 1995 the Environment Committee of the House of Commons conducted an inquiry into 'The Environmental Impact of Leisure Activities in Rural Areas'. In its evidence, the National Farmers' Union did specify several problems, but it also suggested that public access to and public interest in the countryside could bring significant benefits to farmers. The Union pointed out:

On some farms, the agricultural business has now been eclipsed as the main source of income as a result of major recreational developments such as equestrian centres, visitor centres or tourist accommodation. . . . We are concerned that the Committee's terms of reference seem to highlight the negative problematic aspects of leisure in the countryside. Without wishing to underestimate these concerns, they need to be balanced alongside the economic value of recreation and tourism in rural areas. Countryside Commission collated data indicates that total day visitor spending is estimated at approximately £4,500 million (per annum) while total holiday visitor spending accounts for an additional £2,000 million in rural areas. Expenditure by overseas visitors in the countryside is assessed as being in excess of £1,000 million per annum. Thus leisure use is clearly an important source of foreign investment. It is a widely held view that the potential for growth in the recreational and leisure use of the countryside is considerable.[6]

But if access causes some problems for farmers, what are they? A recent study of the views of farmers close to urban areas on public access was the one referred to above conducted by consultants for the Countryside Commission around Alton, Burnley, Clitheroe, and Whitby. One in twelve of the farmers interviewed perceived access to cause significant problems, mainly of damage to property and damage to wildlife; one in three perceived small problems like lesser degrees of damage to property and wildlife as well as damage to crops and livestock. However, one in twelve farmers saw access as bringing significant benefits, in particular goodwill in the local community and notification of problems that might arise for instance with livestock. Two-thirds of farmers perceived smaller benefits citing help in dealing with crime and poaching as well as those already mentioned. Few farmers considered that intrusion by the public significantly influenced the manner in which they farmed.

If the disruption caused by existing levels of intrusion is pretty much balanced by the advantages that the presence of visitors on farmland can bring, what difference would a general right of access make? Farmers in this same survey cited three serious worries: damage caused by dogs, particularly sheep worrying; incursions in vehicles, on horseback, and on bicycles; and vandalism and criminal activity such as theft. The exclusion of dogs from the right of access ought to ease farmers' anxieties, though they might legitimately argue that people armed with a right to walk would be more likely to bring dogs on to their land than people lacking any rights at all. In theory a universal right of access might be expected to enhance opportunities for thieves since their mere presence could not be challenged, but it seems unlikely that this advantage would greatly change criminal behaviour.

An earlier study conducted in the mid-1980s on the attitudes to public access of farmers in North Wales, the Dorset Coast, the East Midlands south of Nottingham, and parts of the Peak District National Park and the Pennines found that many of the 257 farmers interviewed reported annoyances which they considered to be the result of visitor activity, such as leaving gates open (reported by 53 per cent of the sample), trespass (42 per cent), and damage to field boundaries (60 per cent). However, these farmers reported soil condition, climate, and topography as problems much more frequently than anything connected with public access. The percentage of farms where access-related factors were cited as a hindrance to day-to-day running of the farm was as follows: for litter, vandalism, damage to crops, or theft 4 per cent; damage to field boundaries 6 per cent; trespass 15 per cent.[7] 'The results showed visitors and recreational use to be an irritant rather than an impediment to farming,' commented the Countryside Commission in 1995.[8]

One particular theft risk arises from the production of soft fruit like strawberries, gooseberries, and blackberries; grapes; and apples and pears in an orchard. In theory theft is a risk for all types of farm crop, and in some areas sheep rustling is a serious problem. In general, however, while people could even now stop their cars and dig up cabbages, potatoes, or cauliflowers by the roadside, in practice they do not bother. The situation with ripe soft fruit is slightly different. We are often encouraged to pick such fruit, not least at 'pick your own' establishments, while the belief that blackberries and wild strawberries and indeed mushrooms in the hedgerows and pastures are free for all makes it perhaps harder in this area to ensure that soft fruit on farmers' fields is never stolen. Permanent exemption of land devoted to such fruit would not be necessary, since the crops involved are seasonal. Fields of fruit and vineyards can be vast, and blanket exclusion could cause a significant loss of amenity, since these areas can be particularly attractive to walkers. Orchards, particularly under spring blossom, are one of the special sights of the British countryside, and traditional orchards with tall fruit trees perhaps grazed underneath by sheep, still occur in unexpected corners like the Vale of Aylesbury, south Bedfordshire, and Herefordshire and Worcestershire. Many of these surviving orchards have been restored with the help of countryside stewardship funds. The newer orchards which have taken over most fruit-growing areas in Kent, which consist of serried ranks of dwarf trees, are both less visually appealing than the traditional orchards and also offer greater possibilities for theft since the fruit, closer to the ground, is more easily plucked. In all these cases the obvious remedy is temporary exclusion: the right of access would allow people to walk on roads and tracks and round the edges of fields of soft fruit and orchards, but farmers could seek temporary exemption for the whole of this land during the relatively short period when the fruit is ripe.

One other hazard which went unmentioned by the Alton, Burnley, Clitheroe, and Whitby farmers but which might nonetheless concern others is rubbish dumping. Since a right of access on foot involves no extension of vehicle use, the danger is clearly limited. However, if rubbish is dumped on your land, you are unlikely to find out who did it, and if you do the prospect of trying to get the miscreant prosecuted is not encouraging. If the rubbish involved is dangerous, the Environment Agency will take it away. Otherwise you will usually have to put up with the rubbish or take it away yourself. Today, rubbish dumped is less often the old mattresses and sofas of ten years ago: in Leicestershire, to take a typical example, 95 per cent of the population lives within 5 miles of a council recycling and household waste site open for 12 hours a day in summer and 10 in winter. However, the introduction of the landfill tax in 1996 has meant an increase in tipping by traders such as unscrupulous builders who unlike householders have to pay to leave rubbish at a council tip. To counter this hazard, farmers close to urban areas sometimes block gateways to fields with machinery—an act which does not stop people walking through but would prevent somebody driving into a field. A right of access for pedestrians seems unlikely to affect this situation unduly. Littering by walkers is another matter. Visitors to the countryside at present have, however, shown themselves perhaps surprisingly ready to take their litter home, something they are often urged to do by notices erected by bodies which have decided not to station litter bins not only because of the cost of emptying them but also to discourage the habit of thought that the countryside is a place where litter should be deposited. The northern European countries where access is permitted have not found littering a serious problem.

The presence of more people in the countryside, if that were a consequence of a right of access, might help deter not only theft and vandalism but the assaults which, though uncommon, create much anxiety at present. A right of access on foot would bring no new legal rights for riders, cyclists, or four-wheel drivers. Insofar as they misinterpreted the new right, intentionally or otherwise, they might henceforth incur the odium not only of landowners but also walkers, at least some of whom could be expected to note a four-wheel driver's number and report it.

Fears of damage by walkers were specifically addressed in Germany's provisions for access to woodland. In North-Rhine Westphalia, the 'Land' undertakes to pay up to 50 per cent of the cost of reasonable insurance against forest fires. It also guarantees to pay for the cost of removing any rubbish that is dumped. And if public recreation damages the forest or forestry or hunting facilities (with the exception of fire damage) the Forest Commission is required to repair any damage if an owner asks it to do so. If substantial damage occurs which cannot be rectified, the Commission must pay the owner financial compensation. However this approach does have its drawbacks. Essentially it involves legitimizing ongoing vandalism; while at the same time it provides an open-ended commitment for the public purse. A less problematic way of reassuring farmers that vandalism could be addressed would be to make vandalism or damage such as excessive theft grounds for temporary exemption from the right of access. This would enable the access agency to consider offering help, such as war-dening, if a valuable recreation resource were involved. If vandalism really did turn out to be a problem, application for exemption on such grounds would take its place alongside applications for the tempor-ary exemptions farmers might require for activities like camping, cara-vanning, car boot sales, and clay pigeon shooting.

To reduce bureaucracy, exemptions sought for only a few days a year need not be the subject of formal applications to the access agency. A farmer who was going to use his field for a clay pigeon shoot or the owner of a country estate who was going to allow a stretch of his park to be used for car parking at a time when the estate was playing host to some event, like a game fair, could simply be allowed to post up notices of a standard type informing the public that their right of access was suspended on that particular piece of land for that day or number of days for one of a set of reasons listed in the statute. He or she could be required to send in a notice of what was happening to the access agency which could file it in a register of claimed exemp-tions. Any person could challenge such a posted exemption, and in the case of such a challenge the agency would have to adjudicate.

Forestry

Forestry uses much less land in Britain than agriculture and its crop is obviously much less vulnerable to disruption, damage, or theft than farm crops. Forestry does not involve an annual cycle of planting and harvesting operations which may be impeded, but a growing cycle which runs for decades. In farming terms, forestry can be seen as the production of giant vegetables which become so woody that they can-not be chopped down, stolen, or easily otherwise harmed by passers-by. This is not to say however that there are not certain periods in the cycle of timber production during which uncontrolled public access might cause problems.

In most cases the first stage of the forestry cycle involves the preparation of land through ploughing and then the planting of saplings. Such planted areas could be damaged by walkers, who might need to be confined to roads, tracks, field edges, and other land not sown with young trees. This could be achieved in at least two different ways. Plantations of young trees could be treated like growing crops and thus become subject to the blanket exemption. Or they could be identified as a suitable subject for temporary exemption. The forest law of North-Rhine Westphalia permits landowners to fence in nurseries and plantations of young trees and to bar access to them, but for areas of over 25 acres in extent, permission must first be obtained from the Forest Authority. This second approach seems preferable. While a blanket exemption would cut down on paperwork, an exemption that required individual owners to seek an exemption which would normally be granted would provide an opportunity for the administering authority to sort out precisely what public access would exist to a particular plantation during the first years of its life. This could be particularly important in places like the Highlands of Scotland where new plantations can be vast and take over open moor and glen over which people today enjoy *de facto* freedom to roam. Though such a procedure may seem to involve a lot of form-filling, foresters already apply for grants for planting and for permits for felling, so this would be just another form-filling exercise. However, in those plantations in which each individual sapling is encased in a plastic tube to protect it against browsing deer and rabbits, no exemption will usually be necessary and so it is by no means obvious that plantations need all be exempted during their early years. Indeed, the community woodlands scheme makes special provision for access payments to new plantations even though the payments run for only the first ten years of the wood's life.

Once a plantation was established and the trees were above a stated height, temporary exemption would need to be granted only occasionally, for instance when a plantation was being sprayed with herbicide or when trees are being thinned, which may take place once when they are 15 years old and every 15 years hereafter. Finally, exemption would need to be granted when the trees were being chopped down. Felling and thinning clearly present far more hazard to the general public than day-to-day farming operations. Nonetheless, the public can be excluded quite effectively when these activities are under way. Redlands Wood, south of Dorking in Surrey, is a popular wood managed by the Forestry Commission and much visited by people walking their dogs or enjoying a family picnic or simply a stroll outdoors. Visitors to the wood over the Christmas and New Year holidays of 1997/8 found strips of orange tape tied round the wooden posts leading in to the site and a notice barring entry, warning that thinning was under way, explaining its purpose and offering a phone number for inquiries. There was no sign that anyone challenged or objected to their temporary exclusion. Already there are plenty of places in which forestry operations coexist with public access even within the United Kingdom without apparent ill-effect. Public and semi-public bodies like the National Trust, local councils, the Forestry Commission, and the Woodland Trust already have experience of ensuring that the public come to no harm when woods in which they are accustomed to walk are felled for timber production or when new plantations are established.

Pheasant and Deer Shooting

Forestry is, however, far from being the only industry to which our woods play host. Recreational activities, from deer and pheasant shooting to war-gaming, are of growing commercial importance, and public access has always been considered more of a threat to these activities than to the production of timber. From the moment pheasant shooting took off in the nineteenth century, it has been considered sufficient to justify the energetic exclusion of walkers from many of the deciduous woods with their bluebells and primroses which are perhaps the best-loved feature of England's countryside. In 1937, Cyril Joad, the grand old man of 'The Brains Trust', complained that in the woods of southern England 'a pair of lovers may not walk in privacy, a little girl may not go to pick primroses, without being harried and chivvied by angry men, whose sole concern is to ensure that the greatest possible number of pheasants shall be offered every autumn as living targets to the guns of lazy townsmen.'[9] Today, Joad's observation is more rather than less true. In 1992, academics Graham Cox, Charles Watkins, and Michael Winter questioned nearly 400 landholders in Gloucestershire, Nottinghamshire, Buckinghamshire, Cumbria, and Devon who reared and shot pheasants on their land. They discovered that the numbers of birds reared increased by more than three-quarters between 1978 and 1992—a figure which is supported by the increase of 3 per cent each year which we noted earlier (see page 136).[10] To appreciate what this means for public access, and what it ought to mean, we need to know what pheasant shooting entails.

Unlike grouse and partridges, foxes, deer and hares, all of which are also pursued for sport, few of the 12 million pheasants which are shot every year in Britain originate in the wild. Specialist game farms provide 20 million or so eggs and chicks which, when nearly two months old, are placed in release pens in the outdoors, usually in woods. Here, gamekeepers feed them twice a day; between meals they venture out of their home wood into land around, favouring in particular rough grassland, damp fields, ponds, and certain crops like kale and mustard. A few months later, from 1 October until 1 February, the birds are bagged in organized shoots, in which a line of beaters drives hundreds of birds out of the crops in which they are feeding back to the wood in which they were released as young birds and which they see as 'home'. The guns stand in a row under some feature which causes the birds to fly high in the air, like a line of tall trees, and fire at their prey. Birds which are killed are picked up by dogs, which also 'mop up' wounded specimens. Few estates see more than twenty-five or thirty days' shooting a year, and many only about ten.

Although the nesting and shooting seasons are relatively short, the public are normally kept out of pheasant woods all year round. This is a great loss. Pheasants prefer deciduous woods with plenty of undergrowth—precisely those favoured by the bluebell, primrose, nightingale, and therefore walkers and picnickers. When questioned about the reasons for the exclusion of the public, Richard Van Oss, the Director of the Game Conservancy (which carries out research and provides advice on field sports), told a House of Commons Committee in 1989: 'During the nesting season disturbance is disastrous.

It is disturbance by dogs chasing a rabbit or by people. They [the pheasants] need peace. Similarly it is no good with a pheasant covert just closing it on the day of shooting because they need peace for a fortnight before and a fortnight after.'[11] This line is, however, open to question.

Since the vast majority of pheasants which are shot start life in incubators rather than in nests in the woods, disturbance in the nesting season is not quite as significant as might be thought. Only a tiny number of eggs laid in the wild produce adult birds, nearly all of which fall prey to natural factors like the rain, frost, and foxes. It seems sensible to close areas where birds are actually being shot, for safety reasons, but this need not involve blanket closures of whole woods, let alone whole estates. Although public footpaths are uncommon in most woods, there are cases in which public paths cross woods used for pheasant shooting. These paths cannot be closed during a shoot; what happens in practice is that a marshal is placed at either end of a right of way to warn walkers and ask them, for safety reasons, to stop for a few minutes if a shoot is in progress. As soon as the shoot may be interrupted, the marshals ensure that no further firing takes place until the walkers have passed through safely. There have been no recorded cases of members of the public being wounded or harmed in any way in such situations. The Cox, Watkins, and Winter team asked their 400 landholders whether public access along rights of way caused problems for the shoot. The majority reported no conflict whatsoever. If public access can be managed under the noses of the guns in this way, it can certainly be accommodated away from the firing line.

Some estates have to work their pheasant rearing and shooting operations around public access because the land involved supports a relatively high density of rights of way. When Mrs Penelope Greenwood inherited the 4,000-acre Balcombe estate in West Sussex from her grandmother Lady Denman, she found the area criss-crossed by public paths. Her husband is a keen shot and the pheasant shoot has been planned to avoid potential conflict. When I toured it in 1982, 16,000 pheasants were being turned down every year so that the Greenwoods could let out ten days' shooting a year commercially and keep a further ten days to themselves. Although the estate is only 37 miles from Hyde Park Corner and occupies some of the loveliest countryside in Sussex, few problems have emerged. Poaching of game is not a problem: Mrs Greenwood told me that not one pheasant had ever been stolen from the estate. Yet some of the release pens were placed only yards from public footpaths; people often come and watch the birds being fed. Another estate where shooting and access coexist happily is the Arundel estate, 25 miles to the south-west of Balcombe. Here, the Earl of Arundel and Surrey allowed the public to wander freely throughout 1,000 acres of woodland, lakeside, and parkland when I talked to the agent to the estate, Ralph Percy, in 1985. A public footpath $2\frac{1}{2}$ miles long runs through the middle of the park and is of course open all the time, day and night, every day. Freedom to wander anywhere was subject to two conditions: dogs were not allowed; and the estate was closed on one day a year to ensure that the public could not claim other routes across the estate as rights of way by demonstrating twenty years' continuous use. Ralph Percy told me he did not find it necessary to close the estate on the sixteen days a year when its pheasants were shot: 'People are fairly sensible and keep out of the way. Shooting is usually in the middle of winter when there aren't many people walking through anyway.'

Landowners' desire that their pheasants should stay undisturbed before a shoot is understandable. In law pheasants, even those which have been artificially reared, are classed as wild animals, which means that they do not belong to anybody: they become somebody's property only when shot. One of the benefits of landownership is the ability to shoot game on one's own land, and of course to charge others for the privilege of doing so. Once that game settles on a neighbour's land, however, it becomes legally his or hers to shoot. So disturbance which causes birds to move on to someone else's land can be costly for a landowner. During the 1970s this concern fuelled conflict between pheasant-wood-owners and fox-hunters. Landowners who reared pheasants were unwilling to see the hunt pursuing its quarry across land which was about to be shot over lest the pheasants be disturbed and vacate their home territory on the day of the shoot. The British Field Sports Society therefore set up a series of experiments in which packs of foxhounds were deliberately run through pheasant woods a few days before a shoot was to take place. The number of birds subsequently shot was compared with the pheasant bags on previous years. These experiments demonstrated that the pheasant-wood-owners' fears were unfounded. While the pheasants flew up into the air when startled by the hounds they did not leave the wood, or, if they did, they soon returned. In fact, the disturbance caused by hounds seemed to help the shoot by making reared birds more jumpy and readier to take to the wing.[12] Some landowners now capitalize on this finding by deliberately running hounds through pheasant coverts a few days before a shoot is to take place. If pheasants are not frightened away by foxhounds and mounted huntspeople crashing through the undergrowth, it is hard to see people enjoying a family picnic, walkers, or birdwatchers doing much harm. So Mr Van Oss's idea that the public must be excluded for a fortnight either side of a shoot seems dubious to say the least. Effectively this requirement can close a wood for the whole winter, while exclusion during the breeding season closes it for the spring. We must wonder whether it is the owners' desire for privacy rather than the needs of their pheasants which dictates this practice.

In other countries in which pheasant shooting is conducted in the way it is in Britain, there is usually provision for closing areas where shooting is actually taking place even if the access régime is otherwise liberal. Temporary closure for deer shooting is also usually provided for, and public safety during deer shooting would also need to be protected here. While the British method of pheasant shooting involves noisy and conspicuous groups firing shotgun pellets up into the air, deer shooting is done by individuals stealing through the woods and stealthily pursuing individual deer which they dispatch with a rifle bullet fired at the same height as a human being and carrying for a mile or more.

As well as the red deer which roam over the Highlands, considerable populations of some red but mainly other species of deer—roe, fallow, and muntjac—inhabit our woods. Deer shooting in woodland takes place almost entirely out of sight but it is far more widespread and involves far larger numbers than many people realize. David Whitby, head keeper on the Petworth estate in West Sussex, whose ownership is shared between the National Trust and the 2nd Baron Egremont and 7th Baron Leconfield, commented in 1995, 'There's hardly an acre of Sussex that isn't stalked'.[13] Stalking in lowland woods is done in a very different way from that in the Scottish Highlands. In some places sportsmen sit on a high seat specially built near a place known to be frequented by deer and wait for them to appear. Alternatively, they track deer through the woods, following their spoor. Roe deer are night feeders and move mainly between dusk and dawn, so the most productive time to pursue this species is early morning or last light. Fallow deer too tend to remain in the thickest part of thick woods during the hours of daylight, and are most often shot very early in the morning or just before nightfall. This means that in theory one could restrict access to provide for the shooting of deer in woods to a few hours of each day and open the wood for the main part of the day. However, considerable care would have to be taken, for while a stalker taking aim on an open Scottish glen-side can be pretty confident that his bullet is unlikely to hit anything other than the deer, the same cannot be said of the stalker in a wood who cannot see the background to his shot.

In those countries with a general right of access, landowners manage to carry out activities ranging from shooting to forestry without much trouble. Vilhelm Bruun de Neergaard owns a 4,940-acre estate at Skjoldenaesholm, near Roskilde which lies 18 miles west of Copenhagen; his family have owned this estate for 200 years. About three-quarters of it is forest. The estate employs fifty-five people on its woods, on its farms, in a forestry contracting company, and in the conference centre which is housed in the mansion at the heart of the estate. As we have seen, Danish landowners have to put up with a public right to walk along all roads and main paths in their woods, and this right has existed in large woods, like Mr Neergaard's, since 1969. Signs make it clear to visitors not only what they can and cannot do but also that they are welcome. As I drove round the estate in September 1988 I saw several 'Velkommen' to the forest posters and leaflets, which are also posted in schools, nursery schools, libraries, and garages. In the woods themselves are signs issued by central government for use in private woods which explain that access is allowed along all the roads in the forest but only on foot and at the walker's own risk; loose dogs, open fires, and damage to trees and shrubs are forbidden; people must keep 50 metres from houses; and access is permitted only from 7 a.m. until sunset (from sunrise until sunset from November until February), and that breaking any of these rules is punishable by law.

Just what constitutes a road along which people may walk is of course debatable in a forest with different levels of track, few of which are surfaced. Mr de Neergaard told me that the rule he uses is 'if it's a track where you can drive a tractor, people are welcome.' In fact he told me he does not mind if people walk off the tracks: 'If you want to protect a place, just plant it round with thorns or sitka spruce —that keeps people away quite nicely.' Those who wish to drive a car or ride a horse in the woods need special permission: 'Bicycles are not in fact allowed but nobody takes any notice here.' Mr de Neergaard told me that public access created very few problems. To enable potentially conflicting activities to take place, the estate closes woods temporarily. Thus the woods are closed on the one day a year when herbicides are sprayed from a helicopter. Young plantations are closed off until they have become established; but Mr de Neergaard does not find it necessary to close off sections of the forest when clear felling: he simply posts up notices informing people of the danger, while the men doing the felling make sure no members of the public come to any harm.

Two thousand pheasants are shot on the estate every year, but the woods are not closed while this happens. Pheasant pens are carefully placed in places where members of the public tend not to walk: 'It would be very unclever of us to put pheasants out where a lot of people come.' Buck hunting, which takes place with rifles and during a season from 16 May until 15 July, poses a much greater potential danger to the public than pheasant shooting. About 200 roe deer are shot on the estate each year. The estate itself pursues this activity only during the week: most walkers come at weekends, so potential conflict is avoided. However, a group of huntsmen who have leased part of the estate often do hunt on Saturdays and Sundays. They take advantage of the possibility of closing the woods in the early morning and evening (from sunrise until 9 a.m. and from 5 p.m. until sunset), putting up notices to inform the public of the closure.

Such problems as do arise usually involve groups. Mr de Neergaard: 'The problem is not from the normal family coming from Copenhagen —they never give us any problem. The problem comes when you get

orienteers who are running.' Danish access law requires organized
orienteers to seek permission from landowners. The estate allows
some orienteering, but turns down applications for the period from
mid-October until mid-December to reduce stress on the deer: 'Say
you have hunting on the Wednesday of each week and 300–400
people orienteering the following Sunday. In that case the deer will
be stressed twice a week.' A problem is created by dogs let off the lead
which can worry deer. If a landowner captures a dog found roaming
free he can shoot it if he has first put a notice in the local paper on
two occasions and the owner fails to claim it. As far as his arable land
is concerned: 'People don't wander into the crop areas. That's completely no problem.' Litter? 'People don't leave litter in the forests.'
As we have seen (page 272), Denmark has gradually extended the right
of public access to more and more of its private woodlands. It seems
likely that it will eventually introduce free access, day and night, over
all private woodland—the state of affairs already existing in Germany,
Switzerland, and of course Scandinavia. There seems no reason why
the UK should not move immediately to that situation, and there are
several models which could prove useful.

As we have seen (page 271), the House of Commons Environment
Committee found in 1993 that the right of access introduced to the
former Federal Republic of Germany in 1975 was working well. The
Forestry Owners' Association for instance told the Committee that it
fully supported the policy of free public access to German forests.[14]
In 1989 I made my own trip and found that in spite of their early
objections, Germany's landowners seem to have learned to live with
public access in the woods. Dr Albrecht von dem Borne of the
German Landowners' Organization (the equivalent of Britain's CLA)
told me: 'Access is not a general problem for our landowners. They
accept it and have nothing against it because they accept that the
people must walk in the countryside. General access is not in our
discussion, we accept it.' The regional laws which allow the suspension of access to facilitate hunting seem to be little used—despite
the importance of hunting in Germany in both economic and other
terms. Dr Borne: 'There is no restriction on access when hunting is
taking place. It is not necessary in our country in general because before
the hunter shoots he must be sure there are no people and thus no

danger to man or child. . . . German hunters have to pass an examination before they can go hunting and the first rule in this is keep safe: if something is moving check it is not a man and only if you are sure, shoot.'

With a population of 17.4 million people and containing cities such as Bonn, Aachen, Düsseldorf, and Cologne, the 'Land' of North-Rhine Westphalia is one of the most densely populated parts of the country. It is also one in which conflicts arising from public access to woodland seem to be minimal. So what does its own regional law on access to woodland actually say?

The Landscape Law of North-Rhine Westphalia provides for a right for people to walk over all woodland in the state at the user's own risk. Woodland is defined to include not only land supporting trees but also parks containing trees, windbreak strips, and thick hedgerows; it excludes parks in residential areas. Those entering woods must not disturb the forest ecosystem nor forestry practices, nor damage, endanger, or pollute the wood in any way. They must not infringe the legitimate interests of landowners nor the rights of other people for recreation to an unreasonable degree. Dogs must be kept on a lead when they are off public paths although hunting dogs and police dogs are exempted. The use of motorized vehicles is specifically excluded from the right.

For his or her part, the owner of a wood is forbidden to limit access without first obtaining permission from the access agency which is empowered to order the removal of restrictions on access if they have been placed there without its consent. However, the law permits landowners to fence in areas of up to 25 acres of very young trees without permission. In addition, an owner can limit or temporarily restrict access to woodland in the interests of tree felling, game management, or hunting if he first obtains permission from the Forest Commission. He must demonstrate that the restriction is necessary; the law provides that permission may be granted only temporarily and only if the forest authority considers that it is necessary in the interests of tree-growing, forest conservation, game rearing, or hunting. The commission can itself temporarily restrict access to public paths only, in order to prevent forest fires; while if a wood is under great recreational pressure and is sufficiently accessible by public paths or other facilities, public access may be restricted between 5 p.m. and 8 a.m. in order to protect animals or to facilitate hunting. The right of access which Germans enjoy under the federal Nature Conservation Law along all roads and paths (except for those like driveways which pass close to a dwelling or through a farmyard) means that if a walker spots an attractive looking wood which he or she knows will be accessible, he also knows he can take the nearest path to reach it, rather than having to make a long detour and then perhaps proceed without legal sanction as he might have to in Britain.

One other possible model comes from Switzerland. As we have seen, Switzerland first guaranteed its citizens a right of access over all woodland in 1907 and it has thus had more than a century of experience of upholding such access. In 1991 a new federal forest law introduced the notion of cantons being empowered to restrict access to forests for the general protection of the arboreal environment. Under this heading, they can require that permission be obtained from them for public events such as mass jogs or festivals, and also when felling is taking place or new plantations are being established. Hunting is not considered an acceptable reason for excluding walkers.

War-gaming

Woodland is almost always the preferred environment for the increasingly popular recreation of war-gaming. In 1988, 44 English woods were given over to war-gaming; by 1990 the figure had risen to 372.[15] The sport arrived in Britain from the United States in the early 1980s and in its earliest manifestations did not involve the countryside. Enthusiasts staged team battles inside buildings, firing laser guns at pads on their opponents' chests which, if hit by the laser beams, disabled their wearers' guns. That at least was the theory. Unfortunately the technology proved unreliable, and successful marksmen often found their supposedly disarmed victims firing back energetically. The simpler technology of the paintball gun proved more reliable: once splattered with paint from an exploding pellet a successfully targeted opponent could not convincingly claim he had cheated pseudo-death. Unfortunately, a paintball gun makes almost as much noise as a real firearm, and in the confines of a building, a paintball battle was deafening. The answer was to transfer the sport out of doors, a move which brought with it additional attractions for the participants. Woodland, with the opportunities it provides for taking cover, provided the obvious environment. Broadleaved woodland endowed with thick undergrowth and if possible the occasional pond, marsh, and muddy trench was best of all. So the woods that are best for war-gamers are also the ones which ramblers like best too.

Like pheasant shooting, war-gaming need not preclude access for walkers at all times, though it undoubtedly creates conflicts with rambling when the activity is actually under way. The Wayfarers' Walk public footpath passes through the middle of the 70-acre Bulls Bushes Copse outside Basingstoke in Hampshire, which has been used at weekends for war-gaming. Users of the path have not enjoyed being caught up in the combat. Such problems do not, however, justify the total exclusion of walkers from war-gaming woods. However, as with pheasant shooting, war-gaming tends to bring tougher curbs on public access. During the 1980s when paintball games became a fashionable management training exercise, picnickers could suddenly discover padlocks barring them from what had been a much-loved resort. When people pay to go shooting in Britain, whether they are shooting pheasants or each other, they expect sole use of their hunting ground. Though only a small number of woods have so far been claimed by war-gaming, the impact on walkers has been disproportionately great. Because it is the urban population who play war-games, the woods selected tend to be close to population centres, which are of course the woods most sought after by walkers. Outer London is not over-endowed with woodland, but in 1993 war-gaming was claiming two of the largest stretches of woodland that have survived in the borough of Bromley—Badgers' Mount and Hollows Wood—both of which lie on the doorstep of a small country railway station, which make them an ideal target for Londoners seeking a walk in the woods. On the edge of south-west London, a whole cluster of woods around the junction of the M25 and the A3 in Surrey had become war-gaming sites by 1997.

Even a bar operating when gaming is under way would deny walkers many important opportunities. Although the total number of woods in which war-gaming takes place is only a small fraction of that used for pheasant shooting or deer shooting, it takes place much more frequently, often on several consecutive Sundays and sometimes on Saturdays and on midweek evenings as well. If public safety and the effective operation of the sport require that people should be kept out of woods when war-gaming is actually in progress, there seems no reason why they should be barred outside these times. War-gaming does not require the preservation of vegetation in pristine condition, as on golf courses. The introduction of the general right of access would render woods which are at present used for war-gaming open to the public outside times when they were in use when temporary exemption would presumably apply. Clearly, the dates when such use was occurring would need to be carefully publicized, but the red flags used by the M.o.D. when live firing is under way on their ranges provide an already well understood means of achieving this. The loss of access accompanying war-gaming while actually in progress would be something local authorities could bear in mind when considering applications for change to this use in woods with amenity value for local communities.

Deer Stalking

Deer stalking may not be as widespread as pheasant shooting, but it is the main land use—along with sheep farming—over a very large area of the United Kingdom—3.5 million acres of the Scottish Highlands and Islands. While pheasant shooting rarely plays a central part in the economy of rural estates, but is often essentially a recreation for owners,[16] deer stalking can be the mainstay of Highland estates which have little other productive use.

There are plenty of people from both Britain and abroad who are prepared to spend hundreds of pounds to stalk deer. Part of the attraction is the trophy, usually a pair of antlers, which they are allowed to take home with them, and part is the attraction of taking part in an elaborate operation. Deer stalking is a complex art: hours of climbing and stalking may be required to line up a target. The stalkers' prime consideration is to avoid getting downwind of the deer, which might otherwise pick up their scent and take flight. For the owner of a deer forest (in fact such 'forests' are usually treeless expanses of moor) the flight of the deer can present real financial loss, so the impact of walkers is a matter of real concern to them. The deer of the Highlands do not in law belong to landowners: they are *res nullius* in Emperor Justinian's terminology (see page 117). One of the benefits of landownership, however, is that owners are allowed to kill certain wild animals which happen to be on their land and red deer are such animals. If the deer are disturbed and escape onto a neighbour's acres, they are lost to the original owner's stalker and sportsmen.

Despite the appeal of the creature itself and the prestige attached to deer stalking, it is actually a form of pest control. Unlike grouse, which have to be encouraged to breed on a sufficient scale, and unlike pheasants which are artificially reared in the countryside by the millions each year so they can later be shot, Scotland's deer have overpopulated the habitat to which they have been banished. Not that this is any fault of the deer. Humans exterminated the wolves which were the deer's natural predator and cleared away the broadleaved and pine woods which were their natural home leaving them to make do on barren slopes devoid of the bark, leaves, and other rich pickings of a woodland environment as well as the shelter it affords. Once deer stalking had become a prestigious and profitable pursuit in the nineteenth century, Highland estates started boosting deer numbers artificially by putting out food for them in winter while keeping out other animals, like sheep, which might compete with them for the often impoverished upland grass which was their only food. The result was a large increase in total numbers of red deer in Scotland, though on their new sparser diet they became only a dwarf version of their woodland forebears. Today individual deer hardly ever reach the natural size of the species, though their foraging has swept the Highlands and Islands of many of their native plants. The extent of this devastation can be assessed by comparing open hill country with areas from which deer are fenced out. On the Creag Meagaidh estate east of Fort William, owned by Scottish Natural Heritage, part of the 10,500-acre site has been fenced off completely. Here, the flora has been enriched dramatically, with a profusion of heath-, spotted- and marsh-orchids, melancholy thistle, grass of parnassus, and bluebells. Waves of cotton grass, a particular favourite of red deer, are spreading over wet flushes on the hillside, while hazel, alder, rowan, holly, birch, and willow are all returning.

Making it Work

Most Highland estates now acknowledge that hill walking is a considerable money spinner for the Highlands, bringing in far more income for hotels, restaurants, shops, and so on than deer stalking. It was partly in recognition of this that the Scottish Landowners' Federation signed the Concordat on access in 1996 which provided for freedom to roam over stalking areas within limits set by restrictions providing for the management of estates. The Concordat does not spell out what restrictions are to be considered reasonable, and there is very wide variation in the periods over which estates seek to restrict walkers. Though the main deer stalking season runs only from mid-August until mid-October, some estates seek to restrict access for much longer periods including the period from 20 October until 16 February when estate workers cull surplus hinds. An access agency administering a legal right of access could vet and co-ordinate applications for temporary exemptions from the right during the stalking season and ensure that notices gave accurate information. Estates could put forward the dates and areas over which they would like to restrict access through the temporary exemption machinery, but the agency could bear in mind other factors, including the availability of alternative walking areas.

Despite the practice of restricting walkers when deer are being shot, there is little evidence that the deer are rattled by hikers to any significant extent. Research suggests rather that stalking, understandably enough, frightens them much more than hiking. 'There are no data available to suggest that current levels of disturbance to red deer in Scotland affect their survival or population performance,' wrote Robert Staines and David Scott in research into the impact of recreation on red deer commissioned by Scottish Natural Heritage in 1994. 'There would be concern if red deer were endangered, but their numbers are rising and, it is generally agreed, too high.'[17] Deer are disturbed by walkers but the disturbance tends to be brief: they soon return to their grazing, resting, care of their fawns, or whatever unless the form of disturbance is unusual (walkers appearing perhaps in unexpected places such as a ridge-top or very close to an individual animal) or the disturbance arises from a cause the deer have reason to fear. Thus Staines and Scott report that the deer 'remained where they were but watched alertly' when their landrover was present and 'they only retreated if we stopped too long or left the vehicle'. However, 'they retreated from the stalker's vehicle immediately it was seen'.[18] Insofar as walkers affect deer in the Highlands, it is inconvenience to the stalking process itself which seems to cause most annoyance. But although this meant that individual stalks were sometimes affected by the presence of walkers, Staines and Scott found that few days were completely lost.

The bodies responsible for administering a right of access would need to consider findings like this carefully. They might conclude that restricting the public was sometimes justified, sometimes not. They could determine the extent of restrictions sought by landowners to meet the claimed needs of deer stalking and other activities, like fishing and shooting. At present, at the height of the holiday season people often find the possibilities available to them narrowed by a combination of restrictions imposed by different owners to meet the supposed needs of a series of different sporting activities.[19]

Red Grouse

For some moorland estates, red grouse are as commercially important as red deer are to others. Renting out shooting rights to groups of men from the city or, as happens increasingly nowadays, to parties of foreigners, can be lucrative. The capital value of moorland estates in places like the Scottish Borders, Angus, North Yorkshire, and Derbyshire depends to a considerable extent on the number of grouse bagged in recent years—just as the value of Highland stalking estates can depend on the number of stags shot. However, if deer are over-abundant, the red grouse needs a lot of care and attention. It is prone to population crashes, which have been the subject of considerable research and which are now thought likely to be related to the life cycle of parasites to which the grouse is prone. Grouse are fussy eaters: they prefer fresh green shoots of heather to heather which has grown up to be high and woody. For this reason, grouse moors are burned periodically. Grouse cannot be reared artificially like pheasants because the cocks are highly territorial: once they have claimed ground they keep every other male bird off that area. So the protection of birds nesting in the wild takes on an importance unknown to the owners of most pheasant woods.

The other main challenge for gamekeepers who have to provide a regular supply of grouse for the butts is the fox. David Parkinson, who has worked as a keeper on grouse estates in Durham and North Yorkshire, told me in an interview in 1990, 'The biggest threat to nesting grouse is the fox. If there is a family of foxes then anything within one square mile will be hoovered. Foxes carry mouthfuls of chicks away, so fox control is top priority. If you manage foxes then you can afford to forget birds of prey.'

Pressing though the threats to the well-being of grouse are, they do not seem to include walkers. Yet the owners of Britain's grouse moors have been amongst the most vigorous opponents of access rights. Since moorland has become the prime target of access campaigners in England and Wales, grouse moor owners have become leaders of the resistance. In 1996, the Radio 4 programme *Common Ground* tried to find out why. Kate Ashbrook, then Chairman of the Ramblers' Association, debated with Sir Anthony Milbank and Martin Gillibrand, the Chairman and Secretary of the Moorland Owners' Association. Both Sir Anthony Milbank and Martin Gillibrand stressed not the demands of the red grouse *per se* or the challenge of producing as many birds as possible for the guns but the needs of other wild birds which happen to nest on heather moorland.[20]

There are indeed nature conservation issues on moorland, which we shall come to, and it is not surprising that Gillibrand and Milbank chose to rely on these rather than the needs of their grouse. Red grouse do not take flight as soon as they perceive the presence of a human being. Dr Roger Sidaway, who has carried out a review of research on the impact of walkers on birds, observes, 'Given the habit of nesting grouse to "sit tight", it would appear that casual recreation disturbance is only likely to be occasional in occurrence and no more than a side-issue in the clash of interests between shooting and access bodies.'[21] Paul Woodhouse, a former hunt-servant who has worked on estates in Yorkshire told me: 'How can two or three people walking across several thousand acres of moorland disturb the grouse? I can't see how they can, and I've been in the country all my life. You're not likely to stumble over a grouse nest—if you do it's a chance in a million. Most game birds—pheasant, partridge, grouse—when you come to them when they're nesting, they lie ever so low and only when you're on top of them will they move. Mostly they won't, they'll remain stationary. Unless you actually stand on the nest you haven't disturbed them and if you do disturb them they'll perhaps fly away twenty yards, they'll settle down and then they'll run back through the undergrowth to their nest. So why close a whole moor down for fear of disturbing a bird for a few seconds?'

It is not surprising that no scientific data have ever been produced to demonstrate that the presence of the public reduces the number of grouse shot. Grouse continue to thrive on Barden Moor and Barden Fell, for instance, although it has been enjoyed by hundreds of thousands of walkers since 1960. The only scientific study carried out, by Nicholas Picozzi of the Nature Conservancy Council in 1971, compared breeding success and public access on moorlands in the Peak District. He could find no significant difference in breeding levels or shooting bags on moors with or without public access. If anything, the birds on moors open to the public did rather better than their counterparts elsewhere.[22] More recently, Dr Peter Hudson, now the Manager of Upland Research for the Game Conservancy, sought to uncover any relationship between the level of disturbance on moors on fifty estates in northern England and the numbers of grouse shot there during the 1960s and 1970s. Dr Hudson discovered there was no significant difference in the average grouse bag between moors with low and high levels of public access. His studies also revealed that there was no significant disturbance to breeding grouse by walkers along a public right of way.[23]

In view of all this, the concern voiced by grouse moor owners about walkers may seem surprising. Yet there is more to grouse shooting than shooting grouse. Maintaining a grouse moor is a rich man's hobby. Scotland for instance had 486 grouse moors in 1989, each 9,100 acres in extent on average. The average income for each moor from lettings was £12,000 per year; the average outgoings £20,000. This gives a total annual loss across the grouse moors of Scotland for the year of £3.7 million.[24] Such losses may have been mitigated by the abolition of sporting rates in 1995, but running a grouse moor is still a loss-making activity. Because of the subsidy needed owning grouse moors is therefore part of the lifestyle of the rich. The people involved, paying as they do vast sums for the privilege of owning grouse moors, cannot be expected to welcome the intrusion of the lower orders onto territory over which they pursue their expensive hobby even if it can be demonstrated that any direct impact on the grouse themselves is likely to be limited.

In view of the evidence on grouse and access there seems no reason why the public need be excluded from grouse moors except on those days when shoots are actually taking place. A considerable amount of valuable experience has already been built up by Lancashire County Council and the Peak District and Yorkshire Dales National Park Authorities in particular in managing areas of grouse moor subject to access agreements. As we have seen (page 255), the new access agreements which will be signed as a result of the renegotiation between the Peak Authority and the Moorland Owners' and Tenants' Association in the park provides for the drawing up of shooting management plans, which should ensure that particular moors are no longer closed for a whole day but different sections of the moor are closed at different times of the day. Thus in the case of large moors of which one side is being shot over in the morning and the other side being shot over in the afternoon, only half of the moor will be closed for any particular half-day; and in situations where grouse moors fall down below ridge paths, the Peak Authority hope that the ridge paths will not need to be closed while the shooting takes place on the moor below. Temporary exemptions provided under a new right of access regime could regulate shooting in this way on grouse moors throughout the UK, with red flags and standard warning notices posted up on the days when shooting is actually taking place, as they already are at access agreement sites like Barden Moor and Barden Fell.

Fishing

While grouse and pheasant shooting allow the separation of sportsmen and walkers, fishing does not. Angling is not a group activity but involves individuals spread over large areas. Many fear that the presence of the public would frighten away the fish they are pursuing.

Some, particularly the high-rent fly fishermen of the trout streams, if not the coarse anglers crowded round urban reservoirs and along canalsides, also value the seclusion which may be an important part of their fishing experience. Anglers invest skill on a scale more comprehensive than that displayed by shooters or even stalkers, who usually leave the strategy of the stalk to a ghillie. Wading into a river, selecting the pools or shallows on which to concentrate whether from the bank or midstream, the type of fly to be used and the length at which to cast it all require considerable engagement with the environment of the prey and an assessment of the behaviour of the quarry. Not unnaturally, fishermen and women do not like being disturbed just at the moment when they are about to cast their fly or when they stand waiting expectantly for a tug on the line. All this is reflected commercially. Lettings from prime fishing sites bring in large sums of money (£62,000 a year for a 1.5-mile stretch of Perthshire's River Tay, say) and in resisting extensions of access for walkers and other groups like canoeists along rivers, particularly those favoured by salmon and trout, the owners of fishing rights have been protecting the value of substantial financial assets.

Any potential conflict between walking and angling cannot be resolved neatly by simply segregating the sportsmen and walkers while the sport is in progress as with grouse or pheasant shooting. Although there is a close season for fishing, it is not of a length or at a time of year which would allow a sufficient access for walkers. The close season for salmon runs from November until January; for trout from October until February, which means that both species can be fished through spring, summer, and early autumn. The statutory close season for coarse fishing is more helpful for walkers in its timing (mid-March until mid-June) but not in its total length.

So how far do passing walkers really reduce the angler's chances of a catch? On a lake or reservoir it is hard to see that walkers round the edge are likely to have much impact. Anglers argue that fish like trout can be 'spooked' or frightened away by a silhouette from the bank since they can see clearly and through a wide angle. However, on a body of water there is enough wave action to spoil the vision of the fish. On a narrow stretch of river, things could be different. But are they? There is surprisingly little evidence that walkers on riverbanks cast shadows and thereby frighten the fish away on a significant scale. In 1986 the Centre for Leisure Research carried out a study for the Countryside Commission on the potential conflicts not, unfortunately, between walkers and anglers but between anglers and canoeists (who might be expected to cause more disruption to fishing than people walking along the banks). At present canoeists are even more restricted than walkers along Britain's rivers, and the team asked anglers and their representative organizations why they felt they must keep the rivers to themselves. Their objections fell into two categories: technical arguments, and what the team called 'ideological objections'; both, the team found, were subject to much dispute. On the first, they observed,

Anglers argue that fish have acute senses and are disturbed by any movement on or near the water. Thus, fish 'go down' on the passage of a boat, take time to resurface and take a hook, and the angler's fishing is devalued. Anglers claim that they may spend hours 'building up a swim' and coaxing fish to bite, and that this can be destroyed instantly by a few passing canoes. These arguments remain unresolved by empirical research, and it is difficult to disentangle the two arguments. Some of the discussions appear to combine elements of fact with the sacred and mythical.

Of the ideological objections, based on a view of fishing as a contemplative pastime, they reported,

From this perspective, a central part of angling is 'peace and quiet', a 'communicating with nature', which is disturbed by canoeists, especially if they pass in small groups over a long period of time.... Such arguments relate to collective values and attitudes which are not amenable to rational discussion. Anglers either feel disturbed or they do not. In terms of actual events, reports support both sides of this argument, with stories of anglers being both friendly and irate at the presence of canoes. Much depends on goodwill and mutual respect for each others' requirements.[25]

Canoeists do of course violate the element into which anglers are reaching out. Walkers behind them might be expected to pose less of both a practical and an ideological threat. In fact, there are plenty of places where walkers and anglers seem to coexist happily. Excellent fishing including trout and grayling can be had on many canals alongside which the British Waterways Board permit people to walk.

The late actor Sir Michael Hordern used to maintain that walkers did not intrude on fishing. Hordern was not only a committed walker (he was a life member of the Open Spaces Society) but also a committed fisherman with a cottage by the River Lambourn near Newbury. While quoting this opinion, Hordern would refer to the case of the River Wylye, the Wiltshire river which is supposed to have given its name to the county, and which supports excellent fishing despite accommodating many short stretches of riverside public footpath.[26] The author of the classic *The Rivers and Streams of England*, published in 1909, and himself both a walker and a fisherman, A. G. Bradley, also observed of the Wylye that this 'naturally fine trout stream can be seen by any strollers upon the bank' and went on to speculate about the reasons. He wrote:

The smaller trout of wild rapid streams, who take the fly so much more readily, rush madly for safety the moment you show yourself upon the bank above a pool. But the big chalk-stream trout, so much more wary of the deadly fly, is comparatively indifferent to the mere spectator. Possibly the superior education that has quickened his perception in the matter of artificial flies and their method of presentation has also taught him that in them alone danger lurks, and in mere man as such there is none whatsoever. So it comes about that in the Wylye you may look down in places through three or four feet of crystal water, and at quite close quarters watch over movement of a score or so of great trout or grayling of from 1 to 2 lbs. weight, as they lie poised above the clear gravelly bottom.[27]

As with other activities, the machinery of the temporary exemption should provide for satisfactory resolution where anglers could demonstrate that their sport was damaged by walkers. Ramblers or other groups like perhaps ornithologists would be able to oppose applications if they believed the claim of disturbance was bogus. The access authority might opt to introduce some spatial zoning. This would not only be possible around lakeshores or the edges of reservoirs, but on watercourses too. Anglers do not generally fish the whole length of a river but frequent spots or pools where, perhaps because of the presence of deep holes where the fish can lie in cooler water, or bushes, or the presence of food, they know from past experience a catch is likely. Even if walkers found themselves restricted to one bank of a river for certain stretches of particularly favoured fishing beat, this would mean a far greater degree of access for them than exists in many areas at present.

It is not possible to pretend however that the fisherman would not be deprived of the seclusion he currently enjoys were a meaningful right of access to be introduced. If seclusion were to be deemed an adequate reason for exemption in the case of angling, then there would be no way of denying exemption to any landowner who wanted privacy for any reason. Our rivers, reservoirs, and lakes simply form too large and too significant a potential recreation resource for the whole community for restrictions on access to operate over long stretches in the interests of just one group.

Walkers should, however, have a responsibility to minimize the impact of their presence on angling, as anglers should be required to minimize their impact on walkers. Casting flies can endanger walkers, and anglers should be told in a Country Code-like way that they should not cast in a manner which could endanger others. Similarly, the public should be told that they should not cast shadows unnecessarily across the water, or disturb the angler. The fictitious J. R. Hartley recounted an experience while fishing along the River Coln near Fairford in Gloucestershire:

The river was ten to fifteen yards wide where we fished, three to five feet deep, flowing sinuously over beds of water crowfoot and water milfoil. In good conditions it would be gin clear, with occasional dark pools tucked in beneath overhanging willows. From a selfish point of view, it was a snag that there was a public right of way along the bank. All too often an uncomprehending walker would stop to engage us in well-meant discussion after the inevitable greeting, thrown from twenty yards, of 'Any luck?' Spencer, though he was a courteous man, could not resist responding 'Up till now.'[28]

Privacy and Security

If a right of access must coexist with existing land-use activities so too must it coexist with the right of all individuals to reasonable privacy. The notion that each individual is entitled to a certain amount of private space seems to be an instinctive part of our behaviour as a species. Out of doors we all seem to feel that privacy ought to be respected. In a park we do not approach the stranger sitting reading or simply musing under a tree. For that short period of time the place where he or she is sitting and a certain area around them, whose boundaries we all instinctively know, is not public property in the sense that we all feel we can walk freely over it. It is theirs. Even on a crowded public beach in the height of summer there is still a sense in which patches of beach, however pocket-handkerchief-sized, in some sense belong briefly to those who have claimed them. In railway carriages we demand a degree of privacy even though we are sitting only a few feet away from complete strangers.

At present, those who plan our public open spaces see the need for each person to have some sense of individual privacy or psychological distance from others as extremely important. Here is Marcus Galey, South Norfolk District Council's Public Rights of Way Officer, talking about his vision for a 150-yard belt of marsh and low-lying pasture which is being given to the council as part of a planning gain deal involving the development of an industrial estate on the eastern edge of Diss:

I have this theory that people actually want to be on their own in the country-side: they don't actually want lots of other people around. And so if you can see lots of other people on the site that's not as attractive as feeling that you are on your own. As it's a pasture field, it's absolutely open. So that once you get three or four groups of people on there it will feel very full. But if you can screen it, break it up a little perhaps with trees or ponds you can get lots more people in there without it feeling full. That's something I want to try to create with the people here in Diss.

This approach is not very different from the thinking of those who created the town parks of Victorian times: given a level site in a crowded industrial city, they would set about building mounds and hillocks not only to cut off views of the built-up area and thus create the illusion that park users were in the middle of the countryside, but also so as to enable individuals to feel their own personal space was not being infringed, even though the park might contain hundreds of other people all under the same illusion.

We all want privacy in our own homes and the freedom to engage in activities in our own back garden unseen by our neighbours or anybody else. However, we can manage to cope with considerable incursions into our privacy. When those who live in flats or in terraced housing venture into their back gardens they are actually on show whether to other people living in the same block of flats or along the same row or to other people passing along public footpaths and roads or using other publicly accessible space like a playground or allotments. Here people are protected by the instinct of others to respect their privacy. If we happen to see our neighbour in his or her back garden, we instinctively avert our gaze.

A general right of access will intrude into some people's privacy some of the time but clearly should only be allowed to do so up to a point. An exemption from any general right of access should clearly exist for houses, their immediate surroundings, and gardens. In Sweden it is generally considered acceptable for walkers to come within 15 metres of a summer house in a forest clearing and closer still if there is obviously no one at home. An ordinary occupied home would normally be given 100 metres' berth. This rough and ready approach seems to work perfectly well and no one seems to feel rigid rules would improve matters. In Denmark there is a rule that walkers must not come within 50 metres of a house when they are exercising their right of access along the shore and 150 metres in woods and on heaths, but this creates conflicts with other principles, such as the idea that beaches, woods, and heaths ought to be accessible. In both Sweden and Norway gardens are much less energetically fenced and hedged than they are in Britain so people there have more reason to feel vulnerable to intrusion. Their failure to do so ought to reassure us.

If an exemption on grounds of privacy were extended as far as some landowners would like, it would, however, make nonsense of the right of access itself. As we have seen (page 133), Lord Brocket liked to feel private in his 'patch' of land even though that patch extended to 5,000 acres of woods, fields, parkland, lake, and river as well as a mansion and garden. Landowners like him would have to sacrifice some privacy. What though of large private gardens which merge almost imperceptibly into a private parkland? At this particular margin there would doubtless be continued scope for argument. On the whole, owners would probably get away with claiming extravagant areas as gardens much of the time, but where a citizen wanted to challenge this he would obviously need the opportunity to do so. The bodies managing the right of access would therefore have to adjudicate claims that exemptions were being claimed unfairly. Ultimately it would also be necessary for it to be possible to test the adjudicating body's verdict in the courts.

Nowadays, security is often used as a justification for exclusion, and of course the exclusion thus secured incidentally provides privacy. The desire for undue privacy should not be allowed to masquerade as the demand for necessary security. Nonetheless, there will very occasionally be a convincing case for the pre-emption of the right of access to safeguard the security of people or property. The entire grounds of Chequers could clearly not be opened to the public when the Prime Minister is in residence, nor could Balmoral. It is less obvious that the inner park at Windsor could not be open when the Queen is not in residence. These dilemmas are already faced with the routeing of public footpaths. A public footpath passed close to John Major's home near Huntingdon, but the Cambridge Constabulary which was responsible for the protection of John Major as Prime Minister wrote to the Ramblers' Association:

It is not our intention to prevent members of the public or, indeed, ramblers, from using the footpath in the vicinity of the Prime Minister's home at Great Stukeley. However, as you quite rightly express, there may be occasions when it is necessary, as a purely temporary measure, to divert members of the public from their normal route. I stress this will be on very few occasions and only as a temporary measure. In the normal course of events, the Police Officers tasked with the Prime Minister's security will be only too pleased to see members of the public and local people using the public footpaths. This gives the opportunity for additional 'eyes and ears' to be present in the area. I would urge any of your members who witness or see anything suspicious to contact our Force Control Room immediately at Police Headquarters, telephone number ... In conclusion, I would hope that I have answered your queries and allayed any fears that the normal rights of ramblers will not be compromised by the Prime Minister's security, as I would not wish that to be the case.[29]

The notion that the public interest in access along public paths should be upheld unless the security case is very strong indeed is an important principle which should not be eroded. At present plenty of people put up with—or enjoy—the sight of walkers using public paths close to their homes, even though those homes may be in fairly remote rural areas and even though they may harbour possessions of considerable value. As we have seen (page 197), even such a prominent and wealthy person as Lord Lloyd-Webber was not allowed to reroute a public footpath close to his home to improve his security. Decisions about exemption from a right of access on grounds of security would face a similar process of scrutiny.

Wildlife Conservation

One of the most serious problems confronting a right to roam is the suggestion that free access to the countryside might endanger wildlife. One of the reasons for visiting the countryside in the first place is to see and hear its wildlife. To imperil that wildlife by making its habitat accessible would clearly be absurd, and it is understandable that opponents of a right to roam have made much of this possibility even when their own concerns lie elsewhere. But do walkers really threaten our wildlife? If so, how and when, and can any genuine danger be averted?

Perhaps the first point to acknowledge is that the presence of virtually any creature in an environment will affect that environment and the other creatures which live there to some degree or other. Man is not unique in this regard. Predators—whether they be foxes, domestic cats, or the garden frogs which may in turn fall victim to cats—affect populations of the species on which they prey. Grazing animals, whether domesticated like cattle and sheep or wild like deer and rabbits, affect the composition of the ground vegetation enormously. People walking in the countryside can have an impact, though the effect is of course normally far more localized than that of grazing animals and therefore unlikely to have a significant ecological impact. Nonetheless, public use of popular sites at some times can be sufficiently intense to change the composition of the underlying vegetation. The unsightly white gashes which have appeared from time to time on hillsides at beauty spots like Box Hill, Dunstable Downs, and Ivinghoe Beacon are unarguable evidence that walking can have an impact on the countryside. In places like this, plant species which are unable to withstand much trampling die out and are replaced with other more resistant species. In very heavily used spots, even resistant species are unable to survive the trampling they receive and the bare ground which is exposed may be eroded by wind and rain. Some underlying vegetation is particularly ill-adapted to withstand large amounts of trampling. Peat bog, such as occurs along parts of the Pennine Way, is quickly turned into a quagmire by heavy visitor use. As walkers seek to skirt the impassable stretches the area affected expands. And while mountain tops may seem indestructible, their thin soils can be eroded away by only a moderate amount of trampling whose effects can be exacerbated by rain and frost.

Fortunately, heavily used paths whether at the top of Snowdon or on the side of Box Hill can be repaired. Temporary fencing off of the areas concerned while their habitat is restored or paths made more robust through improved drainage and surfacing is normally all that is needed to cope with what is usually only a very localized problem. Chalk downland turf such as occurs on Box Hill and sites on the Chiltern scarp like Ivinghoe Beacon and Dunstable Downs is actually more resistant to trampling than lowland heathland; much grassland, like parkland, is pretty robust, as is much woodland. Sand dunes represent one of our most vulnerable habitats. The parts most susceptible to vegetation change and even alteration of the underlying dune structure are not only the pathways through the dunes along which most use is concentrated as people make their way to the sea, but also a zone about two-thirds of the way landwards where little humus manages to develop in the soil which could afford it some protection, yet where seasonal drought also frequently occurs. A moderate amount of sun-bathing and walking in this zone can cause serious problems. In fact, those dunes which have been seriously altered have usually suffered from something more than visitor pressure, such as military training. Nonetheless dunes do pose a particular problem for habitat protection: they cover only 0.2 per cent of the land of the British Isles, yet people like to wander all over them, the higher dunes offering viewpoints and the sides offering an inviting slope to slide down.[30]

In spite of these particular problems, the impact of current walking on wildlife habitats in the countryside seems to be small. Even in the most heavily used areas, like London's parks or Arthur's Seat and Holyrood Park in Edinburgh (itself a designated site of special scientific interest or SSSI), careful management of visitors can enable huge numbers of people to use a relatively small area without grinding it to dust. Box Hill, perhaps our most celebrated countryside site and one which has been frequented by city dwellers for 300 years, not only provides a playground for people but also a sanctuary for wildlife. No fewer than seventeen orchid species flourish here and these are as numerous as they were in the 1950s.[31] Dr Graham Bathe, the official of English Nature then responsible for wildlife conservation in London, explained to me in an interview in 1993 that Richmond Park, Hampstead Heath, and Wimbledon Common are all SSSIs which attract millions of visitors every year (3.5 million in the case of Richmond Park, 5 million at Hampstead Heath). 'By and large people don't have a significant impact on the wildlife interest of these SSSIs,' he told me. 'We don't have any anxiety to reduce or control visitor numbers and there is great interest for people in cities to see wildlife.'

In 1995 the House of Commons Environment Committee studied the impact on the environment of all leisure uses, not just walking. It concluded:

Despite these sorts of cultural conflict, despite the public perception that the environment is under immediate threat from leisure use, and despite the potential of individual activities to spoil the natural heritage, however, we have found no evidence that leisure and tourism pose a serious, immediate or intrinsic threat to the environment. . . . Leisure and tourism are less of a threat to Sites of Special Scientific Interest and Areas of Outstanding Natural Beauty than industry or other developments. According to English Nature's records, no Sites of Special Scientific Interest have been lost through tourist activity and most of any damage done is short- rather than long-term. . . . The Countryside Commission also noted that damage to the environment by industrialisation, farming and urbanisation 'heavily exceeded' the damage caused by recreational activity. These views were supported by, among others, the Ramblers' Association, the Natural Environment Research Council and New Forest District Council.[32]

Overall impacts on particular habitats are, however, easier to assess than impacts on populations of animals. Take the erosion of vegetation to bare earth. For some burrowing wasps, bees, and ants, this can be beneficial. For other creatures there may be other effects which we are only beginning to understand. Dormice move around in woods along aerial runways such as occur in hedges and in undergrowth. They dislike and often refuse to cross bare earth, even if it is only a few feet wide. So if a wide path is cut through woodland or perhaps an existing path is allowed to become bare and wide through concentrated passage of walkers, serious results could ensue for dormice. If a population of dormice finds its habitat lost, say through the clearance of timber and undergrowth, a wide path could form an uncrossable barrier, isolating the community so it cannot colonize other areas and eventually threatening its survival as inbreeding undermines its gene pool. The extent to which paths, particularly wide or deeply rutted ones, form a significant barrier threatening the survival of other small mammals, amphibians, reptiles, and invertebrates is simply not known.[33]

More is known about the extent to which larger, easily visible creatures like ground-nesting birds are disturbed by walkers. As we have seen, organizations like the Moorland Owners' Association point to the damage walkers may do to such creatures. In woods, wild birds are relatively unaffected by walkers. There are a few, like the black grouse, which do seem sensitive, but even ground-nesters like the woodcock choose such dense undergrowth that they are to all intents and purposes inaccessible to casual walkers. Tree-hole nesters and birds of the woodland canopy do not seem much bothered by the presence of people beneath. In open country, on the other hand, where the ground is often the only place available for nesting, disturbance by walkers is a much bigger potential threat. Important species of our upland moors like golden plover, dotterel, red grouse, and curlew have to nest on the ground. Walkers are unlikely to trample over nests as they are so widely scattered, but if they get close enough to scare a sitting bird off the nest, they may expose eggs or young to an increased risk of predation, particularly if their numbers make such disturbance frequent. This is less of a problem for birds which sit tight when threatened, like the rare dotterel, but can be fatal for flighty species like the curlew. On our lowland heaths, the rare woodlark seems surprisingly tolerant of walkers, but if walkers cause fires in the breeding season all species could suffer badly. It is not only while breeding that wild birds can be affected by walkers: strollers along the tide-line can frighten off flocks of wading birds in winter which are feeding between high and low water mark. When these birds, such as redshank, dunlin, knot, grey plover, and so on fly up and resettle they use up valuable energy and therefore reserves of body fat while losing the feeding time they need to replace these. When day lengths are short and estuaries may be frozen this can put their lives at risk. None of these considerations mean, however, that the needs of walkers and wildlife cannot be reconciled.

Changing Attitudes

Over the past thirty years, wildlife organizations have changed their attitudes to visitors. During the 1960s and 1970s, wildlife conservationists were as ready as anyone to blame the townsman for the ills of the countryside.[34] Townspeople were ready enough to accept the role of villain and were content to be corralled in semi-rural playgrounds called 'country parks' close to towns, where it was hoped they could disport themselves without doing too much damage to wildlife or anything else rural. Wariness of visitors permeated the national wildlife agency, the Nature Conservancy, later the Nature Conservancy Council, which concentrated on selecting and designating a network of key wildlife locations which it called sites of special scientific interest. The Conservancy managed to secure some proprietary interest in a small number of these sites, either through leasehold or freehold ownership, and these were called national nature reserves. These reserves were managed during the 1950s, 1960s, and 1970s largely as outdoor laboratories—places where scientists could keep records and carry out research, and where they could safely leave scientific equipment without the public damaging it. They did not expect outsiders to understand their esoteric world, nor did they imagine that many of them had much interest in it, and in any case their ideal laboratory was usually an environment devoid of human influence. Often they did not see the human race as itself one of the species making up the nation's wildlife but as a particularly alien creature which should be kept out of the 'natural' world. 'I recall as a student', wrote one-time Deputy Director of the Nature Conservancy Sir Martin

Holdgate, 'that the conscious or sub-conscious aim of all "real" ecologists was to study plant and animal communities as little disturbed
by human influence as possible.'[35] George Barker, who worked for
the NCC and is now national urban adviser to English Nature, the
body which succeeded it in England after reorganization in 1992, added
in an interview with me in 1993: 'Also the wardens had all these places
as their territory. Some had an antipathy to the general public. They
liked to have privacy—an attitude like that of the landed gentry.
So there was resistance to access, particularly to opening up places
which were inaccessible.'

Soon, though, wildlife conservationists found they could not exist
in a closed world. Their sites of special scientific interest turned out
to be as vulnerable as the countryside beyond to the widespread destruction of habitat which occurred during the 1960s and 1970s as a result
of the intensification and expansion of agriculture and forestry. Even
where the sites themselves escaped damage, wildlife populations suffered because they needed to range beyond the sites' confines. So conservationists came to realize that safeguarding wildlife would mean
concerning themselves with the whole countryside and building
public support for this project. That meant coming to terms with public access. Dr Barker, then warden/naturalist at Old Winchester Hill
in Hampshire, was one of the first to see this. He was also anxious
to see SSSIs in the hands of an owner sympathetic to conservation,
which would not sell the site on to somebody else and which would
respond to his recommendations for management at a time when the
NCC had no grant-aiding power to encourage proactive management
of sites. During the mid- and late 1960s, Barker encouraged the land
agent for Hampshire County Council, Colin Bonsey, to safeguard some
of the larger SSSIs by acquiring them as public open spaces. As a result,
the council bought not only the important downland landmark
of Butser Hill but also Crab Wood outside Winchester (a haunt of
solomon's seal and lily of the valley) and a 4-mile stretch of the hanger
woods and grasslands which run between Petersfield and Selborne (now
with a memorial to the poet Edward Thomas who lived nearby). All
are still SSSIs, and all are far more accessible to the public than they
were before purchase by the county council. Dr Barker explained to
me: 'We did expect to lose a bit—to trampling, car parks—and there

might be odd bits of malicious or accidental damage. But these are probably not significant in contrast to getting management appropriate to the site. So we got a trade off: we lost an area to car parking, a few sparrows, rats and litter (aesthetically damaging but not damaging ecologically), and in return we secured the long-term survival of the site.'

As wildlife conservationists looked to the urban population for support for rural conservation, they found, much to their surprise, that a number of valuable wildlife sites survived in the inner areas of cities. Necessarily, these were not sites which had survived as untouched wildernesses safe from the hand of man; what is more, many of them were attracting hundreds of thousands of visitors every year without suffering any obvious environmental harm. In many places towns were found to be providing a refuge for wild creatures driven out of the countryside by agricultural change. While numbers of frogs and toads diminished in rural areas they increased dramatically in the suburbs; sparrowhawks, which had been driven out of rural areas by gamekeeping and pesticides, moved into the hearts of cities. Mass membership organizations like the Royal Society for the Protection of Birds already depended on city dwellers for much of their support, and when other wildlife organizations began to look to towns they discovered there a constituency which, if marshalled on the side of wildlife, could increase their political clout. Years of wildlife programmes on television had fostered great concern for wild creatures, and the growing democratization of society was encouraging people to take a more proprietorial view of their environment.

A trail blazer in opening and interpreting wildlife reserves to the public was the Suffolk Naturalists' Trust. In 1986 it appointed ecologist Jane Madgwick to consider whether and if so how the Trust's network of reserves, access to which was then restricted to the Trust's few hundred members, should be widened to take in the general public. At the time there was very little scope for people who were not members of the Trust to visit its reserves or even to find out where they were. There were few signboards, leaflets telling people where to go, or reserves handbooks written for people who were not knowledgeable naturalists. But in 1989 the Trust published a reserves handbook written for the general public providing details of the forty-eight sites to which they were and still are welcome. When Miss Madgwick started work, many of the voluntary wardens responsible for individual sites disliked the idea of opening them to all comers. By the early 1990s, they had changed their mind: they did not consider the increased numbers of visitors had had any significant harmful impact on wildlife in the reserves and a significant number felt that access could be increased further without threat of harm.

Yet in Suffolk wildlife habitats have been much reduced and fragmented by post-war agricultural change. Redgrave and Lopham Fens, a 320-acre stretch of reed bed, sedge bed, wet heath, waterways, pools, and woodland south of Diss was one of the first trust sites to be opened, Miss Madgwick told me. This is the largest remaining tract of valley fen in Suffolk, providing a habitat for many plants and animals which have become rare as fenland has been drained and turned over to intensive farmland. To facilitate public access, the Trust created 11 miles of pathway which are now open all the time; in addition it welcomes school parties and other groups. Despite initial fears, some of the most valued species of the fens—reed warblers, sedge warblers, and dragonflies for example—have proved happy to tolerate the public. Although the Trust has had some trouble with people looking for the species for which the site is most famous, the great raft spider, its population does not seem to have been affected by visitors. Rather, its survival depends on the maintenance of water levels in the calcareous pools in which it lives and of saw sedge around their edges in which it builds its nursery webs. However, dogs are not allowed to run free at Trust sites: in twenty reserves they must be on a lead while at the remaining twenty-eight they are barred. Jane Madgwick: 'I would actually prefer, apart from the public footpaths (where dogs are allowed), not allowing dogs in reserves because I do think that not only creates far more disturbance for wildlife because a dog will cover ten times as much ground as a person will and be noisy, but also it ruins the enjoyment of other people. It's a difficult area. Then there is the mess that they create when you get ten dogs in a wood every night and then you take kids in to do plant rubbings and fiddle around on the ground.'

Fox Fritillary meadow near Debenham might seem even more vulnerable to visitor damage than Redgrave and Lopham Fens. This is a site of special scientific interest covering a mere 6 acres, celebrated for its spectacular display of the rare snake's head fritillary. Here 300,000 fritillaries bloom in late spring amongst cowslips, cuckoo flower, and ragged robin while short-eared owls roost in the hedgerows. The need to conserve the fritillaries is very great indeed: once abundant in Suffolk they have been virtually eliminated outside this site through the drainage and ploughing of the wet meadows in which they lived. The wetness of the site makes it vulnerable to erosion, while the fritillaries themselves are extremely fragile. The Trust cordons off a metre-wide pathway around the edge of the meadow when the flowers are in bloom which allows between 3,000 and 4,000 people to view them on any one day without causing significant damage.

At Reydon Wood and Green Lane, another Suffolk Trust reserve, this time an ancient hornbeam and ash wood covering only 40 acres near Southwold, different visitor management techniques have been developed. This is the only wood with open access in a large stretch of Suffolk and it was crucial that the Trust, in developing their management strategy, should ensure that visitors did not damage the plants on the woodland floor, including six species of orchid, as well as those of the wet areas in the wood like the water violet and the fine-leafed water dropwort. Jane Madgwick: 'What we did was to create a carefully designed nature trail round the wood which would allow people to see the various aspects of it but not for instance to get them to trample right up the middle of a wet, marshy rise but to get them to go along the sides so that they can see it but not walk on it.' Thousands of people visit the wood every year yet blackcap, woodcock, hares, rabbits, weasels, and woodmice continue to do well. Jane Madgwick again: 'I was in the wood when there was an open day and there were 800 people during that day walking round and I went off to sit away from the nature trail in a glade and as I sat there a fox casually walked through and I thought this is ridiculous, there's hundreds of people in this wood and it's just not bothered at all.'[36]

The Suffolk Trust's experience at Reydon Wood is paralleled by that of the Woodland Trust. It opens all but one of its 918 properties to the public as a matter of course, even though most are small and close to population centres. Dr Hilary Allison, the Trust's Corporate Affairs Manager, told me in 1998: 'The Trust's own experience is that the conservation of wildlife, except in exceptional circumstances, is not compromised by allowing public access to those woods which are important habitats. In some cases if a habitat is particularly sensitive, it may be necessary to divert paths to reduce the likelihood of any accidental damage or disturbance. It is the Trust's general experience that those enjoying quiet recreation offer no threat to wildlife. Most walkers follow existing paths (permissive or rights of way) in any event and leave wildlife undisturbed.'

In some cases, the Trust has found that the wildlife value of woods has actually increased rather than diminished after the wood concerned has been opened to the public. Bramingham Wood in Luton is a case in point. This 45-acre ancient woodland is almost encircled by housing estates (50,000 people live within 1 mile of its boundaries). It was managed for at least part of its history on the coppice-with-standards-method, its ancient oaks being allowed to grow to full height amid hazel coppice. Stroll in the wood today and you may well see one of the resident tawny owls observing you from the branches of one of the oaks, maples, or tall ash trees, to the accompaniment of the drumming of another resident bird, the great spotted woodpecker. January in the wood sees the snowdrops in flower, followed by colts-foot, primroses, wood anemones and dog violets, and in late spring, a carpet of bluebells, red campion, and yellow archangel. In high summer, red admiral, peacock, small tortoiseshell, brimstone, speckled wood, and comma butterflies flutter in the glades while dragonflies dart and hover around the ponds.

In the early 1980s, Bramingham was just another private fenced, inaccessible wood, albeit subject to trespass and vandalism. It might be thought that throwing open the wood to all would exacerbate such problems, but the Trust's local officer, Andrew Thompson, told me in 1987: 'The people who were causing damage don't want to be seen doing it, so the more people you get into a wood like this the less damage you get.'[37] The Trust has harnessed the enthusiasm of local people by forming a Bramingham Wood Volunteers' Group which has reintroduced coppicing, not for the commercial sale of timber but for the effect the process has on enhancing wildlife: the cutting of the coppice timber allows light through woodland canopy and thus allows plants of the woodland floor like primroses and wood anemones to flourish. As a result, the wildlife diversity of the wood is actually greater than it was before 1985. Two years after the wood was opened, one local volunteer reported to me: 'We are finding that the variety of birds has actually increased over the last year, and several plants have been found which, though not great rarities, are fairly uncommon in this part of the world. These have been found because we have been clearing paths so people could have access, and this has been of tremendous benefit. Natural historians and a lot of people are now coming in with their cameras and their notebooks and recording what they see around them. Last autumn we found a species of fungus in the wood which is in fact new to Britain.'[38]

Today the vast majority of national nature reserves are open to the public, and the nature conservation agencies as well as local authorities run programmes of guided walks as well as promoting interpretation centres to enable every citizen to enjoy nature. In addition people enjoy access to land in the ownership of bodies like the National Trust, significant amounts of which are of outstanding wildlife value. The opening up of the national nature reserves has however not been matched by any improvement in access to important wildlife sites in private ownership. The growing numbers of people wanting to visit the countryside and experience wildlife at first hand have thus been concentrated into a small number of sites, some of which are the best examples of particular habitats, and some of which are vulnerable to visitor pressure.

In the face of this overall picture, the introduction of a general right of access to the countryside, if done properly, could end up improving rather than damaging the position of wildlife. Obviously the protection of wildlife would be a prime reason for either the temporary or permanent exemption of particular areas from a right to roam. And the understanding that exclusion was occurring for the benefit of wild creatures rather than to safeguard landowners' privacy over a wide area might enhance rather than reduce people's willingness to comply with restrictions designed to protect wildlife. Instead of creating the idea that people can trample over everything in the countryside, a general right of access ought to instil the notion that people can go where they will not do harm. At present people sometimes damage the environment because they resent being kept out of so much of it for the benefit of the privileged. If people understood that they could go anywhere in principle, they might be more rather than less willing to respect a sign telling them to keep off a stretch of shingle on which terns were nesting. At present open and close seasons are well understood and respected in the world of country sports. Temporary exemptions under a right to roam could create similar close seasons during the breeding season on moors used by curlews and in the winter on high-tide wader roosts. What is more, the creation of more accessible areas could spread the visitor load and relieve some of the most important wildlife sites currently attracting people who merely want somewhere to go in the countryside. Putting access on the more organized footing which a general right of access and its exemptions would bring might result in the countryside being used in such a way as to create a better overall balance between the needs of recreation and conservation.

Managing Out Threat

Already local authorities are taking more and more steps to channel visitors, through the relative promotion of different sites, the provision of cycle hire facilities, the promotion of public transport, and the restriction of excessive car use. One shining example is Norbury Park.

Surrey County Council bought Norbury Park, a country estate, in the 1930s to prevent the land being sold for housing at a time when councils could prevent urban development only by paying landowners compensation. The estate, which hugs the southern edge of the sprawling settlements of Leatherhead and Fetcham, covers 1,300 acres of spectacular scenery. A steeply sloping hillside covered in beech, oak, and yew woods gives way at its foot to pasture grazed by sheep and cattle interspersed with arable land. Bordered on its east by the winding River Mole, the estate contains amongst its woods and farmland stretches of chalk downland turf together with a sawmill, a nursery, and twenty-five dwellings, mainly old gamekeepers' cottages and farmhouses. Before the county council acquired it, the estate was very private and inaccessible. The council opened it to all, and today permits free access over pasture as well as woodland, downland turf, and riverside. Yet four commercial tenanted farms exist here along-side a forestry operation as well as commercial fishing and clay pigeon shooting. Special events like farm open days and a craft fair are accommodated, while an access agreement provides for canoeing on the River Mole during the close season for fishing. The only categories of land from which visitors are permanently excluded are areas under crops or close to buildings. When trees are being felled, the areas involved are temporarily blocked off and warning signs go up. People are not completely barred from plantations: these are encircled by rabbit fencing but accessible through self-closing gates. A large part of the woodland at Norbury Park is a site of special scientific interest but the council has not found it necessary to restrict access in order to protect the rare plants which grow here. Deer and badgers are both common on the estate and the hunt is allowed access. The farm tenants have two licences apiece to carry out rough shooting while the council culls deer when necessary.

The site is easily accessible by road to the millions of people who live in the nearby urban centres of Gatwick/Crawley, Epsom, Guildford, Leatherhead, and south London; and Boxhill railway station (with direct access to Waterloo and Victoria) lies close to its boundary. The site attracts more than 100,000 visitors every year, but it suffers no significant erosion nor any other apparent visitor damage. Publicity is, however, relatively low key: the site appears in lists of recreation land owned or managed by the county council, but no special effort is made to promote it except through guided walks and the staging of particular events there, like sheepdog trials. Motorists are not particularly encouraged: no notices proclaim that Norbury Park lies just off the road. The council deliberately under-provides car parking and the three small car parks are at the edge of the site. Ranger Graham Manning explained to me in an interview in 1990: 'There is no one big car park in the middle and people have to make an effort to get in.' Only the disabled may drive into its heart. Well-signposted paths with information boards and maps lead from the car parks and from Boxhill station into the estate for walkers, cyclists, and riders. The council has also made a positive decision to refrain from allowing a permanent refreshment site in the heart of the estate (there is one site with toilets at a farm just inside). No litter bins are provided anywhere on the estate, since the council believes that the presence of litter bins would attract more litter and dumping.

Damage

Intruders into the countryside can harm more than wildlife. They may harm all manner of other features in the countryside. They may dig up prehistoric burial mounds and raid them for buried treasure. They may vandalize property and machinery. Their cars may clog up roads and damage roadside vegetation by parking on it. They may light fires which get out of control and destroy property. And when their numbers are particularly heavy they may create erosion scars, which, even if not damaging to wildlife, can be unsightly and reduce the attractiveness of the countryside. Many of these activities are of course already illegal. If you dig up a wild plant or raid a scheduled ancient monument for treasure trove, you can be prosecuted. Vandals and arsonists can of course also be taken to court. But might the creation of a general right of access increase the incidence of these activities?

While common sense suggests it might, common sense is not altogether reliable. People who are going to poach game or vandalize property do not necessarily wait for a legal right of access before going about their business. Frances Griffiths, Secretary of the Council for British Archaeology, for instance, told me on the subject of the raiding of scheduled ancient monuments: 'It's an illegal activity. Whether there is a component of trespassing or not is completely irrelevant.' In other words, she considered that giving greater public access would not lead to more raiding or to greater use of metal detectors. And any increase in such activity flowing from greater access might be offset by reductions it might cause. As we have seen, the experience of the Woodland Trust at Bramingham Wood has been that the vandalism which used to occur when the woodland was a fenced-off private domain has disappeared now that all are welcome there. Nobody knows precisely why this has happened, but it may very well be that the presence of the well-behaved majority alongside the irresponsible minority who caused damage in the past has deterred the second group from carrying out the damage in which they used to indulge. Or it may be that they no longer feel angry and frustrated at being barred from an attractive woodland near their homes. Either view might be borne out by the experience of Norfolk landowner Robin Combe. Mr Combe owns an 1,800-acre estate north of Holt in the Glaven Valley and during the 1990s he improved public access to his estate by laying out a 4-mile permissive footpath, as well as 10 miles of toll-rides available to people who pay an annual subscription. Mr Combe told a reporter for the landowners' magazine *Country Landowner* in 1996 that his estate has experienced fewer problems than before he made this extra access provision: 'At one time, we had people digging up the bluebells, along with other minor acts of vandalism. Since opening the rides and the permissive path, I can honestly say we've had no trouble. Most users have the interests of the countryside, and therefore, the interests of the estate owner at heart. They act as your unofficial wardens. If there is anything out of order, they will tell you'. [39] This can range from warnings about the presence of suspicious vehicles to the discovery of creatures which are in distress. In the summer of 1996, for instance, a Dutchman camping in the New Forest found a distressed bat and handed it in. The creature turned out to be a rare Bechstein's bat and as a result of this information scientists were able to locate the first breeding colony of Bechstein's bats in Britain for 100 years.[40] Or people may discourage illegal activity: badger setts close to public paths are less likely to be disturbed by diggers and baiters than those in more remote sites.[41] The presence of the public could also increase the chances that a smouldering fire on a dry heath or moor might be spotted before it got out of hand. Illegal egg-collecting or the illegal persecution of birds of prey by gamekeepers are other anti-social activities which might be more readily detected.

Highway authorities already have powers to manage recreation traffic in particularly popular areas. They can restrict car parking; they can prevent roadside parking by installing barriers or short wooden stakes in the ground; and they can ban traffic entirely. Whether or not a general right of access is created, it seems very likely that highway authorities will deploy such powers to a greater and greater extent, not only pedestrianizing particularly popular areas in the way that town centres have been barred to the car, but also slowing and restricting traffic elsewhere.

Though Britain has not gone as far as, say, Germany in this field, considerable expertise has built up over the years in dealing with traffic in the countryside—expertise which could be used elsewhere. One of the leaders in this field is the authority responsible for the national park which receives the highest number of day visits (22 million a year)—the Peak District. Here the Peak National Park Authority seeks to restrain the use of private cars by visitors and, as a complementary measure, to foster public transport and cycling. It spends £75,000 each year on revenue support for bus services, both to increase the mobility of country dwellers and to improve access for townspeople who do not own cars, or who own them but who are prepared to forgo their use. The authority has published an integrated bus and train timetable to promote these services (this task is now undertaken by Derbyshire County Council); it continues to issue special tickets—like the Derbyshire Wayfarer day-rover ticket, which is valid on services run by thirty-six different bus companies as well as trains.

The national park authority also promotes and supports the use of the Hope Valley railway for leisure purposes. This railway line cuts across the centre of the park, connecting Sheffield on the park's eastern boundary with Manchester on its west. It runs past some of the most attractive scenery of the national park—along river valleys, beneath the gritstone edges of the Dark Peak, and within walking distance of the limestone caverns of Castleton. The little country stations which punctuate its route provide ideal springboards into the surrounding countryside. Support for the railway thus allows the authority both to enable townspeople without cars to get into the heart of the park and to offer the ultimate in park-and-ride: instead of asking motorists to leave their cars at car parks in the country and take minibuses to popular sites, it allows them to leave their cars at a station in or near their home town. The authority has part-funded a project officer to run the Community Rail Partnership which brings together the rail operator, user groups, the county council, the Park authority itself, and the local tourism association and youth hostels. The Partnership has refurbished stations, installed lighting, and improved station approach roads. It promotes the service with interpretation boards at stations, guided walks (many led by park authority rangers and offering the opportunity for people to do linear walks rather than the circular ones required for return to cars), and special events like music on trains (a folk band can attract an extra 200 passengers). In other areas the authority's park-and-drive aims are more modest. Thus in the Upper Derwent Valley motorists have to leave their cars in car parks on summer Sundays and bank holidays and either walk, hire a bicycle, or travel on a minibus along a road which runs alongside Ladybower, Derwent, and Howden reservoirs and is surrounded by accessible moors and woods. One option in the Upper Derwent Valley is for motorists to hire bicycles, and the authority has its own cycle hire scheme here and in four other places. Some other councils have engaged in less obvious but nonetheless still remarkably successful means of curbing visitor traffic. Thus in the Surrey hills Surrey County Council provides only a small number of fairly small car parks, prevents roadside parking in many areas with physically unobtrusive barriers, and promotes and publicizes special recreation bus services.

Visitors will undoubtedly continue to be attracted to the many country parks, National Trust-owned land, and other particular attractions which absorb most use at the moment. British people tend to be rather timid about venturing into the countryside and it may be some time even after the introduction of a general right of access before the public visit in appreciable numbers areas to which they are at present barred. It is important, however, that some safeguard is provided to cope with a situation in which for one reason or another very large numbers of people congregate on a particular area of land to such an extent that it is causing appreciable damage, not only to wildlife but also if it is affecting the owners' ability to enjoy and use his or her own property. One way of dealing with this problem has been recently advanced by a country that already provides a right of access to the countryside.

In 1996 Norway passed new legislation refining the procedures available to local councils to deal with this sort of thing. The procedure now is as follows. If an owner is concerned that too many people are using his or her land, the first option which is tried is the introduction of the equivalent of by-laws. The local authority and the landowner together work out rules designed to keep peace and quiet, to protect animal and plant life, and to provide for health and sanitation where necessary. If this does not solve the problem, then either the council or the owner can initiate a rather more drastic course of events: they can exclude the area in question on a temporary basis. An owner can only do so with the permission of his local council and this council (the 'commune') can close an area only with the say-so of the county council. Furthermore, the legislation lays down that an area cannot be closed off if subjected to a normal level of use: use has to be extreme or inflict considerable damage or prevent the owner from using his own property. The council can close an area completely or just partly—it might for instance simply close a road which crosses it. The temporary closure is limited to a maximum of five years at a time. Furthermore, the law stipulates that even if all possible reasons for closure obtain, then councils still have to evaluate them carefully, and this is not a decision to be taken lightly.

If an owner wants to close off his property and the council is reluctant to allow him to do so, or if relations between the owner and the council become difficult, the council may offer to buy the property concerned in order to secure its use for the public. They have powers not only to acquire by agreement but also to secure some other legal agreement over the land, or to buy it compulsorily. In fact, a legal agreement and with it a regulatory plan for the area can often be an effective means for resolving these conflicts. If the owner is still dissatisfied, and wishes to have his property closed off, or if closing off does not work as intended, the landowner himself may demand that the local council buy the area.

Liability

In seeking to demonstrate that a general right of access would materially and visibly—and unfairly—disadvantage them, landowners have made much of one issue. 'The public liability obligations on occupiers would be extended considerably, unless specific provision was made to limit these', maintained the Country Landowners' Association in its document *Access 2000* in 1996.[42] If people are to have the right to wander over others' property, more are likely to do so. More are therefore likely to come to harm, and in an increasingly litigious age seek redress against the owners, who already owe a duty of care to others on their property even if they are trespassers.

It is important not to get carried away with this point. Walking in the countryside is not a very dangerous business, and few walkers seek, or are likely to seek, redress against owners for ills which befall them. If a walker tears his or her clothes climbing over a stile or even barbed wire, he or she does not usually try to sue the landowner. Nonetheless, if the stile was faulty or the barbed wire hidden, they might arguably try. If a man fell into a pit which was undetectable to a prudent walker and was killed as a result, his dependants might well seek recompense, and they could do so today even if the walker was trespassing.

An owner with a deep water-filled gravel pit on his land might be wise to put up a warning sign. If children have access to the area though, is this enough? Fencing the pit would obviously be a bigger undertaking than putting up a warning sign. Removing all hazards from the countryside completely would obviously be impossible and undesirable. So the risk that a landowner will face claims remains real if small. Insuring against this is standard practice and enables the cost of the burden to be quantified.

Landowners' liability for unfortunate incidents befalling others on the land (other than workers, who are of course provided with additional protection) was codified for England and Wales in 1984 when Parliament extended a general duty of care on landowners from those present by invitation, like workmen, family, friends, employees, or paying visitors, to everybody else, including trespassers. Before then a landowner owed no duty of care to a trespasser, but a court case in the 1970s involving a child who had climbed through a broken stile on to a railway line where he was hit by a passing train left legislators feeling that landowners should be held responsible for harm befalling anyone on their land which they could and should have prevented. 'Allurements' to which children might uniquely be attracted were seen as a particular problem. Now that the 1984 Occupiers' Liability Act is in force, a trespasser—even a burglar or a poacher—who injures himself can sue the landowner if he believes that the landowner has been negligent—in other words aware of potential dangers but failing to warn others of them. If a landowner has entered into a contractual arrangement with other people—for instance by charging horse-people to use special rides on his land—he incurs a separate, higher level of liability, just as a householder is more responsible for a lodger than a burglar, though he still has obligations to the latter. If a rider's horse stumbles on uneven surfacing on a toll-ride and he is thrown and injured, he might sue the landowner; similarly, if somebody twists their ankle on uneven ground on a public footpath they may sue the highway authority responsible for maintaining it if their injury arises out of the authority's negligence.[43]

Creating a right of access to the countryside need not convert landowners' existing obligation to avoid placing walkers at unnecessary risk into a level of responsibility comparable to the highway authority's responsibility to users of public paths or a private landowner's responsibility to users of toll-routes. The access legislation could specify that the right of care due at present to trespassers was the same as that due to people exercising the new right. We are left then with the extra liability which would arise if a general right of access increased the numbers of people walking on others' land and perhaps their adventurousness in doing so. In 1997 the insurance industry in England did not consider that the government's plan to create a right of access over mountain, moor, down, heath, and common land would make much difference. The general feeling was that premiums should stay unchanged until some sign emerged that claims were increasing. Certainly the introduction of the Concordat in Scotland in 1996 does not seem to have had any impact on insurance premiums. Nonetheless a right of access—particularly one which provided for greater passage over farmland and thus close to hazards like slurry lagoons, farm machinery, and ponds—does create some potential extra burden on landowners.

Landowners are understandably anxious to avoid bearing this burden if they can. One way of achieving this which appeals to landowners would be for the state to pick up any increase in the liability burden. As we have seen (page 323), the regional government of North-Rhine Westphalia undertakes to cover up to 50 per cent of the costs of reasonable insurance against forest fires. However, no government would welcome open-ended commitment of this kind, especially as its existence would doubtless encourage the insurance industry to ratchet up its premiums. There might however be a case for a limited fund to which landowners could apply for reimbursement if they could prove that they had suffered substantial damage as a result of public access. Such research as has been carried out on the costs landowners and land occupiers incur from the presence of the public shows that the vast majority suffer little in the way of cost, but that a few can suffer quite large amounts. In 1994 Robert Crabtree led a team of researchers who carried out a postal survey of more than 600 farms and nearly 200 estates in Scotland in an attempt to find out what financial burdens landowners and farmers found themselves having to bear as a result of public access. They found that 85 per cent of farms and 51 per cent of estates which received no income from access (the other landholdings had commercialized access to some degree or other) suffered no or very low costs, reflecting the limited impact that access had on the majority of the properties. However, in a minority of cases, the level of extra costs or lost income arising from access was substantial, exceeding £5,000 in a few cases.[44] The forest law of North-Rhine Westphalia provides for financial compensation for landowners in individual cases where substantial irreparable damage occurs. A similar system exists in Denmark. Claimants have to provide police reports and documentary evidence of the value of items like tools or firewood which have been stolen, and a committee of representatives of the relevant government ministry, the Forest Owners' Union, and the Danish Outdoor Council advise on payments which come out of a finite predetermined budget— £50,000 in 1997 for example. A first port of call for cases in which landowners complained of excessive loss or damage could be to consider a temporary exemption for the land in question. However, the additional facility of a limited compensation fund might be helpful in hard cases. Such a fund would however need to remain small not only to keep costs down but to avoid instilling the idea that a dropped toffee wrapper ought to be cause for compensation.

Another way of relieving landowners would to be to place more of the burden on walkers. Margaret Ewing's and Paddy Tipping's bills on access, as well as the Blair government's 1998 consultation paper for England and Wales, all talk about any new rights of access for walkers being used 'at their own risk'. It would be possible to change the current balance of responsibility between landowners and walkers so that a successful action could be brought only if it could be demonstrated that the landowner had been, say, 'grossly negligent'. In other words, the negligence test which currently operates would be stiffened. Any increase in the burden on landowners caused by an increase in the number of walkers would thus be offset by a reduction in the duty owed to all of them. The walkers would have to pay something for their new right in a cut in protection.

Yet there are good reasons to avoid tampering with a well-established and successful balance to tackle a problem which is likely to be of minimal importance. One danger is that a loophole could be created which would enable landowners who were unsympathetic to the new right to try to obstruct it by deliberately creating hazards which might scare walkers. Already the keepers of animals tend not to be liable for damages for injury by a farm animal unless they are deliberately negligent or the animal involved is a member of a dangerous species or is individually known to be vicious,[45] a fact usually demonstrated through its having bitten somebody on another occasion. Farmers can keep frisky stallions and many breeds of bull in fields with footpaths running through them, and if they do so even when alternatives are available, walkers can do nothing about it. If they were also allowed to unleash frightening animals with impunity, some might take advantage of the opportunity to use this means of continuing to exclude walkers. Nonetheless, the idea that walkers should gain new responsibilities in return for their new right is not in itself unreasonable. On the contrary, new obligations on walkers could do much to meet landowners' claim that they would be unfairly disadvantaged, not just over liability but in other ways.

Duties for Rights

It has become a mantra of the age that rights should be matched by duties. In principle this is questionable. Should a fair trial be denied to a man who has shown himself to be a bad citizen? But whether or not people ought to enjoy an absolute right to walk in the countryside, there are good grounds for increasing the responsibilities expected of them on communitarian grounds. Walkers ought to behave responsibly towards themselves, landowners, and society generally whatever rights they enjoy. The most basic duty walkers ought to shoulder is responsibility for themselves and those for whom they are responsible. They should take steps to inform themselves of the dangers and should look neither to landowners nor the state to protect them from hazards from which they can protect themselves. Mountain and moor, the kinds of countryside top of the list of government access targets for England and Wales, do hold dangers. Those who walk there should take adequate precautions and carry adequate equipment rather than calling up the emergency services on their mobile phones as soon as they get lost. Having to pay for emergency service call-outs when walkers had been negligent might help inspire responsibility.

After duties to oneself come duties to landowners. A new right of access should be subject to respect for landowners' and land occupiers' interests. However, walkers will not be able to discharge their obligations towards landowners unless they understand what landowners' interests are.

The Country Code already enjoins users of the countryside to take their litter home, fasten gates, guard against risk of fire, keep dogs under close control, and eight other things.[46] Little research has been conducted on the extent to which the Country Code is known and understood in the UK. When Scottish Natural Heritage asked 1,000 households in Scotland about the Country Code in 1996, they found that although the majority (70 per cent) had heard of it, most could name only one or two of its strictures.[47] However representative this survey, as a nation we expend far less effort than many other countries in explaining to people what lies behind the Country Code. In Sweden, education about rights and responsibilities in the countryside starts at the age of 5, with the help of a doll, Mulle, invented by the Society for the Promotion of Outdoor Life. Mulle is a male troll who helps injured animals and clears up litter so that it will not injure the beasts of the countryside, which are his friends. The Mulle class for 5–7-year-olds is succeeded by three further stages, culminating in the class for children of 14 and over who are taught how to survive in the wilderness and how problems like acid rain can be addressed. Statens Naturvårdsverket, the state agency comparable to our Countryside Commission, educates adults, whether native

Swedes, immigrants, or foreign visitors, providing explanations for the behaviour it advocates. A leaflet on Allemansrätt explains, 'Never put your rubbish bags down beside a full wastepaper basket or rubbish sack. This is because wild animals are likely to tear them to pieces and pull the rubbish out. Bottles, cans and bottle tops can injure both people and animals, while plastic bags can cause a lot of suffering to animals if ingested.' So unless a rubbish bin is provided, a Swede will carefully gather up his or her rubbish and take it home with him.

Britain's Country Code has nothing to say on rights of access in the countryside. Although attempts have been made by the Countryside Commission and similar organizations to explain to people their rights of access in the countryside,[48] this has not been done in a form as well known as the Country Code, and a replacement ought to explain such rights, whatever they are at the time, as well as promulgating admonitions. It could also go beyond discouraging individuals from damaging landowners' interests to urge them to take proactive action as well. While on someone else's property, walkers are likely to encounter all kinds of situations which threaten the interests of that owner. Suppose you see somebody else's dog worrying sheep. Suppose you see smoke suggesting a fire has started. Suppose you come across a gate which has been left open though a notice on it says the owner wants it shut. Suppose you come across stock which have escaped and invaded a field of crops. Should you not be expected to take steps to inform the landowner if he provides you with a means of doing so? Walkers could act as the eyes and ears of the landowner, and the more of them there are the more effective they could be. Today, when there are so few farmworkers, there is often no one to notice trouble but the stray walker. Education by public authorities and a few phone numbers from landowners might turn such efforts into a real benefit for the latter.

After duties to oneself and the landowner come duties to society in general. Criminal activities like fly-tipping, cruelty to animals, or egg-collecting would become harder if the culprits thought any stray observer might feel obliged to pass details of what he or she had seen to the authorities. The countryside plays host to antisocial activities ranging from badger-baiting and digging up wild flowers to disposing of murder victims' bodies. Why shouldn't walkers provided with access to the countryside by society be expected to support society's interest in return? It may be objected that it would be hard to enforce any obligations of this kind. In some countries bystanders are required by law to help out on occasion. Some of the photographers attending the crash which killed Princess Diana faced the possibility of prosecution on the grounds that they failed to give help at the scene of an accident. It might not be practicable to make failure to report fly-tipping a criminal offence, but that does not mean there would be no value in establishing the principle that walkers were expected to do that sort of thing. Social pressure can achieve much, and even if some people ignored their obligations, others would not. Those contemplating fly-tipping, taking a four-wheel-drive vehicle down a footpath, or treasure hunting with metal detectors, would not know whether the walkers they might encounter would be good citizens or not. Certainly walkers who valued their new right would be aware that behaving responsibly would reduce the possibility that it might subsequently be removed.

Hard though it may seem to imagine at present, there might come a time when landowners and farmers might welcome walkers as an asset rather than a liability. Not, of course, that all this good citizenship would be wholly to landowners' advantage. Walkers might discover farmers burying bovine carcasses infected with BSE, laying poisoned baits for birds of prey, polluting watercourses for instance by spreading slurry on fields which drain into nearby streams, erecting or changing the use of buildings without planning consent, ploughing up sites of special scientific interest, felling trees without a felling licence, or dumping dangerous materials on their land. If as a result of more civic awareness on the part of walkers these things came to light, farmers might not like it but society would benefit. Environmental crime is one of the most difficult of all types of crime to detect simply because there are so few witnesses. At present, if you cycle or drive past a wood in which some rubbish has been dumped and there is a clear indication that as a walker you are not welcome there, you tend to pass on, telling yourself that it is not your affair. But a similar sight in a wood which you know is owned by the Woodland Trust elicits a different response. If a right to roam turned us all into concerned citizens of our whole country, so much the better for us all.

Institutional Apparatus

A right to roam would require an agency to administer it, and to help people make use of it, whether such a body was part of central or local government or free-standing. Such a body's prime tasks would be enforcing the new right by, for example, ordering and if necessary effecting the removal of obstructions, adjudicating applications for exemption and temporary exemption, and trouble-shooting—perhaps, for example, buying up any sites which turned out to be overrun with visitors. A separate entity could deal with appeals from individuals or organizations aggrieved by the administrative agency's actions or inaction.

The agency could also promote the new right, explaining its scope and encouraging people to use it. In Britain, people are wary of venturing far off the beaten track in the countryside. Without positive encouragement they might fail to make much use of their new right. Promotion of a right of access would be best carried out in conjunction with other rural recreation functions such as the acquisition of land, the designation of country parks, and the preparation of rural recreation strategies, so the access agency ought either itself to be the body which handled such matters or have close links with those that did.

So should the access agency be part of an existing or new government department, local councils at either county and unitary or district levels, part of a countryside agency like Scottish Natural Heritage or the Countryside Commission, or a new single-purpose body, centrally or locally organized? Uniformity might be most easily achieved by a central institution. Central control might also better serve the interests of the urban majority, as local bodies in the countryside have shown themselves susceptible to the influence of powerful landowners. On the other hand, implementing access to the countryside might be a challenge not only well suited to local democracy but one which might help to invigorate it. Not only administrative convenience but the experience of related matters in existing institutions argues against the creation of new bodies.

Uniformity, although something people seem to expect in the exercise of rights, is not intrinsically necessary in this case. At present, the area of public administration most akin to the new function, the interpretation of public rights of way policy, takes place at county and unitary authority level (and also sometimes at district and national park authority level where the function has been delegated). Different authorities have different policies on, for example, the signposting of paths; different authorities give different levels of priority to the prosecution of landowners who flout path law; in Scotland different authorities spend different amounts of time on mapping paths. But although varying levels of diligence in these areas give rise to unfavourable comparisons from time to time, nobody really objects to differing local standards in what amounts to maintenance of part of the Queen's highway.

Local authorities thus seem the most obvious bodies to administer a general right of access to the countryside. But what level of council should be involved? The tier of government with its ear closest to the ground as far as local access needs and problems are concerned in England is the parish and the community in Wales, and there are moves about to increase the responsibilities of parish and community councils. However, parish and community councils have no paid staff and do not even exist in 15 per cent of the parishes and communities of England and Wales. They are not in a position to assume complete responsibility for a considerable administrative task. In the field of public paths parish councils do nonetheless enjoy considerable powers which most of them do not use. Under John Major's premiership they were encouraged to use these powers more and to play a larger role in path management under a 'Parish Paths Initiative', promoted by the Countryside Commission, under which Parish Paths Officers approached parish councils and local voluntary groups to get additional help in path management as part of an overall strategy aimed at pushing power down to the lowest possible level. John Gummer, the then Secretary of State for the Environment, declared in 1995, 'We start from the presumption that local people know best. . . . We want to push power down to the lowest possible level. Isn't it about time we heard a great deal more about the Parish Councils? If the best of them want to do a bit more—take on a bigger role—then I'm determined to help them do it.'[49] A similar role might be possible in managing access, but there would be dangers in shifting too much power in this direction. Because parish councils are so closely influenced by local landowners they may hesitate to assert the access rights and needs of the wider community. When it fell to parish councils in the 1950s and 1960s to map their local rights of way, many well-used paths went unclaimed. Even where parish councils are not under the sway of landowners, they may give too much emphasis to local patterns of use at the expense of the wider community. They tend to be particularly concerned, for example, about paths which are convenient for dog-walking rather than paths which would serve the needs of specialist groups, like, say, butterfly enthusiasts, who might not be represented in the parish. At the same time, access might often be outweighed by some pressing local priority, and a parish council might sacrifice the wider community's interest in access for some local economic or social gain. They might, for example, go soft on a landowner prepared to make land available for an affordable housing scheme or to provide money to upgrade the village hall even if he was flouting access rights. Although public paths are local, their importance goes much wider, and responsibility for them should reflect this fact. The same would be true of a right of access.

All these considerations apply to a much lesser degree in respect of district councils, but there is still some reason to prefer the remote county (or unitary) level for the administration of a right of access. Other considerations also point to the suitability of this tier, one of the most important of which is that it would ensure proper representation of the urban majority from whom most users of the right of access would actually come. In countries where a right of access already exists, it is usually administered at the regional level, and unless and until regional government comes to Britain, county administration is our nearest equivalent.

It is counties and unitary councils in Britain which have accumulated the expertise in fields like farming, forestry, archaeology, and wildlife conservation which ought to inform access administration. It is also the counties and unitaries which handle the local authority work most akin to enforcing access, the implementation of public path law. In England and Wales this is already provided under highways acts and is the responsibility of the highway authority, normally county or unitary councils. These councils usually deal with path matters through a rights of way unit within a highways department, whose main task is of course the planning and management of roads. These units have been discharging the challenging duty of arbitrating between landed and non-landed interests over rights of way for over half a century. Though often understaffed and underfunded, they have managed nonetheless to command respect on both sides of the fence, being felt to act fairly most of the time. The staff involved have considerable knowledge and experience of public path law, a not uncomplicated field and one which the law relating to a new right of access would inevitably resemble. Where urban unitary authorities have taken population centres out of counties (as Bristol and Bath have been taken out of Avon) a joint committee of neighbouring councils ought to be created to enable the townspeople to have a say over access to the countryside around them. The Countryside Commission has proposed similar committees to give townspeople a say in the planning of areas of outstanding natural beauty, so that, for example, the people of Luton and High Wycombe can have some say over the fate of the Chiltern Hills and the people of Brighton, Worthing, and Eastbourne over the Sussex Downs. At present, the Department of the Environment, Transport, and the Regions carries out inquiries into appeals over public path decisions (with the Welsh Office, the Scottish Office, and the Department of the Environment for Northern Ireland taking a similar role elsewhere in the UK). It would seem entirely natural to make this government department the body to which people could appeal if they felt aggrieved by decisions taken by county and unitary councils administering the access right.

Though county or unitary authorities may be the right bodies to administer access rights, they should not just be lumped in with highways under the county surveyor, as happens in many councils in England and Wales. What this means is that there is an administrative split between footpaths, dealt with alongside roads, and recreation planning and management and often the management of public open spaces as well. If the administration of a right of access were attached to public paths in the highways department it would be dwarfed by road matters and cut off from council departments responsible for wider countryside management and recreation. It would make more sense to move the rights of way units into wider departments dealing with other countryside matters including access. As we have seen, South Norfolk District Council's rights of way functions, for example, sit side by side with its responsibility for common land and other forms of leisure and recreation provision. Hampshire County Council has done something slightly different but from which lessons could also be learned. It has reorganized its countryside departments so as to provide a closer link between the rural land which the community owns and manages itself for conservation and recreation and the promotion of rural recreation. Hampshire's new Countryside and Community Department not only has responsibility for the county's 8,000 rights of way, but it is also responsible for the management of sites which the council owns ranging from small picnic sites to extensive country parks, the protection and management of archaeological sites and nature reserves, the promotion of countryside sites through guided walks and other events and activities, the provision of opportunities for schools and colleges to experience the countryside, the development of partnerships with other local authorities, and support for voluntary groups.

In Scotland less would need to change. Responsibility for public footpaths, such as they are, lies with the planning departments of the unitary authorities which have administered Scotland since 1996, since that is where Scottish law reposes this function. Thus the local authority department which is responsible for preparing development plans and any rural recreation strategies is also the department charged with the care of public rights of way.

Aberdeen City Council came out in support of a general right of access to all types of countryside in 1998. Its Assistant Director (Environmental), Robert Reid, chaired a group set up by the Convention of Scottish Local Authorities to prepare a response to the recent debate on improving the law on access to the countryside in Scotland. Mr Reid told me he considered that the local plan which embodies planning authorities' policies and proposals for five-year periods on a map base would be an ideal vehicle for the rural recreation planning which the introduction of a right of access would require. The statutory requirements of public participation in the plan-making process and the provision for a public inquiry into the plan would provide a firm base of accountability.

Facilitation

In Scotland many of those urging the introduction of a general right of access have argued that one of the main benefits would be the delivery of an effective path network. Look at the countryside behind Aberdeen from aerial photographs and you will see a structured network of paths and roads; look at the map of rights of way around the city and you will see, in Robert Reid's words, 'chopped up sphagetti' —in other words lots of little bits of path which do not go anywhere. Once a right of access was in place, these private paths could become an important part of any new strategy for managing access. Most people prefer to walk on paths anyway; landowners and land managers would want them as a tool for concentrating visitor use; local councils would be happy to see routes which had been private opened up to all. The Ramblers' Association in Scotland would like to see the most important paths designated 'heritage paths' in local plans and given priority treatment and funding.

While these paths at present exist on the ground but simply need to be opened up through a change in the law, there would be other places in which land to which the public would have a right of access would in practice be inaccessible unless steps were taken to make paths, clear rides through woodland, hack back undergrowth at watersides, and so on. Owners would have little incentive to facilitate the exploitation of a right extracted from them against their will. County and unitary councils as well as district councils could, however, organize the necessary work and negotiate with landowners to arrange it, paying them for their co-operation where they judged this worthwhile.

Money would naturally help ensure that the best possible use was made of a new access right. This could of course be provided centrally or locally, but the advantages of doing it locally are impressive. Facilitating rural recreation could take its proper place against other claims on a local authority's purse, in the light of local debate. Urban unitary authorities should, however, be expected to contribute to the costs incurred by rural unitary and county councils on activities from which their own citizens may benefit. Where councils decided to spend little, walkers would have to make the best use they could of their new right. But many might decide to spend quite a lot. Robert Reid told me in 1998 that Aberdeen City Council (70 per cent of whose area is countryside) finds it difficult to find ways of spending the money it already has available for rural projects. The main cost involved is the salaries of rangers, countryside project officers, and local council estate workers: if the council wants to surface a footpath or put up a signboard the cost of labour far exceeds that of the materials. Mr Reid maintains that existing local authority rangers and project officers could in most cases take on board the management of the countryside in the light of the introduction of a general access right. He told me in an interview in 1998: 'I don't think there would be any extra costs on what we spend already on access strategies, countryside projects, paths and rangers' projects.' Aberdeen City Council has a considerable budget for rural work because it is one of the majority of councils in Britain which is also a waste disposal authority and which has taken the option open under the Finance Act, 1996 to defray 20 per cent of the landfill tax it would otherwise have to pay on environmental projects. The current landfill tax liability for the 1,200 landfill operators in the UK is estimated at £450 million, which means that about £90 million is available for spending on the environment, so long as the landfill operators provide their 10 per cent or £9 million. This represents a potentially rich source of funding for access. The young people now available through the environment taskforce set up under 'Welfare to Work' would be an additional source of labour. Another possible source of funds would be the money saved from spending on access payment schemes like countryside stewardship and the like. As we have seen, millions of pounds are spent in this way at present, part from the UK taxpayer, part from the European Union. Once these payments were phased out, the money saved from the UK element could be redeployed towards providing and enhancing rural access facilities, and hopefully the European element could in due course be redirected too as CAP reform gathers steam.

Public authorities would not of course be the only source of help to enable people to use their new right of access. New walking guides would emerge taking in places hitherto unknown because inaccessible. Painters, photographers, poets, and writers would start producing work revealing the new world which had opened up. Guides for birdwatchers and botanists would bring in places hitherto effectively off the map. All of this ought to benefit not only 'ramblers' who wish to cover much terrain quickly and normally progress along fixed routes, but many others ranging from picnickers to archaeologists, birdwatchers to artists, or individuals simply out to refresh themselves in the open air. In time, we might all develop completely new mental maps of our own areas as places from which we were shut out before or deterred from entering on foot became available. The idea of exploring these new worlds—the other world which is on one's doorstep but has been virtually unseen till now—might fuel a new wave of home tourism. It could open up a new awareness of the world akin to the change in perception of scenery both here and abroad that was prompted by the discovery of Italian landscape and painting by the eighteenth-century aristocrats who embarked on the Grand Tour.

Local councils could enhance this process by running or encouraging others to run guided walks which both explain to people the extent of their new right and suggest places in which they could enjoy it. These new walks would link the paths and places with which people are already familiar with the others once out of reach but which people might be nervous of entering alone. The presence of others or even better those already knowledgeable about the area could embolden them to venture further. A growing number of local authorities already run programmes of guided walks during the spring, summer, and autumn in which local experts, often the rangers responsible for particular sites, encourage those who might not otherwise use the countryside to do so. At the same time, councils might perhaps offer advice to specialist groups like local branches of the Ramblers' Association and county naturalists' trusts who already organize events for their own members about new places to which they might care to draw their members' attention. Councils could also provide car parking where it would be needed and encourage the provision of special bus services for recreation. Such services could be accompanied by leaflets with suggestions for walks, and even guides knowledgeable about the local area. The more such services were built up the more car use could be discouraged, with car parking being withdrawn in some places once bus services reached a satisfactory level.

The presence of other people could embolden wary souls nervous about taking full advantage of their new right.

Cost

Not all local authorities would be as well placed as Aberdeen City Council to meet any new costs arising from funding and facilitating a right of access. All would however have to meet the core cost of enforcing the new right and dealing with exemption applications. Stephen Jenkinson of the Institute of Public Rights of Way Officers told me in 1988 that he considered that the introduction of a new partial right covering mountain, moor, heath, down, and common land would involve councils having to employ three new members of staff during the first two years and two thereafter. He estimated that this would cost £81,000 annually for the first two years and £51,000 thereafter. These figures consist of salaries and associated staff costs like building accommodation and mileage payments: they are based on the current costs of employing officers to protect the rights of way network and keep the definitive maps up to date. Mr Jenkinson envisaged that the extra members of staff during the first two years would be employed plotting the boundaries of land to which the new partial right would apply. There would obviously be far less scope for such dispute and necessity for any kind of register if a universal right was implemented. However, a general right would of course cover far more land than the partial right the government is considering for England and Wales, so Mr Jenkinson's estimates might still be on target.

If rural recreation strategies were to be drawn up as part of local plans, this would also increase staff costs. Robert Reid told me this cost could easily be absorbed: 'There may be a slight increase in the cost of processing local and unitary plans since there would be a new chapter in the plans dealing with access. This would be no more than a very marginal extra cost at most. Local plans have to go to public inquiry, so we would be talking about the cost of an extra couple of days at the public inquiry.'

Clearly, a right of access would involve some extra financial burden on local councils: even if the cost of managing access could be absorbed, the fair administration of the new right would require additional staffing. However, the cost would not be excessive. Agencies like Scottish Natural Heritage, the Countryside Council for Wales, and the Countryside Commission should offer guidance to councils on the administration of the new right; however they already do much in the rural recreation sphere and it seems unlikely that the new right would add very much to their existing costs.

Compensation

Some landowners argue that if a right to roam were introduced, they should receive financial compensation to reflect the expropriation of the exclusive enjoyment of their asset. In their document *Access 2000*, the Country Landowners' Association asserts: 'A legal challenge [to a right to roam] would be inevitable—e.g. on the grounds of unfair discrimination between landowners. Compensation payable to those who lost the ability under a "right to roam" to exclude visitors from some or all of their land could be very costly.'[50] Such a case would be stronger in the case of a partial right of access than of a universal one, as landowners affected could claim they were being subjected to arbitrary discrimination. In either case, the idea that landowners would suffer loss cannot be contested. A right of way running through a wood can reduce its value significantly. The privacy landowners currently enjoy is so attractive that some foreigners not so blessed come to Britain to enjoy sporting pleasure in private.

However, legislation constantly imposes loss on people without compensating them. The state could argue that compensation was unnecessary because exclusion was a privilege owners should never have been awarded as it is contrary to natural justice. If however it nonetheless wanted to soften the blow, it could follow the example set when planning control was introduced in 1947, a comparable erosion of the benefits of landownership. This would mean setting up a fund from which special payments could be made to landowners who could demonstrate hardship during the early years of the new right. It was specifically indicated that the disbursements under the 1947 fund should be considered as the alleviation of hardship rather than compensation.

Pay Walking

A general right of free access to the countryside is clearly incompatible with charging people to go on land. Once such a right had been enacted, fencing land so that people could be charged to enter it (rather than to restrain stock, say, or to protect young trees) would become an infringement of the new right. If the new right were to be meaningful, it would have to be accompanied by laws making it illegal to construct such fences, with powers for the access agency to order their removal or to prosecute if such orders were ignored. At a stroke the practice of charging visitors to waterfalls and stretches of river valley, farmland, and coastline and so on would be wiped out. Equally ravaged would be the schemes under which the government through bodies like the Forestry Commission and the Ministry of Agriculture pays landowners for granting access to the public, though fairness would presumably require that owners in existing contracts should continue to receive their payments till the expiry of their terms. The access tier of the countryside stewardship and environmentally sensitive areas schemes, the community woodland supplement, and other forestry access payments as well as the whole of the two countryside access schemes rest on the notion that landowners should expect remuneration for allowing others to set foot on their land. So does the idea of exemption from inheritance tax in return for access. Once the public could walk on that land as of right, there would be nothing for the government to pay for.

Landowners who do make money from walkers, either through turnstile charges or government grants, cannot be expected to welcome this aspect of a right to roam. As it happens, more and more farmers, foresters, and landowners are supplementing their incomes in this way, and the landowning community likes both the money and the control this activity entails. Plenty of other people will be happy to see it nipped in the bud, however, and not only because walkers and taxpayers would like to save a bit of cash. Former Director-General of the National Trust Angus Stirling is, as we have seen (page 218), one of several prominent people who have come out against charges for access, while several organizations including the Woodland Trust, the Forestry Commission, and the John Muir Trust have chosen to forgo income they could have generated through charging for entry in order to support the principle that access to the countryside should be free. There are even those in the landowning community who are uneasy about turnstiles. While the Country Landowners' Association sees charging as the key to managed access, its sister organization in Scotland, the Scottish Landowners' Federation, takes a different view. The SLF is not in a position to control the actions of its members but in a policy paper in 1993 it said: 'The issue of charging for access has been difficult and requires sensitive treatment. Each case must be justified on its merits and carefully explained. The charge should reflect the facilities being supplied and *should not be made for individual pedestrian access where no special facilities or management are provided*' (my emphasis).[51]

The effective abolition of payment-for-access would release public funds currently supporting the access elements of agriculture, conservation, and forestry subsidy schemes. At the same time, it would of course also remove an incentive for landowners to create spaces suitable for walkers, though this effect would not be large since most access grants take the form of top-up payments where land is being dedicated to a particular purpose in return for other grants. It would of course also still be possible for grants to be paid to landowners and land occupiers to carry out capital works to help people take advantage of their new right, like building additional footbridges, surfacing paths, sign-boarding, and providing car parking. Ideally the public money saved from payment for access itself could be made available to the access agencies and diverted to this purpose. Payments for facilitating access in this way could be made wherever the agencies saw fit rather than only in places where a scheme devised for another purpose happens to be operating, as is the case with most of the current access subsidy schemes. This change would remove the unfairness that currently allows some owners to charge for access while others find their land happens to be crossed by rights of way. Under the countryside stewardship scheme, grants for the provision of facilities to owners already receiving access payments reflect only part of the cost of the work; under new arrangements, grants of 100 per cent could be provided, or more than 100 per cent where the access agency wanted to provide an incentive. A challenge funding system could enable landowners to compete between themselves for the money available. Thus money at present used to pay for nothing more than the privilege of allowing access to land could instead facilitate free walking as effectively as possible.

As with public subsidy for access, so with direct charges to walkers under private turnstile schemes. They are already effectively outlawed in those countries where rights of access are already in place, and also in some other countries where societies are anxious to preserve the idea of free access to particular features. Thus in Tobago, where access to the beach is guaranteed to all, a payment booth at the entrance to the prime beach at Pigeon Point can issue tickets only for the use of facilities: visitors can still walk round the shore to access the beach without payment. Where a scheme offers not just access to attractive landscape but some facility such as the opportunity to view rare breeds or use hides for watching birds or badgers then charging could still be permissible. Charging for car parking could also continue to provide substantial opportunities for owners to make money from walkers, so much so that some might still find it worthwhile to create features like nature trails. The owners of large estates would still be able to charge not only for car parking but for special exhibitions and access for people other than walkers, like riders or motorbike scramblers. At Highclere, for example, the Earl of Carnarvon charges for entry to the house and gardens and a stretch of parkland next to the house. The house and gardens would fall within the definition of permanently exempted land while the stretch of park involved would probably fall within the definition of curtilage and thus also be exempted. The Earl could carry on charging for entry to these things for as long—or as short—a time as he chose. However, he would have to put up with the presence of the public over much of the remainder of his estate and over land from which access is at present barred—like private roads and tracks, parkland and lakeside—all year round, subject to any exemptions he was able to negotiate with the access agency, for instance when pheasants were being shot or trees felled. If he feared that he might lose some receipts because some visitors were content to visit the grounds without visiting the house he would be able to counter the problem through car parking charges. At private country parks where the visitor passes through a turnstile, owners would in future have to look to recouping charges from car parking, refreshments, or the use of other facilities.

A grey area might emerge where landowners operated turnstile schemes on the argument that entry to an area involved access to facilities like lavatories, gravelled paths, picnic benches, and so on. In practice it should not be difficult for the access agencies to develop rules of thumb for adjudicating such cases. It might also be considered sensible to allow a transitional period during which schemes already established by the time a right to roam came into force could be allowed to continue to charge.

Not all the landowners affected by the outlawing of charges for access would be seeking profit. Many of the wildlife trusts offer their members entry to a network of sites rich in wildlife from which the general public are barred as one of the main benefits of membership. The Royal Society for the Protection of Birds charges non-members for entry to some of its reserves. Such organizations would be able to claim exemption from a general right of access on the grounds of disturbance to vulnerable wildlife, but such a claim would not, on the face of it, allow charging for entry. If a right of access were to be completely unrestricted, such bodies would be faced with a choice between opening their facilities to all for free and closing them to everybody by securing an exemption.

There might well be circumstances in which this would be unsatisfactory. Charging for entry does not only generate revenues which can help pay for the upkeep of nature reserves, archaeological sites, and landscape features. It also provides a means of controlling access to ensure that those who are actually interested in the special characteristics of the site are able to enjoy what it offers without it being overrun by people whose needs could be met in less vulnerable locations. Public parks can be 'captured' by dog-walkers, skate-boarders, or gay cruisers at the expense of other groups. Wildlife reserves and archaeological sites would need to be able to protect themselves from a similar fate. Charging for car-parking might often effectively replace charging for entry as a means whereby the owners of specialist facilities could continue to select visitors. Where this would be insufficient, however, an exception could be made, though it would need to be policed to ensure it did not become a loophole through which a general right of access could be avoided. In Norway, an amendment to the Outdoor Recreation Act of 1957, passed in 1996, specifically forbids landowners from taking money from people who are using their right of access. However, it specifies circumstances when people do more than simply exercise this right—for example obtain access to facilities of some kind, in which a landowner can require payment. Landowners must however first obtain permission for such charging from their local council, which will not only grant or withhold permission but also adjudicate on the scale of the charge.

In Britain, the access authority could be given responsibility for considering applications for charging for access to wildlife and archaeological sites and vulnerable landscape features, and, as in Norway, controlling the level of any charges. It would simply have to decide whether it was in the public interest that a charge should be made rather than letting the general right of access apply. The charges levied by the Royal Society for the Protection of Birds on non-members for access to its popular reserve at Pulborough Brooks, West Sussex, could be replaced by charges for car parking under a right to roam. If, however, this proved inadequate as a means either of controlling access or raising revenue, the RSPB could apply to the access agency for the right to continue to charge for entry and its case could be judged on its merits. An individual landowner would be able to make a similar case for charging for access to a beauty spot, but his own profit would clearly not be considered part of the public interest.

Public Paths and Other Existing Access

It may seem that a general right of access to the countryside would make redundant such guarantees of access as already exist. Arrangements opening up particular places under 'access agreements' between local authorities and landowners would indeed become unnecessary, though councils might still choose to make arrangements with landowners to make access more practicable through the provision of facilities like gates, stiles, and pathways. They might still establish country parks to absorb visitor pressure in particular areas. Toll-payment schemes would of course become illegal. Yet by far the most important guarantor of access to the countryside at present is our rights of way network—public footpaths, bridleways, roads used as public paths, and byways open to all traffic. And even with a general right of access there would still be a vital role for this network, just as rights of way continue to operate separately in other countries which have provided general access rights.

This is essentially because access provided under rights of way offers something more than would be provided under a general right. A right of way enshrines the right to pass along a predetermined slice of the earth's surface for all time: the use of the land over which that way runs cannot be changed in a way which would interfere with the route. If an owner is granted planning permission to build a house in a wood, then the land covered by the house, its curtilage, and its garden would probably be automatically exempted from any general right of access. If, however, a right of way crossed the land, the owner could not build across it or otherwise obstruct it without a successful application to divert or extinguish it. Thus public paths do sometimes run through gardens, very close to houses, and through farmyards —all locations which would not be opened up under the right of access. Public rights of way exist in places which even with a general right of access would otherwise be inaccessible. They connect isolated farmhouses and old gamekeepers' cottages which are not only landmarks but also of interest to those keen on vernacular architecture and the history of agriculture. Their owners have had to put up with an ancient right of passage and should continue to do so.

Not only is the access provided under a right of way more permanent than could be expected from a general right of access, it is also more comprehensive, applying every day of the year. Rights of way are not subject to seasonal closure, and as we have seen, even operations which could threaten public safety, such as a pheasant shoot or paintball manœuvre, cannot be used as reasons for securing the closure of a path. True, public paths can cease to be apparent on the ground for up to a fortnight after first ploughing in cases where they cross arable fields, but even during that period the citizen has a right to use them. On land subject to the right of access, on the other hand, citizens will find certain types of terrain closed at certain times of the year. The other major difference between rights of way and the public's rights on access land concern maintenance and as a result the extent to which the citizen can expect the land involved to be usable. A right of access would give citizens a right to be present but one which they would not always be able to assert. This might be because the land is physically impenetrable, perhaps consisting of shale scree or peat hag; or perhaps in high summer when encroaching vegetation from hedges will block field edges. Councils may manage land as best they can to make it more navigable, but they clearly could never keep all the countryside physically passable all the time. A right of way, in contrast, normally guarantees not only that a citizen has a right to travel but also that passage will actually be possible on the ground. This is because of the responsibility imposed on all of the highway authorities in England and Wales to maintain the surface of public footpaths and bridleways so that they are usable by the public at all times. This is however less true in Scotland and Northern Ireland where the obligations on public authorities to maintain public paths are less onerous and where paths are nothing like the major recreation resource which they embody in England and Wales.

Another reason why the rights of way system should remain separate from a general right of access is that its history affords it a measure of entrenchment which a general right would take a long time to acquire. Rights of way have long been respected by governments of all parties, and they are unlikely to be abolished or significantly encroached upon. A right to roam would take many years to become similarly established, and until it did it would be vulnerable to revocation or emasculation.

There is, however, one way in which the paths system and the right to roam system could interact which would need attention. At present, citizens can claim routes as new public paths on the grounds that they have been used without let or hindrance for at least twenty years. A general right of access would thus enable citizens to claim countless new routes as rights of way once twenty years had elapsed, if this rule were to persist. Many of these new routes might be genuinely incompatible with perfectly acceptable activities which might require the temporary exclusion of the public. Highway authorities would find their responsibilities suddenly extended to a potentially vast new set of routes of whose utility they might be unconvinced. The effect would be to downgrade the standing of the whole rights

of way network. Respect for the system would decline and important paths which had been kept open and in use for centuries might
well suffer.

New legislation for a general right of access ought therefore to include
some provision which could override the twenty-year rule. One mechanism which might do the job is already in operation in England
and Wales and could be extended to Scotland and Northern Ireland.
At present, landowners may if they wish deposit with their highway
authorities a 'section 31 statement'. Such a statement, provided under
section 31 of the Highways Act 1980, indicates such routes as a landowner admits as being public paths and announces that he or she does
not accept that any other routes are in the process of being dedicated.
Such statements, which must be renewed every six years to remain
valid, in effect prevent new paths being claimed by walkers even if
they are moving freely over land in question. Many landowners have
not heard of these statements and are not making such depositions,
but a number of large estate owners who employ advisers have spotted
the usefulness of the provision and have made statements. Even owners
who happily allow access but wish to ensure that such permissive access
is not entrenched as a right have made section 31 statements. The
Woodland Trust and the Suffolk Naturalists' Trust are two examples.
A clause in any new access legislation embedding similar machinery
might prevent some new paths coming into being which would otherwise be welcome, but this seems a price worth paying for maintaining
the overall integrity of the public paths network.

Landscape Change

If a right of access would inevitably provide an exemption for certain types of land use, we must be alive to the possibility that some
owners would seek to change the use to which land is put in order
to secure exemption from the right of access. Clearly this might in
theory at least entail landscape change which might be undesirable.
Ploughing up downland turf, heath, cliff roughland, or moor, or draining wetland to create cropland would be accompanied not only by
the financial rewards which already exist but by the new advantage
of reclaiming the right to exclude.

Existing regulation would impose some brake on this process. Anyone who wanted to build, extract minerals, install a golf course or racecourse or make other changes which would turn, say, a woodland or a stretch of rough, open grassland into some other category of exempted land would have to apply for planning consent before he or she could go ahead. Planning authorities would be able to take any loss of recreation opportunity into account. Where woodland clearance was involved, landowners seeking to clear more than the equivalent of eight large oak trees every year would need to obtain permission to do so from the Forestry Commission. On land designated a site of special scientific interest some protection would exist. Normally, however, changes of use which cut recreation opportunities might also erode or destroy important wildlife habitats because most farming and forestry operations fall outside the scope of any regulation. Chalk and limestone grassland and lowland heath in particular are now rare and fragmented and of outstanding natural history importance. It would be unfortunate if the prospect of the introduction of a right of access to these types of land were to cause their destruction, and a partial right singling out down, heath, and common as its only lowland targets would maximize this risk. As long ago as the 1950s the danger of prompting landscape destruction by imposing access agreements was being recognized. Local authorities which entered into access agreements with landowners over stretches of chalk downland turf sometimes inserted clauses forbidding the conversion of the 'open country' concerned to 'excepted land' as defined in the 1949 National Parks and Access to the Countryside Act.

Today, the most effective solution to this problem would be to extend planning control to all farming and forestry operations which can have a far-reaching impact on the landscape whatever their effect on public access.[52] Such operations might include ploughing stretches of semi-natural grassland, clearing woodland, piping streams underground, afforesting land, and draining wetland. This would of course be a considerable step in its own right, comparable in scale with introducing a general right of access itself. It is, however, a move which has its own logic in the light of the devastation wrought on landscape, wildlife, and archaeological remains by agricultural practices over the last half-century. The development of aerial photography and geographic information systems as well as the satellite imagery techniques which the Ministry of Agriculture has developed to control fraud under the set-aside scheme would make the monitoring and enforcement of planning controls over land-use changes easier than they would have been only ten years ago. The treatment of planning applications could be covered by policies set out in plans prepared locally within Whitehall-inspired guidelines, as happens within the existing planning system. An applicant refused permission before, say, the removal of a copse or the conversion to arable land of a wetland, could have a right of appeal to the Secretary of State for the Environment, Transport, and the Regions as he or she would with a building scheme.

The whole idea that one consequence of a right of access to the countryside might be the threat of deliberate destruction of landscape features may seem far-fetched. But like the more obvious consequences considered earlier, it deserves to be thought through. Though simple in conception, access by right would change not only a fundamental principle but myriad practical realities about the way the countryside works. Experience from abroad can reassure us that none of these changes need pose insuperable problems, yet we owe it to land-owners, our wildlife, and ourselves to ensure that the introduction of the new right is as trouble-free as it ought to be.

CONCLUSION

So is the right to roam over not just part but all of Britain's countryside about to be restored to us?

The present Labour government has raised hopes and disappointed them at different stages but left the issue firmly planted in the mainstream of national debate. Its choice to concentrate only on mountain, moor, heath, down, and common was essentially mistaken, yet the problems this has generated serve perhaps only to highlight the advantages of a universal right of access to the whole of the countryside. The government's decision to put even a limited right of access on hold while inviting landowners to advance the case for a voluntary solution looked like weakness. Yet requiring landowners to prove that rights of access are unnecessary presented them with a challenge that they were bound, sooner or later, to fail.

Even more significant than the government's own proposals on access may be its decision to grant Scotland a Parliament of its own. Scots are elegantly side-stepping some of the muddles into which the government has trapped itself. It may well be that the Scots will give themselves a universal right of access to the countryside before the English. If this happens their example is likely to be followed before long south of the border. Examples from Sweden, Norway, Switzerland, and Germany may have been ignored, but neither the English, Welsh, nor Northern Irish are likely to stand by while the Scots recover a birthright all should enjoy.

Fateful though the present moment may seem in the history of access to the countryside in Britain, it takes on a different colour when seen against the long struggle in which it is just one episode, though an important one. The people of Britain were battling against landowners for rights in land during the Middle Ages. Bills which would have enacted a right of access to some of Britain's countryside were debated at Westminster in the nineteenth century. Men went to prison after a bloody mass trespass in the 1930s. A committee sitting during the Second World War formulated a right of access to the countryside from which we could still learn today.

Over the last half-century, the people have been let down time and again by political leaders unwilling to take on the power of the landowning lobby. But through that period there has developed a combination of forces which seems destined to ensure that full victory is only a matter of time.

When the Diggers of the seventeenth century articulated the rejection of absolute ownership of land, they could not have envisaged a world in which the sanctity of the environment as the home of the human species had become an article of faith all over the planet. Nor could they have imagined a world in which democracy was to become an unstoppable force, steadily reclaiming what the strong had stolen from the weak in the dying era of privilege.

The outcome of the present government's actions remains to be seen. What we know however is that the British people care about their countryside and intend to enjoy it as never before. Visiting the countryside is now the most popular outdoor activity after gardening and way ahead of watching and participating in formal sports like football. The culture of deference which sustained the landowning élite through a century of nominal democracy has faded away and it is hard to believe it will ever return.

In the face of these realities, access to our countryside cannot stay much longer out of reach. Our trespass laws look increasingly like other leftovers from our feudal past which are steadily being swept away. Already, every landowner who puts up a 'Trespassers will be Prosecuted' sign now offends against the as yet unlegislated but nevertheless unarguable spirit of the age. We can be confident that, sooner or later, those signs will be coming down for ever.

NOTES

Chapter 1

1. J. A. Jolowicz, with T. E. Lewis and D. M. Harris, *Winfield and Jolowicz on Tort* (London: Sweet and Maxwell, 1971), 306.
2. P. W. Birts, *Remedies for Trespass* (London: Longman, 1990), 35.
3. This was reported in *Common Ground*, BBC Radio 4, 26 Sept. 1996.
4. M. Shoard, *This Land is Our Land: The Struggle for Britain's Countryside* (London: Gaia Books, 1987), 91, 462–3.
5. (1972) AC 877, 904, quoted by T. Bonyhady, *The Law of the Countryside: The Rights of the Public* (Abingdon: Professional Books, 1987), 162.
6. See W. M. Gordon, *Scottish Land Law* (Edinburgh: W. Green & Son, 1989), J. Rowan-Robinson, with W. M. Gordon and C. T. Reid, *Public Access to the Countryside: A Guide to the Law, Practice and Procedure in Scotland* (Edinburgh: Scottish Natural Heritage, n.d. (1990s)), and D. Laird, 'Access and Trespass' in *Countryside Concerns Seminar 1995* (Edinburgh: Law Society of Scotland, 1996). An alternative view on trespass in Scotland has recently been put forward by Alan Blackshaw in a report on the history of trespass. Mr Blackshaw asserts that for much of the early part of the twentieth century, until 1967, no effective law of trespass existed in Scotland and walkers could move around in many areas, particularly over open upland, under a form of 'implied consent'. He argues that in 1967 a government statement introduced the 'hard' view of trespass which exists in England, Wales, and Northern Ireland today, when a Minister sought to justify the introduction of legislation to Scotland providing for access agreements and the like. Mr Blackshaw says that although a harder view on trespass was prevalent from 1967 onwards the government today acknowledges a position on trespass in Scotland reflecting the position of the 1950s. Whatever the rights and wrongs of the matter, Scotland's landowners seem to be able to eject trespassers from their land and to secure interdicts to prevent repeat trespass. For further details see A. Blackshaw, *Scotland's Distinctive Laws and Traditions of Access or Going Back to the 1950s*, available from Scottish Wildlife and Countryside Link, Rhu Gianach, Kingussie Road, Newtonmore, PH20 1AY.
7. House of Commons, *Hansard*, 13 April 1994, col. 367.
8. Labour Party, *A Working Countryside* (London: The Labour Party, 1995), p. 26.

9. For further details of the law on rights of way see J. Riddall and J. Trevelyan, *Rights of Way: A Guide to Law and Practice* (London: Ramblers' Association, 1992); Bonyhady, *Law of the Countryside*; Countryside Commission, *Rights of Way: An Action Pack* (Cheltenham: Countryside Commission, 1992, CCP 375) (which contains the useful publication *Out in the Country: Where you can Go and What you can Do*); Countryside Council for Wales, *A Guide for Farmers and Landowners: Managing Public Access* (Bangor: CCW, 1995) (a similar document is issued by the Countryside Commission); Scottish Rights of Way Society, *Rights of Way: A Guide to the Law in Scotland* (Edinburgh: Scottish Rights of Way Society, 1996); Gordon, *Scottish Land Law*; Rowan-Robinson *et al.*, *Public Access to the Countryside*; Environment Service, Department of the Environment for Northern Ireland, *A Guide to Public Rights of Way and Access to the Countryside* (Belfast, Department of the Environment, 1998). Some local authorities have published booklets outlining the law on rights of way; a model of its kind is *A Brief Guide to Public Rights of Way* by the Community Leisure Team, South Norfolk Council, last edition in 1997.

10. These figures are taken from Scottish Rights of Way Society, *Mapping and Recording the Rights of Way of Scotland Project* (Edinburgh: Scottish Rights of Way Society, 1998).

11. This point is discussed more fully by Bonyhady, *Law of the Countryside*, pp. 123–9.

12. J. P. Rossiter, 'An Analytical Study of the Public Use of Private Land for Outdoor Recreation in England 1949–1968', unpublished Ph.D. dissertation (University of Cambridge, 1972), 293–8.

13. House of Commons, *Hansard*, 29 Mar. 1996, vol. 274, no. 80, col. 777.

14. Inland Revenue Budget 98, *Inheritance Tax: Better Public Access to Heritage Assets* (London: Inland Revenue, 17 Mar. 1998).

15. J. P. Rossiter, 'Analytical Study of the Public Use of Private Land'.

16. House of Commons Select Committee on Agriculture Session 1996–7, *Second Report: Environmentally Sensitive Areas and Other Schemes under the Agri-Environment Regulation*, Vol. ii, House of Commons Paper 45-II (London: HMSO, 1997), 16.

17. Gloucestershire Trust for Nature Conservation, *Wildlife in Gloucestershire: A Habitat Survey* (Stonehouse: Gloucestershire Trust for Nature Conservation, 1981), 83.

18. Ramblers' Association, *Countryside Stewardship Scheme: Public Access Sites* (London: Ramblers' Association, 1995). This study is referred to in more detail in Chapter 5.

19. Countryside Commission, 'Community Forests Open New Gates for Millions of People', News Release 4 Nov. 1997 (Cheltenham: Countryside Commission).

Chapter 2

1. 'Ramblers' Right of Way Surveys', *Footpath Worker*, Vol. 16, No. 4 (Dec. 1995) (London: Ramblers' Association), 2.

2. 'Path Surveys', *Footpath Worker*, 17/4 (1996), 2–3. This article refers to the Countryside Commission's *Second National Rights of Way Survey: The Findings from 1993/4* (Cheltenham: Countryside Commission, 1996).

3. 'Walkers Banned from 135 Square Miles of Woodland', London: Ramblers' Association News Release, 14 Nov. 1995. This release refers to the answer to a parliamentary question tabled by Paddy Tipping, MP, and reproduced in House of Commons, *Hansard*, 25 Oct. 1995, cols. 685–7.

4. 'Ramblers Publish New Research Showing Almost Half the Number of Forestry Commission Woods have been Sold', London: Ramblers' Association News Release, 17 June 1996.

5. Countryside Commission, *Study of Informal Recreation in South East England* (Cheltenham: Countryside Commission, 1978).

6. The Forestry Trust for Conservation and Education, *Woodlands to Visit in England and Wales: A Guide to over 700 Woodlands and Forests where Visitors are Welcome for Enjoyment and Education* (Theale, Berks.: The Forestry Trust for Conservation and Education, 1995), 19.

7. C. Watkins, 'Woodlands in Nottinghamshire since 1945: A Study of Changing Distribution and Use', unpublished Ph.D. dissertation (University of Nottingham, 1983).

8. G. Bedell, 'War Starts over the Woodland Warriors', *The Times*, 7 July 1990, p. 17.

9. Countryside Commission, 'Great Western and Marston Vale Community Forests Approved by Government', Cheltenham: Countryside Commission Press Release, 7 Feb. 1995.

10. I examine the attraction of moorland scenery in more detail in M. Shoard, 'The Lure of the Moors', in J. Burgess and J. Gold (eds.), *Valued Environments* (London: Allen & Unwin, 1982); and M. Shoard, 'Lie of the Land: Marion Shoard Assesses the Present Situation Regarding Access to Moorland in Britain', *Environment Now* (April/May 1988).

11. M. Senior, *Portrait of North Wales* (Llanrwst, Gwynedd: Gwasg Carreg Gwalch, 1987), 100.

12. For further details see M. Shoard, *This Land is Our Land: The Struggle for Britain's Countryside* (London: Gaia Books, 1997), 330–3.

13. Ramblers' Association, *Keep Out: The Hundred Year Struggle for Public Access to the Hills and Mountains of Britain, 1884–1984* (London: Ramblers' Association, 1984), foreword by Tom Stephenson.
14. For further details see D. Hollinger, 'Action for Access: Towards a Realistic Strategy for Countryside Recreation in Northern Ireland', unpublished B.Sc. dissertation (Jesus College, Cambridge, 1997).
15. A total of 12,000 acres of moorland—one-fifth of the total on Exmoor—were squared off and converted mainly to inaccessible ryegrass fields between 1947 and 1976 alone. For further details see M. Shoard, *The Theft of the Countryside* (London: Maurice Temple Smith, 1980).
16. *Rambling Today*, No. 6 (Autumn 1992), 12.
17. Vaughan Cornish, *The Preservation of our Scenery* (Cambridge: Cambridge University Press, 1937), 79–81.
18. Nature Conservancy Council, *Nature Conservation in Great Britain* (Peterborough: NCC, 1984), 51. See also R. M. Fuller, 'The Changing Extent and Conservation Interest of Lowland Grassland in England and Wales: A Review of Grassland Surveys 1930–84', *Biol. Cons.* 40 (1987), 281–300.
19. Nature Conservancy Council, *Nature Conservation in Great Britain*, 52.
20. Devon County Council, *The Changing Face of Devon* (Exeter: Devon County Council, 1979).
21. D. Bangs, *The Case for a Downland Freedom to Roam*, available from D. Bangs, 4 Hamilton Road, Brighton BNI 5DL, 1998.
22. D. Lowenthal and H. C. Prince, 'English Landscape Tastes', *Geographical Review* (New York), 55/2 (Apr. 1965), 192.
23. I calculated this figure by scrutinizing *Hampshire's Countryside Heritage: Historic Parks and Gardens* published by Hampshire County Council in 1983. In a descriptive list of historic parks and gardens in Hampshire, the County Council noted whether a particular parkland was open to the public. I have omitted from my examination those sites which were clearly gardens. The areas I have given in this chapter and elsewhere in the book are based on the extent of parkland shown on Ordnance Survey maps.
24. D. Valentine (ed.), *Historic Houses, Castles and Gardens in Great Britain and Ireland* (East Grinstead, West Sussex: Reed Information Services, 1997).
25. These figures were worked out from examining *Historic Parks and Gardens of Cheshire* by Dr I. Laurie (Department of Town Planning, University of Manchester, 1985).
26. His Grace the Duke of Wellington (ed.), *Stratfield Saye House* (Stratfield Saye, Reading: Wellington Enterprises, n.d., *c.*1997).

27. I discuss access to Broadlands in more detail in Shoard, *This Land is Our Land*, 227–9 and 250–1.

28. L. W. Carnegie, *Andrew Carnegie: My Own Story* (Dunfermline: The Carnegie Dunfermline Trust, 1984, first pub. 1920), 151.

29. For further details of the ownership of land by the Crown Estate, see Shoard, *This Land is Our Land*, 123–6.

30. J. N. Moore, *Edward Elgar: A Creative Life* (Oxford: Oxford University Press, 1984), p. 32.

31. B. Booth and E. Mehew (eds.), *The Letters of Robert Louis Stevenson*, vol. iii (New Haven: Yale University Press, 1994), 188.

32. S. R. B. Jackson, 'Navigation Rights after the Derwent Case', *Rights of Way Law Review*, Section 6.3, June 1992, 19–23.

33. I discuss these changes in more detail in M. Shoard, 'Access: Can Present Opportunities be Widened?', Countryside Commission, *Countryside for All?* (1979), papers given at a Countryside Commission Conference, York University, 20–1 Sept. 1978.

34. J. Skellern, 'Countryside Recreation in Berkshire: A Study Asking Whether Current Trends in Countryside Recreation in Berkshire are towards the Reinforcement of an Exclusive Countryside', unpublished dissertation, M.Sc. Town and Country Planning (University of Reading, Department of Land Management and Development, 1993), 26.

Chapter 3

1. The boundaries between the 'champion' landscapes of large villages and open fields which dominated lowland England and the 'woodland' landscapes of early enclosed fields are discussed in T. Williamson, 'Explaining Regional Landscapes: Woodland and Champion in Southern and Eastern England', *Landscape History*, 10 (1988), 5–13.

2. G. C. Homans, *English Villagers of the Thirteenth Century* (New York: Russell & Russell, 1941).

3. This is discussed in further detail by J. Barrell, *The Idea of Landscape and the Sense of Place 1730–1840: An Approach to the Poetry of John Clare* (Cambridge: Cambridge University Press, 1972), 99. Other theories of the origin of the open-field system are discussed by T. Williamson, 'Explaining Regional Landscapes'.

4. D. Whitelock (ed.), *English Historical Documents c.500–1542* (London: Eyre Methuen, 1979), 401.

5. Royal forests were created later in Scotland than in England: the first extant references to royal forests in Scotland occur between 1136 and 1144.

For further details see J. M. Gilbert, *Hunting and Hunting Reserves in Medieval Scotland* (Edinburgh: John Donald Publishers, 1979).

6. For further details of royal forests and private hunting chases see: Gilbert, ibid.; L. M. Cantor (ed.), *The English Medieval Landscape* (London: Croom Helm, 1982); J. C. Cox, *The Royal Forests of England* (London: Methuen, 1905); R. Cunliffe Shaw, *The Royal Forest of Lancaster* (Preston: Guardian Press, 1956); C. R. Young, *The Royal Forests of Medieval England* (London: Collins: The New Naturalist, 1979).

7. Cantor, *The English Medieval Landscape*.

8. L. M. Cantor and J. D. Wilson, 'The Medieval Deer Parks of Dorset', *Proceedings of the Dorset Natural History and Archaeological Society*, 83 (1961).

9. L. M. Cantor and A. Squires, *The Historic Parks of Leicestershire and Rutland* (Newton Linford, Leicestershire: Kairos Press, 1997).

10. R. Muir, *Old Yorkshire* (London: Michael Joseph, 1987), 169.

11. I describe the struggle over land rights in Britain in greater detail in *This Land is Our Land: The Struggle for Britain's Countryside* (London: Gaia Books, 1997).

12. For further details of the development of common rights see W. G. Hoskins and L. Dudley Stamp, *The Common Lands of England and Wales* (London: Collins, 1963); J. M. Neeson, 'Common Right and Enclosure in Eighteenth Century Northamptonshire', unpublished Ph.D. thesis (University of Warwick, 1977); and J. M. Neeson, *Commoners: Common Right, Enclosure and Social Change in England, 1700–1820* (Cambridge: Cambridge University Press, 1993); Lord Eversley, *Commons, Forests and Footpaths: The Story of the Battle during the last Forty-five Years for Public Rights over the Commons, Forests and Footpaths of England and Wales* (London: Cassell and Co., 1910).

13. M. K. Ashby, *Joseph Ashby of Tysoe, 1859–1919* (London: Merlin Press, 1974), 38.

14. J. Clare, 'Sunday Walks', *c.*1820.

15. J. Clare, *Early Poems* II, 170, quoted by J. Goodridge, 'Pastoral and Popular Notes in Clare's Enclosure Elegies' in J. Goodridge (ed.), *The Independent Spirit: John Clare and the Self-Taught Tradition* (Helpston, Cambs.: John Clare Society, 1994), 141. For further details of the impact of enclosure on John Clare's life and poetry, see also J. Barrell, *The Idea of Landscape and the Sense of Place 1730–1840: An Approach to the Poetry of John Clare.*

16. J. S. Henslow, *Suggestions Towards an Enquiry into the Present Condition of the Labouring Population of Suffolk* (Hadleigh, 1844), 24–5, as quoted

by R. W. Malcolmson, *Popular Recreation in English Society 1700–1850* (Cambridge: Cambridge University Press, 1973), 116.

17. R. A. Slaney, *Essay on the Beneficial Direction of Rural Expenditure* (London, 1824), as quoted by Malcolmson, *Popular Recreation*, 108. In 1833 Robert Slaney successfully moved that a select committee be appointed 'to consider the best means of securing open places in the immediate vicinity of populous towns as public walks calculated to promote the health and comfort of the inhabitants', *Parliamentary Reports*, 15 (21 Feb. 1923), col. 1056.

18. E. J. T. Collins, 'Agrarian Industries: The Coppice and Underwood Trades', in G. E. Mingay (ed.), *The Agrarian History of England and Wales*, vi: *1750–1850* (Cambridge: Cambridge University Press, 1989); and E. J. T. Collins, 'Farming and Forestry in Central Southern England in the Nineteenth and Early Twentieth Centuries', in H. Brandl (ed.), *Report of the International Union of Forestry Research Organisations Group S6.07: Forest History* (Freiburg: International Union of Forestry Research Organizations, 1993), 290–305. I am grateful to Dr Collins for explaining to me the process by which woodland was enclosed in England.

19. Notice at Hampshire Record Office, 8M/62/72, quoted by P. Horn, *Labouring Life in the Victorian Countryside* (Dublin: Gill & MacMillan, 1976), 229.

20. For further details about the thinking behind eighteenth-century park creation see Cantor, *The Historic Parks of Leicestershire and Rutland*; T. Williamson, *Polite Landscapes* (Baltimore: Johns Hopkins University Press, 1995); J. H. Hunter, *Land into Landscape* (London: George Godwin, 1985). For discussions on this subject I am grateful to Dr Ivan Hall, author of *Burton Constable Hall: A Century of Patronage* (Beverley: Hull City Museums and Art Galleries, 1991), and Dr Eric Till, author of *A Family Affair: Stamford and the Cecils 1650–1900* (Rugby: Jolly & Barber, 1990).

21. R. Muir, *The Lost Villages of Britain* (London: Michael Joseph, 1985), 220.

22. T. Williamson and L. Bellamy, *Property and Landscape* (London: George Phillip, 1987), 138.

23. T. Williamson, *Polite Landscapes*, 105.

24. T. Rowley, *The Making of the Shropshire Landscape* (London: Hodder & Stoughton, 1972), 130.

25. C. Morris (ed.), *The Illustrated Journeys of Celia Fiennes 1685–c.1712* (London: Macdonald and Co., 1982).

26. A. Crowe, *The Parks and Woodlands of London* (London: Fourth Estate, 1987).

27. R. Schlatter, *Private Property: The History of an Idea* (London: Allen & Unwin, 1951), 17.

28. Ibid.

29. Virgil's *Georgics*, translated by Dryden, quoted by Schlatter, *Private Property*, 26.

30. Schlatter, *Private Property*, 25–6.

31. For further discussion of the Justinian basis of Roman law and its application to Britain see K. Miller and P. Robson, *Property Law* (Edinburgh: Green/Sweet and Maxwell, 1991); and J. O. Grunebaum, *Private Ownership* (London: Routledge & Kegan Paul, 1987); and W. N. Gordon, *Scottish Land Law* (Edinburgh: W. Green & Son, 1989).

32. Schlatter, *Private Property*, 23–34.

33. St Thomas Aquinas, *Summa Theologiae*, vol. xxxviii, trans. Marcus Lefebure, OP (New York: Blackfriars/McGraw Hill, 1975), 2a 2ae, 66, 2, as quoted by J. O. Grunebaum, *Private Ownership*, 51.

34. J. Locke, *Of Civil Government* (London: 1690), Bk. II, ch. v, 'Of Property', as quoted by R. Schlatter, *Private Property*, 155.

35. W. Blackstone, *Commentaries on the Laws of England*, Book II, 1st pub. *c*.1767, as quoted by Schlatter, ibid. 164.

36. Bacon, as quoted by D. Hay, P. Linebaugh, and E. P. Thompson, *Albion's Fatal Tree: Crime and Society in 18th Century England* (London: Allen Lane, 1975), 191.

37. For further details of the operation of the game laws during the eighteenth and nineteenth centuries, see P. B. Munsche, *Gentlemen and Poachers: The English Game Laws 1671–1831* (Cambridge: Cambridge University Press, 1981) and Hay, Linebaugh, and Thompson, *Albion's Fatal Tree*.

38. For further details of the development of pheasant shooting in nineteenth-century Britain see S. Tapper, *Game Heritage* (Fordingbridge, Hampshire: The Game Conservancy Trust, 1982).

39. For details of the development of grouse shooting and deer stalking during the late nineteenth century, see R. Eden, *Going to the Moors* (London: John Murray, 1979); R. Longrigg, *The English Squire and his Sport* (London: Michael Joseph, 1977); D. Hart-Davis, *Monarchs of the Glen* (London: Cape, 1978); G. K. Whitehead, *Hunting and Stalking Deer in Britain throughout the Ages* (London: Batsford, 1980); W. Orr, *Deer Forests, Landlords and Crofters* (Edinburgh: John Donald, 1982).

40. For details of changes in the ownership of land in nineteenth-century Scotland see T. M. Devine, *Clanship to Crofters' War* (Manchester: Manchester University Press, 1994), 63–83.

41. E. A. Baker, *The Forbidden Land* (London: Witherby, 1924), 9. See also E. A. Baker, *The Highlands with Rope and Rucksack* (London: Witherby, 1923).

42. T. Stephenson, 'The Battle of Glen Tilt', *Rucksack*, 10/1 (Winter 1980).

43. Country Landowners' Association, *The Future of Landownership* (London: CLA, 1976).

44. National Farmers' Union of England and Wales, *He Cares* (London: NFU, n.d., early 1980s).

45. W. Smethurst, *The Archers: The First Thirty Years* (London: Eyre Methuen, 1980), 191.

46. Quoted at greater length in Shoard, *This Land is Our Land*, 400.

47. J. Bugler (producer/director), *Power in the Land* (London: London Weekend Television for Channel 4, 1987).

48. Ibid. For further discussion of landowners' attitudes to access, see *This Land is Our Land*, chs. 6 and 11, and M. Shoard, 'Robbers v. Revolutionaries: What the Battle for Access is Really All About', in C. Watkins (ed.), *Rights of Way: Policy, Culture, and Management* (London: Pinter, 1996).

49. Lord Montagu of Beaulieu, *Beaulieu Palace, House and Abbey* (Beaulieu, Hampshire, 1978), 1.

50. Broadlands (Romsey) Ltd., *Broadlands: The Home of Lord Mountbatten* (Romsey, Hampshire, n.d.), 1.

51. B. Sample, 'No Choker on this Yokel', *The Field* (Oct. 1990), 87–8.

52. S. Courtauld, 'Whose Land is it Anyway?', *Daily Telegraph*, 3 May 1993.

53. Tapper, *Game Heritage*, 43–4.

Chapter 4

1. D. Herlihy, *The History of Feudalism* (London: MacMillan, 1970), 265.

2. Further details in M. Keen, *The Outlaws of Medieval Legend* (London: Routledge, 1961).

3. B. Bird, *Rebel before his Time: The Story of John Ball and the Peasants' Revolt* (Worthing, Sussex: Churchman Publishing, 1987), 65.

4. For a longer discussion of the nature and development of this unofficial social contract over the countryside see M. Shoard, *This Land is Our Land* (London: Gaia Books, 1997), 24–47.

5. R. Manning, *Village Revolts: Social Protests and Popular Disturbances in England, 1509–1640* (Oxford: Clarendon Press, 1988). See also A. Charlesworth (ed.), *An Atlas of Rural Protest in Britain 1548–1900* (Beckenham, Kent: Croom Helm, 1983).

6. Manning, *Village Revolts*, 27.

7. C. Hill, *The World Turned Upside Down: Radical Ideas during the English Revolution* (London: Penguin Books, 1975), 244.

8. Ibid. 244.

9. C. Hill, *Gerrard Winstanley: The Law of Freedom and Other Writings*, (Cambridge: Cambridge University Press, 1983), 26.

10. Ibid. 29.

11. Ibid. 127.

12. Ibid.

13. Ibid. 38.

14. Hill, *World Turned Upside Down*, 107.

15. Hill, *Gerrard Winstanley*, 78.

16. Hill, *World Turned Upside Down*, 132–3.

17. Hill, *Gerrard Winstanley*, 49.

18. N. Mann, *Petrarch* (Oxford: Oxford University Press, 1984), 28.

19. As quoted by K. Clark, *Landscape into Art* (London: John Murray, 1949), 7.

20. H. Bloom, *Petrarch* (New York: Chelsea House, 1989).

21. K. Thomas, *Man and the Natural World: Changing Attitudes in England 1500–1800* (London: Allen Lane, 1983), 249.

22. D. Elliston Allen, *The Naturalist in Britain: A Social History* (London: Allen Lane, 1976), 29–30.

23. Ibid. 24.

24. W. Wordsworth, 'To My Sister' (1798).

25. Quoted by J. Dunn, *Democracy: The Unfinished Journey, 508 B.C.–1993 A.D.* (Oxford: Oxford University Press, 1992), 126.

26. Ibid. 127.

27. J. J. Rousseau, *Discussion on the Origin of Inequality between Men* (1753).

28. See S. Edwards (ed.), *Selected Writings of Pierre-Joseph Proudhon* (London: Macmillan, 1969), 33.

29. For further details see Shoard, *This Land is Our Land*, 7–11.

30. J. Bateman, *The Great Landowners of Great Britain and Ireland, with an Introduction by David Spring* (Leicester: Leicester University Press, 1971), 63.

31. Lord Eversley, *Commons, Forests and Footpaths: The Story of the Battle during the last Forty-five Years for Public Rights over the Commons, Forests and Footpaths of England and Wales* (London: Cassell & Company, 1910). Baron Eversley was the title conferred on George Shaw-Lefevre in 1906.

32. W. H. Williams, *The Commons, Open Spaces and Footpaths Preservation Society 1865–1965: A Short History of the Society and its Work* (London: Commons Society (now the Open Spaces Society, based at Henley-on-Thames, Oxfordshire), 1965).

33. For a fascinating account of the struggle over Epping Forest see the newspaper reports assembled in *Epping Forest: Then and Now: An Anthology*

Compiled by Winston G. Ramsey with Reginald Fowkes (London: Battle of Britain Prints International, 1986). Lord Eversley, *Commons, Forests and Footpaths*, also contains a comprehensive account of the struggles to secure access to commons and other areas of open land in the late nineteenth and early twentieth centuries.

34. For further details of the activities of the Corporation of London in conserving open spaces near the capital see G. Cumberledge, *The Corporation of London: Its Origin, Constitution, Powers and Duties* (Oxford: Oxford University Press, 1950); Corporation of London, *The Official Guide to Burnham Beeches* (London: Guildhall, Corporation of London, 1992); and Corporation of London, *The Official Guide to Kent and Surrey Commons* (London: Guildhall, Corporation of London, 1992).

35. For further details see M. Mabey, *A Little History of the Lickey Hills* (Birmingham: Lickey Hills Society, 1992).

36. O. Hill, *Our Common Land* (London: Macmillan, 1877), 106.

37. Ibid. 137–8.

38. Speech given by Octavia Hill on 15 June 1888 at which she helped persuade the Commons Preservation Society to extend its campaign from open spaces to footpaths, as quoted by R. Legge, *National Trust Centenary* (Wincanton, Somerset: Wincanton Press, 1994), 15.

39. Ibid. 15–16.

40. R. Douglas, *Land, People and Politics: A History of the Land Question in the United Kingdom, 1878–1952* (London: Allison & Busby, 1976), 44.

41. T. M. Devine, *Clanship to Crofters' War: The Social Transformation of the Scottish Highlands* (Manchester: Manchester University Press, 1994), 64. For further details of the Highland Land War see J. Hunter, *The Making of the Crofting Community* (Edinburgh: John Donald, 1976); and Douglas, *Land, People and Politics*.

42. T. M. Devine, *The Transformation of Rural Scotland* (Edinburgh University Press, 1994), 61.

43. *Oban Times*, 24 May 1884, as quoted by Hunter, 159.

44. D. E. Meek, 'The Land Question Answered from the Bible: The Land Issue and the Development of a Highland Theology of Liberation', *Scottish Geographical Magazine*, 103/2 (1987), 84–9.

45. H. George, *Progress and Poverty* (London: Hogarth Press, 1966).

46. For further details see Shoard, *This Land is Our Land*, 55–71 and Douglas, *Land, People and Politics*.

47. See Douglas, *Land, People and Politics*.

48. G. B. Shaw, *Fabian Essays in Socialism* (London: Walter Scott, 1889).

49. For further details of the life of James Bryce see H. A. L. Fisher, *James Bryce* (London: Macmillan, 1927); E. Ions, *James Bryce and American Democracy 1870–1922* (London: Macmillan, 1968); obituaries of Bryce and Bryce's own books.

50. House of Commons, *Hansard*, 4 Mar. 1892, col. 94.

51. House of Commons, *Hansard*, 4 Mar. 1892, col. 93.

52. House of Commons, *Hansard*, 4 Mar. 1892, col. 97.

53. House of Commons, *Hansard*, 4 Mar. 1892, col. 94.

54. House of Commons, *Hansard*, 4 Mar. 1892, col. 98.

55. House of Commons, *Hansard*, 4 Mar. 1892, col. 98.

56. House of Commons, *Hansard*, 4 Mar. 1892, col. 99.

57. House of Commons, *Hansard*, 4 Mar. 1892, col. 99.

58. House of Commons, *Hansard*, 4 Mar. 1892, cols. 96–7.

59. House of Commons, *Hansard*, 4 Mar. 1892, cols. 102–3.

60. House of Commons, *Hansard*, 4 Mar. 1892, col. 128.

61. *Hansard's Parliamentary Debates*, 13 Apr. 1888, cols. 1287–8. To see Tom Ellis within a wider context of the land reform debate see J. G. Jones, 'Select Committee or Royal Commission? Wales and "The Land Question", 1892', *Welsh History Review*, 17 (1994–5), 205–29 and J. G. Jones, 'Michael Davitt, David Lloyd George and T. E. Ellis: The Welsh Experience, 1886', *Welsh History Review*, 18 (1996–7).

62. Further details of the Knole Park case can be found in D. Killingray, 'Rights, Riot and Ritual: The Knole Park Access Dispute, Sevenoaks, Kent, 1883–5', *Rural History*, 5/1 (1995), 63–79.

63. Ibid., reference 4.

64. Further details from the Birmingham Association for the Preservation of Open Spaces and Public Footpaths annual reports for the 1880s and 1890s, which are lodged in the British Library in London.

65. See for instance *Footpaths and Roadside Wastes: A Bill for the Better Protection of Footpaths and Roadside Wastes*, Bill 238, 1888.

66. T. Stephenson, *Forbidden Land: The Struggle for Access to Mountain and Moorland* (Manchester: Manchester University Press, 1989), 140.

67. For further details of the history of the campaign to secure public access to the Peak District moorlands, see J. P. Rossiter, 'An Analytical Study of the Public Use of Private Land for Outdoor Recreation in England 1949–1968', unpublished Ph.D. dissertation (University of Cambridge, 1972); P. A. Barnes, *Trespassers will be Prosecuted* (Sheffield, 1934); H. Hill, *Freedom to Roam* (Ashbourne, Derbyshire: Moorland Publishing, 1980); Stephenson, *Forbidden Land*; and B. Rothman, *The 1932 Kinder Trespass* (Altrincham, Cheshire: Willow Publishing, 1982).

68. Rothman, *1932 Kinder Trespass*, 13.
69. Quoted by Hill, *Freedom to Roam*, 16.
70. For further details see M. Shoard, 'The Lure of the Moors', in J. Burgess and J. Gold (eds.), *Valued Environments* (London: Allen & Unwin, 1982).
71. Barnes, *Trespassers will be Prosecuted*, 9–11.
72. Rothman, *1932 Kinder Trespass*, 11.
73. *Hayfield, Kinder Scout and District Footpaths and Bridleways Association Annual Reports*, lodged in the British Library.
74. Rothman, *1932 Kinder Trespass*, 36. However, Tom Stephenson maintains that the trespassers never reached the summit of Kinder Scout itself but, as they were unfamiliar with the terrain, held their victory meeting at the highest point of the Snake Path, 2 miles from and 400 feet lower than the top of Kinder itself. See Stephenson, *Forbidden Land*, 157.
75. This estimate was made by leading campaigner G. H. B. Ward and is referred to in Hill, *Freedom to Roam*, 85.
76. Stephenson, *Forbidden Land*, 165.
77. Hill, *Freedom to Roam*, 86.
78. Ministry of Town and Country Planning, *National Parks in England and Wales: Report by John Dower*, Cmnd. 6628 (London: HMSO, 1945), 35.
79. Ibid. 6, 28.
80. Ministry of Town and Country Planning, *Footpaths and Access to the Countryside: Report of the Special Committee (England and Wales)*, Cmnd. 7207 (London: HMSO, 1947).
81. House of Commons, *Hansard*, 31 Mar. 1949, col. 1485.
82. Ibid. 150.
83. See Rossiter, 'Public Use of Private Land'.
84. Rossiter, 'Public Use of Private Land', 244–50.
85. Ibid. 251–61.
86. Sussex Wildlife Trust, *A Vision for the South Downs* (Henfield, West Sussex: Sussex Wildlife Trust, 1993), 29.
87. Nature Conservancy Council, *Nature Conservation in Great Britain* (Peterborough: NCC, 1984), 52.
88. Sussex Wildlife Trust, *Vision for the South Downs*, 29.
89. For further details see S. Webb and B. Webb, *The Story of the King's Highway* (London: Frank Cass & Co., 1963).
90. Ibid. 232.
91. Dower, op. cit. n. 78, p. 37.
92. For a longer discussion of the effect of parish councils and parish meetings on the definitive maps, see Shoard, *This Land is Our Land*, 271–3.

93. For details of some cases where path creation orders have been made, see pp. 232–3, 244.
94. M. Dower, *Fourth Wave* (London: Civic Trust, 1966), 167, 201, 123.
95. I discuss the development of this recreation planning orthodoxy in more detail in M. Shoard, 'Metropolitan Escape Routes', *London Journal*, 5, No. 1 (1979), 87–112 and 'Access: Can Present Opportunities be Widened?' Countryside Commission, *Countryside for All?: Papers given at a Countryside Commission Conference, York University, 20–1 Sept. 1978* (Cheltenham: Countryside Commission, 1979).
96. For further details of the approach of planning authorities to rural recreation provision in the 1980s, see Shoard, *This Land is Our Land*, 325–8.

Chapter 5

1. 'Stroll Toll Proposed', *The Times*, 25 Feb. 1993, p. 2.
2. 'Rural Access: Permit Scheme Back', *Aberdeen Press and Journal*, 22 Mar. 1991.
3. 'Craven's Country', *Radio Times*, 23 Apr. 1994.
4. Country Landowners' Association, *Access 2000: Queen Elizabeth II Conference Centre, 27 November 1996* (London: CLA, 1996).
5. Countryside Commission, *Conservation Walks: Southern England* (Cheltenham: Countryside Commission, 1995).
6. Ramblers' Association, *Countryside Stewardship Scheme Public Access Sites: A Report into the Value for Money and Effectiveness of Purchasing Public Access to the Countryside via a Government-funded Experimental Scheme* (London: Ramblers' Association, 1995).
7. Channel 17, *Debate Presented by Colin Campbell* (Croydon, Surrey: Telewest Communications), broadcast 25 Mar. 1998.
8. 'Ramblers Rubbish Sir Fred's Fresh-Air Tax', News Release, London: Ramblers' Association, 18 May 1991.
9. 'National Trust Chief Blasts Tolls for Ramblers', *Evening Standard*, 8 Mar. 1993, p. 14.
10. Hampshire County Council, *Hampshire Farming Study Summary Report* (Winchester: Hampshire County Council, 1997), 7.
11. Countryside Commission and Sports Council, *Access to the Countryside for Recreation and Sport: Report to the Countryside Commission and the Sports Council by the Centre for Leisure Research* (Cheltenham: Countryside Commission, 1986), 63.
12. G. Cox, C. Watkins, and M. Winter, *Game Management in England: Implications for Public Access, the Rural Economy and the Environment* (Cheltenham: Countryside and Community Press, 1996).

13. M. Shoard, *This Land is Our Land: The Struggle for Britain's Countryside* (London: Grafton Books, 1987; updated and expanded edition London: Gaia Books, 1997).

14. See note 7.

15. Department of the Environment, Transport, and the Regions, *Access to the Open Countryside in England and Wales: A Consultation Paper* (London: HMSO, 1998), 4.

16. 'Access: The Pace Quickens', *Country Landowner* (Mar. 1998), 5.

17. See note 4.

Chapter 6

1. Country Landowners' Association, *Access 2000: Queen Elizabeth II Conference Centre, 27 November 1996* (London: CLA, 1996).

2. A. Phillips and J. Worth, 'Developing a Strategy for Leisure in the Countryside', *Institute of Leisure and Amenity Management Conference Proceedings*, 11 June 1985, available from the Countryside Commission.

3. R. Jefferies, *The Amateur Poacher* (1879), ch. 6, 1.

4. 'Path Surveys', *Footpath Worker* (London: Ramblers' Association), 17/4 (1996), 2–3. This report analyses the Countryside Commission's *Second National Rights of Way Survey: The Findings from 1993/94* (Cheltenham: Countryside Commission, 1996).

5. 'Sorry State of Welsh Footpaths', *Rambling Today*, No. 13, Summer 1994, 10. Results of the survey on the condition of rights of way in other parts of Wales are to be published shortly by the Countryside Council for Wales, which is based in Bangor, Gwynedd. These are expected to show that one-third of public paths in Wales were obstructed in 1992–3.

6. 'Ramblers' Rights of Way Surveys', *Footpath Worker* (London: Ramblers' Association), 16/4 (1995), 3.

7. I examine the impact of social and agricultural change on public paths in greater detail in M. Shoard, *This Land is Our Land* (London: Gaia Books, 1997), 283–7.

8. Section 263 of the Highways Act 1980 states that 'every highway maintainable at the public expense . . . vests in . . . the highway authority'. This covers all public footpaths and bridleways except those dedicated by a landowner since 16 Dec. 1949 without the participation of the highway authority. The surface of most public paths is thus owned by ('vested in') the highway authority.

9. Countryside Commission, *Local Authorities' Expenditure on Rights of Way 1990–1* (Cheltenham: Countryside Commission, CCP 395, 1993), 6.

10. In 1997 Norfolk contained 1,592 miles of public right of way in an area of 2,073 square miles (a density of 0.7 miles of path per square mile of land) while Suffolk contained 3,295 miles of path in an area of 1,467 square miles (a density of 2.2 miles of path per square mile of land).

11. Ministry of Town and Country Planning, *Footpaths and Access to the Countryside: Report of the Special Committee (England and Wales)*, Cmnd. 7207 (London: HMSO, 1947).

12. T. Sharp, 'Planning the Countryside', *Out of Doors* (Winter 1945–6).

13. J. P. Rossiter, 'An Analytical Study of the Private Use of Public Land for Outdoor Recreation in England 1949–1968', unpublished Ph.D. dissertation (University of Cambridge, 1972), 171–3.

14. House of Commons Environment Committee Session 1994–5, *Fourth Report: The Environmental Impact of Leisure Activities*, vol. i, House of Commons Paper 246-I (London: HMSO, 1995), p. xxxiii.

Chapter 7

1. Chief Seattle, spokesman for the Duwarmisha and Suganish Indians, in reply to the Washington government's offer to buy their land in 1852.

2. For further details of access in Sweden see M. Shoard, 'Harmony in Sweden', *Rambling Today* (Winter 1995), 21–3. For further details of access in northern Europe as a whole see M. Shoard, 'Northern Rights', *Outdoors Illustrated*, 3/16 (Mar. 1993).

3. Det Kongelige Miljøverndepartement, *Om lov om friluftslivet av 28. juni 1957 nr. 16*, Rundskriv T-6/97 (Oslo: Statens forurensningstilsyn, 1997).

4. H. G. Wells, 'On War Aims: The Rights of Man', *The Times*, 25 Oct. 1939, 6.

5. C. Hall, 'Jack Ibbott', *South Eastern Rambler*, 19 (Spring 1997), 4.

6. G. M. Trevelyan, *The Call and Claims of Natural Beauty: The Third Rickman Godlee Lecture* (University College and University College Hospital Medical School, London, 26 Oct. 1931).

7. I examine the attraction of moorland scenery in more detail in M. Shoard, 'The Lure of the Moors', in J. Burgess and J. Gold (eds.), *Valued Environments* (London: Allen and Unwin, 1982).

8. I explore the selection of national parks in England and Wales in more detail in M. Shoard, *The Theft of the Countryside* (London: Temple Smith, 1980), 136–43.

9. See Shoard, 'The Lure of the Moors'.

10. Further details ibid.

11. For further details of access in Germany see M. Shoard, 'The German Way', *Rambling Today* (Winter 1991), 27. For details of access in a range

of European countries, see P. Scott, *Countryside Access in Europe: A Review of Access Rights, Legislation and Provision in Selected European Countries* (Edinburgh: Countryside Commission for Scotland, 1991).

12. House of Commons Environment Committee Session 1992–3, *Report on Forestry and the Environment*, House of Commons Paper 257-I, p. xxxiii.

13. For further details of access in Denmark see M. Shoard, 'Access the Danish Way', *Rambling Today* (Autumn 1992), 40–1.

14. For further details of access in Switzerland see M. Shoard, 'Walkers' Rights in Switzerland', *Rambling Today* (Spring 1992), 36.

15. E. A. Baker, *The Forbidden Land* (London: Witherby, 1924).

16. 'Ramblers Issue Strong Call for Public Access to Set-aside Farmland', Ramblers' Association Press Release, 25 Jan. 1988 (London: Ramblers' Association).

17. Ramblers' Association, Janet Street-Porter speech, Forest of Bowland rally, 25 Sept. 1994 (London: Ramblers' Association).

18. 'Big "yes" for Access Bill', *Rambling Today* (Summer 1997), 7.

19. For the debates on Paddy Tipping's Access to the Countryside Bill, see House of Commons, *Hansard* (London: HMSO, 30 Jan. 1996), cols. 779–85 and (23 July 1997), cols. 967–71. The bill was no. 49 in session 1995–6, ISBN 010 304 9967.

20. The Access Forum, *Scotland's Hills and Mountains: A Concordat on Access* (Edinburgh: Scottish Natural Heritage, n.d.). The Concordat was signed by the following organizations: Scottish Sports Council, Scottish Sports Association, Scottish Natural Heritage, Scottish Landowners' Federation, Scottish Countryside Activities Council, Ramblers' Association Scotland, National Farmers' Union of Scotland, Mountaineering Council of Scotland, Convention of Scottish Local Authorities, and the Association of Deer Management Groups.

21. J. Major, 'Views of the Man Who Holds the Reins', *The Field* (Mar. 1997).

22. M. Heseltine, 'Deputy Prime Minister's Speech at the Country Landowners' Association's Access to the Countryside Conference, 27 November', *Access 2000 Conference: Countryside Recreation and Access into the Next Millennium* (London: CLA, 1996).

23. Countryside Commission, *Common Land: The Report of the Common Land Forum* (Cheltenham: Countryside Commission, CCP 215, 1986). The following organizations and individuals were signatories to the Forum's report: Association of County Councils, Association of District Councils, Association of Metropolitan Authorities, British Horse Society, Byways and Bridleways Trust, Council for National Parks, Council for British Archaeology, Council for the Protection of Rural England, Council for

the Protection of Rural Wales, Country Landowners' Association, Countryside Commission, Crown Estate Commissioners, Dartmoor National Park Officer, National Association of Local Councils, National Farmers' Union, Nature Conservancy Council, National Trust, Open Spaces Society, Ramblers' Association, Sports Council, Association of Welsh Commoners and an individual English commoner. Maurice Mendoza was chairman.

24. P. Tyler, 'Access: Searching for the Common Ground', *Access 2000*, op. cit. n. 23 above.
25. H. Hill, *Freedom to Roam: The Struggle for Access to Britain's Moors and Mountains* (Ashbourne, Derbyshire: Moorland Publishing, 1980), 26.
26. Socialist Countryside Group, *Access to the Countryside* (London: SCG c/o Socialist Environment and Resources Association, 1983).
27. 'Labour Launches Plans for Public to Enjoy the Countryside', Labour Party News Release, 29 Aug. 1990 (London: Labour Party).
28. C. Smith, 'Labour Pledges "Right to Roam" Law', London, House of Commons: Chris Smith Press Release, 26 Sept. 1994.
29. 'Speech by Chris Smith MP, Shadow Secretary of State for Environmental Protection, Introducing the NEC Statement "In Trust for Tomorrow"', Blackpool: Labour Party Conference 94 news release, 1994.
30. E. Morley, 'Speech to the CLA Conference on Access, 27 November 1996', *Access 2000 Conference: Countryside Recreation and Access into the Next Millennium* (London: CLA, 1996).
31. Department of the Environment, Transport, and the Regions, *Access to the Open Countryside in England and Wales: A Consultation Paper* (London: HMSO, 1998).
32. Ibid. 7.
33. R. G. Jefferson and H. J. Robertson, *Lowland Grassland: Wildlife Value and Conservation Status* (Peterborough: English Nature, 1996), 5.
34. C. Board and B. Morgan, 'Parks for People', *Geographical Magazine* (June 1971).
35. Snowdonia National Park Committee, *Map Cadwrath Adran 3, Section 3 Conservation Map* (Penrhyndeudraeth, Gwynedd: Snowdonia National Park Authority, 1991).
36. Department of the Environment, Transport, and the Regions, *Access to the Open*, 6.
37. Even recognition of a moor is not always as easy as many might suppose. The term 'moor' is given not only to a stretch of upland rough pasture but also to a low-lying bog, as at Thorne Moor near Doncaster and Sedgemoor in the Somerset Levels.
38. Jefferson and Robertson, *Lowland Grassland*, 20.

39. Jefferson and Robertson, *Lowland Grassland*, 6.
40. Department of the Environment, Transport, and the Regions, *Access to the Open Countryside in England and Wales: A Consultation Paper*, 6.
41. S. Hedley and J. W. Aitchison, *Biological Survey of Common Land*, No. 22: *Somerset* (Peterborough: English Nature, 1992).
42. K. A. Crowther and J. W. Aitchison, *Biological Survey of Common Land*, No. 26: *Derbyshire* (Peterborough: English Nature, 1993).
43. Country Landowners' Association, *Access 2000*, 11.
44. Ministry of Town and Country Planning, *Footpaths and Access to the Countryside: Report of the Special Committee (England and Wales)*, Cmnd. 7207 (London: HMSO, 1947), 41.
45. M. Shoard, 'The People's Countryside', *New Statesman* (30 Apr. 1982), 6–8.
46. F. Harrison, 'Keep Out', *New Statesman* (22 May 1987), 29.
47. G. Monbiot, 'Whose Land?', *Guardian* (22 Feb. 1995), 5 and G. Monbiot, 'Fences against the People', *Guardian* (19 June 1995), 15.
48. These are: English Nature, the Countryside Council for Wales, Scottish Natural Heritage, and the Department of the Environment for Northern Ireland.
49. J. Bugler (producer/director), *Power in the Land* (London: London Weekend Television for Channel 4, 1987).
50. S. Jenkins, 'Where Cash is the Main Crop', *The Times* (13 Nov. 1993).
51. Scottish Countryside Access Network Conference at Battleby, Perth, 23 Apr. 1998.
52. Dr Hunter describes this attitude to landownership in *On the Edge of Sorrow: Nature and People in the Scottish Highlands* (Edinburgh: Mainstream Publishing, 1995), 60–5.
53. Mrs Ewing's bill was debated in the House of Commons on 22 Mar. 1994. See House of Commons, *Hansard* (London: HMSO), cols. 137–9.
54. The Access Forum, *Rights and Responsibilities in the Countryside: A Review of Access for Open-Air Recreation* (Edinburgh: Scottish Natural Heritage, 1998).

Chapter 8

1. Sandwich Bay in east Kent and Wimbledon Common in south-west London are respective examples. In Stockport, Greater Manchester, the courses of six golf clubs are crossed by public paths; in two of these the course is also surrounded by public open space, and in one case the course is crossed by no fewer than five public footpaths.
2. Unless of course it were used subsequently for some other purpose granted automatic exemption like a housing estate.

3. This information is from the presentation made by the MVA Consultancy at an event organized by the Countryside Commission on 21 Oct. 1996. In 1997 the Commission expected to publish the report of the research shortly.

4. Countryside Commission, *Recreation 2000: Enjoying the Countryside: A Consultation Paper on Future Policies* (Cheltenham: Countryside Commission, CCP 225, 1987), 15.

5. Bulls may legally be pastured in fields crossed by rights of way so long as they are either less than ten months old or, if of non-dairy breeds, accompanied by cows or heifers (when they are supposed to be less aggressive towards humans). Any bull over the age of ten months is forbidden on its own, and any bull of a recognized dairy breed is prohibited even if accompanied by cows or heifers.

6. House of Commons Environment Committee Session 1994–5, *First Report on The Environmental Impact of Leisure Activities*, vol. ii (London: HMSO, HCP 246-II, 1994–5), 309.

7. Countryside Commission and Sports Council, *Access to the Countryside for Recreation and Sport: Report to the Countryside Commission and Sports Council by the Centre for Leisure Research* (Cheltenham: Countryside Commission, CCP 217, 1986), 56–64.

8. House of Commons Environment Committee, *First Report on the Environmental Impact of Leisure Activities*, ii. 155.

9. C. E. M. Joad, 'The People's Claim', in C. Williams-Ellis (ed.), *Beauty and the Beast* (London: Dent and Sons, 1937), 76.

10. G. Cox, C. Watkins, and M. Winter, *Game Management in England: Implications for Public Access, the Rural Economy and the Environment* (Cheltenham: Cheltenham and Gloucester, 1996), 31.

11. House of Commons Agriculture Committee Session 1989–90, *Second Report: Land Use and Forestry*, vol. ii (London: HMSO, HCP 16-II, 1989–90), 214.

12. T. H. Blank and J. Meads, 'Hunting and Shooting', *Shooting Times and Country Magazine*, 4 Dec. 1971, p. 22; T. H. Blank, 'Co-operation in the Thurlow Country', *Shooting Times and Country Magazine*, 30 Dec. 1972, p. 18; and T. H. Blank, 'Foxes and Pheasants: Cubs in Coverts', *Shooting Times and Country Magazine*, 17 Nov. 1973, p. 20.

13. D. Hart-Davis, 'The Majestic Heads of Petworth's Deer', *The Field* (July 1995), 80.

14. House of Commons Environment Committee Session 1992–3, *First Report: Forestry and the Environment*, vol. i (London: HMSO, HCP 257-I, 1993), p. xlviii.

15. G. Bedell, 'War Starts over the Woodland Warriors', *The Times*, 7 July 1990.

16. Cox, Watkins, and Winter, *Game Management in England*, 38.

17. B. W. Staines and D. Scott, *Recreation and Red Deer: A Preliminary Review of the Issues*, Scottish Natural Heritage Review No. 31 (Edinburgh: Scottish Natural Heritage, 1994), 16.

18. Ibid. 3.

19. For an idea of what this can mean for people living in the Highlands see M. Shoard, *This Land is Our Land: The Struggle for Britain's Countryside* (Stroud: Gaia Books, 1997), 242–3.

20. Radio 4, *Common Ground*, broadcast on 28 Sept. 1996 (London: BBC Radio).

21. R. Sidaway, *Birds and Walkers: A Review of Existing Research on Access to the Countryside and Disturbance to Birds* (London: Ramblers' Association, 1990), 15.

22. N. Picozzi, 'Breeding Performance and Shooting Bags of Red Grouse in Relation to Public Access in the Peak District National Park, England', *Biol. Cons.* 3, No. 3 (1971), 211–15.

23. Sidaway, *Birds and Walkers*, 16.

24. P. Hudson, *Grouse in Space and Time* (Fordingbridge: Game Conservancy, 1992), 215.

25. Countryside Commission and Sports Council, *Access to the Countryside for Recreation and Sport*, 105.

26. *Open Space*, vol. 25, No. 5, Spring 1996, 13.

27. A. G. Bradley, *The Rivers and Streams of England* (London: Adam and Charles Black, 1909), 83.

28. J. R. Hartley, *Fly Fishing: Memories of Angling Days* (London: Michael Russell, 1991), 26.

29. Quoted by C. Hall, 'Tangled Webber', *The Countryman*, 101, No. 4 (1996), 15.

30. D. S. Ramwell and R. Boar, *Coast Dune Management Guide* (Huntingdon: Institute of Terrestrial Ecology, 1986), 31–2.

31. These orchids are described by Geoff Chapman and Bob Young in their book *Box Hill* (Lyme Regis: Serendip Books, 1979). David Kennington, the Property Manager for the National Trust North Downs Area, confirmed that these species remain as numerous today in a telephone interview in 1998.

32. House of Commons Environment Committee, *First Report on the Environmental Impact of Leisure Activities*, vol. i, p. xxvii.

33. Sidaway, *Birds and Walkers*, 6.

34. See p. 201.

35. M. Toogood, 'Semi-natural History', *Ecos*, 18, No. 2 (1997), 62–3.

36. For further details of Jane Madgwick's views, see J. Madgwick, 'Nature Reserved for Whom?', *Countryside Commission News*, No. 30 (Jan./Feb. 1988), 3.

37. J. Bugler (producer/director), *Power in the Land* (London: London Weekend Television for Channel Four, 1987).

38. M. Shoard, 'Lie of the Land', *Environment Now* (Oct./Nov. 1987), 25.

39. N. Rowland, 'Landowners Lay Down New Routes', *Country Landowner* (Apr. 1996), 14.

40. BBC Radio 4, *The Natural History Programme*, 6 July 1996.

41. S. Jenkinson, 'Badgers and Access: Problems or Protection?', *Byway and Bridleway*, 10 (1995). See also S. Jenkinson, 'The Influence of Public Access on Badger Sett Sustainability and Disturbance (in West Yorkshire, England)', unpublished M.Sc. dissertation, Manchester Metropolitan University, 1994.

42. Country Landowners' Association, *Access 2000: Countryside Recreation and Access into the next Millennium* (London: Country Landowners' Association, 1996), 11.

43. The law on liability in Scotland is slightly different and is set out in W. Gordon, *Scottish Land Law* (Edinburgh: W. Green & Son, 1989), 852–8.

44. J. R. Crabtree, N. A. Chalmers, and Z. E. D. Appleton, 'The Costs to Farmers and Estate Owners of Public Access to the Countryside', *Journal of Environmental Planning and Management*, 37/4 (1995), 415–29.

45. See Animals (Scotland) Act, 1987.

46. The other admonitions are: enjoy the countryside and respect its life and work, keep to public paths across farmland, use gates and stiles to cross fences, hedges, and walls, leave livestock, crops, and machinery alone, help to keep all water clean, protect wildlife, plants, and trees, take special care on country roads, and make no unnecessary noise.

47. System Three Scotland, *Public Awareness of the Country Code* (Edinburgh: Scottish Natural Heritage, 1996).

48. See in particular Countryside Commission, *Out in the Country: Where you can Go and what you can Do* (Cheltenham: Countryside Commission, CCP 186, 1990).

49. Conservative Party News, *Speech by the Rt. Hon. John Gummer MP (Suffolk Central), Secretary of State for the Environment, Speaking at the 112th Conservative Party Conference at the Winter Gardens in Blackpool Today* (London: Conservative Central Office, 10 Oct. 1995).

50. Country Landowners' Association, *Access 2000*, 11.

51. Scottish Landowners' Federation, *Access: Towards Access without Acrimony* (Edinburgh: Scottish Landowners' Federation, 1993), 13.

52. I discuss this proposal in more detail in M. Shoard, *The Theft of the Countryside* (London: Temple Smith, 1980), 205–25.

INDEX

Index

Index

Index

Index

Index

Index